D0203001

WITHDRAWN
UTSA LIBRARIES

The Life and
Death of Industrial Languedoc,
1700–1920

Looking down the Lergue–Lodève's southern factory district

The Life and Death
of Industrial Languedoc,
1700–1920

CHRISTOPHER H. JOHNSON

New York   Oxford
OXFORD UNIVERSITY PRESS
1995

Oxford University Press

Oxford   New York
Athens   Auckland   Bangkok   Bombay
Calcutta   Cape Town   Dar es Salaam   Delhi
Florence   Hong Kong   Istanbul   Karachi
Kuala Lumpur   Madras   Madrid   Melbourne
Mexico City   Nairobi   Paris   Singapore
Taipei   Tokyo   Toronto

and associated companies in
Berlin   Ibadan

Copyright © 1995 by Oxford University Press, Inc.

Published by Oxford University Press, Inc.,
200 Madison Avenue, New York, New York 10016

Oxford is a registered trademark of Oxford University Press

All rights reserved. No part of this publication
may be reproduced, stored in a retrieval system, or transmitted,
in any form or by any means, electronic, mechanical,
photocopying, recording, or otherwise, without the prior
permission of Oxford University Press.

Library of Congress Cataloging-in-Publication Data
Johnson, Christopher H.
The life and death of industrial Languedoc, 1700-1920/
Christopher H. Johnson.
p. cm.
Includes bibliographical references and index.
ISBN 0-19-504508-4 (alk. paper)
1. Industries—France—Languedoc—History—18th century.
2. Industries—France—Languedoc—History—19th century.
3. Industries—France—Languedoc—History—20th century.
4. Plant shutdowns—France—Languedoc—History—19th century.
5. Plant shutdowns—France—Languedoc—History—20th century.
6. Languedoc (France)—Economic conditions.
7. Languedoc (France)—Social conditions.
I. Title.   HC277.L2J64   1995
338.4'767'09448—dc20   94-29309

1 3 5 7 9 8 6 4 2

Printed in the United States of America
on acid-free paper

Library
University of Texas
at San Antonio

For Lois, Leslie, and Abigail—who lived it

Preface

This book began over twenty years ago and has evolved with my thinking about the nature of social change. My original interest in the woolen textile towns of lower Languedoc, especially Lodève and Bédarieux, grew from their explosive history of worker militance during the July Monarchy and the Second Republic that leapt from the pages of the judicial reports in series BB[18] and BB[30] in the Archives Nationales. They seemed to present a rather "pure" version of class struggle, one that culminated in 1848–51 with a socialist *prise de conscience*. My focus at the time was directed to the problem of proletarianization, and they provided an example of urban workers in a rapidly mechanizing industry whose depth of residential stability, immigrant integration, and cultural homogeneity, along with the new competitive pressures faced by their employers, created the bases for an experience actually validating Marxist expectations.[1] In less than a generation, however, young Jules Guesde could write from Lodève that the workers of the region were "without energy," that radicalism had evaporated. Within another generation, while a certain political revitalization was evident, class-struggle socialism was being replaced by a politics of regional defense in which industrial workers barely had a role: the vine, its owners, and its artisans had come to dominate the life of lower Languedoc.

What had been unfolding was the transformation of the economy from a diverse industrial base—with woolens the leading sector—to an era of decline compensated to some extent by the vast, though erratic, expansion of a vin ordinaire business that would become the identifying hallmark of the coastal departments of the Aude and the Hérault in the twentieth century. Thus, increasingly, I oriented my work toward an understanding of the process of deindustrialization and its implications for the lives of those, at all levels of society, who lived through it. This project was fascinating not only because Languedoc's was the first deindustrialization in a region that had previously experienced mechanization and was virtually unstudied,[2] but also because my own environment, Detroit and the auto-industrial American upper Midwest, was in the late 1970s traversing the same harrowing terrain. And simultaneously, I had undertaken a project that allowed me to study the glory years of worker militance and left politics in *this* world, lending substantial depth to the comparative dimensions of my interest.[3] Thus, in the story of the life and death of industrial Languedoc, an example of a completed cycle could be analyzed and open the way toward a more profound understanding of a phenomenon that has become obvious as an explanation of capitalism's obstinate resiliency: its seemingly endless capacity to move from region to region at will, seeking out low-wage, unorganized, or otherwise oppressed work forces while leaving militant, often class-conscious workers behind. Capital's mobility was perhaps more cumbersome in the nineteenth century, but it was no less effective in setting region against region, state against state, and worker against worker, undermining proletarian solidarity at every turn. Its principal leavening effect was to set the colonized against the colonizers, a struggle that is today largely completed— only to be followed by a new round of capital export (and cheap labor import) that sets region against region, state against state, and worker against worker, now usually those of a different color and faith.[4]

The pathways of regional deindustrialization and capital migration, it turned out, were no less political than those of industrialization had been. Politics and the role of the state, in fact, became the primary focus of my research, calling upon me to give greater and greater attention to both the intricate workings of power at the level of the central state and the micropolitics of lifeworld struggles at the local level. At every stage of the story— the original rise and decline of the Levant trade and the bellwether role of Lodève's highly rationalized military cloth specialization under the old regime, the petty entrepreneurship encouraged by the Revolution then dashed under the Consulat, the process of mechanization and the social upheaval of the first half of the nineteenth century, the explosive denouement of the Second Republic, the tortured efforts to create a viable rail system to serve industry and the emergent coal mines at Graissessac, and finally, deindustrialization and the subsequent *défense viticole*—the political designs of the governors and lobbyists in Versailles and Paris, the political battles of regional notables for Languedoc's interests, and the political struggles of the people animated by corporatist, Jacobin, social-Christian, trade-unionist, démocsoc, Marxist, syndicalist, and Occitan-populist visions shaped the economic trajectories of the region profoundly.

The world explored here stretches across two hundred years, though detailed analysis already published on the Old Regime and Revolution is only summarized in the Prologue. I have followed a research strategy that comprehends in a general way the three main departments comprising the lower half of old Languedoc, the Gard, Hérault, and Aude, though of necessity includes work on the uplands (Causses) above Lodève and the southern Tarn, especially Mazamet. The Gard becomes rather a foil in the story, tied, as it became, to northern interests, above all, Paulin Talabot, the Rothchilds, and the Paris-Lyon-Mediterranée railroad complex, while the Aude, whose history motivated Claude Fohlen and a long line of historians and geographers in the wake of his brief article of 1949[5] to make the argument that the vine wiped out a barely industrialized woolens industry throughout lower Languedoc, fades rapidly from the scene. But the Hérault and especially the twin cites of Lodève and Bédarieux and their surrounding areas of the Lergue, upper Hérault, and upper Orb (including the Graissessac mining district)—the department's "piedmont"—occupy center stage, for here occurred the ongoing history of industrial Languedoc, and here too will we watch it unravel. Only in the final chapter will we descend, even though most of the piedmont's proud inhabitants did not, into the vast fields of rotgut vines that became lower Languedoc's destiny.

Although I have given detailed attention to the rest of the piedmont region, I have ransacked the archives and libraries of Paris, Montpellier, and the "picturesque" little city on the Lergue for every shred of evidence I could find on Lodève. It became, as best I could make it, my laboratory in historical anthropology. In 1975, my family and I lived for six months in a village to the north of the town called Pégairolles de l'Escalette. The kids went to school, Leslie in Lodève to the C.E.S., where she arrived as La Parisienne and became a Lodévoise, complete with accent, and Abby in a one-room schoolhouse in Lauroux with M. Espalier, who played the guitar and taught her to love nature. Then, and in several later sojourns, we got to know the people of town and country, learned the accent (but no Occitan, since everyone there—if not the intellectuals in Montpellier—now disdained it as "patois"), and visited every site there and in the Orb-Jaur valleys across the great ridge of the Escandourgue where my people lived and worked a century, three centuries ago. I also explored their houses, many of which still stand largely unchanged, roamed the streets, followed paths of demonstrators and assassins, and examined the remaining shells of their factories, their mill ponds, and the intricacies of their sluices. At Graissessac, now silent, l saw rusting machinery, abandoned sidings, and the cutoff mountain tops that last-ditch efforts at strip-mining bequeathed to the present in one of the wildest and most beautiful natural settings in France. I also spent an afternoon with a old miner at the cafe and still have on my desk the piece of coal I picked up that day. History without locality is dead. To have been there, to sense the humanity of your subjects in their haunts and in the eyes of their descendants makes your documents more than so many "representations." It makes them breathe.

I would thus like to begin a rather long list of acknowledgments with the people of the Hérault: the Daumases and Combarnouses of Pégairolles and the Boisse de Blacks down the road; M. Hugounenq at the "Midi Libre" (as we always called his bookstore), with whom I spent long hours in conversation about the history of the region; old Emile Appolis, "l'historien," as he was simply known in the city, who lived in a turreted house overlooking the Lergue's largest millpond smack in the center of the city; Jean Mercadier, socialist mayor of Lodève (before and during Mitterand) and his wonderful staff, especially Mme Paul, at the état civil and cadastral offices as well as the municipal library who showed me everything they had; the Miquels and the Villebruns of Le Lau, a hamlet where we lived another time, who taught me a great deal about the interior life of piedmont families; M. et Mme Pierre Jean, descendants of woolens workers and Bédarician migrants to Montpellier, whose good cheer, graciousness, and wistfulness made me think a good deal about the human impact of deindustrialization; successive archivists and staff members at the Archives Départementales de l'Hérault, especially Mme Jacob, who never failed to direct me to the appropriate series or to root out prime documents from unclassified material, and the archival photographer who saved me from banishment from French archives when a bureaucratic error caused a bill not to be paid; Gérard Cholvy, Jean Sagnes, and Rémy Pech, whose unsurpassed knowledge of the department's history guided me in areas beyond my field of primary research. I thank them all and the dozens of others who made the Hérault a part of me. Finally, two transplanted Héraultais, my cousin Jean Ann and Klaus Erhardt, a German, along with their children, have been involved in this book from the beginning and contributed enormously to our acclimatization to the Midi. Since the mid-1960s, they have restored Bardou, an abandoned hamlet above the former outworking center of Mons, to its eighteenth-century authenticity, making it today internationally famous as a historic site as well as a working sheep farm, thus contributing to the revitalization of the traditional ovine culture in the Monts de l'Espinouse. Their example, their intelligence, and their love inform this book in ways impossible to specify.

My debts to institutions that provided financial support are significant. Fellowships from the National Endowment for the Humanities and from the John Simon Guggenheim Foundation combined with Wayne State University sabbaticals to allow full years in France in 1974–75 and 1981–82. A Wayne State Summer Grant (1969) first took me to the Archives Départementales de l'Hérault and an NEH Summer Stipend (1984) pretty much wrapped up the research on the later nineteenth and early twentieth centuries. Although American Council of Learned Societies and Wayne State summer grants in 1986 and 1987 were largely in support of my new topic on family and small business, I stole some time for research and writing on Languedoc during the tenure of both, while a Wayne State Distinguished Graduate Faculty Award provided aid in the summers of 1990 and 1991 during which the writing of my original thousand-page manuscript was completed. Obviously, this book would not exist without this generous assistance, and I am deeply grateful to all agencies and their always helpful staffs.

My most difficult task is to thank (and indeed to remember!) all those colleagues and friends who contributed in so many ways to this study. Conversations with Emmanuel LeRoy Ladurie about doing a book on the origins of mass wine production in France and California helped to crystalize my decision to approach the problem from the other side. Charles and Louise Tilly's constant encouragement and critique of my work as it progressed in the 1970s and early 1980s was invaluable, and Chuck's recommendations I know carried enormous weight with funding institutions. I have a similar debt to Robert Forster and Peter Gay and thank them all for their direct aid as well as the shining example of their scholarship. My welcome and intellectual sustenance from friends in France has been a special delight and I would especially like to thank Annette and Serge Vincent, Michelle Perrot, Jean-Paul and Michèle Bertaud, and Yves Lequin. At various junctures, scholars invited, read, and critiqued my papers and/or provided me with insights and source information. Besides those already mentioned, let me acknowledge with gratitude Pierre Deyon, Franklin Mendels, James Thomson, Colin Jones, Susanna Barrows, Robert Schwartz, Yves Leclercq, Isser Wallach, Elinor Accampo, Ronald Aminzade, Michael Hanagan, Peter Amann, Leslie Page Moch, William Sewell, Jr., Carlo Poni, Stuart Wolfe, Laurence Fontaine, Michael Sonenscher, Leo Loubère, J. Harvey Smith, Laura Frader, Chris Waters, Whitney Walton, Tessie Liu, Donald Reid, Edward Berenson, Lynn Lees, Haim Burstin, Christopher Clark, Tom Safley, and the students in David Sabean's European history seminar at Cornell. Theoretical discussions, exchanges, and critiques that helped shape my arguments were contributed directly and in print by several of the above, as well as Robert Wheeler, Sanford Elwitt, Bernard Moss, Eric Hobsbawm, Standish Meacham, Jacques Rancière, Steven Kaplan, Jürgen Schlumbohm, Geoff Eley, Keith Nield, Mahfoud Bennoune, William Reddy (whose divergent point of view has been a constant stimulus), and Lenard Berlanstein.

Other friends and family have read and/or discussed aspects of this book and rendered the support and comradery that accompany close ties. So here's to Roger Price, Bonnie Smith, Bob Smith, David Sabean, Len Rosenband, Carol Agocs, Marc Kruman, Alan Raucher, Tom Klug, Austin Johnson, Pam Woywod, Ted Kotila, Lynn Parsons, Mel Small, Sam Scott, Nancy Macy, and Bob Painter. Finally, from the day we discovered that we were both forty-eighters in a little bar across from the B.N., through many adventures intellectual and gastronomic, with the warmth and depth added to our friendship after he married Carol Payne (along with their wonderful hospitality), with the constant support on all fronts that he gave, and finally on to the grueling task of reading the monster in its original totality (and crabbing about Habermas), John Merriman has been a wonderful friend. Thanks, John.

The multiple drafts of the manuscript were typed by Ginny Corbin, who not only knows her craft, but the English language. My deepest thanks to her and to Susan Smith of the Wayne State Word Processing Center, who put the final, much-revised version on a disc. No significant portion of the current book has been previously published. Cartographers Jeffrey Barthlow and Bonnie Talaga prepared the graphs and maps with precision and attractiveness. I would specially like to thank Nancy Lane, of Oxford University Press, who edited my first article published in the United States when she was with the *American Historical Review*, for her patience and good will as the due date for this book kept being revised and for her stern command to cut it to reasonable proportions. As she knows, I was not happy about this, assuming that if this were to be my magnum opus, it had to be *big*; now, of course, I realize that we have a much better product. The editorial staff at Oxford, especially Anna Taruschio, Colby Stong, and my copy editor, Susan Glassman, improved the book in many ways.

Then there is the crew who made this book with me. A photograph that I took of Lois and the girls sitting in the grass somewhere in Languedoc during the summer of 1969 sits on my file cabinet. The bumper of my father's camper is off to the side. We had picked the car up in Malaga, where my mother had died the previous year, and were making our way around archives in the Midi, searching for a topic. We found it in Montpellier. Since, we've been back many times, and the reams of research notes grew and grew along with the many experiences of living and loving France. My appreciation of the role of their love, their insight, and their sacrifices (for it was not always easy, especially when the Mistral started to blow) in the making of this book has only deepened over the years. The women in my life have had to wait a long time for this dedication. But I wanted to make it special—because they are.

Detroit   **C. H. J.**
September 1994

Contents

Maps and Photographs

Maps

Photographs

The Life and
Death of Industrial Languedoc,
1700–1920

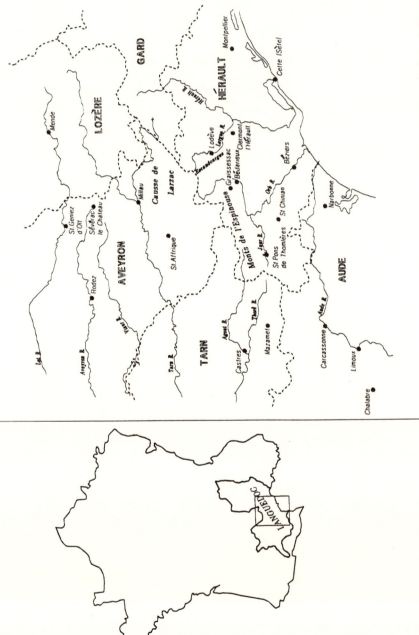

Drawn By: Bonnie S. Talaga

Prologue: Industrial Languedoc from Colbert to Chaptal

"Upper Languedoc has grain and this country [lower Languedoc] harvests oils, besides its manufactures. But everyone knows that the fruits of the earth . . . are exposed to a thousand hazards before they reach maturity, and that it is not the same with manufactures, [for] they depend on the artistry, industriousness, and application of men."[1, 2] Thus did Intendant Henri d'Aguesseau, a Colbertian through and through, reassure skeptics in the Estates of Languedoc in 1681 that their interest-free loans to the Royal Manufactures of fine woolens at Saptes and Villenouvette would bear fruit. The export of well-regulated manufactured goods would result in the influx of precious bullion. D'Aguesseau's successor, Nicolas de Lamoignon de Basville, stressed the capacities of the people of Mediterranean Languedoc to carry out Colbert's mission of development, praising them for their "activity, industrial and commercial intelligence, and dedication and tenacity in business." These characteristics unfortunately were accompanied by a disdain for letters and the sciences and a distinct lack of generosity of spirit: "avid for gain," they were "little inclined toward gratitude." Nor did religion make much difference. Remarking on the Nîmois "converts" after the Revocation in 1685; "if all these merchants are still bad Catholics, at least they have not stopped being good businessmen."[3] Thus, the whip of *le sol ingrat* on the Mediterranean side of southwest France's watershed[4] and the beneficent hand of the state would guide these hard-working Languedocians toward prosperity for region and nation alike.

When a later Intendant, Jean d'Asfeld LeNain, wrote his general report on the state of the province's economy in 1745, that promise seemed fulfilled. He reported production figures significantly higher than had Basville, a doubling of manufacturing values to £38,000,000.[5] Textiles accounted for over 90 percent of this, followed by leather (£1,300,000), twelve iron forges (£350,000), twenty-three paper mills (£260,000), and thirteen glass-works (£120,000). Dyestuff production, largely verdegris, accounted for £360,000. The commercial agricultural product, £11,000,000, was probably underestimated, but the market value of the vine to the economy of the region, though significant, was not a great deal more than that produced by the busy hands of the lace makers in the mountains of Le Puy (£2,600,000 to £2,000,000). It obviously paled in comparison to the textile industries.[6] Within the textile sector, despite silk's recovery from post-Revocation troubles,[7] wool was dominant. Not only was it the principal ingredient of woven cloth (£17,000,000), but it provided the base for three-quarters of the knitwear industry (£10,600,000) as well. The four million livres in Languedoc wool sold and processed in the industry sufficed for less than two-thirds of its needs. Most of the strong, workable wool from the classic mouton de Languedoc went into *bonneterie*, common grades of broadcloth (*draps*), and *petites étoffes* (narrow gauge, usually unfulled cloth sold locally and shipped overseas, especially to clothe slaves and servants). Blankets and some of the lesser cloths used coarse wool shipped in from the eastern Mediterranean. The top of the Languedoc line, above all, draps de Levant, imported much of its wool from Spain, largely shorn from merino sheep.

The dependency of the region on textile production was high, but the range of products large. This diversity meant that only a general downturn in the economy would have broad effects. Demand patterns were rooted in differing circumstances from line to line. Bonneterie, sold mainly through fairs and destined for interior consumption, possessed a clientele largely distinct from silk goods. Draps de Levant, an export product carefully regulated by the state, responded to the vicissitudes of international commerce, while broadcloth for domestic consumption sold primarily in the south, again through fairs, and was purchased by the middling sort. Military cloth had an entirely different demand pattern, one on the whole complementary to export cloth, since war generally cut into maritime commerce. This underlines the centrality of Lodève in the industrial system of Languedoc, for it always served as a kind of ballast in difficult times for civilian demand.

The problem of the role of the state in industrial Languedoc's history is central to this book. Its focus on Lodève, a "defense industry" town, assures this. But in the eighteenth century (and in the nineteenth) virtually all industries—including wine production—received aid from the state, saw their products regulated by the state, and their marketing facilitated and often directed by the state. Some projects were stillborn; copper and lead mining, which appeared so promising, failed largely because the richness of the deposits was vastly overestimated. Others succeeded strikingly. The Levant trade, despite its later problems, was one. But coal mining and glass production, both promoted by the state, made respectable progress in the last thirty years of the Old Regime. And modern chemicals—carefully regulated from the beginning—emerged as an industry; Jean-Baptiste-Antoine Chaptal, scholar, entrepreneur, and future architect of rational administration and economic promotion under the Consulat, worked hand in glove with the state in developing his flourishing chemical works at La Paille on the outskirts of Montpellier.[8]

Dirigisme as such was not the key to growth, and mere state privilege was hardly progressive. Colbert himself clearly understood that his task was to set in motion industrial growth through encouragement and protection and then let industries become increasingly free and competitive.[9] In many respects Colbertism succeeded. The ideal was to guarantee a quality standard that would reassure the customer, while at the same time to encourage price competition rooted in manufacturers' efficiency and the skill of their workers. In times of market expansion and stable costs of production, this worked well enough and explains the happy middle years for the woolens industry. But regulations became shackles as the product demand and materials supply situations tightened. From the late 1750s on, this became a growing problem in the Levant trade, and many manufacturers cheated on the regulations to maintain themselves. This simply made matters worse, and the reputation of French cloth in the Ottoman Empire plummeted. Only Royal Manufacturers and enterprising newcomers from Bédarieux (allowed to enter the trade fully only in 1758) stayed the course of quality. Meanwhile, the other key branch of the industry, military cloth, despite a few contentious moments, kept the allegiance of its chief customer by carrying out major productivity gains through structural rationalization and cheaper labor costs. With the American War of Independence (1776–83) and the suspension of quality controls during Controller-General A.-R.-J. Turgot's brief experiment in freedom of production, Lodève boomed, Clermont and Carcassonne collapsed, and Bédarieux captured significant portions of the remaining Levant trade. Meanwhile, on the flanks of the industry, a new and potent force, the cheap goods industries of Mazamet and Castres, emerged. Simultaneously, other old industries (silk, leather and skins, dyestuffs production) held on, and new industries (coal, "black" glass, cotton, chemicals) began to make their way. There is no question that virtually all economic activity, including the wine trade, slowed during the decade before the Revolution, and that the 1790s were for Languedoc, as for most of the rest of France, a depressed era. The political upheaval played havoc with national and international economic relations and encouraged a flight of capital from France without parallel until the early 1980s. But Languedoc, like the nation, survived. Some of its earlier assets appeared permanently destroyed, others only weakened, while others possessed the potential for growth. Unlike upper Languedoc and most of the southwest, lower Languedoc showed considerable industrial resiliency after 1801. This vitality, though shaken by a variety of economic and political countercurrents, would not finally dissipate until the 1860s.

In a nutshell, the preceding paragraph lays out the contours of the life and death of industrial Languedoc as I see it. It is a picture that is at variance with existing interpretations, though virtually all the studies done heretofore can be integrated into it. It is less a question of error on their part than an inability to overcome the traditional time barriers that plague French historiography. By beginning my research in the middle (for reasons initially that had nothing to do with the problem of deindustrialization) and working backward, then forward, I became much more impressed with the significance of the revolutionary age, 1789–1851, in Languedoc's general history. It is symptomatic of the general problem that the history of the region's economy in the eighteenth century is rather well known. The work and influence of Emmanuel LeRoy Ladurie, Louis Dermigny, Georges Frèche, Charles Carrière, and, most recently, James Thomson built upon the studies of Léon Dutil, Emile Appolis, Paul Marres, and others of the older historical geography tradition to create a solid picture of the scope and movement of both upper and lower Languedoc's economy in the eighteenth century.[10] For the period after 1789, scholarship on Mediterranean Languedoc is relatively sparse. Toulouse and its region have certainly received enough attention, and the failure to make the modern industrial turn there—rooted in a shortage of key natural resources and a social structure combining low global demand due to poverty and a landed elite relatively short on investment capital[11]—seems fairly well understood. The "borderland" between the two Languedocs, the Tarn and Aveyron (though most of the latter was never officially in Languedoc, it forms a natural part of the region, especially in terms of labor supply and population flows) are increasingly known, thanks to the work, among others, of Rolande Trempé, Joan Wallach Scott, Rémy Cazals, and Donald Reid. Cazals and Reid, especially, are interested in problems of development. In the former's books on Mazamet, we have a picture, perhaps, of what might have been: a highly innovative and energetic industrial bourgeoisie confronted in the late nineteenth century by a working class both militant and concerned about local development who in their struggles and compromises created a town at once prosperous and progressive. Reid, on the other hand, has written a history of the most viable coal basin in the region, Decazeville, and carries its quite different history of growth, bitter labor strife, and deindustrialization down to the present.[12]

Lower Languedoc's economic and social history from the Revolution to the mid-nineteenth century has been addressed in three ways, none of them sufficient to answer the main questions posed in this book. First of all, dozens of specialized studies, from Diplômes d'etudes supérieures to published monographs such as Robert Locke's *Fonderies et forges d'Alais*, have explored local developments. Second, considerable amounts of useful information can be gleaned from important studies dealing with other subjects in which the demographic, economic, and social-structural framework has been sketched. Third, there is the sweeping synthesis of geographer Raymond Dugrand, *Villes et campagnes en Bas-Languedoc*, whose focus is contemporary (as of its date, 1963), but who alone has sought to deal with

the historical problem of deindustrialization in a global fashion and therefore assesses Languedoc's early nineteenth-century history in a larger context. It is in many ways a remarkable achievement, and its influence, not
only on historians but on regional planning policy, has been immense.
Building on an idea developed in Claude Fohlen's 1949 study of the Aude,
Dugrand's central argument was that as the nineteenth century wore on,
the vine emerged as a much more appealing investment than industry. Urban
capitalists in Languedoc abandoned, he claims, often thriving industrial
concerns to throw their money into the cash crop that the railroad made so
easily transportable to the north. His judgment of the Languedocian bourgeoisie is a harsh one: they took the path of least resistance, one more re-
warding socially as well (here echoing André Armengaud), and turned
Languedoc into a species of colony, while they themselves often transferred
their principal residences to Paris. Dugrand, popular with the regionalist
left, thus made the case for a nineteenth-century transition and the treason
of the modern bourgeoisie.[13] The problem, however, is that Dugrand's
historical analysis is sketchy and incomplete and takes little account of the
larger economic and political forces that took hold in the nineteenth century. This makes his discussion of causality questionable. Eighteenth-century
historians would revise the entire story backwards and argue that the trends
seen by Dugrand were already in place, at least embryonically, in their
period. Dermigny, in particular, argues that the *emprise* of the vine over
woolens can already be seen in later eighteenth-century price trends and
that most Montpellier capitalists were already oriented toward safe havens
of investment seventy-five years before Dugrand's rush to the land.[14]

Questions of timing, causality, and indeed of fact thus exist. What needs
to be done is to back away and look at the problem quantitatively and comparatively, to take seriously the opinions of contemporaries, and, especially,
to avoid letting the depth of one's knowledge of a period, area, or activity
skew one's interpretation. Naturally insight flows from depth—my own
perspective owes a great deal to my interest in the Lodève-Bédarieux region and the social conflicts there in the nineteenth century—but one must
not allow it to overwhelm one's analysis. It is time for a balanced perspective that draws and expands upon excellent research already done.

The most important thing, perhaps, is to place Languedoc's economic
performance in a national context. If there was evident "decline" in its textile industries in the period after 1770, this was also the case nationally. If
the first glimmerings of modern coal extraction operations may be seen at
the same time, so did other, more mature coal basins boom. Late eighteenth-
century Languedoc in fact was rather average, a sort of microcosm of French
economic development and its vicissitudes as a whole: some industries were
in real trouble (leather and draps de Levant), others held their own (interior woolens, silk), others expanded (cotton cloth, coal, chemicals); agricultural products showed similar unevenness (olives in decline, wheat holding its course, wine on the ascent); levels of commercial activity as reflected
in traffic on the Canal du Midi, sales at the fair of Beaucaire, and depar-

tures from Cette again seem quite "national."[15] Only in the area of banking perhaps, may a significant problem be located: Montpellier was much more caught up in *la finance*, that is to say, public finance, and thus dependent on the increasingly shaky state of the French government, than in private banking operations. Even so, this did not differentiate the city from many others, nor did it necessarily predict a dismal future.[16] Certainly, if one looks hard enough, it is possible to see in eighteenth-century Languedoc problems that augur its long-term deindustrialization, just as one can isolate characteristics of French economic life as a whole that predict the nation's more gradual entry into the industrial age. But the 1815–1860 period is crucial in understanding Languedoc's destiny. This was the period during which the struggle to industrialize unfolded; only after that did the trend toward a *Languedoc viticole* become ineluctable.

The following figures, drawn only from the woolens industry, provide the necessary grounding for the entire study. The Levant trade and Lodève's largely military production comprise most of the broadcloth production for eighteenth-century lower Languedoc. Maxima occurred in 1763, 1764, and 1776—115,000 and (twice) 106,000 bolts of about twenty-five meters for the Levant trade, along with 10,000 to 20,000 bolts of military cloth.[17] If one adds another 10,000 bolts of miscellaneous broadcloth (4,000 from Bédarieux alone) for interior commerce, we can say that 125,000 to 145,000 bolts of fulled and finished woolen cloth was the top production for any year in the eighteenth century. Military and commercial cloth production varied inversely with each other, an obvious consequence of war. In "good" years for Lodève (1744–47, 1758–62, 1778–82), its production made up a much larger percentage of the total, but it never dominated.

It was otherwise in the Revolutionary/Imperial era. The Levant trade virtually disappeared. Military cloth became the motor of what was left of the cloth industry: 60,000 pieces in the Year III, for example, were produced in the Hérault and Aude, with 41,688 from Lodève alone. Bédarieux's reemergence—copying the *nouvautés* pioneered in Reims—brought the total to a wartime peak of 100,000 bolts in 1810, still well below the apex of the eighteenth century. Following the peace of 1815, disaster was evident, with production down to less than 50,000 bolts in 1821 with military cloth accounting for only 11,500.[18] It never topped 60,000 throughout the Restoration. Then, the key—and overlooked—fact in the economic history of the south, came a true boom during the July Monarchy, one rooted in mechanization. Not only was military cloth in great demand, but an important Mediterranean broadcloth trade had reemerged. The industry in the Aude collapsed (thus providing the basis for the Fohlen-Dugrand thesis), but the Hérault more than compensated, and if one includes the thriving industry of Mazamet along with the small totals for Castres and the Aude, over 200,000 bolts of good woolen cloth, as much as five million meters, were produced annually by the Languedoc industry.[19]

I have published my analysis of the growth, stagnation, and survival of industrial Languedoc during the Old Regime, Revolution, and Empire elsewhere[20] and will offer only a brief summary here. The general economic argument has already been presented. Lodève and the military cloth industry became the flagship of survival in the critical 1780–1820 period identified by Serge Chassagne.[21] But it was complemented by the entrepreneurial vitality evident in Bédarieux's export and domestic woolens production. Together they paved the way to a nineteenth-century revival.

Old Regime

Lodève, an ancient episcopal city and fortress of the Counter-Reformation, had a wool textile history stretching back to the Middle Ages. The natural setting—its proximity to the sheepraising Grandes Causses to the north, the Lergue and the Soulandres, its twin streams of soft, clear, and rapidly flowing water, and its easy access by road to the plains—provided its hard-working hillfolk with the bases of industrial prosperity. Although stimulated by Colbert's policies toward Languedoc as a whole, the key moment in its history came in 1729, when Cardinal André de Fleury, the son of a Lodève wool merchant, created a privileged role for his native town in the production of cloth for the French military, a speciality it had developed over the previous century. This move accompanied a series of legal victories by Lodève's *corporation* of merchant-manufacturers (called *fabricants* after 1708) that undermined the rights of the weavers' guild by restricting their contract options and that accorded the merchants the right to put carding and spinning out to villages far and wide in the region.

With the coming of war in 1740, Inspector of Manufactures Le Mazurier issued a report detailing these shifts,[22] followed by a new set of regulations virtually eliminating the privileges of the weavers' guild and encroaching on the rights of Lodève's most powerful producers' guild, the cloth finishers called *pareurs.* The latter's protests in 1749 fell on deaf ears, only exacerbating tension generated by the murder of a weaver by the local inspector, Henri de Sauclières, after an altercation during Carnival the previous year. In every respect, the French state made it clear that it not only stood on the side of the fabricants' guild's drive to create capitalist relations of production (without relinquishing their own corporate protections), but even gave impetus to the process, a phenomenon that Gail Bossenga has documented in Lille and perhaps the key to understanding the structured capitalism that emerged in larger-scale manufacturing in later eighteenth-century France.[23] Savings in labor costs and economies of scale paid off as Lodève withstood challenges from Sedan and Louviers in the post-Fleury era and became a model of efficient production for its prime customer.

Weaving naturally found its way into the countryside after 1740, and the principal consequence of the fabricants' dominion was the marked decline of the independent master weaver in Lodève itself. By the American War of Independence, weavers' sheds had sprung up in or near the fulling mills of most of the major manufacturers; new hires or distraught home-weavers manned looms that they "rented" from the *patron*. Moreover, weavers need not be men. *Tisserande* enters the vocabulary of woolens manufacturing—although women had long "assisted" husbands or fathers—and by 1798 (our first census), forty-three single women and many more (unlisted) wives worked as loom-shed weavers. The locale of pareurs' work, already in space rented in fulling mills, did not change, but their ability to bargain with different fabricants and to control their own procedures had been restricted. Independent dyers (never incorporated) were also under fire as fabricants increasingly took over this activity themselves.

Well before the Revolution and without the least change in machine technology, Lodève was moving toward the factory system. After a period of industrial dispersion, which served to undermine the power of the urban guilds, its manufacturers were able to concentrate much of their production again in the city. Complex manufacturing establishments had grown around fulling mills. The only elements in the process that now fell outside the direct oversight of the fabricant were carding and spinning and perhaps half the weaving; both operations were so carefully regulated that little could happen without the bosses' knowledge. Up and down the Lergue and stretching back into the narrow valley of the Soulandres, the *usines* of the Lodévois captains of industry dotted the landscape. Images of the Colne valley of the West Riding or of the Vesdre and Verviers come to mind.[24] The city's influence had also guided military contracts elsewhere in Languedoc, including the old royal manufactories of Villeneuvette, Saptes, and Montesquieu, as well as Clermont, Bédarieux, and the Jaur valley towns of St. Pons and Riols.[25]

The social consequences of these shifts in Lodève's economic structure were profound. A working class, whose distance from the owning class became ever greater and in which craft distinctions became less and less important, was in formation. Marriage and residence patterns allow one to assess the growth of this class cohesion, the social foundation of Lodève's prodigious worker solidarity of the future.[26]

As was true of eighteenth-century artisans everywhere in Western Europe, occupational endogamy and intergenerational continuity marked the city's experience. Less typically, newly arriving woolens workers, drawn heavily from declining Levant-trade towns, tended to marry local women, mostly from woolens-worker families. Chain migration was virtually absent since professional opportunity, not kin connections, largely motivated migration. Because of their marriage patterns, new men located near their wives' relations in the heart of the city's working-class districts. By 1798, the population had swelled to 9,500 (from 7,500 at mid-century), largely due to workers' migration.

The town divided rather sharply between larger and newer residences around the cathedral of St. Fulcran and in the exclusive Bouquerie district to the north, and the lower city in the parish of St. Pierre and the faubourgs of Carmes, Montbrun, and Montifort across the rivers, where housing was mostly older, tightly packed, and subdivided into flats. Fabricants, profes-

sionals, many better-off non-woolens artisans, a minority of woolens workers, and many farmers (on the edges) lived in the former, while woolens
workers and poorer people generally dominated the latter. This bifurcation
thus possessed both geographical and religious significance, because the
St. Pierre parish nurtured artisan lay brotherhoods separate from the
Cathedral's tutelage and drew priests sympathetic to the concerns of working
people. Thus, if eighteenth-century changes in the relations of production
augured growing proletarianization, patterns of marriage and residence
demonstrated a potential for cohesion among workers and a distance from
the world of the town's emerging industrial capitalists.

Still, despite huge differences in wealth, it would not be accurate to
describe the woolens workers of late eighteenth-century Lodève as poverty-
stricken. Home ownership was one indicator. In general, 72 percent of all
houses in Lodève were owned by a person or persons living there. Absentee
landlords normally came from the professional ranks, especially—*notaires*,
and not from among the fabricants, so little "company town" atmosphere
existed. Indeed, property ownership in Lodève was rather widely distributed. According to the census of 1798, 38 percent of the woolens workers
were home owners; of these, however, slightly fewer than half owned part
of a dwelling.[27] Houses in the woolens-worker neighborhoods were small,
normally selling for less than a thousand livres. Elaborate subdivision
arrangements, with specifications for the use of doors, stairways, and kitchen
facilities, were detailed in notarized contracts.[28] Overall, about one-third
of all dwellings in Lodève were possessed by multiple owners.

Lowest access to home ownership existed among *brassiers* (agricultural
workers), 10 percent of whom owned a single house and 8 percent part of
one. Artisans and tradespeople enjoyed access ratios similar to those of
woolens workers, while virtually all manufacturers and professionals owned
homes, usually single-family dwellings. As a percentage of all home owners, migrants had a lower access rate than their total percentage in the city,
23 percent as opposed to 34 percent. But that of woolens-worker migrants
was almost the same, 37 percent, as all other woolens workers. Thus they
shared a very important characteristic with the woolens population at large.
Few woolens workers were rich, but their condition indicates a picture of
settlement, stability, and integration in a context of mediocre opportunity.

In general, agricultural workers, almost one-fourth of the population,
were the least integrated group in the city, rarely intermarrying with woolens workers and other city residents. On the other hand, Lodève's artisan
and shopkeeper population, while generally located in the central city
for commercial reasons, had close ties to the woolens workers. The latter
were their principal customers and their shops often served as gathering
places for socializing and discussion, especially during the Revolution.
Moreover, intermarriage between people in woolens and the trades was not
uncommon.[29]

Although we shall examine the world of the city's industrialists in detail
in chapter 3, a few remarks on this elite group on the eve of the Revolution

are necessary. Four characteristics stand out. The first was the remarkable continuity of dozens of fabricant families, dating back to the early seventeenth century. The great names seem almost timeless: Teisserenc, Martin, Pascal, Menard, Soudan, Rouaud, Fabreguettes, Vallat, Vinas, Calvet. Newer arrivals often came from big-city merchant families or from regional woolens dynasties; examples include Faulquier, Fournier, Barbot, Vitalis, Fraisse, and Labranche.[30] Second, these men were dedicated industrial capitalists. No Buddenbrooks cycle here! Their investments were heavily committed to ploughback and improvement.[31] Their concentrated establishments represented significant capital outlays. Some fabricants did invest in land, but especially in tracts of sheep pastureland, thus vertically integrating. The contrast with Thomson's discoveries about the fabricants of Clermont could not be sharper. Although some migrated to Lodève and Bédarieux, most withdrew from the trade, investing especially in vineland in the Hérault valley, a process Thomson erroneously generalizes to include all Languedoc.[32] Third, business was family and family was business. Lodève's fabricants' firms were almost exclusively family partnerships that changed often due to shifting alliances based on new marriages, largely within a circle of equals (including local aristocrats), while also pulling in new wealth and talent from elsewhere. Marriage contracts elaborate investment networks.[33] Daughters who could not effectuate business connections often remained unmarried, although their fathers sometimes set them up in independent living situations. Self-sacrifice for the family interest was expected.[34] Finally, from all indications, the fabricants of Lodève were frugal and austere, but cosmopolitan. They were in constant touch with Montpellier, Lyon, and Paris, educated their children there and abroad, and drew spouses from as far as America. They were fluent in French (though undoubtedly spoke to their workers in Occitan) and well read, particularly in theology, with a preference for Jansenism.[35] They lived cloistered in their nuclear-family homes, hiring only the bare minimum number of domestic servants from the poor villages roundabout.[36] It was a bourgeoisie dedicated to careful planning and to capital accumulation.

Their confrères in Bédarieux, while lacking their pedigrees, certainly shared their outlook. In the later eighteenth century, an enterprising group of merchant-manufacturers, many of them from families of dyers (for Bédarieux had long had the right to dye cloth made elsewhere), moved into the Levant trade at a time when the fortunes of the traditional centers of the industry were declining. Carcassonne, Saint-Chinian, and especially Clermont had responded to the difficulties posed by shifts in international demand and unscrupulous Marseille shippers by cutting quality. The problem became an epidemic during the brief period of free trade under Turgot, and their reputations never recovered. Bédarieux became virtually the only trusted name by the 1780s. Clermontois were even prosecuted for putting their cloth on the market under Bédarieux's label.[37]

Historically, the organization of the cloth industry in Bédarieux had been rather primitive. In 1713, one merchant-manufacturer, Seymondy, had won the right to establish a privileged manufacture for the Levant trade and organized along typical putting-out lines. In the 1770s and 1780s, the Martel brothers developed a centralized establishment for all operations except spinning and weaving and several times demanded the title "royal manufacture." But the typical Bédarieux draper had been little more than a merchant, having agreements with dozens of independent subcontractors, weavers and finishers especially. It was the classic *Kaufssystem*, which, as James Thomson argues persuasively, gave verve and freshness to Bédarieux's expanding business community. Only in the last decades before the Revolution did the more successful merchants move toward putting-out patterns.[38]

While the drapers had long had a guild (quality control for government-approved goods had to pass through their *jurande*), the carders, weavers, and finishers did not possess officially recognized *corporations*. The weavers and finishers had organized *confréries*, however, and attempted to regulate their trades through these less formal brotherhoods. In the 1780s, weavers, increasingly pressured to work exclusively for one fabricant, sought to tighten the "guild" controls and in 1784 petitioned for recognition as a corporate body. This drive to unite against the fabricants and to resist the proliferation of weavers who were not members of their confrérie came at the moment when protoindustrial capitalism was coming into its own in the little city. The key problem in the weavers' complaint was the widespread use of weavers in the rural communes of Le Poujol, Colombières, Saint-Vincent, and Mons, villages down the Orb valley.[39] As in the Lodévois, spinning had long been done in the countryside, but under the charge of independent carders who sold the thread to weavers. Now, however, the fabricants increasingly dominated those operations as well, thereafter putting out the thread to cheaper rural weavers. Thus the Lodève pattern unfolded, but at a fifty-year remove. Bédarieux entered the Revolutionary era just as its rural phase of protoindustrialization was reaching full flower.

Revolution and Empire

The Revolution created the most troubling era faced by the Languedocian economy since the mid-seventeenth century, delivering the final blow to the Levant trade and crushing the upland petites étoffes. These developments, however, were not immediately apparent, and what was lamented instead by the most progressive *fabrique* in the region, Bédarieux, was the continuing grip of *Colbertisme*. Jacques Cère, author of a long *mémoire* to the National Assembly dated 5 December 1789, argued for the abolition of all regulations and duties, the end of the inspection system, free and direct trade from the cloth centers, and new trade treaties with Russia and Portugal to match the widely reviled Eden Treaty of 1786.[40] This spirit of enterprise was echoed in Limoux, another recent interloper in the Levant trade, and in Mazamet, a town that had nothing to lose since it had been effectively shut out of regulated commerce under the inspection system.[41] In the mining district of Graissessac, surface proprietors, many of them independent nailmakers, saw in the Revolution the end of the concession system whereby wealthy notables monopolized the underground by virtue of royal grants.[42] And, as we shall see, many Lodévois welcomed a new era of opportunity for those practitioners of the cloth trade—weavers, pareurs, dyers, and lesser wool merchants—too undercapitalized to participate in the Old Regime army cloth contract system.

For many, then, in this land of people "avid for gain," the Revolution represented an era of economic opportunity in which all men of talent and daring might have a chance to profit. The d'Allarde Law abolishing the guilds had been a foregone conclusion, and the months following its adoption in March 1791 passed without incident. With the declaration of war in 1792, army cloth orders boomed and Lodève naturally rejoiced. Jacobin politics rapidly took hold and proved perfectly compatible with the emergence of a whole new set of woolens entrepreneurs. Government policy encouraged small producers, and local politicians, most of whom were new faces in the ranks of the fabricants (figures such as former shepherd and weaver Michel and Antoine Causse, père et fils, and the former dyers, Joseph and Jean-Baptiste Rouaud), used their political positions to their own advantage, as well as that of other upstarts, thus creating a new contingent of manufacturers by 1794. At the height of orders late in the Year II, over 200 fabricants plied the trade.[43] The old guard profited as well, usually retaining their positions of volume leadership, but there were naturally conflicts, economic and social, as well as political. Disdain and vituperation were kept to a minimum during the worst moments of the Terror, however, and no fabricant lost his head, the elites actually being protected by their Jacobin compères. And with Thermidor, despite an occasional outburst,[44] reciprocal service was accorded the likes of the Causses and Rouauds. The central government proved less generous, and Lodève's Jacobin reputation caused army orders to be substantially reduced in 1795. A trying period followed in which the Directory farmed military purchases out to huge firms whose job it was to find the lowest bids. This notoriously corrupt procedure seriously wounded Lodève, halving the number of fabricants by 1801.[45]

The history of Bédarieux during the Revolution contrasted sharply with that of Lodève, revealing a situation where the progressive political thrust of the French Revolution threatened to destroy equally progressive economic development. Bédarieux succeeded as a woolens manufacturing town despite the Revolution; its politics reflected this fact.

The Revolution occurred at a moment when its energetic capitalists had just established their reputation as the most reliable producers of draps de Levant. They had also just won their suit abrogating the claims of local weavers to guild status. Thus a process almost inverse to that of Lodève unfolded. The abolition of the guilds was meaningless for all concerned, because the jurande of fabricants had never been terribly strong. Most of the fabricants were comparative newcomers to the business. The local bourgeoisie was young and fluid. But the key fact was the rapid collapse of the

Mediterranean trade, especially after the declaration of war. This meant that the town's enthusiasm for the Republic, indeed, for the Revolution as a whole, became less than ecstatic.[46] There was one segment that greeted it warmly—the Protestant minority. Moreover, a variety of non-Protestant small merchants and artisans, sans-culottes, became enamored of revolutionary ideals. But for the town's top elites, the Catholic fabricants such as the Vernazobres, Martels, or Fabregats, the Revolution had caused nothing but trouble, a sentiment made all the stronger by their initial sense of its promise.[47] Moreover, artisans in the woolens industry were hardly in a position to invade the ranks of the fabricants, as had been the case in booming Lodève.

But the tradition of enterprise remained strong. Aggressive Bédarieux cloth manufacturers had moved into the labor market of the Orb-Jaur corridor and "demand[ed] with vehemence the opening of better roads" there. A new product, *mi-soie, mi-laine* (weft in silk, warp in wool), found a ready internal market and also escaped the *maximum* on prices when it was imposed in 1793. Moreover, Bédarieux won some army contracts. But the fact remained that the number of successful partnership firms in the city remained small, and resentment toward the upheaval in trade caused by the Revolution ran high.[48]

Bédarieux became a hotbed of royalism. The initial catalyst was the imposition of the Civil Constitution of the Clergy, which was resisted furiously. With the coming of the Republic and the levée en masse, Bédarieux and its westward hinterland, the wild mountains of the Espinouse, became a battleground between bands of royalists, often led by priests, and recruiting officers. By the time of the *coup d'état*, the area was a royalist stronghold where conscription was simply ignored.[49]

The Protestants of Bédarieux made up no more than 10 percent of the population and consisted of about a dozen fabricant families, a few members of the liberal professions, and a variety of artisans and retail merchants. There were few woolens workers among them, meaning that the bulk of the city's working class was Catholic. The Revolution opened new vistas for Protestant businessmen, and, as elsewhere they supported it warmly, thus contributing to the largely royalist response of the workers. Cholvy has shown that Catholic consciousness in Languedoc was heightened by the presence of even a small minority of Protestants, especially if they had power.[50] Deferential popular Catholicism/royalism was thus strong in Bédarieux.

The Consulat saved the day for the Languedoc woolens industry, but also, by virtue of its new policy awarding contracts in large lots and payable only upon arrival in Paris, delivered the *coup de grace* to the struggling petty capitalism of Lodève. The architect of the policy was Chaptal, the famous chemist/businessman from Montpellier, friend of the South, and a Federalist saved from the guillotine by some Jacobin allies. His new orientation was reflected in a conflict in Lodève in which he finally sided with the old elites of the city against the Fabreguettes family, one of whose members, Pierre, he had in fact appointed as the Sub-Prefect of the new arrondissement of Lodève. Pierre's brother Michel, the largest manufacturer in the city and a professed democrat, organized the remaining smaller fabricants, along with the more substantial Causses and Rouauds, into a conglomerate that he then invited the old elite elements to join. The conglomerate (the entire fabrique), under the leadership of Fabrequettes, would then handle the distribution of work and guarantee prepayment to those with insufficient liquidity. Chaptal, petitioned by Pierre Menard, Antoine Visseq, Louis Teisserenc, and other members of the old leadership of the city, rejected Fabrequettes' request on the grounds that it created a monopoly and would impede competition. The purpose, of course, was to allow smaller manufacturers a place at all. The outcome was not in doubt—post paid, large-order lots would be the rule. A restricted circle of responsible, well-capitalized associations with good banking connections to cover outlay costs would compete with one another in an orderly, rational process of adjudication. Naturally, the wealthier renegades such as Fabreguettes, the Causses, and Rouards, once defeated, joined in the concept, but small fabricants, former artisans for the most part, found themselves shut out.[51]

Lodève naturally did well throughout the war years, although nonpayment by the government became a growing problem. The association method of bidding gave way quickly to a system that would remain throughout the nineteenth century: for all but the very wealthiest families, the use of shifting partnerships of major manufacturers that bid for quarter-lot orders (or multiples thereof) became the rule. The state continued to demand large orders and postpayment, which meant that only capitalists with high volume operations and good credit did business with it. The petty capitalist age of opportunity was over.

Chaptal, not at all opposed in principle to equality of opportunity, nevertheless followed a policy that discouraged petit bourgeois aspirations in Lodève. He consistently promoted competition, but simultaneously sought the rationalization of the industry by making certain that small fabricants—accused of cheating on quality and known for late delivery— were forced out altogether. The concept of rational competition had overruled his inherent political beliefs.

There was no explicit response to these developments in Lodève, but across the Escandorgue ridge in the Graissessac coal fields a similar drama unfolded.[52] Surface proprietors, nail makers whose only resources in these barren lands were coal and their own ingenuity (their iron came from scrap traded for nails transported by equally enterprising mule drivers), waged war with the concessionnaires, Antoine de Giral and his successor, a notable de clocher from St. Gervais named Bartholémy Moulinier, for control of the mines. The law of 1791 giving concrete rights to surface owners seemed to be on their side, but Moulinier and his associates commanded capital and the support of Robert Mathieu, the state mining engineer whose ultimate boss was also Chaptal.[53] In 1800 and 1801 pitched battles occurred between the petty capitalist artisan-miners and the police, who attempted, unsuccessfully, to close their shallow backyard mines.[54] The following year, the government put the whole basin up for concession bids. An association of five nailmakers, backed by some outside capital, sought an area, where most of them lived, called the Devois de Graissessac. One of the outside capitalists, a former Jacobin and regicide Conventionnel named Michel Azéma, supported the claim with a ringing defense of the "democratic" principles of free competition that the Revolution had supposedly ushered in.[55] Interestingly, the nail makers won their concession, but it alone was saddled with the responsibility of making coal available at cost to all unassociated nail makers. Moreover, its operating costs were high. It was cut off from decent paths (there were no roads within ten kilometers), and any deep mining would incur staggering timbering expenses. Inevitably, it would fail and be swallowed up as part of the "Quatre mines réunies" under Moulinier's control.[56]

Such experiences with the failed promise of free enterprise did not immediately manifest themselves in outward protest, but unquestionably deepened social fissures as the disenchanted fell back into the world of the laboring classes.

Religion exacerbated the gap. The nailmakers of Graissessac were mostly Protestants; although some of their number would make their way to Bédarieux and even prosper, most struggled on in their traditional craft in a state of permanent antagonism with the mine company. Virtually none of them or their descendants would work for it; they formed the front line of later political radicalism in the district. Only during the Second Republic would the Catholic mine workers, many of them in-migrants, begin to see that their interests also lay in that political arena.

Religious lines of social division also rose to view in Lodève. A by-product of Jacobinism that did not sit well with many of the city's artisans, most of whom lived in the lower city, was the closing of the parish church of St. Pierre and the confréries associated with it. The Constitutional services were held in the former cathedral, thus forcing those believers who supported the *régime decadaire* to attend church in the bailiwick of the fabricant elites. Some among them, however, joined Roman Catholics in clandestine services ministered by nonjuring priests or acted out their confréries' rituals without authorization. Popular piety had a deep tradition in the city and remained an important mode of self-expression (and solidarity) among the people. The Concordat of 1801 brought resentments out into the open. The laboring classes even gave support to the installation of a former non-juring priest as the curé of Saint-Fulcran. But, above all, mass demonstrations pressed for the reopening of St. Pierre, which had fallen into serious disrepair, and for the legalization of confraternities. Both goals were finally realized a year later, but the whole affair confirmed and accentuated the religious division of the city. On one side ranged a majority of the bourgeois who had accepted the Constitutional Church and on the other, the people, whose Roman Catholicism emphasized festive events and participatory religious practices. There was also a third strand—elements of the old elite whose politics were royalist and religion was orthodox Catholic, men such as Guillaume Rouaud, Pierre Menard, or Fulcran Lagare. Their religious beliefs would occasionally serve as a conduit to the workers.[57]

During most of the Empire, however, despite the losses, disenchantments, and fissures, few Lodévois could complain about their economic fortunes, for the army-cloth city bulked large in Languedoc's woolens economy. Serge Chassagne's research on woolens production during this era shows clearly the near collapse of the industry nationwide early in the Revolution, followed by an Imperial revival. But Languedoc did not keep pace, dropping from 30 percent to 22.7 percent of the national product from 1790 to 1810.[58] Champagne—above all, the miraculous case of Reims—accounted for the lion's share by virtue of innovative designs, a focus on la mode, large-scale rural outworking, and imaginative marketing techniques.[59] Languedoc's totals are in fact inflated by petites étoffes production, but this had always been the case,[60] and such cheap materials (though not so much of them) were also included in the official totals for other regions.[61]

Thus, realistically, the production of the draps-producing Languedoc heartland (Lodève, Clermont-l'Hérault, Villeneuvette, Bédarieux, St. Pons, St. Chinian, Mazamet, Castres, Carcassonne, Limoux, and Chalabre) amounted in 1810 to no more than 100,000 pieces of which approximately 90 percent were draps,[62] a drop of about one-third from the 140,000 bolts estimated by Thiomar Markovitch for 1781.[63] But was this, as Serge Chassange argues, "the end of one commercial era, the exportation of the famous draps de Levant," now succeeded by a new one, "that of the Ternaux and the Croutelles"?[64] In the broadest sense, the answer is yes, for the north *did* overtake the south in the course of the nineteenth century. But if we look ahead just to the July Monarchy, one would have to wonder about what Chassagne calls an "inevitable evolution," for Languedoc woolens had made a serious comeback by then, outdistancing in fact its best years of the eighteenth century with figures for the Hérault alone (thus leaving aside for now the burgeoning fabrique of Mazamet, as well as the collapsing world of Carcassonne). In 1838, 162,400 bolts of broadcloth, of which over half was exported to Mediterranean lands, were produced in the department. Totals declined somewhat over the next three years because of the Eastern Crisis, but Lodève army orders picked up some of the slack, reaching 41,000 bolts in 1841. During the 1840s, sales remained around 150,000 bolts, with Bédarieux, which exported 80 percent of its cloth, accounting for more than a third of the total. The value of the products ranged between twenty-four and twenty-seven million francs; the consistent leader during this period was Bédarieux, prospering from the supposedly abandoned draps de Levant. We have here a patient whose vital signs remain strong.[65]

The survival of Languedoc woolens during the troubled years of Revolution and Empire was rooted in the vast demand of France's war machine for soldiers' uniforms. Lodève was at the heart of it, but as the demand mushroomed, most of the old centers gained some contracts, and virtually every woolens-producing town in France got into the act by 1810. And they wanted samples from Lodève, for it provided the standard and indeed advertised Languedoc woolens in general.[66] Lodève's place in the history of Languedoc's industrial development has been played down by historians and geographers who see "defense industries" as somehow "artificial" elements in modern economies. This simply ignores the realities of modern economic growth. How can one discount, for example, the fundamental significance of production for war in the economic history of the United States, beginning with the age of the Civil War? The Great Depression of the 1930s only came to an end with the vast increase in military production in 1940–41; the Second World War, the war in Korea, as well as the continuing Cold War contributed mightily to sustaining the long boom period that followed. Although inherently inflationary and not sufficient to insure long-term growth, military spending has served a crucial function in the history of many economies.[67]

Obviously, the place of government contract work during the Napoleonic period was enormous. In woolen cloth (excluding knitwear) we may—in the absence of reliable general statistics—take the year 1810 as a rough guide. Led by Lodève with 30,000 bolts, the Midi produced approximately 80,000 bolts of military cloth, or 80 percent of its broadcloth production. By that time all the major northern broadcloth towns—Louviers, Elbeuf, Romorantin, Chateauroux, Vire, Sedan, and Strasbourg were the leaders—also produced for the army. Totals can only be estimated from partial orders for that year, but easily another 100,000 to 120,000 bolts were cut into military uniforms. The carnage on the battlefields over the next three years meant an even further increase in demand. Overall, the military absorbed at least a quarter of all woolens production in France and well over half the drap.[68]

Up to the point when Imperial finances went awry, the profitability of the industry was undeniable. By 1810, Lodève's worker population (including extra-muros), had jumped to 14,000—up from 6,000 in 1789. The capital outlay of its manufacturers had quadrupled, the gross value of its 30,000 bolts produced that year was five times that of 1789, and net profits had more than doubled.[69] Although these figures are no doubt mere estimates, there is no question that increasing amounts of money were made by fabricants during the Empire. Business was even better in the following years—50,000 bolts in 1811 and 40,000 in 1813; a report noted that "this important manufacture provides . . . the means of existence for the towns and villages in a circumference of ten leagues."[70] Clermont and Bédarieux weavers worked for Lodève, rural spinning proliferated, and rural broadloom weaving may have even revived.

During the same era, Lodève took the lead in the process of mechanization, again the result of the interplay between government stimulation and local entrepreneurship. We have no direct information on the use of hand-cranked spinning jennies in the Lodévois, but the state's sponsorship of a seminar for Lodève's weavers on the fly-shuttle loom in 1802 may in-

dicate their earlier introduction, for it was only at that point in the history
of spinning technology in woolens that a sturdy enough thread had been
produced by a perfected jenny to withstand the jolt of the shuttle spring.[71]
French manufacturers were skeptical of power spinning devices, and the
state was unwilling to subsidize them until the arrival in Paris in 1804 of
Douglas and Cockerell, a firm of textile machine builders.[72] In 1809,
Lodévois Antoine Causse, the son of the self-made manufacturer and
Jacobin, Michel Causse, took advantage of a quarter-price government
subsidy to install two sets (assortments) consisting of a scribbler, a carder,
a slubbing billy, and four mule-jennies in his finishing shop. Lacking access
to water, the motive power consisted of horses. He formed a partnership
with another young entrepreneur and was further rewarded with an order
for 4000 meters of cloth. Official correspondence makes it clear that many
fabricants resented Causse's move, and someone apparently convinced the
supply department that Causse's delay in delivery of his first order was due
to incompetence, not worker training time as he claimed, for his order was
not renewed. He was able to join with the firm of Costaing, however, in
another order. Again a subterfuge cheated Causse and Privat out of their
due, as the quality of their product was questioned. Whatever the truth of
the latter, Causse's endless correspondence with the administration indicates that there was a great deal of opposition to this upstart. Whether it
was the man who undertook it or the very concept of mechanization that
was the problem is difficult to ascertain. It was probably a little of both.
Prefect Nogaret certainly thought that Causse was a victim of "intrigues
and envy." Causse and Privat, although they participated in two more
fournitures (1813 and 1814), took their skills, energy, and assertiveness to
Bédarieux in 1816, where they went on to consistent success in the commercial market for the next thirty years.[73] Causse pioneered mechanization
there as well—in all, an impressive record for the son of a shepherd.

Lodève, however, did respond to the challenge of mechanization. "In
1811, two English machine builders came to Lodève; the first decided
to create an establishment of his own and spin on contract; while he carried out preliminary construction plans, his compatriot contracted an agreement with some fabricants; he offered to furnish the machines which would
be paid for only after a trial of several months. . . . When the machines were
in operation and one could calculate their advantages, several fabricants
and capitalists decided to follow the example given."[74] By mid–1814, five
water-driven spinneries with a total of twenty-five sets of machines were in
place. The new leader was Etienne Faulquier, whose firm alone possessed
twelve assortments capable of spinning sufficient thread for 4,000 bolts of
cloth. Doubts remained nonetheless. "Several enlightened persons," wrote
the Prefect during the First Restoration, "seek to throw disfavor on these
establishments by claiming that they are harmful to the people. . . ."[75] Thus
there remained a core of unbelievers among the fabricants, but established
people like Faulquier had converted. The machine had come to stay in
Lodève.

The interrelationship between the rise of mechanical spinning, which produced a higher quality yarn because of the evenness of the draw, and fly-shuttle weaving has already been noted. Unfortunately, the details of the rise of the new weaving device escape us, but by the early 1830s, it— along with the cuts in ratio between weavers and looms, the growing number of women weavers, and, because of the capital investment involved, the rapid completion of fabricant-owned, factory-housed weaving—dominated the craft.[76] The impact of fly-shuttle weaving on the workers of Lodève was significant, but subtle. Many weavers were already used to working on machines that they did not own, and women weavers were hardly unusual. Indeed, for those who continued to work at home, the elimination of the assistant (by now always a woman or youth) made the acquisition of a second loom and nearly twice as much production possible. The same, theoretically, could be said for those families working in weaving sheds. But the potential material benefits depended on increased overall production. The late Empire, despite the growing payment problem, provided a great stimulus for all concerned, but the coming of peace and the Restoration saw drastic cutbacks—and disastrous conditions for Lodève's workers.[77]

The most immediate consequence of the introduction of spinning machinery from 1813 through 1819 was the elimination, very rapidly, of rural outworking. Creuzé de Lesser estimated that each sixty-spindle mule-jenny was "worth twenty fileuses." What was happening in human terms was revealed in this declaration of the Conseil d'Arrondissement de Lodève: "It is understood that it is necessary to absorb the indigents who inhabit the mountainous part of the arrondissement into the ranks of the *ouvriers de fabrique*. The former were until recently woolens workers. This has been forcibly brought to an end since mechanical spinning has been substituted, very advantageously for business but very painfully for them, for hand spinning."[78] Lodève did absorb a good number. Male migrants from Fozières or Soumont or Les Plans were able to establish themselves as spinners and the women migrants, as tenders of carding machines, thus reversing their ancient roles.[79] In general, the demand for *les ouvrières* intensified not only for factory work, but also because many of their traditional jobs (washers, sorters, burlers, and now weavers) remained unmechanized. As overall production increased, so too did the call for their work in these areas. Solid figures on male/female ratios do not exist until the 1830s, but a study in 1838 counted 1,506 men, 2,402 women, and 744 children, a ratio that remained fairly constant until the 1850s, except in boom years when large numbers of male handloom operatives were lured in from other towns.[80] For the rural areas around Lodève, this demand for female labor relieved some of the hardship provoked by the rapid demise of carding and spinning by hand. But spinning factories also went into the countryside, with substantial establishments created north of Lodève, at Soubès (two), St. Etienne de Gourgas, and "Labranche" on the *ruisseau* de Lauroux.[81] In the barren country east and southeast of Lodève ("les Ruffes"), the loss of supplemental industrial work resulted in a permanent force of migrant labor that worked the vines, mowed the hay, and pillaged the forests of the Hérault valley. To the west, work lost from Lodève was replaced by new opportunities in the Orb valley, although wage levels were often pitifully low. Coal mining in Le Bousquet, St. Gervais, and Graissessac stimulated migration from the eastern slopes of the Orb valley, but the main new employer was rural outworking—still carding and spinning as well as weaving—from Bédarieux.[82]

The beginnings of Lodève's "industrial revolution" was thus situated in the Empire and in direct relationship with the state. Despite its specialty, the Hérault city was hardly unique. None of the major woolens centers mechanized without considerable input from the state,[83] and those, like Reims, where direct *primes d'encouragement* were not forthcoming, did not mechanize. It is clear that the state played a quite important role in Lodève in overcoming prejudices and fears, as well as complacency, by giving its stamp of approval (and 25 percent!) to the new technology. That a Causse should take the lead and face the opprobrium was not at all surprising in view of the relationship of his family to past governments and to the socio-political dynamics of their city. The absence of significant worker resistance can best be explained by the sector being mechanized. Little spinning occupied Lodève's workers, and weavers largely benefited from the change. The main locus of conflict over textile machines first occurred in the finishing crafts, and Lodève was no exception. But these battles were still a few years off in 1814, even though a few opening salvos had already occurred in France.[84]

I

INDUSTRIAL CAPITALISM AND SOCIAL UPHEAVAL, 1815–1851

As late as 1824, the Prefect of the Hérault, Hippolyte Creuzé de Lesser, questioned whether the industries of his department could recover from the new crisis caused by British reentry into Mediterranean markets and the Greek Revolution. Yet he held out hope: machines could make all the difference by "saving a great amount of labor and shortening operations, which are also carried out with greater uniformity."[1] And his call was being heeded. Industrialists with the means to do so reacted to hard times and competitive pressures by seeking productivity gains through technological innovation. In their turn, workers reacted. A letter sent to M. Moulinier, a Saint-Pons fabricant, captured their sentiments:

> If, in four days, 3000 francs are not buried in a hole at the corner of M. Tarboureich's house—behind the wall at the first gate, beside the first pile of manure, and marked with a cow dab so I can find it, we are going to break your shearing machine and then you. Don't go out at night if you don't want your throat slit. Your machine will deny us work or at least take our skill away and destroy our independence—this is why I want this sum of money.[2]

The cash was never deposited, and Moulinier and his machine survived; but the tensions expressed here did not dissipate.

Languedoc woolens manufacturers mechanized during the Restoration, and by the early 1830s, Creuzé's doubts seemed groundless. Their struggle to survive, however, turned the region into an arena of bitter class conflict. It had many contemporary parallels, but Languedoc's competitive disadvantages and employers' consequent need to press all the harder made the conflict one of the most virulent in all Europe. These fabled battles ulti-mately made the region the heartland of the démoc-soc movement during the Second Republic. They also made it the scene of a repression that con-tributed to the collapse of Languedoc's industrial foundation. How this interaction between politics and industrial decline played out is the central subject of this book.

1

Restoration Uncertainties

If the political seesaw of 1814–15 gave rise to new horrors in the religion-torn Gard,[1] the rest of lower Languedoc moved grumpily through the up-heavals without any significant resort to violence. Not that its inhabitants were politically indifferent, but politics here was understood to revolve around two essential concerns: material interest and resentment against the French state. When the first received satisfaction, the second abated. Hence the Consulat and the early Empire, providing relative prosperity for most Languedocians, quieted conflicts rooted in antinational feelings. As these conditions waned, saying no to Paris reappeared.[2] Royalism in the Hérault was hardly a matter of ideals. As Napoleon's agent during the One Hundred Days remarked, the Empire found disfavor for one cause only. "People only think in terms of money here. . . . [T]he interruption of maritime commerce has suspended operations . . . and from that derives the ardent wishes on behalf of the Bourbons. If [it] would pick up, . . . those same voices would proclaim 'Napoleon' with enthusiasm."[3] The return of Louis XVIII evoked the same practical response. The Hérault had its share of ultraroyalist and anti-Protestant fanaticism. But incidents in villages and *bourgs* with large Protestant minorities, such as Pignan and Montagnac, were more serious than those in the larger towns or in the capital. And there, in the opinion of the first Prefect of the Second Restoration, royalism largely amounted to lip service. Certainly "all classes, all conditions, all ages discuss the events of the day and the acts of government." But commitment to royalism came largely as "outward expression—songs, cries, flags, and effervescence." It was what they did, not said, that showed the Héraultais' true attitudes. Little of the three million francs pledged "to chase the tyrant," had been paid, and many now claimed this "war tax" was unconstitutional. Ninety per cent of the three thousand returning veterans refused to participate in the royalist Légion départementale. Most seriously, "the indirect taxes are slow in coming in; direct taxes are fraud-ridden, ignored; there is armed insurrection against fishing leases, mining concessions." Tax rebellion had been endemic since Napoleon's abdication, especially in the distraught woolens cities.[4] There was a spirit here, said Prefect Brevannes, that was essentially *frondeur*; it was "a country essentially enemy to authority." Economic revitalization alone would keep them loyal.[5]

Politics in the region's principal woolens towns reflected a similar "effervescent," antiauthoritarian, yet expedient perspective. Bédarieux and Lodève had distinct histories, however. From an economic point of view, Lodève should logically have been Imperialist; but the Empire's default on payments and the promises of the First Restoration government to make them good made such loyalties more problematic. Bédarieux, on the other hand, had experienced its best years under the late Old Regime. Protestant and some Catholic manufacturers had benefited to an extent from the Revolution, but no one in its woolens industry could argue that the previous twenty-five years had been good for it. They had survived through innovation and initiative, despite the loss of the Levant trade. But Bédarieux too had benefited from army contracts and government encouragement of technological progess during the Empire. So from a strictly economic viewpoint, it was natural that opinion in both cities would be divided.

Religion and social tradition complicated matters even more and so did class divisions. As things evolved under the Empire, Lodève emerged with a tripartite elite structure: a traditional, paternalist group of older families who were generally pious Roman Catholics; a middle group of families who had largely emerged with the eighteenth-century boom, had led the capitalistic transformation in labor relations and were practical Catholics, some tinged with Jansenism; and, finally, the new men of the Revolutionary era who were most given to innovation and whose religious outlook was Masonic or freethinking. Bédarieux essentially split into two groupings that cut across religion: the old Catholic elite led by the Martel family, the eighteenth-century pioneers; and the newer elements, both Protestant and Catholic, who had joined the competitive fray since the opportunities opened up under the late Old Regime and the Revolutionary era. These elite divisions were not based upon horizontal levels of wealth, but rather were constellations of middling and poorer manufacturers around a few great families in each. The lower levels continually flaked away, but it was among the entrepreneurial, "arriviste" group in each city where the casualties had been the most numerous. All groups had their clients among the professional bourgeoisie, although in both cities there seems to have been a certain independent esprit de corps among lawyers, notaries, and doctors. The woolens working classes of each town—closely tied to artisans and shopkeepers that served them much more than the elites, who did much of their shop-

ping elsewhere—were qualitatively different. Lodève's was largely proletarianized, while Bédarieux's remained more clearly artisanal. Ideologically,
Lodève's workers passed through Agulhon's penitents-to-sans-culottes
phase and, to an extent, back to a more Catholic perspective—but it was
their Catholicism, practiced in their parish, St. Pierre, and would play a key
role in the future history of class conflict in the city. Bédarieux's Catholic
working class was much less exclusive, joining the Catholic elites in a single
parish and subject to the latter's practiced paternalism. The Protestant presence among Bédarieux's bourgeois and service artisan population was no
doubt the key factor cementing this relationship.

Thus, while internal divisions existed, the logic of the economic, social,
and religious histories of each city meant that Lodève would shade toward
a mild Bonapartism and sympathy toward the Revolutionary tradition shorn
of its anti-Christian content, while Bédarieux would be more clearly favorable to the Restoration. Conflict occurred during the 1814–16 transition,
but it was largely jostling among the elites influenced only marginally by
"the people," and it was tempered in both cases by the larger consideration
of what the regime might bring for the woolens industry.[6]

Painful Growth

As the political crisis subsided, did the troubled state of the Hérault's
economy follow suit? In general, the answer was no. This was certainly the
tenor of Creuzé's massive study, published in 1824. But at the moment
that the book appeared, a turnaround was becoming visible. For the leading sectors of the economy, sustained growth would then continue for a
generation.

Woolens production during the first half of the Restoration hovered
around 30,000 bolts, less than half the output of the late Empire.[7] The
most obvious fact was the collapse of the production for the army, Lodève's
specialty, which had also become the stock in trade of Clermont and Villeneuvette and a factor in Bédarieux's activity as well. Lodève's spinning capacity remained important despite the losses in sales of finished cloth. The
vast expansion of handspinning in the countryside during the Empire now
shrank precipitously, and reports of distress in the villages throughout the
cloth region were numerous as the supplemental income it provided dried
up.[8] Rural disturbances became endemic. Most obvious were the illegal
incursions into communal woods and wasteland by poor people seeking
firewood, cutting live oak, which was sold to *cercliers* to make barrel hoops,
or reaping wild hemp, used to make a rough cloth worn as an overgarment.[9]
The highways were dangerous, as bands of "brigands" reappeared in the
Lodévois.[10]

The wool towns themselves, particularly Lodève, were not immune to
trouble. Petty crime by the poor and insecurity among the well-to-do became facts of life. The criminal docket showed an alarming number of minor
thefts of money, bed linens, and even food. Stealing wool and thread was a

common problem in any era, but the number of cases that came to trial in 1815—seventeen—appears higher than usual.[11] The high cost of food, caused by poor harvests, naturally was keenly felt, and public relief did little to assuage distress. The most basic responses to the hardships of these years was family restriction and out-migration. The number of marriages in Lodève dipped significantly in the years after 1813 and birth rates fell from an average of 35 per thousand in the period 1804–1817 to 29.2 per thousand in 1818–23.[12] Lodève's working population in woolens dropped precipitously from over 5,000 in 1812–1813 to 1,540 in 1816 to 910 in 1817.[13]

Where did they go? Bédarieux, a long-standing trading partner in labor, took up some of the slack. In 1820, city officials argued that more gendarmes were needed "because of the large number of workers who arrived daily to seek in this city the livelihood that the lack of work in the other manufacturing towns keep them from gaining." Total population jumped from 3,737 in 1815 to 5,402 in 1821, 5,805 in 1828. According to Jean-Marie Oustry, there was a steep increase, from 24 percent to 50 percent, of people marrying in Bédarieux who came from elsewhere in the period 1815–1820. Although local villages supplied a substantial proportion of these, the number of partners from further away in the department increased from less than 5 percent in 1815 to 20 percent in 1826 and 1827, with Lodève, Clermont, Avesnes, Ceilhes, Gignac, Béziers, St. Chinian, Abeilhan, and Servian, in that order, leading the list. Almost twice as many grooms as brides came from these towns. Lodève's complementary relationship with Bédarieux comes into view, but now the migrant flow was reversed.[14] Marriage figures, of course, give only the vaguest notion of movement; temporary migration would have accounted for many more.

Lodève's place in the woolens economy of the Restoration, however, remained stronger than outright cloth production would appear to indicate. This was due to the growth of the city's spinning capacity, which employed 700 to 1,300 people during the period 1816–23. As a percentage of the active work force, spinnery workers were more stable, and more kept their jobs when cloth production was low in Lodève.[15]

Why had Lodève achieved this advantage? Because its manufacturers had been willing, despite misgivings, to mechanize. So had their counterparts in Bédarieux and elsewhere in Languedoc. New market opportunities arose as well. If *draps de troupe* was no longer as lucrative an avenue as it once had been, the demand for lighter broadcloth and mixed materials was strong in France, and the export market for new, lighter draps de Levant was again open in the Mediterranean. The response to these opportunities, typically, was marked by action that sought stable continuity, careful experimentation, and a tendency to look to the national government for aid, yet to mistrust its sincerity in offering it.

Progress in mechanization was steady. Table 1–1 reproduces Creuzé de Lesser's report of the number of "filatures mechaniques."[16] The numbers in parentheses are not of "mechanical spinning mills," but of assortiments, (one scribbler, one carding machine, one slubbing billy, and four

Table 1-1 Numbers of Filatures (assortiments)

	Lodève	Clermont	Villeneuvette	Bédarieux	Saint Pons	Saint Chinian	Riols
1810	1						
1811	2						
1812	2			(8)			
1813	5	1	1	(14)			
1814	5	1	1	(22)	(6)		
1815	4	1 (4)		(22)			
1816	5	1 (4)	1 (2)	(16)	(8)	(4)	
1817	6	1 (4)		(24)	(9)	(4)	
1818	10	2		(24)	(9)	(5)	
1819	10	2		(30)	(9)	(4)	
1820	12	2 (6)		(30)	(9)	(4)	
1821	12	2 (6)	1	(30)	(10)	(4)	1 (2)
1822	12	2 (6)	1	(30)	(10)	(4)	1 (2)
1823	12 (68)	3 (9)	1	(25)	(10)	(4)	(2)
1824	12	3	1	(35)	(10)	(4)	(2)
1825	14	3	1	(40)	(10)	(8)	(2)
1826	15	3	1	(30)	(12)	(8)	(2)
1827	15	3	1	(35)	(18)	(8)	(2)
1828	15	3	1	(35)	(18)	(8)	(2)
1829	15	3	1	(35)	(18)	(8)	(2)
1830	15	4	1	(42)	(20)	(8)	(2)
1831	15	4	1	(35)	(20)	(12)	(2)
1832	15	4	1	10	(20)	(13)	(2)

mule-jennies). If we assume a proportional expansion of the numbers of assortiments per filature where they are not listed and take the price paid by Philippe Pascal of Lodève in 1816 for four *assortiments complets* (Fr 55,200) as a standard, woolens fabricants in the Hérault invested something approaching two-and-one-half million francs in spinning machinery alone during the Restoration. To this one must add the often extensive changes needed in building structures, canals and weirs, and hydraulic machinery, as well as legal costs in the often bitter fights for water rights.[17]

The fabricants of Lodève, despite the slow repayment by the Bourbon government of the Napoleonic debt, now put the profits from the Empire to work in modernizing and restructuring, a task made all the more urgent by growing competition, especially from Sedan. By 1824, success was obvious. A survey of Lodève's thirteen largest firms revealed the extent of mechanization since the first timid efforts fifteen years before. Eleven spin-neries were outfitted with sixty-six scribbling and carding machine units, sixty-nine slubbing billies, and 231 mule-jennies with 16,440 spindles al-together. Sixty-six reeling frames and the same number of warping frames provided thread for thirteen weaving sheds housing 226 broadlooms and thirty-three petites-étoffes looms. By contrast, work was put out by these firms to city home workers using only forty-five broadlooms and fifteen knitting frames. The finishing mills counted four hydraulic-powered gig-mills and five hand-turned gig-mills, two transversal cropping machines and twenty-five water-powered cropping shears, eight mechanical brushes, and six hydraulic steam presses. In all, these firms operated 589 pieces of ma-chinery run by water.[18] Such a level of mechanization compares favorably with Louviers, Elbeuf, and Sedan at the time and was far ahead of Roubaix, which only began its ascent in the 1830s.

This was only the beginning. In 1824, the Administration also insti-tuted the "fifty-thousand meter rule." This meant that each contracting company had to have the capacity, with the use of water-driven machinery and the latest fly-shuttle handlooms (which were fast becoming standard),[19] to produce 50,000 meters of cloth per year (about 1,650 bolts). These stipu-lations brought about a flurry of new companies in the later 1820s, as indivi-dual fabricants searched for combinations that would gather sufficient resources together. It appears that without at least Fr 350,000 in fixed and liquid capital, even a bid for one 50,000 meter *lot* was impossible. Some of the biggest names in Lodève's manufacturing elite had to come together to reach that figure. For example, eight members of the Fabreguettes, Jourdan, Martin, and Labranche families pooled their resources in eighteen shares (23 September 1829). The Teisserencs, Calvets, and Visseqs brought their weighty interests together in another society, but later expanded to include Etienne Brun-Fabreguettes and Fulcran Martin for 21 percent and a total capital of half-a-million francs (25 September 1829). If a society failed to gain a contract, it would dissolve and a new one would be formed. There were also a number of exclusive lease arrangements made by these enlarged companies with dyeing establishments. A typical agreement between Vallat, Faulquier et Gauffre and Fulcran Grimal, *teinturier*, provided the follow-ing: a five-year *bail à ferme* at Fr 600 per year payable in advance, mainte-nance and equipment repairs at the expense of the lessee, and six-months' renewal notice. Grimal, from an ancient family of dyers, would also serve as a piecewage earning employee of the company and maintain his own staff of assistants. The state had again imposed regulations that forced ever-greater consolidation of capital, while undermining independent subcon-tracting.[20]

The dyer's situation clarifies the difference between true contract work and *marchandage*. Grimal could no longer seek competitive bids for his services. His relationship to his underlings became that of a "master worker," rather than an independent employer. This distinction should be under-scored because it was an important step in the transformation of the social relations of production as industrial capitalism developed in the nineteenth century. It might appear to be a good bargain for Grimal because he had a guaranteed situation: besides his annual rent, he no longer had to worry about the costs of plant and equipment maintenance, his wages were pure profit (greater or lesser depending on what he paid assistants), and he no longer faced the insecurity of searching for jobs among different cloth makers. But he definitely did not see it this way. After the July Revolution, he petitioned the new regime for a release from his contract, saying that he faced "ruin." His request was denied. On this aspect of industrial rationalization at least, both governments agreed.[21]

Larger and more efficient fabricants, such as Barbot and Fournier, Vallat, Faulquier, or Labranche, seemed perfectly happy with the new government requirements. They did not figure among the members of the city council who complained loudly in 1829 about the pressure to consolidate. Mayor Guillaume Rouaud and his Catholic royalist circle dominated city politics. Nevertheless, royalist fabricants suffered disproportionately under the government to which they lent their political support. This was an irony hardly limited to Lodève, but it can be viewed with clarity here. Moreover, one can also observe the Restoration government's inconsistent economic policies that unquestionably contributed to its own demise.

The Restoration government exhibited many of the contradictions of the late Old Regime with regard to economic development. On one hand, it recognized the importance of providing support for growth, whether it be in social overhead capital, promoting French exports through diplomacy and subsidies, or engendering rationalization. The statistical information gathered by the Restoration probably exceeded that of the Empire. None of the institutions of economic and technological promotion founded by Napoleon (from schools to chambers of commerce) was eliminated, and more were founded. On the other hand, the Restoration government's political base lay with landed interests for whom property was regarded more as patrimony than as capital or with older commercial and manufacturing families who were more interested in government protection than in entrepreneurial stimulation.

Government contract work showed the dilemma in the most glaring manner, for here favoritism and privilege, so easy to grant, directly confronted the state's own interest in getting the best price possible for services rendered. The Restoration government tried to merge the two. Thus, despite protest from towns that had been awarded contracts under the Empire, the Restoration government finally settled on Lodève as its principal army supplier for its much-reduced needs, while constantly pressing for greater efficiency. Privilege was won at a price.

Lodève experienced a number of anxious moments. In 1817, the Duc du Feltre, the Minister of War, proposed a return to the "entreprise générale" system of the Directory. Here politics saved the day as Rouaud went off to Paris and, with the support of dedicated royalist deputies from the Hérault, convinced the Minister to abandon the idea. A new alarm arose in 1820, when the War Ministry questioned buying so much from Lodève, "situated at the extremity of the kingdom where few troops are stationed." Creuzé reminded Interior Minister Elie Decazes (a friend of the south) of the "tacit and reciprocal agreement" that had long existed between Lodève and the government, one that must be maintained or the political allegiance of Languedoc to the King would be threatened. Then came the campaign in 1823–24 to encourage more bids from northern manufacturers while imposing the 50,000-meter mile. A Faulquier mémoire argued convincingly that large, multiproduct northern concerns could easily underprice the more specialized industries of Lodève or Clermont, in effect, by dumping army cloth to destroy the south, only to increase their prices later. The administration compromised. Remaining adament on the 50,000-meter rule, it kept the bulk of its orders in the south, despite the passage of the Ordinance of 21 April 1824, which supposedly created competitive bidding. Once more in 1829, the government threatened to revive the "general enterprise" system, but a political counterthreat worked again, as Lodévois were amazed to see their "paternal government" propose a system created during the Revolution![22]

The process of concentration, however, seriously weakened the royalist fabricant elite. From 1813 to 1822, the number of people paying *patentes* (the business tax) as fabricants fell from seventy-eight to fifty-three. Changes in the rolls during the early Restoration (1816–21) saw six substantial manufacturers identified with the royalist right retire, while only one liberal quit. Fifteen other small fabricants dropped out as well. Only two newcomers, one a Vinas, began paying the patente during this period. The middling group among the elites and the *nouveaux riches* seemed to survive in larger numbers than the old guard. Significantly, the number of butchers either quitting their trade or receiving a reduction of their tax was also unusually high (25 percent), another blow for royalism in Lodève.[23]

In 1823, a shocking event rocked the city. Jean-Louis Cauvy, deputy mayor whose business partner was the other deputy mayor, Pierre Gauffre, declared bankruptcy. Cauvy was a fabricant of only modest proportions, but a respected figure and a key leader of the old royalist right. Gauffre survived his partner's fall, but never fully recovered. A close look at Cauvy's business activities, a rare treat afforded by an unusually complete record of his bankruptcy proceedings, gives an idea of the type of manufacturer doomed to oblivion as the machine revolution took hold. He might just as well have been one of the Revolutionary artisan entrepreneurs who failed, but his commercial pedigree extended far back into the past.[24]

Cauvy produced about two hundred bolts per year in the early Restoration. In 1819, his "paternal home" on the rue de la Calvarie was valued at Fr 5,500. It opened in the rear on the boulevard des Caves and the quai de Soulandres. In its large courtyard there would have likely been his warehouse for wool and cloth storage and closer by the house, his workshop.[25] There he employed three to five hand-jenny spinners and, intermittently, wool sorters. All other operations were put out. Washing was carried out by a *laveur* off the premises. Weaving was the major expense, and he used four to eight *tisserands à domicile* depending on need. All finishing activities were done either by one of the few remaining independent artisans (Cadilhac et frères, pareurs, received Fr 150 "pr compte sur leur ouvrage" on 20 July 1819, for example) or by large companies (packing and shipping was done by Michel Fabreguettes). Cauvy also bought machine-spun thread from large companies. He sought weavers both in Lodève and outside and, as he slipped toward bankruptcy, went further and further afield to locate cheap weaving. But his main activity appears to have been the relentless search for wool at good prices. He had dozens of sources—local fabricants who were overstocked, sheep growers in the nearby hills and causses, and major wool merchants in Montpellier. Like many of his colleagues, Cauvy owned some land and dabbled in grain speculation. His household goods and the contents of his *cave* were evaluated at Fr 4,100.

Finally, Cauvy bought on credit and borrowed heavily, using his property as collateral. In a desperate move, impelled by the logic of the age, he and Gauffre bought into a small mechanized mill early in 1822. His spinning work there lasted only two months and it appears that this venture broke his back. In his bankruptcy declaration, his major debts were owed to local fabricants acting in the capacity of short-term bankers, but he also used the services of two major Montpellier financial houses, Mourgue and Vidal et Querrelle, who regularly advanced Lodève fabricants money against their pending military orders. But Cauvy had gone consistently beyond his assured return. In the end, the amount owed in interest alone (some seven thousand francs in 1822) was more than double his gross income. In his last year of operation he tried every conceivable method of cost-cutting. The lower wages and the constant turnover of people working both in his shop and outside indicate that the vicious cycle of employee exploitation, quality deterioration, and diminishing sales had taken over. Cauvy resigned his municipal post and died shortly thereafter, though he managed to hold on to his house. His partner struggled on, only to follow the same path in 1834–36.[26]

Pierre Ménard was a much more important manufacturer and long a major force in the Catholic royalist camp. If he did not fall, he certainly reeled under the pressures of growing industrial concentration. Ménard and his partner, J.B. Salze, did not measure up to the Administration's expectations and were unceremoniously dropped as suppliers in 1827. In a long letter of 7 February 1828, they pled for consideration in the following adjudication. Both came from families that had been producing cloth "père et fils" since the time of Colbert. For four years they had been in the "first rank" among the contractors of the city. "This status and the economies they produced for the government caused the hate and jealousy of their rivals." The new pressures were breaking a code of honor that existed especially among the old guard. They were accused of lowering standards, and then came "several delays caused by the constant rainfall in the winter of 1826—and contracts . . . were cut off!" Their petition pulled out all the stops in praise of "throne and altar" and trumpeted the ancient role that they had played in the service of France. Alas, it was not enough. Politics (for individuals, at any rate) was less important than performance. The Minister sternly rebuked them not only for the delays, but for having provided "false information" to the government, and turned them down.[27] But Ménard was not so easily beaten. In 1829, he tried to put together another society with fellow royalist Auguste Jourdan, another loser of 1829, failed again, but finally made a successful bid in 1830 with Frédéric Martel and Auguste Soudan. Martel was a relative of the deeply royalist Martels of Bédarieux, but, significantly, Soudan was a scion of Lodève's less ideological middle group of practical businessmen. Ménard survived into the next regime.

Such trials did not trouble the acknowledged leader of Lodève's Catholic royalism, Guillaume Rouaud, for he had taken a third path, one which elevated him above the daily struggles of a Cauvy or a Ménard. He became a banker. At the time of his death in 1833, he had credits totaling Fr 49,902 on loans to Zoé Granier, Montpellier's most active industrialist and (by then) member of the Chamber of Deputies; Fr 55,637 out to Barbot et Fournier, Lodève's most enterprising company; Fr 41,731 owed by Pierre Gauffre, whose bankruptcy case was pending; Fr 26,010 by Jean-Pierre Fabreguettes, fabricant and now Orleanist commissaire de police; 33,739 by M. Lugagne-Jourdan, receveur des finances de Lodève; Fr 15,375 by Vitalis frères; and a variety of smaller loans, all made in the department of the Hérault, which included investments in several Montpellier banking houses. Finally, he served as the *mandataire* for Tessié and Sarrus, Montpellier bankers, in Lodève. He had Fr 154,000 in 5 percent government bonds as well. His total *mobilier* wealth was Fr 673,005. His real estate was modest by comparison: his Fr 12,000 house in Lodève, which he left to the Frères de l'école chrétienne; his "domaine," Le Permelet, worth Fr 150,000; and a vineyard of 20 hectares and its cave valued at Fr 15,000. He had sold his cloth business in its entirety.[28] But far from returning to the land as one might expect of a wealthy royalist, Rouaud had remained an active capitalist to the end. With the exception of the loans to his old deputy Gauffre, his money was placed with the most vital houses in Lodève and Montpellier, whatever their politics or social status.

In sum, Lodève survived the post-Imperial crisis by undergoing major changes in the character of its industry, both technological and structural. Heavy concentration had occurred, accompanied by a new abandonment of rural outworking. An overall belt tightening took place as well. The main victims among the fabricants were first, the small businessmen, whatever their economic and political values, and second, certain individuals from among the old royalist elite who found themselves unable to adjust to the new competitive demands of the nineteenth century. Finally, Lodève manifested a troubling general trait, one shared by almost all its manufacturers. This was a hesitancy to diversify. Although some production for the Levant and the interior commercial market occurred, the lure of the military

business held such tendencies in check. The town failed to reach its potential during the Restoration because of this.

Industrialization in Bédarieux took on a different complexion. The figures cited in Table 1–1 indicate that the city embraced mechanization, although the number of assortiments installed came to about half of Lodève's
total by the late 1820s. Its impact was similar. "Before mechanization,"
wrote the Comte d'Orfeuille Foucaud, Sous-Préfet of Béziers, in 1818, "the
poorest part of population [of the upper Orb area], which numbers about
3600 souls, found in spinning an assured resource. This resource no longer
exists and its mountainous terrain does not present to the laboring class
the same advantages as [the land] of the southern part of the arrondissement;
mechanical engineering has been fatal to it." He thought that work in the
mines might be of some help, but at current levels of employment there
(fifty-three full-time miners in 1822), this seemed a bit optimistic.[29]

On the other hand, Bédarieux itself was in full expansion, attracting
workers for its industry at unprecedented rates. Great numbers came from
nearby villages, a majority of them female, meaning that the rapid decline
of the by-occupation in the countryside drove young women to the textile
center.[30] There was work to be found, particularly in low-paying washing,
sorting, preparation for spinning, and as *époutieuses* (burlers/pickers). The
small size of the mule-jennies meant that a piece-rate earning male spinner
and a single family member (wife or child) did most of the machine work.
Slubbing billies were also run by men, but fed by a family member. Only
carding machines were a female preserve. Later on, sex ratios would change
substantially with the introduction of more complex machinery.[31]

The numbers of people employed by Bédarieux fabricants in spinning
and its preparatory crafts declined from 1812 to 1820, but thereafter the
volume of wool spun in Bédarieux skyrocketed,[32] finally outdistancing
Lodève. According to a survey of 1818, the early leaders in the spinning
revolution were Pierre Martel (620 spindles—perhaps 2 assortiments), Verny
et Gaston (700), Antoine Causse (1,300), Prades et Grand, frères (780),
Amefield (1,200) and Jean Belagou (670), a total of 5,220 spindles.[33] Of
this pioneering group, the two largest were outsiders, Causse from Lodève
and Amefield from Paris (originally from England), while only one, Martel,
came from Bédarieux's old elite. In time, the other cloth merchants would
follow, although the number of assortiments in use increased quite slowly.

Hand-loom weaving naturally benefited from the growing capacity in
spinning. The number of looms at work in Bédarieux itself changed little
during the 1820s (between 250 and 300) and the small, outworking *atelier* remained the rule. But rural weaving exploded, making up family income lost with the decline of spinning, but at rates well below those paid
in the city. In 1822 there were 264 broadlooms at work in Bédarieux itself,
while another 256 dotted nearby villages.[34] As late as 1851, 5-to-10 percent of the villagers in Le Poujol, Faugères, and Camplong listed textile
work as their main occupation.[35] It was in communes further along down
the Orb, however, that village outworking really flourished in the 1820s

and 1830s. Colombières-sur-Orb, a village sixteen kilometers west of Bédarieux, owed its good fortune to the Bédarieux spinning revolution as well as the establishment of two filatures on its own territory, one owned by Bédarieux's Fabrégat family. Here, according to marriage records, a good quarter of the grooms were handloom weavers, although we cannot determine how many worked specifically "for Bédarieux."[36] Another important weaving commune was Mons. Bédarician fabricants included Mons in their orbit, but the villages and hamlets comprising it also took work from nearby mills at Prémian and Colombières, as well as Riols and even St. Pons further to the west.

In 1836, 166 people, or 28 percent of Mons's active population, were listed in the census as weavers, 108 males and 58 females. Of these, only 44 men and 1 woman headed households. Table 1–2 reveals the structure and role of outwork weaving in this commune, which may be taken as typical of the region.

Seventeen of the male heads wove alone, or were assisted only marginally by family members, for this census taker was assiduous in recording the occupations of all working family members twelve and over. As indicated in the table, the other weavers headed households with multiple loom operators. (Though we cannot be certain that each listed member worked his or her own loom it is likely, because by that time—indeed a decade earlier—the fly-shuttle, single-operator loom had become standard in the region.) Younger single children dominated their ranks, with a slight edge to daughters. Wives only occasionally wove full-time and would usually be listed as ménagères if they were not heavily employed in agricultural work. The most interesting finding, however, is the large numbers of weavers at work within families headed by farmers and tradesmen (and by widows without listed occupations). Indeed, weaving occupied exactly twice as many household members of nonweaver heads as members of weaver-headed families. It is clear therefore that weaving was not an occupation separating its practitioners from other rural people. This was also the case spacially within the main village of Mons and its dependent hamlets. It is true, however, that those households relying on weaving exclusively (the weaver heads) were less solidly seated in the locality and would later disappear most rapidly from census listings.[37] Weaving was therefore an ideal family-supplement occupation, but more precarious as a main profession, yielding insufficient profits to purchase land, commercial operations, or craft shops. A final point: few weavers were found in the hamlets of La Trivalle and Tarassac, where the vine (then largely for eau de vie production) predominated. Both labor demands and higher income levels meant that finding outworkers in woolens was less likely. Thus, while weaving served as an important supplement to the family economy, it supported full-timers poorly and appealed little to well-off people because wages were too low.

From the perspective of the fabricant these low wages were the main basis of his prosperity. The urban weaver, more expert and working on fancier goods, made, in the 1820s, around one franc twenty-five per day.

Table 1-2 Relationship of Weavers to Heads of Household (Mons, 1836)

Relationship and Marital Status of Weavers

Occupation/Status (chef de Ménage)	Single Sons Under 30	Single Sons 30+	Married Sons	Single Daughters Under 30	Single Daughters 30+	Daughters-in-law*	Sibling M	Sibling F	Wife	No Obvious Relation	Total
20 Cultivateurs	16	3	5	17	2				1		
6 Propriétaires	3			4	2				1		
1 Journalier									1		
27 Total agriculture	19	3	5	21	4				3		55
6 Service tradesmen†	3	1		4				1		1	10
10 Widows (no occ.)	5	2	4	3	0	1					15
43 Total non-weavers	27	6	9	28	4	1		1	3	1M	80
28 Weavers‡	11	2	6	15	0	1	1	1	3	1F	41
17 Weavers alone											
Totals: Dependent weavers	38	8	15	43	4	2	1	2	6	2	121
Chef weavers											45

Total males 108	Total females 58		166

*One son-in-law. There were no married daughters among weavers living with their parents.

†1 Maréchal (blacksmith), 2 voituriers (carters), 1 boucher (butcher), 1 tailleur (tailor), 1 ex-instituteur (teacher) (in those days the status of this post was about the same as an artisan).

‡Twenty-seven males and one female (a widow).

Women, used generally for more common types of cloth, could clear seventy-five centimes for the same amount of input. In the countryside, men's rates would bring in eighty-five centimes for a twelve-to-fourteen-hour day, while women and boys averaged around fifty centimes and were given less demanding work. The quality level of men's work was in fact little different from that demanded of city men, but complaints were widespread by the later 1830s that the source of Bédarieux's emerging reputation problem was an overreliance on rural outworking.[38] In the 1820s, however, it paid to take work to places like Mons. Transport raised the cost somewhat, but agents of the companies made regular rounds up and down the valley and into the hills as part of their various tasks. The trips normally had a dual purpose, for local wools also came from many of these villages. Cauvy of Lodève, our famous bankrupt, picked up olive oil in places like St. Saturnin on his trips to his weavers in Nébian and Clermont and wool in St. Michel, where he also occasionally gave work to a weaver. Such travel was worth their while.[39]

Bédarieux's boom was founded on work in town and country. The dimensions of its rapid economic growth were reflected in official statistics. But the short description by the traveler Renaud de Vilback, made in 1825, captures the feeling of the time.

> This little city is open and well-built and will become quite pretty if the prosperity of its cloth manufacturing establishments continues; it owes this prosperity to machines, the installation of which cause grumbling and threats from the people. Two hundred houses have been built in eighteen months. Bédarieux also has two paper-mills whose products are worth forty-five thousand francs. The best inn is the Cheval-Vert, chez Boudet.[40]

Bédarieux's sales during the Restoration moved in three phases: a brief Levant-trade revival coupled with expansion of its earlier "interior cloth," followed by the growth of thread production already noted, and then the emergence of a diversified line of products for the French market that competed well with northern producers.

The Levant trade, of course, was the hope of all the Languedoc industry. Already in 1816–17, the French ambassador to the Sublime Porte, the Marquis de la Rivière, felt confident that Languedoc woolens could retake their rightful position in the Eastern trade. But two things needed to happen to achieve full success: the production of lighter cloth of the "Belgian" style, as pioneered by Flottes of Saint-Chinian and now copied by the Bédaricians, and the bypass of Marseille, to deal directly with Constantinople and Smyrna and set up export control in Cette.[41] The Languedoc port, silted badly under Napoleonic neglect, needed much attention. Creuzé projected a new seawall in 1819. Three years later, he threw the first stone in the project that all hoped would begin Cette's advance as an alternative to Marseille.[42] The Levant trade did indeed revive, as the industry sold almost 5,000 pieces in 1816 and 1817. Bédarieux predominated, but St. Pons, Clermont, and even Lodève contributed. Still, an old problem was haunting the trade. One

Emmanuel Biso, a Jewish trader, lodged a formal complaint with the French consul in Salonika late in 1816 about six pieces of cloth made by Laisset et Guiraud of Saint-Pons, which were "filled from one end to the other with mends and blemishes." A warning went out forthwith. Jean Verny, manufacturer and mayor of Clermont, immediately responded that it was not "our fault," for "these Jews and Greeks are always trying to cheat" us. If Clermont's whining was to be expected, both Bédarieux and Lodève took a careful look at the situation and emphasized the need to expand interior production simultaneously.[43] One can imagine that the Bédaricians did not want to be burned again by the transgressions of their less scrupulous neighbors. This may also be a better reason for Lodève's hesitation to reorient much of its production toward "quality" work than its alleged entrapment in "routine."[44] Production for the Levant declined in 1818 and 1819. Then came the Greek Revolution, which, in the words of Clermont's mayor, "totally destroyed our principal industry."[45] Nevertheless, the Levant trade did not die. By 1824 and 1825, St. Chinian and St. Pons were using the outworking possibilities of their region to produce reasonably-priced "Belgian" cloth of decent quality that sold well not only in the eastern Mediterranean, but also in Italy and North Africa.[46] Marseille still monopolized exports, however, a situation that was not to change, especially as it was the only quarantine facility on the French Mediterranean coast. To the 5,600–6,000 pieces produced in the western Hérault in 1826, Carcassonne's 3,000 and a reviving Clermont's 2,200 should be added. One Lodève house, Barbot and Fournier, kept their hand in, sending out 250 pieces that year.[47]

Bédarieux merchants seemed little interested (they sold 286 pieces to the Levant in 1825, 60 in 1826), for this was their age of expansion in spinning and in cloth production for the "interior," then marketed largely through the Beaucaire fair. Like Mazamet, Bédarieux had its agents scouting northern centers of production for new ideas and establishing outlets in Paris and in smaller towns in the center and west, which increasingly marketed the city's fabrics at competitive prices. Its manufacturers also benefited from excellent connections with wool suppliers, especially in Spain, giving them a distinct advantage over northern houses. Soap and oil costs were lower as well. But the rush into the countryside for labor, following upon intelligent mechanization in town, made the biggest difference. Table 1–3 shows its production and that of Lodève for the remainder of the Restoration.[48]

These developments in woolens were fortunate, for the story of other industries in the Hérault was not a happy one. The Montpellier cotton industry just held its own during the Restoration. The little town of Aniane had several mechanical spinning mills that worked for it, but the handkerchief business that was the capital's stock in trade remained at about 12,000 dozen and that, plus some *toile*, created a total value of about Fr 400,000 per year. Silk weaving collapsed in the Hérault. By 1830 Ganges, its main center, was counting by the hundreds the pairs of stockings produced per year. Tanneries had a similar history. The paper industry did somewhat

Table 1–3

	Bédarieux		Lodève	
	Pièces	Workers Employed	Pièces	Workers Employed
1822	15,740	3,317	12,000	2,220
1823	10,650	2,912	12,000	2,305
1824	18,230	4,785	4,000	1,075
1825	29,000	5,605	4,500	2,020
1826	27,560	5,317	9,900	3,575
1827	22,000	4,500	9,000	2,950
1828	14,000	3,300	15,000	4,700
1829	13,156	3,985	7,000	1,440
1830	20,040	3,415	26,500	5,200

better, adding five new sites and doubling production in the fifteen-year period.[49] Finally there was coal. The Alès basin in the Gard was on its way to the modern world, but its Hérault rival, Graissessac, remained moribund. Overall, in the 1820s, industrial Languedoc was largely sustained by the woolens enterprises of Lodève and Bédarieux. Their ability to respond creatively to a general political and economic crisis that might have brought the region's industrial history to an early end had been striking. It also engendered the first round of a workers' resistance movement that in the end would profoundly influence its future direction.

Luddism and Modernization

Lodève's working class had already undergone a long process of proletarianization that dated back to the old regime. By the late Empire, even the elite finishing crafts were succumbing. A working class in the modern sense of the term was largely in place before significant mechanization had occurred. The smaller fabriques of Clermont and Villeneuvette generally followed suit, although Villeneuvette's planned community provides a special case. The woolens towns to the west, Bédarieux, St. Chinian, Riols, Saint-Pons, and Mazamet, on the other hand, relied heavily on rural weaving for that crucial stage in the production process while mechanizing spinning. The finishing crafts remained relatively autonomous. Everywhere, however, the arrival of machinery was greeted with fear, despair, and finally with violence by the people who did the work.

Disquiet over the question of machines began to be expressed by workers from the moment of their introduction. In January of 1818, two placards were posted in Clermont urging destruction of "mule-jennies" and dire consequences for their owners if they were not dismantled and returned. Eight men were arrested, one of whom, a weaver named Souleyrac, had gone to Lodève to seek support for their movement. Two of those arrested were known royalists and members of the National Guard. Urging severe punishment, Creuzé also authorized a total of Fr 3,000 for distribution among the unemployed in the Clermont area.[50] In 1819 and 1820, a series of anonymous notes and placards were distributed by woolens workers in St. Pons, St. Chinian, and Riols, all threatening bodily harm to machine owners and destruction of the machinery, whatever it might be. If we are to judge from arrest records, the resistance to the sets of equipment suitable to mechanical spinning[51] was orchestrated by men in diverse woolens professions, and, in the case of Clermont, they enlisted the aid of a teacher. They made efforts to generalize the struggle geographically as well. The threat posed by new machinery should not be underestimated. Independent male carders and warpers worked with their wives and daughters who spun on the *grande roue*. Moreover, for weft thread production, hand-cranked jennies might be set up in the home. The advanced sixty-spindle jenny, its preliminary carding and slubbing machinery, all adaptable to water-powered drive shafts, along with factory-installed warping frames, displaced not only part-time spinsters, but entire family workshops in the first phase of cloth making. Indeed, although documentation is vague, it is likely that the first impact of the hand jenny was to enhance independent artisan production, as it did in the cotton industry of the Choletais[52] and the woolens industry in Yorkshire,[53] a circumstance making mechanization all the more painful.[54] All in all, however, the mechanization of spinning in lower Languedoc had its chief effects in dispersed villages and did not give rise to violence there. It stimulated female emigration as supplementary spinning work disappeared, but it also rather quickly provided new opportunities in hand loom weaving for both men and women.[55] What might have been lost in independence was (again) regained in remunerative work.

By 1820, however, the first textile machine directly threatening a large number of urban, skilled, male workers had arrived in Languedoc. This was the shearing machine. Various *tondeuses* had been on the market for more than a decade. The "longitudinal" machine sheared from end to end, required a male/female team to operate, could shear thirty cloths per day (as opposed to the two-man teams of hand shearmen's rate of three per day), but was very expensive and did rather uneven work. The "transversal" or "helical" machine, a device operated by a single man with a child assistant by which several power-driven shears set in a frame were maneuvered across the cloth, was cheaper and did a better job, but could only work twelve cloths per day. Besides provoking resistance in the woolens districts of England, such machines, but especially the more practical transversal, had already been the subject of a number of confrontations in France, especially at Louviers, Sedan, Chateauroux, and Vienne.[56] In the early 1820s, the scene shifted to Languedoc.

Although the first open conflicts did not occur until May 1821, trouble had been brewing for a long time. Earlier discontent had arisen largely during Carnival. So in February 1821, Mayor Rouaud decided to ban both transvestite apparel and masks from the festivities altogether, but was overruled by the Prefect who put curfews on these traditional practices of ridicule.[57] It is possible that news of the imminent arrival of Lodève's first transversal shearing machine was already afoot.[58] In any case, arrive it did. Etienne Faulquier, prize-winning fabricant and a consistent leader in mechanization,[59] had one installed on a trial basis by Montolieu, an agent for John Collier et Cie, a Parisian machine builder. This new Faulquier venture was complicated by the fact that his more conservative partners for army contract work,[60] Mayor Rouaud himself and Beaupillier, were apparently not enthusiastic about his decision. As members of families dominating both the municipality and the local Church, Catholic paternalism mixed with the desire for public order in their thinking.

In any case, shearmen liked it even less, and at 9:30 on the morning of 5 May 1821 (a workday) they organized a mass demonstration near Faulquier's factory. It was dispersed by the police, but the workers reassembled and "went to the factory of le Sieur Faulquier, forced the doors, and broke the shearing machine." They then pitched the parts into the river. The crowd consisted not only of shearmen, but of men and women from other occupations. This public act took place with little resistance from the vastly outnumbered gendarmes. The National Guard was apparently not even called out. Only later, after troops of the line were sent from Montpellier, were five arrests made. One arrested was a shearman for Faulquier, the others worked elsewhere. Almost immediately the Sub-Prefect began to suspect that Faulquier himself was not all that upset about this turn of events; perhaps he had contractual arrangements with Collier that he could now conveniently sidestep. The loss, in any case, was the supplier's, not his. On the evening of 27 May a crowd, urged on by woolens workers Ramondenc and Cadilhac, attacked the jail, but were repelled by line troops stationed there. Gendarmes, pelted by stones thrown by women and called "brigands" as they rode out, chased these "perturbers" into the hills, but all escaped. National guardsmen, among them Beaupillier himself, according to the Examining Magistrate, "seemed to take pleasure" in the whole affair. Finally, a few arrests were made amid further public hue and cry. The newly arrested people and the original inmates were escorted to Montpellier by regular troops and put on trial in August. But even there, sympathy seemed to be with the machine breakers: the jury (by law made up of men of substance and education) acquitted them. Prefect Creuzé de Lesser tore his hair.[61]

Indeed, the only men who became exercised in the course of this affair were nonnative officials and perhaps Faulquier, although Creuzé thought him complacent. The Prefect himself was an arch-supporter of machine industrialism. He also thought it "very bad politically to back down before the people," and hoped that another fabricant would try to install a shearing frame so that the government could properly protect it![62] His hardheaded attitude contrasted sharply with Lodève's perception of the issue. There were certainly fabricants committed to technological development. But the unreliability of the National Guard (consisting principally of fabricants) is a sure indication that this machine—which threatened to disrupt well-understood work relations, cost more than many could afford, and, by workers' violent responses, promised property destruction and general disorder—was not welcomed by the majority. No doubt, paternalism played a part for some, simple traditionalism for others, but many saw this as the route by which a few big fabricants would get bigger and they, unable to make the capital outlay, would be destroyed. So their "moral economics" was no doubt reinforced by a hard look at the books. Finally, they were fully aware that Montpellier bankers, who lost heavily because of government defaults during the Empire, were still hesitant to advance money to Lodévois. Round one went to the workers.

In Bédarieux, plump with prosperity, most manufacturers were less hesitant—and their credit less restricted. The concerns of workers over the introduction of machines fell on deaf ears locally. Thus, good royalists that they were, the "carders and shearmen" sent a petition in 1821 to fatherly Louis XVIII, whom they humbly beseeched to pass a law "prohibiting the use of all machines" in the fabrique of Bédarieux. The response, however, might as well have been written by Adam Smith. Its author was the Minister of the Interior, le Comte Simeon.[63] First of all, it said "the law" (meaning the Revolution) does not allow intervention in the internal affairs of manufacturers, but even if it did, such an interdiction would destroy the competitive position of Bédarieux. Its companies, "being at a disadvantage in the [competitive] struggle, would close down its shops one by one and thus deprive workers of their means of existence, workers who otherwise, even after the introduction of machines, they would have been able to employ." The whole region was being told: modernize or perish.

Although difficult to gauge precisely, this grim logic began to sink in. Workers, while continuing to use the threat of machine destruction, increasingly sought to influence the process of its introduction and gain compensation for jobs lost. In March 1822 at St. Pons, a shearmen's placard tacked to the church door first called for the "removal" of the shearing machine of M. Molinier under pain of "disasters that will befall you," but then (still with a threat of death) sought money in recompense. In August, with a burst of orders due to the Spanish crises, Lodève workers struck en masse for higher wages and specifically identified the impact of spinning machines on family incomes. The Lodève city council had also shown concern, not only requesting funds for poverty-stricken rural outworkers, but considering ways to compensate or retrain Lodève skilled men. In 1823 came the moment that Creuzé had been waiting for: a shearing machine was ordered (and paid for) by Joseph and Jean-Baptiste Rouaud. The November installation received protection from 100 Swiss Guard. The Rouauds made certain no shearman was immediately laid off. Cloth finishers had also organized to protect themselves: in 1822, Lodève's first mutual aid society—of "tondeurs, presseurs et foulonniers"—was formed.[64]

Over the next five years, a relatively prosperous period, a number of transversal machines were introduced without recorded incident. The first precise count that we have is in 1838, at which point there were forty trans-versal, one longitudinal, forty-five "Garrigue system hydraulic shears," and forty-seven hand shears operating in Lodève's woolen industry, meaning that the vast majority of work was by then being done by machine, with the hand-directed Garrigue shears and old hand shears moved by muscle power alone doing only fine work. Also, fifty-five updated gig-mills had replaced most hand-napping.[65] The introduction of machinery, however, was gradual enough and the increases in production significant enough that jobs lost to new technology were not numerous.[66] But the workman's con-trol over the process and pace of work had been considerably reduced, and the psychologically critical work team of two skilled shearmen was being replaced by a man and a child. The latter might be the shearman's own son and called an "apprentice," but the human situation of the work was dras-tically altered and what was left of the corporate character of the shearman's craft fast dissolving.

Hand-shearmen's responses moved from threats against the machine to intimidation of shearing machine operators. The last recorded incident with a Luddite flavor in Lodève occurred in the wake of the Revolution of 1830 and during a boom in army production that encouraged the installa-tion of new machines simply to keep pace. On 29 May 1831, "several fin-ishers, nappers, and shearmen other than those employed on hydraulic-power machines" assembled in a field near the village of Soumont "to deliberate on the means to adopt in order to stop the work of those who operate the said machines." So began the testimony of Jean-Pierre Fabre-guettes, Lodève's chief of police, at the trial of eight shearmen, a napper, and a presser. Thereafter, the hand-workers undertook a systematic effort to convince or frighten machine operators not to report to work. They raised money to provide assistance to the men who agreed to quit. Many of the hand-workers also laid down their tools. The point was "to force the bosses of the fabrique of Lodève to suppress the use of hydraulic machines called shearing frames and gig-mills and to increase the wages of the hand-shearmen." They sought to bring about a general assembly of the industry to discuss measures to deal with the machine issue.

The level of organization and the sophistication of their action and proposals were striking. If they could not intimidate a machine operator himself, they focused on his young aide. Pierre Laux, a presser's apprentice at Rouaud frères was promoted to journeyman presser when the former occupant of the slot, Bouissac, was shifted to a shearing frame abandoned by Etienne Bousquet, who quit voluntarily once the movement began. Bouissac proved immune to intimidation, so Laux became the focus. He was stopped on the way to work "by a rather tall, well-dressed woman of around thirty who counseled him as a friend not to continue his job as jour-neyman presser if he wanted to avoid being beaten up." If the tenor of this entire affair was new, the methods were as ancient as the charivari. Men in animal skins and other disguises prowled the night looking for machine workers, while fires of conspirators flamed in the hills. When some of them were finally rounded up and tried, the jury proved sympathetic; they got three days in jail and fines averaging thirteen francs each.[67]

A transition was being made. No longer the "collective bargaining by riot" that characterized the 1821 upheaval, Luddism now merged with carefully articulated strike activity and a focus on a general program to control technological change. Clearly, the "suppression of all hydraulic machines" constituted a maximum demand. That the strikers also called for compensatory increases in the piece-wage rates of struggling hand-workers indicates that they doubted whether machines really could be eliminated. Lodève workers were moving toward machine-age trade unionism.

It was typical that Lodève's shearmen should lead the way toward a coherent program for dealing with the impact of machinery. Although direct evidence is lacking, the coordinated character of the shearmen's action betrays the subterranean influence of their mutual aid society–legally limited to relief activities, but, as with its counterparts in Lyon, serving a much broader organizational function.[68] By 1831, the various economic and demographic forces at work in the formation of Lodève's working class were now being translated into associational links of solidarity tested and refined through the confrontation of crises posed by the evolution of the city's economic life. Evidence of a new consciousness and a working-class culture would soon be manifest. It would contrast sharply with that of its neighbor on the Orb, but in time, as objective conditions changed in Bédarieux and beyond, a wider worker movement of profound significance spread across the Languedoc piedmont.

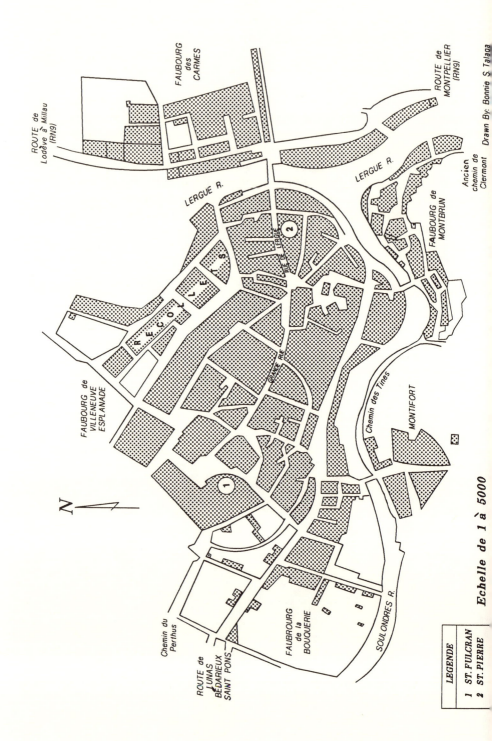

N

ROUTE de Lodève à Millau (RN9)

FAUBOURG des CARMES

ROUTE de MONTPELLIER (RN9)

LERGUE R.

LERGUE R.

FAUBOURG de MONTBRUN

Ancien chemin de Clermont

Drawn By: Bonnie S. Talaga

RECOLLETS

RUE DE L'ERGUE

GRANDE RUE

FAUBOURG de VILLENEUVE ESPLANADE

Chemin des Tines

MONTIFORT

Chemin du Perthus

ROUTE de LUNAS BÉDARIEUX SAINT PONS

FAUBOURG de la BOUQUERIE

SOULONDRES R.

LEGENDE

1 ST. FULCRAN
2 ST. PIERRE

Echelle de 1 à 5000

2

Crucible of Conflict: Industrial Languedoc Under the July Monarchy

The complex interplay among market forces, the changing power structure of the French state, and conflict at the point of production that made the history of industrial Languedoc moved to a new and climactic stage during the July Monarchy. As in so much of France, the Revolution of 1830 marked a fundamental economic and social—as well as political—turning point in the Languedoc woolens district. For its chief towns, it ushered in an era of unprecedented economic growth, Lodève benefiting immediately from huge army and National Guard orders, Bédarieux skyrocketing from 18,000 pieces to 50,000 from 1831 to 1833, as commerce responded to Orleanist stability. The 1830s and early 1840s turned out to be the glory years for both towns, and their complementary relationship served them well: Lodève's stimulus was war or threats of it, Bédarieux's peaceful commerce. One spun for the other when its own cloth sales lagged, and they also exchanged workers. Overall growth and this relationship are seen in Figure 2–1.[1]

Unlike earlier booms, the 1830s witnessed continued industrial concentration. It was more severe in Lodève because its military cloth manufacturers faced an even more stringent adjudication process than under the Restoration, further accentuating the trend toward large, efficient, and technologically advanced companies. Even the most substantial fabricants, such as the Barbots, Fourniers, Vitalises, Teisserencs, and Faulquiers found it advantageous to form complex partnerships. Further weeding out occurred, a fact of ongoing social and political relevance, for in Lodève the losers continued to be from the oldest, most Catholic, and most paternal-

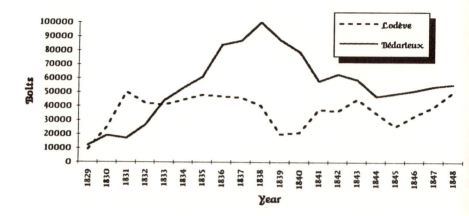

Figure 2-1   Cloth production (draps), 1830–44, Lodève and Bédarieux

istic families whose relations with their workers, like Cauvy's, were friendly
and personal, but whose talents as nineteenth century capitalists left something to be desired.[2]

Concentration also occurred in Bédarieux, but with different victims.
The great majority of fabricants here were "new" men whose business dated
back no more than three generations. Many of the biggest names were indeed royalists, then legitimists, but there is little evidence that they were
less economically progressive than anyone else. They shared their Lodève
coreligionists' putative concern for the workers, promoting Catholic chari-
ties and mutual aid societies. As in Lodève, there was also a group of successful "men on the make." *Nouveaux-arrivés* of the Revolution and Empire such as the Antoine Sicard and Jean Prades, while of common roots,
entered this city's more open elite circle.[3] Most, like their counterparts in
Lodève, became dedicated Orleanists. The Protestant fabricants assumed a
position paralleling people like the Rouaud brothers in Lodève. More
marginal socially, they made a solid economic contribution, a place won
by tough bargaining, creative salesmanship, and heavy demands put on their
work force. Hard workers themselves, they expected the same of their
employees. The true victims of concentration in Bédarieux were generally
newcomers to the industry, mostly Catholic, independent spinners and
small-scale fabricants who rose from artisan ranks during the booming
1820s. Their low volume of operations kept costs high when compared to
the vertically integrated businesses of the *grands.* These marginal industrialists also appear to have been the most extreme exploiters of the workers
and were the targets of a bitter strike in 1835, which helped to send several
of them into oblivion.[4]

By the early 1840s there were only eighteen companies in each city.
There were more, and more stable, extrafamilial partnerships than in the
past. In Lodève the four smallest companies had an annual product of

around Fr 200,000, while the largest (Vitalis) grossed Fr 700,000; most averaged around a half million. In Bédarieux, the figures ran about 25 percent less overall, although Sicard, the largest, produced an annual value of Fr 600,000.[5] The scale of operations in Lodève and Bédarieux placed both towns among the most advanced woolens producers in the nation. In general, the French industry did well, compared to cotton, in confronting English competition during the July Monarchy. This was due in part to its stylistic innovations and in part to its growing adaptation to mechanical spinning. The southern cities were in the forefront of these developments, with technological levels similar to Sedan, Elbeuf, and Louviers in draps production. All were more mechanically sophisticated than worsted producers because until the critical combing stage was mechanized in the 1840s, Reims and Roubaix (and their counterparts in Yorkshire) were little inclined to sink money into spinning machinery whose efficiency was mediocre, at best. The Languedoc industry, as will be argued in more detail in chapter 3, not only remained viable, but was technically and organizationally more advanced during the July Monarchy than the future woolens leaders of France. This was the context in which its remarkable history of social upheaval occurred.

1830

Outwardly, the political consequences of the Revolution of 1830 were straightforward. Almost immediately upon the arrival of the news that a new regime had been established (1 August), the excise tax collector's offices were attacked in both towns. This was the only immediate manifestation of violence, though in Bédarieux an angry crowd later liberated those arrested from jail. Antifiscal riots were endemic throughout lower Languedoc and continued into 1831. In Lodève, former Revolutionary activists and Bonapartists reemerged to capture city hall. Antoine Causse briefly occupied the Mayor's office and was replaced by Joseph Rouaud in December. That these parvenus and industrial mavericks had sufficient local backing is indicative of the liberal-Bonapartist character of the municipal revolution in Lodève.[6] Both were dedicated capitalists whose popularity with woolens workers was problematic. Rouaud held on until early 1832 and was then replaced by the more conservative and respectable Gaspard Barbot. Fifty-nine years old, Barbot came from a family of merchants that, although not wealthy, "occupied nonetheless an honorable rank in the *cité*." Using his good name, he had linked himself first to the ancient Rouch family of small fabricants, then to the Fournier brothers whose father had married into the Lodève business aristocracy late in the old regime. By 1830, Barbot was among the richest manufacturers in Lodève, an advocate of industrial innovation, a living symbol of careers open to talent, but a well-connected *notable*. In short, he was the perfect Orleanist. He remained mayor of the city until his death in 1845, choosing *adjoints* and backing candidates like himself for the city council.[7] Lodève's older elites also remained politically active. The industrialists in the Teisserenc and the Ménard families rallied to Louis-Philippe without much problem and became powerful voices in the new régime. Legitimism gathered little elite support, although Guillaume Rouaud's circle was kept under surveillance. Typically, its most evident activity was a willingness by some to risk fines for selling cloth to the Spanish Carlists.[8]

In Bédarieux, the new mayor, Jean Prades, was the son of a starch merchant, a middling fabricant, and good friend of Sicard. He had been a lukewarm Bonapartist who rallied to the One Hundred Days, but had cooperated with Mayor Fabrégat to keep order during the tense months after Waterloo. For this he won the respect of the major fabricants and royalists who ran Bédarieux during the Restoration, a time in any case when industry, not politics, was the main concern.[9] Prades's accession to power, while it again brought in a typical Orleanist, marked somewhat less of a change than in Lodève. Legitimist agitation in Bédarieux had no echo in official documents. In neither city did the new regime connote a fundamental shift in the power structure.

If the ever-practical business elites were mending political fences, truly revolutionary events began to unfold in the wake of the "Revolution" itself.[10] This, in fact, was the age of an awakening working-class consciousness in both cities. Its political content remained vague.

In the first place, the change in government unleashed a variety of nonpolitical illegal acts, collective and individual. Hunting violations multiplied, simple theft doubled in the Lodève area from the previous, harder year, counterfeit money abounded, attacks on policemen became a regional sport, and *bois communales* and private heaths became scenes of nearly constant "invasions" by the poor. Traditional youth group rivalries burst into flame as well in several villages. In Graissessac hand nailmakers once again helped themselves to coal on their own property assuming that finally *this* revolution had put an end to the monopoly rights of mine concessionaires. Antiauthoritarianism, an "esprit frondeur," as one official described it, was once again evident.[11]

Anticlericalism added to the mix, but was largely the work of young middle-class radicals stirred by memories of the Great Revolution. In the Lodévois, priests were insulted in Canet and Claret, while at Gignac a number of Frères de l'Ecole chrétien were menaced by a group of youths. At Autignaquet, a mountain hamlet above Lodève, a malcontent removed the steps from the church during high mass, and two months later the curé physically attacked a man who had heckled him in Church. In Lodève itself, priests were mocked as they passed in the night. During Lent in 1831, some young bourgeois sang bawdy songs during a service.[12]

There is no evidence of worker anticlericalism in Lodève, nor should one expect it. Workers seemed happiest when religion and support of the recent revolution could be harmonized. At the 1833 commemoration of July, the "worker population came *en masse*," to a religious service at St. Fulcran, the church of the upper town's elites, while attendance among the bourgeoisie was spotty and the curé was downright disrespectful, wearing "old and ragged" vestments.[13] More important, Lodève's workers had their own Catholic institutions. Most went for regular Sunday services not to St. Fulcran but to St. Pierre, which also sponsored a very active lay brotherhood, the *Penitents bleus*. It had its own chapel, and we have seen its importance at the time of the Concordat. Moreover, Lodève's second mutual aid society for woolens workers developed under its aegis in the late 1820s. But above all, the Penitents bleus, with their regular round of public festivities, funerals, and charitable activities, kept members in constant touch with one another. They were not all workers—Joseph Rouaud, for example, was probably a member—but in Lodève it appears likely that the two confraternities, Penitents bleus and Penitents blancs, split by parish and thus by class.[14] While legitimist ideas no doubt circulated in the former, it is unlikely that it served a function of elite cooptation. And as a *political* force it gave raise to no known groupings.[15]

In Bédarieux, the situation was much clearer. The bulk of the woolens workers, old Catholics from town, new Catholics from the country, if they had any political views at all, were old-style royalists. This did not stop them from participating in antifiscal riots or protest gatherings against machines after the Revolution of 1830. The response was swift; curé Miquel, urged on by the legitimist elite, organized a mutual aid society under the auspices of the Confraternity of the Holy Cross. Miquel, by all accounts a saintly person and the chief of the large St. Alexandre parish that included the entire town, was an enterprising builder of charitable organizations of all sorts. His roots were in the local peasantry, but his principal benefactors were from the legitimist establishment of the city. A look at the statutes of the society is revealing. The list of members included all of the big names among the legitimist fabricants. Article 16 told the story of its structure: "The President, Vice President, Treasurer and Receiver should be men who are financially solvent; they will be chosen from among the best off of the brothers." Jacques Donnadille, the third richest man in town, was duly elected President and remained in office for years. Moreover, among the reasons for excluding a member was "slandering one's superiors." The organization expanded to create another branch, the *Frères Cadets*, two years later.[16]

At this time, we may assume that these institutions appealed to all workers. Soon, however, an important change would occur, for Bédarieux's working class would follow the lead of Lodève into a protracted trade union struggle. And it was in this battle that a revolutionary working class, one that would reshape the evolution of industrial capitalism in Languedoc, was forged. These dramatic conflicts, among the most striking of the early industrial age, were indeed the product of willful action by men and women consciously seeking to change their world. These people were explorers in uncharted territory; they were creators of concepts of the strike and other strategies in the battle for control of production and its rewards; they were architects of new social values and political ideals consonant with their sense of economic justice; and by the late 1840s, they had become a class in a subjective, conscious sense, a group of people united in the belief in their power to revolutionize social relations through political action. What makes the workers of the Lodévois and the upper Orb so fascinating is that much of this process grew out of their own immediate experience with little apparent influence from Paris or Lyon, although obviously certain notions filtered in as time went by. Only during the Second Republic, however, does what might be termed their "folk socialism" merge with formal theory and political blueprints. It happened rapidly and thoroughly, making these towns a frightening antithesis to the bourgeois order.

Class Struggles

In November 1830, with orders cascading in, the weavers of Lodève organized their first modern strike. There was no threat to their jobs from machines: they were on the offensive. Sous-Préfet Eugène Brun reported that when it began on 17 November, it had been "plotted" for several days. Weavers in two workshops started it and walked en masse to others. "By example or by threat" they got the rest to leave their looms by noon. Weavers in each company then went on to demand a three-franc-per-cloth raise, up to eighteen francs. Brun, under general orders from Paris to be as conciliatory as possible in labor disputes[17] said he knew who the leaders were, but would seek to convince workers to return to their jobs. He plastered posters all over town calling on workers "to act wisely" and recognize "their errors." Such an approach proved fruitless, so he increased the number of national guardsmen on duty and closed the cafés, the workers' habitual gathering places, at 8 P.M. Brun apparently also talked to some of them and pointed out that they cleared two francs a day, which was much better than agricultural work and far less debilitating. That evening, when the cafés were closed, weavers "and workers from other branches" surged about town, making noise and intimidating fabricants whenever they could. While he recognized that there was no manifestation of hostility toward the government, Brun nevertheless called for troops, which arrived on 19 November. The following day, workers began to return to their shops.[18] But Brun did not realize that agreements were being made by the fabricants for wage increases. For how much, at this point, we do not know, but a retrospective comment in 1845 noted an increase from fifteen to eighteen francs per piece "granted" to weavers in the early 1830s.

The spinners followed in April 1831. These were men (some 200 altogether) in charge of the various machines in spinning factories. Their goal was to equalize wages throughout the local industry at the two-francs-fifty level being paid by the major companies, Barbot et Fournier and Visseq, in other words a *tarif*. Their strategy was to strike selected low-paying companies while the others continued to operate. Yet workers from all were involved in the overall operation. They met in cafés in the evening. The police finally got an agent into a big meeting at Guiraud's café and discovered that they were led by elected officers. (What he was observing was doubtless the board of the yet unknown mutual aid society that the spinners formed in 1830.) Then another spy reported on the meeting of eighty men at Carel's house in the faubourg Montbrun. Both were able to observe the involvement of men from various companies, but it was clear from the large number of its workers present that the big Vallat establishment was the main target. Since there was no further action taken by the authorities, despite the obvious functioning of an organized "coalition," we can only assume that the spinners returned to work with gains in hand.[19] The equalization issue, however, remained a subject of contention throughout the July Monarchy and was raised again in 1848.

Both these movements provoked immediate responses from fellow workers in Clermont, although the details escape us. Bédarieux was also probably aware of Lodève's successes. Finally, these actions gave courage to the shearmen and nappers of Lodève in their renewed war against the machine in 1831, discussed earlier. Overall, the first year and a half of the July Monarchy had meant success for Lodève workers. The mayor specified in a retrospective report of January 1832 that wages in general "had increased" since the July Revolution.[20]

In Bédarieux, all was not so happy. Despite the boom that got underway in the last quarter of 1831, wage cuts during the depression of 1828–29 had not been rectified and finishing machinery of all sorts was arriving daily. Although we have distressingly little information on it, a veritable Luddite war occurred in mid–1832 with "several" machines being burned. Radical Carlists were accused of promoting the mayhem, a theory that made some sense since Protestant fabricants seemed to be the main victims. Also, such action—if the disease did not spread—could not but help the fortunes of the Catholic elites largely mechanized already.[21]

In spite of this fiery beginning, Bédarieux's first strike had an air of calm and dignity. The spinners formed "a society" in August 1833. They sought a one-franc-fifty per quintal of thread increase, citing booming conditions and recent price hikes by companies. The threat proved sufficient and the spinning masters capitulated. Then, after the return to work, the firm of Gaston et Donnadille undertook to fire the leaders one by one. Their workers thereupon walked out "en masse." The rest of the fabricants then closed down. This lockout lasted only a few days, as the bosses realized, according to union leaders, "their mistake." Just as it seemed that the matter was settled, the Sous-Préfet (Béziers) decided to press charges against the spinners for coalition and arrested ten men. This move reflected the growing repressiveness of the Orleanist regime in the wake of the great upheavals in Lyon and Paris from late 1831 on. Nationally, both legitimism and republicanism were on the ascendant.

The ten published a remarkable letter from Béziers jail to their "comrades" on 10 October 1833. "To be forced to give our sweat for a piece of bread, that is slavery; to be in a position to refuse work which is not sufficiently paid, that is liberty." And "the condition of that liberty, it is our unity which will be our force." This ringing statement of solidarity was then followed by some fascinating modifications that identify the mentality of this working class at the time: "Comrades, we are all brothers! Let us live as a family. God wills it, so who dares to oppose it." But their concept of association went beyond the workers. "Let us be united not only among ourselves, but with our masters; let us make them understand that their interests are ours: are they not workers like we?" This sentiment, possibly Saint-Simonian in origin (they also attack *les oisifs*), but more likely drawn from the experience of intimate daily contact with their employers and from Christian sentiments, demonstrates a frame of mind clearly not yet ready for class confrontation.[22]

Still, the spinners had already moved to break with masters' influence, forming their own mutual aid society. The weavers of Bédarieux would do the same the following year. Both took on religious names, "St. Etienne" and "Notre Dame de Février," but the workers sought to control the organizations themselves and obviously would use them to back a job action. The break with the legitimists was beginning. Two letters written after the imprisonment of the strike leaders—to Sicard and to Prades—remind these bosses of their "worker origins" and speak of a "republican" future in which roles will be reversed. Where these letters came from is unknown, but it meant that already a rival opposition politics existed.[23]

In 1834, the scene shifted back to Lodève, this time for a strike with few parallels in French labor history to that point. Both the sophistication of strike strategy and the changing relations with the authorities merit attention.

Begun by handloom weavers objecting to an uncompensated increase in the size of the cloth, this strike quickly turned to a variety of demands. A single twenty-four-loom weavers' shed, that of Jourdan, was selected as the focus, and its strikers were supported with small contributions from the rest of the weavers. As Jourdan, pressed with heavy orders, began to waver, his machine spinners and carders went out, and the weavers upped their demands to include an indemnity for the time they had lost while on strike. This was followed by another selective strike by spinners at Pascal's, then by one by weavers at Lagare's. The Sous-Préfet was convinced that this intercraft action was planned in advance and supported by the bulk of the town's woolens workers, who would then seek to generalize the wage standards set at Jourdan's.

Such unity became clear when, on 27 January 1834, a huge demonstration of 700 Lodève workers was organized to protest the failure of Mayor Barbot to validate work passports of four Jourdan weavers who wanted to go to Bédarieux to seek jobs. What occurred at the end of the march, on the route to Bédarieux, symbolizes the new dimensions of the class struggle in Lodève. The national guard had not been called out because it was unreliable; as an earlier police report noted, the guardsmen "are mostly small proprietors and artisans who are little disposed to show favor to the fabricants against the workers." Thus only the Sous-Préfet, Brun, and a few policemen were there to meet the crowd. Brun declared the entire body of marchers under arrest, to which their leader, the weaver Jacquesjean, responded that they were merely exercising their historic rights as *compagnons* to see their brothers off on the Tour de France. The humor of it all escaped Brun, as did the next incident: a spinner named Ollier dashed from the crowd, grabbed a *garde champêtre's* sword, and scurried back waving it over his head to the laughter of 700 voices. Police Chief Jean-Pierre Fabreguettes saved some face for the other side by wading into the crowd and retrieving it. Brun then proceeded to try to arrest the front row of demonstrators, who quickly pinned his arms to his sides and then quietly disarmed him and his men. The farce was over. Brun and his companions were left sputtering in the twilight as the crowd disappeared into the streets, courts, and doorways of the city.[24]

This series of events shows an intriguing admixture of new and sophisticated tactics that were becoming part of the corpus of modern strike strategy and expressions of social conflict legitimated by older norms, a phenomenon also apparent in the shearmen's struggles of 1831. Two points stand out. First, to challenge the legal right of the mayor to refuse to validate *livrets* of workers, the possession of which was required by recent law, Lodève workers relied on the time-honored rights (or rites) of the *compagnonnage* for justifying not only their confrères' departure but for the festivities accompanying it. Certainly such celebrations had long been an accepted part of the ancient institution.[25] The only problem was that there is no evidence that the compagnonnage ever existed among woolens workers in Lodève, although it was quite familiar to building tradesmen. Second, there was the disarming/counterdisarming sequence. On one level it can be seen as a simple test of power that grew out of the situation and as an aspect of the strikers' challenge to the boss-dominated municipality. But more deeply, it likely was an expression of the community's disdain for the gardes champêtres, those symbols of the state's police powers over "traditional" community rights, who were often incompetent bullies as well. The tradition here, of course, was a complicated one, since it involved above all the freedom to hunt at will, a perceived revolutionary right that was more generally viewed as the vindication of community right against noble privilege. The mockery and relative good humor, at least as far as the crowd was concerned, in these events also smacks of Carnival (though it had not yet begun), and the almost ritual exchange of the weapon, not untypical of past Carnival activities, makes this all the more likely.[26] In general, our privileged view of this incident, made possible by a remarkably detailed report, allows us to observe precisely how so-called traditional culture was utilized and remolded into forms of protest effective in the struggles of the industrial age. But also, it should be recalled, these same workers used selective targeting of employers in their work stoppages, an "invented" tactic that grew out of the logic of modern industrial conflict itself.[27]

The confrontation of 27 January changed the terrain of the struggle. The fabricants capitulated, for the rush of orders was too great. They even promised not to press for arrests in connection with the demonstration. Brun

and his superiors in Montpellier and Paris, however, were not as cooperative. On 5 February, Brun attempted to arrest the four weavers now back
at work chez Jourdan. They escaped and hid in the hills. Their fellow workers
then organized a two-day, clearly political strike in which the entire woolens industry was closed down in a stroke. In the end, the woolens workers
did not win, since the town was invested with troops. But neither did they
lose. Their economic strike demands had been met, their collective strength
in the community was made obvious, and they had gained an important
psychological edge. A class presence was emerging.

Three other points about these events need to be stressed. First of all,
the fabricants split on each side of a long-visible fault line, politically between legitimists and Orleanists, socially between old-guard paternalists and
the cost-accounting modernizers. Fulcran Lagare, struck early, was an easy
mark not only because of a certain sympathy for the workers (it was said he
saw the "justice" of their first demand), but because, as a smaller company,
he could not afford many days of inactivity. On the other hand, René
Fournier, the brother of the mayor's son-in-law, was the leader of the hard-
liners among the fabricants. Auguste Jourdan, a legitimist, was more conciliatory. In a blistering letter, Neyrat, an agent for the Ministry of War,
berated the fabricants for their divisions. He also introduced the second
point, saying that if the insubordination of the workers was going to prevent the army order from being filled, he would send it elsewhere. He darkly
hinted at reductions in the next order, too. Obviously, this was the ultimate weapon to intimidate workers. Lastly, republicanism finally surfaced
in this strike. Not only was *La Parisienne* sung on several occasions, but
anonymous letters praising the republic circulated. A bit more chilling was
this ditty on a placard hung on 9 February, after the military occupation of
the town:

> Justice for sale, the Sous-Préfet to hang,
> The Mayor to the guillotine, the way the workers do it.
> Let's call the Sous-préfet what he is: a Brigand who
> tries to kill workers on the road, pistol in hand.
>   Les Trois Couleurs
>   Le partage ou la Mort.

This strike was a great testing ground for both sides. Relations could not
be the same again.[28]

The following year Bédarieux experienced the last strike of the prosperous 1830s. Five small companies involved only in spinning were struck
by their 300 workers when they attempted to reduce spinners' wages. They
said their small-fabricant customers were no longer able to meet the competition at the declining Beaucaire fair. The vertically integrated larger rivals
of both could afford to continue at the same rates and thumbed their noses
at these companies. Nevertheless, the small owners had a strategy guaranteed to upset workers: they began to hire scab labor from the mountains.
In a town where weavers were already livid about rural competition and

more than one "stranger" had been beaten up, this policy promised violence. The Sous-Préfet of Béziers committed armed force to protect the
scabs. This was enough to get the spinners to go back. This time, the state
had played a critically negative role. Four slubbers, two men and two women,
still refused to return and were arrested because they were preventing 100
other employees from working. One was Jacques Chalabre, a strike leader
in 1833 and a future démoc-soc militant.[29]

Overtones of republicanism echoed in both Bédarieux and Lodève by
the late 1830s. In the former, Paul Belagou, a lawyer whose Protestant
grandfather had been murdered by royalists during the Revolution, was
ejected from the Frères cadet de Ste. Croix for preaching democracy to
worker members. (Belagou was nominally a Catholic, having married one.)
The organization itself now reflected a growing separation of the common
woolens workers from this instrument of fabricant hegemony. In 1841 only
eight spinners and sixteen weavers were members, although seventy-one
finishing workers, by now mostly gig-mill and shearing frame operatives,
stayed in. The rest of the 180 members were artisans, merchants, and the
handful of bourgeois directors. Fifty women workers were also affiliated.
Essentially, spinners and weavers had their own institutions (each of their
mutuals had about 100 members) and represented the heart of a growing
class consciousness, which would slowly absorb the republican message.[30]

In Lodève, typically, although there were numerous late-1830s reports
of "republican" gatherings in cafés and of night meetings in the countryside, nothing was proved. Clermont l'Hérault, twenty kilometers down the
road, was less covert. Its republican movement was reputed to be the strongest in the department and well established among woolens workers who
migrated in regular streams to the more prosperous Lodève.[31] The eventual démoc-soc leader of Lodève, Moïse Lyon, was a Clermontois. By 1840,
Lodève had at least seven mutual aid associations, including one for women
workers, and no one doubted that while Christian principles informed them,
worker republicans in large numbers were members.[32] Legitimism in fact
was dying a natural death in Lodève. Most of its key supporters of the early
1830s were now deceased. Fulcran Lagare, brother of two priests and father
of another, lived on, but was hurriedly buying land for his retirement.[33]
Smaller companies such as Sumat or Beaupillier were long gone. The field
was now left open to the Orleanists, and their views on industrial relations
increasingly mirrored those of René Fournier. The days of divided loyalties
among the fabricants were ending. The decline of the technologically backward also meant the decline of legitimist ideology and hence of paternalism among the fabricants.[34]

Lodève's strikes in 1839 and 1840—both by weavers—occurred under
these new conditions. In November 1839, weavers at Rouaud frères et Vinas
walked out because they were not being paid twenty francs for working
2,000-thread warps, even though they got eighteen for 1800. Young Vinas,
the grandnephew of Joseph Rouaud with none of the latter's Revolutionary empathy for "his men," followed the law and got a Conseil des Prud-

homme's judgment for twenty-eight francs in damages for several warps left incomplete on the looms. This infuriated the men and encouraged weavers in other shops to go out in sympathy. Vinas employees went to Bédarieux to alert weavers there to reject calls for scabbing. The next day belonged to Lodève women who, in large groups, harassed Vinas with cries of "à l'eau, à l'eau!" and convinced the few Vinas workers still on the job to quit. The upshot was a series of arrest warrants against the strikers and the women for "insults." The escalation of this affair illustrates the growing confrontationist mentality on both sides and the immediate resort to force by state officials.[35]

The strike of September 1840 was an offensive operation, which, if one is to believe officials, "took the lead from Paris," where a great strike wave had just unfolded. Weavers again led the way. While the pretext was the renewed execution of livret regulations, this was in fact a carefully articulated, company-by-company attack plan, the goal of which was a wage increase stimulated, again, by booming demand. The critical point is that officials were outraged by this "audacity" and, even after workers returned to their jobs empty-handed, decided to prosecute anyway. This then provoked a strike against Barbot et Fournier—the workers' way of communicating to officialdom their displeasure at this turn of events. This political strike turned out to have an effect, for the original livret grievance at least was "settled."[36]

With the coming to power of François Guizot in face of the nationwide working class awakening in 1840–41, government policy moderated substantially. Préfets were put under strict orders to remain "neutral" (meaning let the unequal law take its course) in labor conflicts. Roulleaux-Dugage, the new Préfet, and Antonin de Sigoyer, the new Sous-Préfet of Lodève appointed in 1841, were conscientious career bureaucrats who understood, like their chief, that the survival of the July Monarchy might well depend on their action in these matters.[37] This was the setting for the final round of industrial conflict in Lodève and Bédarieux in 1844–1845.

For Bédarieux, the intermittent strikes that unfolded from 7 February to 29 March 1844 demonstrate how far that city's workers had come since the petition to Louis XVIII in 1822. But they also showed the defensive position into which these workers had now been put. About half the weavers of the city walked out in February when their bosses, citing slumping sales, lowered their wages. As they marched through the streets, they sang *La Marseillaise* and *La Parisienne*. Later that morning, several encountered two women who came from St. Martin d'Olargues to collect outwork from the modest Protestant fabricant, François Bompaire, and threatened them. Cut wages, republicanism, the competition of rural weavers: here was the new reality. Still the workers won the initial fight—their wages were not lowered and they were compensated for the two days lost. But they demanded more: the firing of the one worker who had stayed on the job at Sicard's. Mayor Prades exploded and summoned weavers' leaders to the Mairie. Instead, 400 weavers showed up. This was indeed a union. For his part, Sicard decided to fire the scab. The Sous-préfet then forced the poor man to return to Sicard's employ and arrested the strike leaders. The earlier decision not to cut was now rescinded, with only Sicard, who could afford it, still paying the higher wage. Thus the workers moved from apparent victory to defeat, having returned to the bricks for a trade-union principle—the punishment of scabs. The final line, however, was that state officials, despite orders from on high, intervened powerfully to thwart apparent worker success.[38]

The great strike of Lodève, all aspects of which lasted from 1 February to 21 May 1845, was the longest and bitterest in industrial Languedoc's history to that point and ranks among the major confrontations between capital and labor in the first age of European industrialization. Years ago, Frank Manuel called attention to it in an important article stressing the impact of mechanization.[39] Although this certainly became important, the range of issues, of strategies on both sides, of community involvement, and of governmental responses allow us to plumb the depths of early industrial conflict in ways rarely possible. The reports of police and administrative personnel, not fully available to Manuel, articles in the press, especially the recently founded *Echo de Lodève* and *L'Indépendant: Journal du Midi,* and the judicial reports sent on to Paris provide unusually detailed information.[40]

During the mid-1840s, the French military tightened its belt under the budgetary constraint imposed by the *juste milieu* policies of Guizot and his equally sober king. Production in Lodève dropped from 45,000 bolts in 1843 to 38,000 the following year. Further slashes were ordered for 1845. Simultaneously, the army sought to improve quality by demanding an increase from 1800 warp threads to 1900 in their basic gris-blanc material. The city's military manufacturers complied, but, having received no increase in remuneration from the government for the 5 percent increase in warp costs, were unwilling to compensate their weavers for the extra time that it would take them to complete the denser cloth. The eighteen-franc piece rate remained unchanged. This set the stage for the confrontation.

In January, several weavers chez Martel (the Lodève branch of the famous Bédarieux family), made a claim, after seeking the counsel of Sous-préfet Sigoyer, for a one-franc increase to match the increase in warp before the Conseil des Prudhommes. Predictably, the employer-dominated court turned it down. The argument, and not a bad one, was that since the number of shuttle-strokes remained the same, no time would be lost. The workers countered by citing extra preparation time, possible complications with heddles, and more broken threads. After the rejection (on 31 January), the delegation returned to Sigoyer to inform him that several men had already walked out of Martel's weaving sheds and more would follow if the Sous-préfet failed to act. He immediately consulted with other important manufacturers who assured him that it was all a tempest in a teapot and that even the Martel strikers would "end up asking to return" to work.[41]

The following day, forty-two weavers at Clermont's largest firm, Marréaud, Bouquet et Deraux, an army producer, also abandoned their looms and urged others to follow them. The increased warp was not the issue. Rather it was the decision by military producers to cease paying weavers the stipulated francs in advance for each piece. They argued that advance compensation led to "less than desirable" quality and that the new regulations required greater care at work (an admission that Lodève's workers' claims had some validity). Although no evidence of collusion between the weavers in the two cities existed, it was clear that these acts were hardly spontaneous. Marréaud in fact had received three anonymous letters from "*le conservateur*," apparently a weaver disgruntled with the job action, "telling of the existence of a secret society" and of threats against foremen who would not join the walkout. As a "gesture of benevolence," he decided not to turn the letters over to the judicial authorities, however. In Lodève, Mayor Barbot informed Sigoyer of a similar verbal report: "a secret fund, undetected by police investigations, financed by deductions made on [employed] workers wages by their *syndics*, provides, one says, two francs per day for the eighteen weavers who have left . . . Martel." Such organization was also evident in the collective decision taken by workers at Vinas and at Jourdan "to request that the fabricants hold their eighteen-franc pay in escrow until the differences between M. Martel and his workers are resolved one way or the other." Single-firm strike tactics, which Lodève workers had pioneered, were becoming ever more sophisticated. From his side, the frustrated Sous-préfet remarked to his superior that he was "lying in wait" for "these weavers" to make a mistake that would allow judicial action ("to fortify the fabricants") against their "manifest coalition."[42]

By 10 February, the Clermont workers were back on the job, thanks to the "generous and effective intervention of M. Rastoul, *curé* of Clermont," but because the mayor failed to follow through on the agreement (unspecified), they went out again. This stimulated several other companies to lock out their workers. Lodève sent a delegation of weavers to Clermont, and authorities took this as further evidence of a subterranean union including men from both towns. Such ties paid off for the Clermontois, for they had discovered that not only did they receive one franc less per piece, but the length of the "rang" (sections into which a cloth was subdivided) in Lodève was 3 meters, whereas in Clermont it had been incrementally lengthened to 3.5 meters of army cloth over the past fifteen years. This differential—the army no doubt assuming an inferior quality given Clermont's past record, thus demanding a larger quantity—soon became the principal focus of striking Clermontois. Their cause was also aided, reported *L'Independant*, by agricultural workers who helped them find jobs and learn techniques.[43]

In Lodève, positions were hardening, although one fabricant, the "eccentric" Fulran Lagare, had agreed to pay nineteen francs. Officials were beginning to see greater justice in the workers' claims, despite their being the "best-paid draps-de-troupe weavers in the nation." A mid-February visit to the Prefect in Montpellier by three Martel weavers clearly softened his attitude toward them; in a confidential letter to Sigoyer, Roulleaux-Dugage advised him that there seemed to be a "veritable coalition" among the fabricants to reduce wages since weavers "will need one day more" to complete a full cloth of sixty-three meters. They were scarcely making one franc twenty-five a day as it was. He felt that the manufacturers had made a mistake by not seeing the "justice" of the workers' claims in the first place and possibly could have gotten away with a twenty-five centime increase. But now "they dread appearing to have their hand forced and thus to give rise later to new demands. . . ." Sigoyer reiterated that the weavers were "under very skilled leadership" and understood the power of their position. Thus, in a decision taken on the seventeenth or eighteenth, two of the major manufacturers decided to strike back, closing their shops and sending all workers home. Soon they were joined by others, and by 27 February virtually all the major military producers had apparently agreed to a general lockout. This certainly was Roulleaux-Dugage's opinion. Workers in these other plants were not demanding higher pay. Were they "not laid off . . . to give satisfaction to M. Martel?" Was this not "to punish unjustly workers who have until now accepted conditions imposed on them?" If the fabricants have indeed taken concerted action, "it is not only blameworthy in the eyes of equity, but . . . in the eyes of the law." Was this not "an act of coalition?"[44]

Thus did the drama begin. Most Lodévois quickly made up their minds about whose side they were on: "Public opinion," said Sigoyer, "loudly declares itself in favor of the workers."[45] Sigoyer also now seemed drawn in that direction, especially in view of the attitude of the fabricants. In a revealing comment on 4 March, he wrote:

> Since the négociants of Lodève live in a most secluded manner and contact authorities only when it suits their interests, I have, in truth, ties only to M. Vitalis and M. Auguste Jourdan, leaders, to be sure, of our fabricants. As soon as they came into my office, I discretely shared the just and stern warning that you instructed me to carry to several fabricants with regard to the act of coalition. Far from misperceiving it, far from denying it, these gentlemen, particularly M. Vitalis, who became the most emotional, declared that they were indeed linked in coalition and that they thought it fitting . . . to see a judicial investigation undertaken, not only against the workers but against the masters as well, so that the position of one and the other might be well clarified and that one might ascertain exactly which side is wrong.

If Sigoyer was taken aback by this insular arrogance, his superior in Paris, Passy, the current Minister of the Interior, wanted no doubt about the willingness of the state to prosecute if they continued on their current course. Moreover, he wanted the workers of Lodève to know, "despite the insinuations of certain leaders, that the law serves to protect them against masters' coalitions with the same solicitude that it guarantees the latter against coalitions formed by the working class."[46]

The Ministry of War, interested in production, was less concerned about workers' feelings. It sent its regional inspector, one Lainel, out to Lodève on 6 March with eight Montpellier weavers (men temporarily laid off from Granier textiles) whom he installed, with local police protection, at Martel's and oversaw the startup of weaving operations. Although the blacklegs survived the morning, when they went for lunch at their auberge, accompanied by four armed guards, they were harassed and verbally abused by a troop of men and women workers and quickly made the decision to return home. Lainel continued to bluster about, causing considerable consternation among local officials.

The mention of Granier, however, brings up politics, for Zoë Granier was deputy for Montpellier East and a July Monarchy loyalist. His cooperation in supplying scabs is obvious. And it was politics, interestingly, that tipped the scales of official opinion, despite Lainel, back toward the side of the bosses. In a confidential letter to Passy, Roulleaux-Dugage was most sympathetic with his superior's desire to make an example of the employers, but did want to point out some political realities:

> The fabricants of Lodève, army contractors, give the strongest possible support to ministerial policy in elections. Rivals of Maistre of Villeneuvette, . . . it was they who brought about the defeat of M. Maistre, the opposition candidate, in the recent elections. It is thus important for the administration to use great circumspection toward the fabricants of Lodève so as not to alienate their votes and their influence.

Maistre, influenced by Fourier and his own paternalist ancestry, had built a solid business in army cloth around the concept of "honor to work" in the old royal manufactory, complete with cradle-to-grave social security, healthful working conditions and housing, and education and leisure facilities. And he undersold Lodève firms on his one-lot contract. But politically, he promoted democracy and social reform and thus stood against the current regime. Lodévois businessmen no doubt saw him as both an economic and political threat to their ascendancy. The prudent Préfect went on to stress that action against the workers for coalition was also inadvisable given the popularity of their cause in the city. Even the scab-baiters would not likely be prosecuted since the Montpellier weavers would have to file a complaint and "probably would not." Passy agreed immediately and wrote the Garde des Sceaux to have his agents proceed "only slowly and with prudence."[47]

Unemployment began to take its toll. Although the market boomed in the week following the lockout as people stocked up, penury quickly overtook most. Efforts by the Prefect to find work for Lodévois as laborers in Cette failed, and the Fr 1200 relief sent from Montpellier was quickly used up. Now, wrote Sigoyer, "all the unfortunate besiege our gates, led by women, poor mothers especially, while the fabricants discourage us" from giving any aid in order "to gain satisfaction" in their cause. "Yesterday, several spinners (who have more to complain about than weavers, generally better paid and possessing some goods) came to the police station to ask for work." But weavers also were distraught. Many had gone to Castres and St. Chinian for work, but returned quickly from "these towns already abounding in workers." Charity workshops must be created if the city was not to explode.[48]

The situation of the spinners and their response bears underlining. Part of the "new" working class, spinners lacked the traditions and sophistication of the ancient warriors of the handloom. *L'Indépendant* published a letter from a former spinnery clerical employee of Lodève late in March comparing the two. "Spinners are generally hard-working, moderate, punctual, and listen attentively to their boss's observations, having every intention of putting them to their profit." Weavers, on the other hand, wrote the *employé*, caused "all the troubles in our town" and "are indolent and inclined to plot against their masters," while "the least thing suffices to distract them from their work. Whatever happens in the streets, there they are at the windows or crowded at the door to check out what is going on. Finally, to prove the instability of their character, just take a look at most of their livrets, and you will soon be convinced by the number of declarations by their masters or directors that they are only to be found in the workshops where he is not."[49] Avoiding surveillance and causing trouble, the irascible weavers now led the biggest labor struggle in Lodève's history—and the spinners, cashiered by their masters, had little choice but to go along.

A breakthrough had occurred in Clermont and the workers reentered their shops on the basis of an agreement that promised parity with whatever was arranged at Lodève, except that Clermont cloth would be twenty-two rangs (sixty-six meters) in length; advance payment would also no longer be in force. Lainel, who had had a hand in arranging this settlement, now turned to Lodève, proposing a commission acceptable to both sides be formed to examine exactly how much extra time would be needed for the new 1900-thread cloth and set rates accordingly. In the meantime, production would start again under the old eighteen-franc rate. This was supported by all officials, but evoked no response from either side. Finally, after hints that the workers might support it, Vitalis *aîné*, "le plus éclairé et influent parmi les fabricants," came to see Sigoyer at noon on 24 March, telling him why the employers must reject the plan. They feared that "the commission proposed to evaluate 1900-thread cloth production would become a permanent commission from which the workers would call for a decision each time a change in work patterns would be introduced, even though the level of wages should in fact be discussed voluntarily and uniquely between master and worker, and [thus] . . . create multiple barriers to the growth and to the freedom of the industry."[50] Lodève employers were not about to give up their mastery for an uncertain future of arbitrated wages. As if to reinforce this outlook, "an industrialist" published a letter on 23 March the *Echo de Lodève* to let the world know how Lodève's bosses viewed industrial relations: "The manufacturers are the generals of industry, the workers are only the soldiers. When the fabricants command, the workers should obey. Let them submit, and any agreement is possible, but without submission there is no hope for them, for all resources run out, even charity."[51] Sigoyer, in reading this piece, summed up what for us (and Karl Marx and a host of contemporary reformers) might be obvious, but was rather noteworthy in an Orleanist official: the fabricants "regard the worker as a thing, an instrument, an addition to their working stock."[52]

If they were machines, so too might they be replaced by machines. The fabricants (except Lagare) now made their most radical move: they formed a special society to create a collectively owned power loom factory. Naturally this news spread like wild fire. Early April was marked by growing desperation on the part of the workers. Mayors in nearby villages complained of begging, threats, and robberies by wandering groups of unemployed Lodévois. Ateliers de charité were created but were woefully inadequate. The fabricants' determination to crush their foe was obvious to all. On 10 April, 250 workers signed a petition to the Sous-préfet in which they backed down considerably. They focused—as if groping for a fallback position— on two issues receiving little attention before: a five-centime per warp deduction made by some manufacturers for a widows and orphans fund and the problem of truck. The latter had never been an important issue in Lodève, though some fabricants made cloth available in lieu of a portion of wages if workers wished. (Clearly pressure could be brought to bear, however.) Weavers also wanted "something" for the extra work and would accept a "tarif" to be determined later. This confidential petition was shown to Hippolyte Couzin, the deputy mayor, by Sigoyer. Workers were outraged because Couzin immediately let the fabricants know about this weak and poorly formulated negotiating position. The fabricants thus published a triumphal mémoire that made no bones about why they were ready to invest in power weaving: "the projected factory cannot satisfy all our needs; but it is marvelously appropriate to come to the aid of a fabricant put under interdict by workers and henceforth to render impotent attacks against a single [target]." And more generally, they said with disarming candor that as machines spread, "the worker will understand that reason commands him to obey the regulations of the master and work as hard as possible; it further commands him, given what competition does to all things, to renounce the exaggerated wage levels that only men foreign to the realities of today's commerce and industry can dream of."[53]

In face of the fabricants' growing ascendancy, Lodève workers began to seek ways toward an honorable peace. Police Commissaire Nougaret— who seems to have been an honest broker throughout—had pressured a number of fabricants to meet with strike leaders on 18 April; the latter were told that "they would find the masters in a conciliatory mood." Nougaret was aghast when workers stormed into his office that afternoon to report that the curé, Hippolyte Beaupillier, had just said in mass that "he had an agreement with [Nougaret] and that the projected meeting would take place in the cloister of St. Fulcran." Not only was this definitely not neutral territory, but everyone knew Beaupillier's allegiance to the town's establishment. He represented the "official" church. Nougaret tried to convince the workers that he had discussed nothing with the mistrusted priest, but to no avail. The meeting was called off. Beaupillier must have been contacted by hard-line fabricants who desired to sabotage a proposed meeting where they might have to make concessions. Their goal was to crush the workers' union movement. For their side, the weavers had now come to believe, according to Sigoyer, that all officials (including himself, because of the error of giving their petition to Couzin) were "only working in the interest of the fabricants."[54] State, Church, and bosses were united against them.

The demoralization caused by the successive threats of mechanization and shattered hopes of a negotiated settlement led to the lockout's ironic denouement. The bosses' only condition for the end of the lockout was the reoccupation of the Martel weaving shed. The town was slowly starving (credit at bakeries was drying up), nonweavers' solidarity was beginning to wane, and weavers themselves were splitting. If they were to give up, more conciliatory weavers nevertheless had to save face. It was a ritual of the distant past that came to their rescue. The feast day of the weavers was 5 May. The night before, weavers traditionally went to the fabricants' houses, gave them a piece of bread, shook hands, and received a small amount of money. After determining in advance that the manufacturers would accept them, they proceeded with the distribution. The symbolism of the ritual allowed them to swallow the bitter pill; the masters' gratuity was received as "un gage de réconciliation." Weavers slowly returned to Martel. It took another two weeks before the *fabrique de Lodève* was operating again. Weavers were still paid eighteen francs. But bitterness hardly evaporated. On the morning of 6 May, Martel's foreman had to rip this placard from the factory door:

> Martel, aren't you happy now!
> Your slaves are back . . .
> Woe to you!
> Woe to you![55]

Nor did bitterness toward workers who had capitulated abate among the militants who fought the empty-handed return to work. Another placard plastered in the Halle au blé, having cried "Woe to the negociants, those monsters of Lodève," concluded:

> Woe? Three times woe!
> To those perfidious workers
> and their infamous course of action.
> They will all lose their lives.

A skull and crossbones adorned the bottom: "Pensez y bien."[56]

Thus it was that the fabricants, united and actually benefiting from a downturn that meant they did not need high production levels for a while, and the government, afraid to prosecute what was an obvious masters' coalition because it needed Lodève's political support (despite efforts to conciliate and disgust at the employers' tactics), combined to defeat the trade unionism of the workers. The official Church had played a role as well.

In mid-June 1845 a flare-up occurred that foreshadowed the violence of the revolutionary period. A group of workers confronted fabricants returning from a benefit concert for poor children in day care and threw stones at them. They then followed them to the meeting place of *le Circle*, their bastion of social authority, and pummeled it with stones, leaving broken glass and china strewn everywhere. The government, after a frantic search, finally arrested the sullen *malfaiteurs* and sentenced four weavers, including Jean Alias, a key strike leader, to a year in prison, the longest sentences ever given in the labor wars of Lodève.[57]

There is a curious footnote that must be added. On 9 July, the new mayor, Auguste Bérard, aîné, wrote an approving Roulleaux-Dugage requesting the authorization of a *Société des Artistes* that would consist of "artisans, machine builders, clerks, and foremen." He remarked that they were all "good citizens, peaceful and friends of order." They should function "to cement more and more the state of tranquility we currently enjoy since this is the fusion of all the professions included in the second class of inhabitants (the workers of the fabrique and of the countryside excluded.)" He did not have to identify the first class.[58] This last-ditch effort to build a petit-bourgeois social force to mediate class conflict only serves to underline officials' fear and trembling before the divided society they saw. As the downhearted Sigoyer put it when asked if troops of the line dispatched to Lodève during the lockout should be withdrawn:

> The calm that appears to extend across the city exists only on the surface; it is not interiorized, since the germ that had divided and troubled the industry and its work force still subsists, still as alive as ever. You know yourself that it had not been killed.[59]

The evolution of working-class militance in the Languedoc woolens district had parallels throughout France and Western Europe. Among the woolens towns, strong movements grew in Reims, Elbeuf, Louviers, and Vienne as well as in Liège, Leyden, Dresden, and Leeds abroad. But nowhere, with the possible exception of Vienne, was the confrontation of classes so stark as it was here. Let us now turn to an analysis of the reasons why.

3

Le Monde des Fabricants

An explanation of the growing bitterness of class relations in the Languedoc woolens district during the July Monarchy must begin with an assessment of the business activities and social power of its industrial bourgeoisie.

A great deal has already been said about the industrial evolution of the key cities of Lodève and Bédarieux and Figure 2–1 presents the precise figures for the two. We should, however, broaden the discussion briefly in order to set the detailed analysis that follows in context. The southern woolens industry, according to the estimates of T.J. Markovitch, declined from roughly one-fourth of the total national production to less than one-fifth from 1815 to 1851. This occurred despite the excellent progress made by Lodève, Bédarieux, Castres and Mazamet. St. Pons, St Chinian, and the Jaur valley mills stagnated after making considerable investment in plant and equipment during the early 1830s. Nevertheless, they remained viable until mid-century. Carcassonne's share of the woolens business in the Aude shrank throughout the July Monarchy, leaving Chalabre and Limoux in charge of the declining industry there. Fohlen's thesis that the vine progressively replaced woolens, based on research in the Aude, is certainly accurate for that department, but the process was much more complicated if the rest of Languedoc is taken into account. In the Tarn, truly revolutionary events were taking place. Castres continued to produce cloths using traditional methods, but at an ever-larger volume. Mazamet, however, emerged rapidly as the most vital center of woolen cloth production not only in the south, but perhaps in the nation. Called the "Elbeuf of the Midi," its leaders no doubt preferred to think of Elbeuf as the Mazamet of the north.

By 1848 it had passed Bédarieux and Lodève in both total production and value, and by 1860, its Fr 12,000,000 gross output equaled that of the other two cities put together. Mazamet, well-studied by Rémy Cazals, will provide a point of reference (and an ongoing exception) in our entire analysis of southern deindustrialization.[1]

How did the woolens industry of Languedoc compare with other industries in the region and with woolens and worsted production nationally? A fascinating study, ordered by the National Assembly in 1849, provides special insight into this problem. Although by no means universal, the year was one of improving economic conditions. But for Languedoc, including military cloth production, the best that can be said is that things were "stable." The figures are thus somewhat loaded in favor of its rivals elsewhere. The prefects and mayors carried out a detailed census on the number of employees in the ten largest enterprises in each department. Although number of employees is not necessarily the best measure for scale of operation, at least we have a comparative framework that is consistent and does not ask employers to provide information subject to gross manipulation, such as total value or profits.[2] Compared with the rest of France, the Languedoc woolens industry remained quite strong, with nine firms making the top twenty-five (see Table 3–1).[3] Barbot et Fournier of Lodève (which listed no children) and Siau et al. of Clermont (which listed only six children) rounded out the Hérault ten with 222 and 206 employees respectively.[4] For all of Mediterranean Languedoc plus the Aveyron and the Tarn, the only companies larger than the woolens enterprises were in mining and metallurgy—Decazeville with 2,503 and Talabot of Alais with 1,453. Only the Ardennes could boast integrated woolens enterprises of greater magnitude than the Hérault, and even here the average size of the eight firms making the list was 554 compared to the Hérault's average of 394; the inclusion of Cormouls-Houlès would obviously increase that figure. With the exception of the huge cloth-printing and cotton spinning establishments in Alsace, woolens were generally the largest firms in France.

The figures for Reims were relatively low, reflecting the fact that vertically integrated production in worsteds had not yet occurred. Only with the adoption of mechanical combing—then in its infancy—would this development take place. The large enterprises in worsteds and "fantasies," in terms of level of affairs, were still essentially mercantile houses who sold the wares produced by modest putters-out using a work force based largely on artisans. William Reddy, among others, has emphasized the continued significance of this mode of production in much of the cotton and linen cloth industry as well.[5] This comparison confirms the argument made throughout that the Languedoc industry not only held its own during the first half of the century, but in the important respect of integration, concentration, and rationalization, ranked among national leaders.[6]

The fabricants in woolens were among the major notables in the department, and in their own towns, especially Lodève and Bédarieux, no one

Table 3–1

Firm	Location	Product	Employees*
1. Berteche Cheson	Sedan (Ardennes)	Woolens†	1315
2. Paturle, Lupin, Seydoux et Sieber et Cⁱᵉ	Le Cateau (Nord)	Spinning and Weaving	1307
3. GRANIER	MONTPELLIER	BLANKETS	823
4. Tranchot-Fromont	Neuville-lès-Wasigny and Lalabbé (Ardennes)	Spinning	766
5. Paul Bacot et fils	Sedan	Woolens	764
6. CORMOULS-HOULÈS	MAZAMET (TARN)	WOOLENS	738
7. Jourdain et Cⁱᵉ	Cambrai (Nord)	Woolens	721
8. Cunin Gridane et Cⁱᵉ	Sedan	Woolens	653
9. Jourdain et Cⁱᵉ	Louviers (Eure)	Woolens	642
10. Lataille, Duncan et Cⁱᵉ	Chateauroux (Indre)	Woolens	596
11. Deseat-Leleux	Flers (Nord)	Dyeing, Finishing	491
12. Cheuneviere	Elbeuf (Seine-Inf.)	Woolens	398
13. Frédéric Bacot	Sedan	Woolens	394
14. Flanguy	Elbeuf	Woolens	387
15. VITALIS	LODÈVE	WOOLENS	368
16. DONNADILLE	BÉDARIEUX	WOOLENS	359
17. SICARD	BÉDARIEUX	WOOLENS	358
18. MAISTRE	VILLENEUVETTE	WOOLENS	357
19. VERNAZOBRES	BÉDARIEUX	WOOLENS	350
20. d'Espinapoux	Marvéjols (Lozère)	Spinning	302
21. Longeaux	Reims (Marne)	Spinning	295
22. Tessier et Cⁱᵉ	Signy (Ardennes)	Spinning	294
23. FOURCADE	ST. CHINIAN	WOOLENS	277
24. TEISSERENC et al.	LODÈVE	WOOLENS	258
25. Leroy et Raulin	Sedan	Woolens	257

*Children are included—generally the percentages are about the same as in the Hérault.
†As in the Hérault, this means a firm carrying out the entire process of cloth production.

rivaled them in wealth and power. For example, in the canton Lodève there were, in 1846, seventy-four *censitaires,* men who paid over Fr 200 in taxes and therefore had the right to vote under the July Monarchy. Of these, fifty-six owed their wealth to the woolens industry. This figure was arrived at, however, only by combining information from the *cens* list of 1846[7] with prior knowledge of Lodève's leading families and other contemporaneous documentation, especially the *déclarations des mutations par decès.* Use of the cens lists alone is a risky business, as the following analysis shows.

The number of Lodévois who actually listed themselves as "fabricants" or "filateurs" was relatively small (twenty-four). On this basis, the "industrial bourgeoisie" of Lodève might have been recorded as only one-third of the notable population. Another sixteen were *négociants,* which by certain definitions, would seem to designate men of commerce. But in Lodève (and indeed throughout the land), négociant was generally regarded as a more prestigious title or at least it indicated a more diverse economic activity than simply manufacturing. Owners of woolens firms often called themselves such. In fact, in Lodève, there were no négociants on the list who were *not* manufacturers.

Three other industrialists called themselves "propriétaires," a title understood by historians using the cens lists to indicate owners of "landed" wealth. Paternalist boss Fulcran Lagare was one of them. He was then seventy-one years old and an owner who had undoubtedly tired of the labor wars. He *did* own enough real estate to pay Fr 379 in land tax. But he had sufficient movable property to pay Fr 178 on it and, above all, his business tax alone was higher, at Fr 446, than the total tax of more than half of Lodève's censitaires. Although the aristocratic ideal always beckoned, we have no idea why at this particular point he chose the designation "proprietor." When he died in 1848, his probate declaration listed him as a négociant. His total movables, merchandise in stock, and credits were evaluated at Fr 76,500. He was indeed a proprietor, owning some valuable land: a thirty-nine-hectare country estate in nearby Campestre of which the "master house" was evaluated at Fr 6000 and the "meadows, vines, and pastures" provided an annual revenue of Fr 900 (Fr 18,000 cash value); sixteen hectares in Olmet-Villecun commune with vines and pastures also worth Fr 900 in revenue; and, valued at Fr 16,000, a Lodève "house, Grand'rue" with its "attached buildings." The last was unquestionably his old dwelling and its warehouse, but Lagare had passed on his mill to sons Isidore and Eugène after forty years of activity as a fabricant.[8] His total worth was evaluated at Fr 154,500, a tidy fortune, but considerably less than it had been while he was still active in business.

Another would-be "propriétaire" was Adolphe Teisserenc, thirty-seven, who with his brother Jules, a "fabricant de draps," split the business tax on their share of the firm, Teisserenc, Visseq et Calvet, the twenty-fourth largest woolens company in France; he also paid out Fr 224 in mobile wealth taxes along with his large real estate tax of Fr 706. A good portion of the latter was in industrial property, as we shall see. Teisserenc was an inveterate modernizer and among the least popular employers in Lodève. The third "proprietor" on the Lodève cens list, who in reality was an industrialist, was Honoré Calvet, Teisserenc's cousin by marriage and partner. His Fr 168 *patente* connoted an equal share of one-third in their venture.[9] There are several more men in this "landed" category from fabricant families, but they may have shifted some of their capital to land and bonds, a not untypical process, especially among retirees after they passed along their industrial interests to their heirs and were thus propriétaires in a more traditional sense.

Of the other three woolens-industry censitaires, two appear on the list as *teinturiers,* dyers, who might be categorized as "artisans" if we did not know who they were—Joseph Gauffre, a small millowner who leased his dyeworks and fulling machinery to the Ménard interests, and René Fournier, the highest taxpayer in Lodève! Finally, Fulcran Fraisse, a substantial taxpayer (Fr 445) with a Fr 140 patente, listed himself as a *commissionnaire,* normally a term describing a sales employee of a company. It is possible that he had not yet found a company to buy into, but in the following ten years before his death he became one of the key capitalists in Lodève.[10]

Some attention has been given to this matter in order to underline the dangers inherent in the uncritical use of occupational categories to describe a social or economic structure. It seems likely that the reliance on cens lists without other information may vastly underestimate the significance of industrialists among the elites of July Monarchy France. A.J. Tudesq, if read carefully, does not do so, nor does Adeline Daumard. Unfortunately, in using their work, the Cobban school among "Anglo-Saxon" historians has not been so scrupulous.[11]

This does not mean, of course, that this source is not of great value, for it provides a cross section of wealth and its basis among local elites at a given time. The other key source of this order, the probate declarations, has the disadvantage of overrepresenting the aged, people who are often no longer actively involved in their professions. Their combined use generates the most accurate information.

In 1846, Lodève counted twelve men who paid more than Fr 1000 in taxes and thus qualify as "grands notables" according to the schema developed by Tudesq.[12] Another fifteen paid over Fr 500, thus being eligible to stand for the Chamber. One of Lodève's richest men, Gaspard Barbot (Fr 1654 in 1842 cens) had just died. Table 3–2 provides a picture of Lodève's richest individuals and the bases of their wealth according to the cens list.

This list reveals the obvious preponderance of the woolens industry as the basis of wealth in Lodève. And even Lacas and Maurel came from old woolens families, although the Maurels went into the law (first as *notaires*) two generations before. The Lacas family had only recently withdrawn from the industry. Etienne Lacas, Scévola's father, died in 1843 and was still designated a négociant even though he willed no industrial property. He had long been one of the city's leading fabricants. Scévola inherited the Lauroux property called the Domaine des Sièges, which was an old noble estate of several hundred hectares in the highlands above Lauroux and

Table 3–2

Name	Age	Stated Occupation	Location	Property	Personal Property	Business	Other	Total*
René Fournier	65	Teinturier	Lodève	872	160	608	97	1737
Pierre Ménard	86	Fabricant	Lodève	1280	254	—	111	1645
Joseph Vinas	51	Négociant	Lodève	888	103	490	51	1532
Pierre F. Martel	57	Fabricant	Lodève	338	200	248	53	1417
			Octon	265	14	—	31	
			LeBosq	144	—	117	7	
Jules Teisserenc	34	Fabricant	Lodève	305	169	167	98	1391
			Soubès	652	—	—	—	
Eugène Menard	51	Négociant	Lodève	194	146	133	18	1375
			Vendémian	866	10	—	8	
Pierre-Ph.Pascal	86	Filateur	Lodève	1078	92	145	51	1366
Hector Teisserenc	34	Fabricant	Lodève	866	236	111	106	1319
Scévola Lacas	53	Propriétaire	Lodève	189	128	—	55	1151
			Laroux	763	11	—	5	
Adolphe Teisserenc	37	Propriétaire	Lodève	706	224	167	44	1141
Fulcran Etienne Vitalis	51	Fabricant	Lodève	434	290	300	81	1105
J. Fulcran Lagare	70	Propriétaire	Lodève	379	178	446	83	1086
Pierre Faulquier	72	Fabricant	Lodève	677	146	111	60	994
Charles Vallat, Fils	36	Négociant	Lodève	651	128	98	98	975
Honoré Calvet	45	Propriétaire	Lodève	135	191	168	22	874
			Aniane	337	11	—	10	

Name		Profession	Location					Total
Adrien Calvet	52	Marchand de draps	Lodève	130	110	111	38	822
			Octon	141	10	—	9	
Auguste Labranche	51	Fabricant	Lodève	394	74	118	11	753
			Soubès	137	6	—	13	
Emile Maurel	47	Avocat	Lodève	519	94	20	99	732
Frédéric Pascal	54	Négociant	Lodève	352	92	—	—	648
			Lunas	192	—	—	12	
Matthew Puech	50	Négociant	Lodève	126	92	196	33	628
			LeBosq	172	—	—	9	
Auguste Vitalis	32	Négociant	Lodève	140	150	300	52	642
M.J.C. Vallat	63	Fabricant	Lodève	101	128	—	4	608
			Montpaon	342	12	—	20	
F.J.G. Fraisse	40	Propriétaire	Lodève	556	29	—	—	585
Jules André	50	Négociant	Lodève	213	125	196	43	577
Eugène Fournier	55	Négociant	Lodève	259	137	149	29	574
Antonin Jourdan	37	Fabricant	Lodève	248	74	153	54	539
François Pomier	53	Fabricant	Lodève	304	42	132	29	507

*Includes the Door and Window Tax levied on the number of openings in one's buildings and "prestations."

Pégairolles. Since his occupation was already listed as a proprietor on his father's probate declaration, we may assume that the transition had been made before 1843. F.J.G. Fraisse, too, was born into an important fabricant family, but had left Lodève, although he maintained considerable landed property there. The other twenty-four, with the possible exception of Pierre Ménard who may have finally retired by 1846, were actively involved in the industry.

The wealth of Lodève's top elites compares quite favorably to those of northern woolens cities. For example, Sedan, a town almost three times as large, had twenty-seven grands notables of which twenty were négociants or fabricants. Altogether 138 electors voted in its two cantons, compared to Lodève's seventy-four. The major difference was Sedan's extremely wealthy group, which included two of the "plus-imposés" in France, the iron millionaires J.N. Gendarme and Eugène Schneider. But the top woolens manufacturers were comparable to Lodève's major figures.[13]

As in Sedan, the wealth of individual Lodève industrialists was dwarfed by family assets. The Teisserenc, Fournier, Ménard, Calvet, Martel, and Vitalis dynasties had more than one representative among the city's very richest men. But if one descends down the cens lists and then on to the tax rolls[14] a much fuller picture emerges.

The Calvets had no less than five brothers on the cens list. All were sons of Louis Calvet (1762–1840). Adrien and Honoré were joined by Jules, Justin, and Amédée, who paid Fr 422, Fr 262, and Fr 262 in taxes respectively, bringing the total tax of Calvet frères, (all, save Adrien, partners in Calvet et fils et Cie) to Fr 2,642. What does this represent in terms of actual wealth? This is quite difficult to answer. For the Hérault, the average ratio of annual revenue from real property only (*revenue foncier*) compared to the total cens is around ten to one.[15] This would mean that the Calvet's total revenue (if used only for that purpose) from land, buildings, and fixed capital was around Fr 25,000 and, using the inheritance tax assessors' standard of a twenty-to-one ratio, their total wealth in this category was thus about five hundred thousand francs. But they were not taxed on their investments, credits, cash in hand, or current inventories—for businessmen, often a more substantial element in their overall wealth. The patente was a rough measure of their volume of business activity, but represented a tiny proportion of it. According to the *Statistique générale*, Calvet et fils paid a total patente of Fr 830 but put out a product whose value in 1844 was reported at Fr 303,200. Rough calculations put their profit for that year at a low 10 percent. In general, the army cloth companies more often cleared 15 percent and above.[16] But in any case the patente amounted to only 2.5 percent of profits in a bad year and was a tiny percentage of overall revenue from other sources. When their father, Louis Calvet, died in 1840 when he was seventy-eight, he had already passed on three-quarters of the ownership of his mill on the route de Soubès to his sons, but was still an active partner. According to his probate declaration, he left Fr 62,960 in merchandise, credits, and personal movable property and Fr 68,000 in real estate. His share of the Calvet textile works was evaluated at Fr 14,000, meaning the assessed value of the Calvets' industrial property was Fr 56,000. Its annual rental value in 1844, however, was Fr 4,000; using the 5 percent rule, that would put the value at Fr 80,000. Old Calvet had a variety of other property, although, again, he had probably already passed on some of it to his sons.[17] Overall, in his later years of semiretirement, he enjoyed an annual income of close to Fr 10,000 in nonindustrial revenue, as well as a quarter share of the company's profits.

The younger Calvets had already diversified their investments as well. Adrien, the second oldest after Jules, who was born in 1792, paid a very large *cens foncier* on property in Octon, which he leased out. Honoré, the youngest brother, owned almost precisely the same type of property in Aniane, a purchase no doubt made possible by his marriage to Emilie Teisserenc. Both probably included vineyards. It is likely that the two "landed" Calvets could each count on an income of twenty-to-twenty-five-thousand francs and the other three, perhaps twelve-to-fifteen thousand francs. The average working-class family in Lodève who toiled in the mills could make Fr 800 in a good year. The Calvets, collectively, were very well off indeed.

All told, the seventy-four men on the cens lists of 1846 broke down into forty family names. Of these, twenty-two were single individuals. Thus the other fifty-two electors shared eighteen surnames, an average of three per name. Only two, three Arrazats and two Gots, were not in woolens. The other sixteen were woolens families. All were at least cousins, except the seven Martins, who came from two distinct branches. Thus we find two Crouzet brothers, Faulquier father and son, three Fournier brothers and a cousin, two Fraisse brothers, two Granier brothers, four Jourdan brothers, two Labranche brothers, three generations of Ménards (four), Martel father and son, Pascal father and son, Portefaix father and son (of Soubès), two Teisserenc brothers and a cousin, Vallat father, son, and nephew, and two Vitalis brothers. These were Lodève's elites, some of whom we have already met.

Considerable family wealth was also lodged in the hands of women. Not only were they and their dowries central in cementing partnerships, but several individual women figured prominently on the tax rolls and some appear to have been active in business affairs. The rolls of *foncière* assessments for Lodève commune only, completed on 13 September 1846, carry nine of them with assessments over Fr 100, topped by Veuve Jean Teisserenc fils, née Faulquier, at Fr 450. All, save Claire Vallat (Fr 350), were widows.[18] These figures represent substantial wealth because they account for only a portion of the income of those listed. It is likely that most of these women would have been censitaires had they had the right to vote and should logically be added to the family lists above. Although widows head the list, in the fifty-to-ninety-nine franc category there were a dozen single women, and notarial records reveal that many wives operated as independent business women.

To what uses was their money put? Certainly many widows were simply set up by testament with a fixed income largely from state *rentes* and revenues from rental property.[19] But others were actively involved in running their departed husbands' business, as did Camille Barbot Fournier (the daughter of the Mayor) after René's untimely death in 1858. Moreover, her daughter Emma, the wife of Michel Chevalier, inherited a huge portfolio of investments that she further increased, essentially financing her husband's political career.[20] Jean-Pierre Fabreguettes's widow also continued to take an active hand in the operation of Brun-Fabreguettes et Cⁱᵉ. Other widows built upon the income bequeathed to them or which they held in dower by their own right. One of the most interesting figures was Thérèse-Hélène Faulquier, whose husband, Jean-Fulcran Teisserenc died prematurely in 1813. Married in 1803, she was the mother of Hector Teisserenc, and her daughter Zoé would marry Adrien Calvet, thus forming one link in that key alliance. A third child, Melanie, would marry a prominent Montpellier lawyer. Upon Jean-Fulcran's death, his widow used the inheritance from her husband to purchase in 1815 the substantial Domaine de Tréquier for Fr 30,000 and, in 1822, a tract of "vines and arable lands" south of Lodève for Fr 23,000 in the names of her children, as well as two more pieces of land in 1814–15 for a total of Fr 13,700 on her own account. (Her dowry had been Fr 127,000.) Beside providing dowries twice the size of her own for her two daughters, she emerged as one of Lodève's richest people and one of two women to be a member of le Circle (the other was Jules André's mother). In thirty years she had tripled the value of her capital.[21]

Women's money could also be put to work politically. Jean-Pierre Fabreguettes, Guillaume Rouaud's nephew, was not wealthy. In 1834, his mother-in-law, Thérèse Faulquier (widow of Joseph Faulquier), "designated" him, by virtue of the law of 19 April 1831, "to avail himself of the *contributions fonciers*" paid by her in order to become a censitaire. Nonwidows could be active too. Notarial minutes for Lodève are dotted with instances of married women involved in real estate deals. Although their husbands legally had to sign with them, it is likely that they sought out opportunities and carried out the transactions with little male input. Louise and Marie Rabejac, for instance, were the daughters of a fabricant who had invested in real estate. After his death, they used their capital to amass substantial holdings in small properties. The spouse of each was well placed to help them locate interesting deals: Louise was married to Géraud, the notaire, and Marie, to Michel, the Secretary at the Mairie. The frequency of their appearance in the notarial records indicates that they were small-scale but quite active real estate speculators. Their brother Bartolémy complemented their work: he was a small-loan agent who sometimes financed buyers of their land.[22]

Despite these indications of semiautonomous economic activity,[23] the most significant role of women in Lodève's business community was narrowly tied to their gender functions as marriage partners and producers of heirs. As we have already remarked in discussing the town's elite in the late eighteenth century, the wife of a fabricant married young (her husband was usually ten years her senior) and bore him many children. Significant numbers of younger or less desirable daughters never married at all. Such patterns remain evident in the nineteenth century, as a close examination of the census of 1851 reveals.[24]

In one respect, marriage as an element in business practice became even more crucial as the nineteenth century wore on. Large, well-financed companies were becoming more necessary. The place of marriage in cementing business alliances and the financial arrangements of marriage contracts became increasingly significant. Let us look at some of the principal firms and examine the role of marriage in creating them. Two of the most important combinations in Lodève at mid-century were Teisserenc, Calvet Frères, and Barbot et Fournier. The former associated a third family (first Visseq, an old name with aristocratic connections, then the Graniers of Montpellier), but they were minority, silent partners. The Calvet-Teisserenc tie, completed by the merger of 1846, was the backbone of the firm. Of all the Lodève fabricants, they would most successfully weather the disasters of the Third Republic, and their descendents would be the last cloth manufacturers in the city, owning Teisserenc-Harlachol, which finally folded in the 1950s.[25]

During the Empire, there were two branches of the Teisserencs involved in the cloth industry. Jean-Joseph and his son Jean-Fulcran (the enterprising Thérèse Hélène Faulquier-Teisserenc's husband) and Fulcran Justin, the son of Jean-Joseph's deceased brother. With Jean-Fulcran's death in 1813, the elder Teisserenc groomed his grandson Hector (born in 1801) to succeed him but worked with Thérèse-Hélène to find advantageous marriages for his granddaughters Zoé and Mélanie. His nephew, who married Marie Visseq, daughter of one of Lodève's oldest and most prestigious families, produced four children, Jules and Adolphe, the elder brothers, Emilie, born in 1811, and young Prosper, born in 1818. The five Calvet brothers, whom we have already met, were prime catches and the Teisserencs ended up with two of them. The key marriage was that of Adrien Calvet and Zoé Teisserenc in 1827. Not only did Zoé (then twenty-two) bring the Fr 50,000 bequeathed by her deceased father and the Fr 20,000 from her mother, but also a Fr 30,000 gift from her grandfather. Ten thousand more francs in Faulquier money (from her maternal grandmother) also came into the marriage. Emilie Teisserenc, from the collateral branch, married the youngest Calvet, Honoré, two years later, but investment levels were much lower. Adrien emerged as the leader of the Calvet brothers.

Both Jean Teisserenc and Louis Calvet (the founder of the Calvet firm) died in 1840. Hector Teisserenc, Zoé's brother, took over the direction of the family's affairs, but shared the inheritance (Fr 250,000 in taxable assets, plus much more) with his sisters and their husbands. The Teisserenc factory and its appurtenances occupied a prime location on the left bank of the Lergue in the Faubourg des Carmes. The total complex, including Jean's home, was valued by probate at Fr 95,500. He also left over Fr 100,000 in "money, commercial papers, and movable goods." The Calvets' plant was located up-river in a former paper-mill that the patriarch, Louis, and his sons had purchased in the later 1830s, due in part to the Teisserenc investment in Adrien. Its probated value in 1840 was Fr 56,000 and it would continue to appreciate, reaching a Fr 70,000 value in the 1850s. Jules and Adolphe Teisserenc's finishing mill was on the right bank of the Lergue just north of Lodève, and in the midst of the strike of 1834, they leased it to Adolphe's father-in-law, Jean-Pierre Fabreguettes. These brothers remained powerful figures in Lodève's business world, but increasingly as "capitalists" in the nineteenth-century sense and less as active cloth manufacturers.[26]

Besides their industrial property and town houses, both the Teisserenc and Calvet families, typical of all the wealthy fabricants, possessed land of various kinds in the vicinity. Again, the probate records of 1840 are indicative. Jean Teisserenc bequeathed a seventy-hectare, Fr 35,000 "domaine dit le Pradel" in the commune of Dio to the southwest. Located in high hill country, besides providing a country dwelling for the family, it was a working sheep farm. He also possessed a property closer to Lodève (tenement Laroque) which combined a fulling mill, a meadow irrigated by the mill canal, and, above, a vineyard, all valued at a rather modest Fr 3,500. Louis Calvet left considerably more nonindustrial real estate, including three houses besides his own in Lodève (all four worth Fr 46,000) and four vineyards with a total area of five hectares valued at Fr 7,500. Obviously, investments in agricultural property were not the top priority of either, but provided a supplemental source of income. Purchase took place on a piecemeal basis. For example, Louis Calvet bought three *ares* of vines in the nearby hamlet of Soulages for ninety francs in 1833 and paid Fr 900 for thirty ares in Grézac tenement, Lodève, the following year.[27]

On the other hand, their serious land transactions involved investment in plant. Although one finds instances of improvements and additions by means of ordinary transactions throughout the notarial records, for the successful fabricants of the period, the key to large-scale expansion was the distress of others: buying out people threatened with or actually undergoing bankruptcy. Jean Teisserenc, already solidly established in Carmes, did not hesitate to expand. In 1832, Pierre Archimbaud, a tanner facing bankruptcy, sold his extensive water works and buildings near the Teisserenc mill to Jean for the bargain price of Fr 9,500. The fabricant then paid off the old tanner's creditors in a meeting at Notary Clainchard's in April the following year. Archimbaud was one of a dying breed, but he and his family escaped without declaring bankruptcy. Archimbaud actually salvaged about Fr 1,400 out of the deal, although he lost some money in cases before the Tribunal de Commerce of Lodève, headed by Fulcran Faulquier, the brother of Jean Teisserenc's daughter-in-law. Despite the odds against Archimbaud, old Jean had come to his rescue for he *did* buy the property; after all, his wife's dowry was secure, and a son managed to fulfill his marriage contract. It was a meeting of two worlds, of the Lodève power elite and the second level of affairs that had no choice but to render it deference. But what counted for Lodève's economy was that the Teisserencs could now produce cloth in greater volume and more efficiently.

In the 1840s, La Papeterie, which was transformed into an excellent finishing mill, fell into the hands of Adrien Calvet and Hector Teisserenc in a similar fashion; two enterprising young men from Montpellier, Sarrus and Méric, who had modernized the facility, found themselves overextended and were forced into bankruptcy before completing improvements. Brothers-in-law Hector and Adrien picked up the property for a song at auction and finished the installation of machinery, some of which had already been paid for by Sarrus and Méric. The factory soon became an integral part of their operation.[28]

The power and the income of Lodève's fabricants was also enhanced by their regular activities as the town's bankers. The most common entry in the Actes de Notaires (examined in detail for the 1830s) are the various transactions (loans, mortgages, refinancings, receipts) relating to their lending activities. The Teisserencs were especially active in the area of home loans and agricultural credit, large and small. For example, in 1835 young Hector loaned Henry Latreille, a member of a former Lodève fabricant family, Fr 5000 for the purchase of more vine land in the prosperous wine village of Aspiran, south of Clermont, and to Louis Fruit, a farmer, Fr 2000 for improvements on his Lodève property. Both were at 5 percent for five years with their property as collateral. In a more important transaction, he loaned Jean Fulcran Portier, a manufacturer of eaux de vie and landholder, Fr 12,000 for seven years for the development of his affairs. Police Commissaire J.P. Fabreguettes, Portier's brother-in-law, was guarantor in the deal for which Portier's two houses and vine land were put up as collateral. Defaults on such loans, of course, provided another avenue to property accumulation among the fabricants.

The Teisserenc-Calvet relationship proved to be a happy one, at least for the Teisserenc name. After the firms merged in 1846, Adrien Calvet bought out his brothers' interest, so that he and Hector Teisserenc became the sole directors. Then in a marriage reinforcing the family ties, Prosper Teisserenc, Zoé's and Hector's young second cousin (the brother of Adolphe and Jules) was married to Christine Calvet, Adrien's and Zoé's only daughter, in 1849. After Adrien's death in 1854, their son, Louis Calvet, and Prosper Teisserenc emerged as the new generation of leadership. But Louis was cut down by an early death in 1859. He was not married and thus left the bulk of the family concerns to his sister Christine and her husband Prosper, thus paving the way to a reunification of the Teisserenc fortunes (Figure 3–1).

Louis Calvet's probate accounting allows a glimpse at a portion of the family wealth and the distribution of investments by one of Lodève's leading industrialists. His personal property was evaluated at Fr 3,000 and he had another Fr 3,000 in personal credits on small loans. His "interêts dans

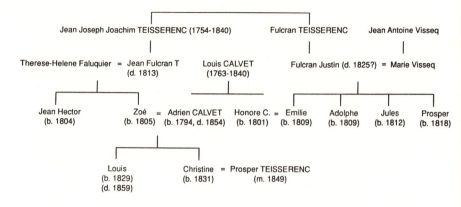

Figure 3–1 Genealogy

la Société de Commerce Louis Calvet, frères, Jean Hector Teisserenc et Cie" totalled Fr 23,421 and he possessed Fr 7,414 worth of 4½ percent government bonds (rentes) of which Fr 1,056 were in "départementales," funds earmarked for use in the Hérault. Local loyalty only went so far, however, for the Calvet heir also held fifteen shares of Paris-Lyon-Méditerranée railroad stock worth Fr 13,594. His real property tripled the value of his *mobilier* (159,000 vs 54,000) and consisted of half interest in La Papeterie and a smaller spinning and fulling mill adjacent to the main complex that the Calvets purchased in the late 1840s (Fr 45,000), a town house worth Fr 29,000, two hectares of vines in Lodève (Fr 16,000) and the "Domaine d'Arrièges," situated in the communes of Octon, Salasc, Mourèze, Liausson, and Clermont—arable fields, vines, meadows, woods, pastures, dwellings— of which the value for the portion in the jurisdiction of the Lodève bureau alone was Fr 68,200. This pattern of investment was quite typical of Lodève fabricants on the eve of the town's decline, combining industry, real estate, stocks and bonds, and personal loans.[29]

The full expansion of the Barbot and Fournier interests, our second success story, also depended heavily on marriage alliances. Unlike the Teisserencs and Calvets, neither family had a deep history in the Lodève cloth business. The Fourniers, originally from Gignac, were dyers who, like the Rouaud brothers, made the transition to full-scale cloth production during the Revolution. Gaspard Barbot came from a merchant family whose business is not clear. In any case, he was orphaned at an early age and, during the Revolution and especially the Empire, became the "artisan of his own fortune," gained, according to his obituary, because "it was to him that was reserved the honor to bring our industry out of its routine ways and most certainly he transformed it, adapting to nearly all its new needs." Although this obviously slights the less acceptable Causse family, it described a reality. Barbot, born in 1773, married Marie Chavière from Magalas, a woman of little fortune. His sister Marianne married Joseph Puech, a fabricant born in Ceyras, but a member of the Puech clan who had long done business in Lodève. Barbot's talents and this connection quickly pushed his fortunes forward. By 1814, he could be found among the larger manufacturers, though by no means in the top ranks. Barbot also busied himself with public affairs, especially as they related to business. A member of the Municipal Council of the city from 1805, he then was appointed a judge of the Tribunal de Commerce upon its transfer to Lodève from Clermont in 1809 and served on it throughout the hard times of the following years. In the late 1820s, he won election to the Conseil d'Arrondissement and, as we have noted, was one of the architects of the July Monarchy's easy acceptance in the region, becoming mayor in 1832.

These activities, however, were probably less important than the marriage he arranged for his younger daughter, Camille, to René Fournier, one of three brothers whose father's history was almost a carbon copy of Barbot's. René, the eldest, was born in 1791 and already directing the affairs of the Fournier company before the end of the Empire. The alliance between the two families was cemented by marriage in 1820. A dowry of Fr 50,000 no doubt was one of the key reasons for the rapid development of Barbot/Fournier interests thereafter.

In 1824, the combined equipment of "Fournier frères, Barbot et Cie et Eugène Fournier" put them among the top five societies presenting themselves for consideration for navy contracts.[30] Over the following decade, the associates maintained separate company designations (Fournier Frères and Barbot), but combined in their society for large contracts. In 1834, at the time of the strike, Fournier frères had 102 employees in weaving and spinning.[31] Barbot, who was mayor at the time, did not list his company's employees in the strike count, but an 1837 prefect's report indicates that "Barbot et Fournier" had as many as 200 employees. As of 1844, the two companies provided the following figures to the *Statistique générale* (annual estimates) (Table 3–3): Together, they did over a million francs in business annually and employed over 500 people. With the deaths of Barbot in 1845 and the eldest Fournier brother, Eugène, in 1846, ownership in both companies narrowed. René, through Camille Barbot's inheritance, became proprietor of Barbot et Fournier, while he and brother Benjamin became joint owners of Fournier frères. The latter would shrink considerably thereafter and finally be absorbed into B et F when Benjamin sold out to his brother in the early 1850s.

The years 1845–46 were also happy ones for both families because of the engagement and marriage of Emma Fournier, Camille Barbot's and

Table 3–3

	Product Value	Employees	Motors (Water)	Machines	Patente
Fournier frères	587,600	338	4	125	538
Barbot et Fournier	422,400	217	4	166	973

René Fournier's daughter, to Michel Chevalier, the well-known political economist. He was familiar with the region through his close friendships with Jules André, of Lodève, and with fellow Limogeaud Paulin Talabot, both Saint-Simonians. There were also several cosmopolitan Lodévois with whom he mixed in Parisian society. Among the latter was the mayor's other daughter, Philippine Barbot Galibert, who had long lived with her lawyer husband in the capital. They were childless and no doubt introduced their niece to Michel, one of the nation's most eligible bachelors. Chevalier, though obviously well connected, was not wealthy. The Lodève link, besides bringing him a woman who was, by all reports, lovely, gracious, and intelligent, opened all of southern high society to him and, as it turned out, immense riches in terms of both industrial and domestic property.[32]

The probate declarations of the Barbot and Fournier older generation reveal a series of inheritances that would have been in prospect for any suitor of Emma. First of all, her children would be the sole heirs to the Barbot fortunes because her aunt's marriage was barren. But even more remarkable was the absence of children in the Fournier clan. René had only Emma, and his brothers, Eugène, married to Elizabeth Vallat, and Benjamin, a bachelor, had no legitimate children at all. Thus, with René's death in 1858, Mme Michel Chevalier inherited the entire Barbot-Fourier fortune.

And a considerable fortune it was. Even before her marriage, her mother (and father) had come into Gaspard Barbot's vast holdings, evaluated at Fr 456,807 in mobile wealth (almost all related to the cloth business—raw materials and cloth, outstanding credits, and some sixty hand looms) and Fr 174,000 in real estate. Besides his town house and Fr 100,000 for his half of the company's property, he owned half, also shared with René and Camille, of the Domaine de Monplaisir, which was described as follows: "Master house, barn, out-buildings, stables, English garden, meadows, fields, luzerne field, vines, woods, thickets, vegetable garden, river bank, greenhouse." This formerly noble property, located south and west of the city and spilling over into the communes of Villecun and Les Plans, was the most beautiful and productive in the immediate area. It had been in the hands of Lodève's most prominent citizens for decades and seemed to follow left-to-moderate political power, moving from Bernard Luchaire to Eugène Brun under the Empire and then to Barbot in 1826.[33] Chevalier and his bride took over its full use—though five-sixteenths of the revenue still went to Emma's aunt in Paris—in 1858.

The deaths of the Fournier brothers heaped immense riches on Emma Chevalier. The main source was her father, but he was the beneficiary of his older brothers who died in 1846 and 1855. Moreover, Uncle Benjamin, in his will, left her Fr 30,000 in cash and set aside another Fr 15,000 in trust for her firstborn, Marie. The Fourniers—along with Chevalier himself—had also bought the former chateau and seigneurie de Cazilhac, a vast domain that comprised the entire commune of St. Martin d'Orb east of the river. At over one-and-one-half million francs, René Fournier's estate was the largest in the probate records of Lodève during the nineteenth century. The records make fascinating reading not only in helping to understand Michel Chevalier's willingness to get along with the powers that be—whatever they might be—but also as a picture of the investments of Lodève's top businessmen at mid-century (Table 3–4).

Despite the significant investments in prestige domestic property and its agricultural revenue, the overwhelming majority of Barbot and Fournier wealth was in their business operations. Even a slight majority of their fortune in landed property was connected with manufacturing. Their investments outside their cloth operations were minimal. Barbot, when he died, had no money in stocks and bonds at all. All of his mobile assets, in fact, except for his share of a big loan to Fabry of Millau (made just before his death) and a paltry two thousand francs in personal property, were in his business. René Fournier was somewhat more sophisticated, but even his stocks and bonds account for only 18 percent of his nonlanded wealth. And profit potential, not security of investment, was what attracted his money. He held almost nothing in government bonds, but invested heavily in major railroad companies, including the highly promoted Austrian system.[34] Even venture capital (the ill-fated Olonzac lignite mines) exceeded money in rentes. The Barbot-Fournier world was thus far removed from that of Guillaume Rouaud, who, despite the obvious intelligence of his late-life banking operations, essentially withdrew from active business affairs, and from that of the more prudent Teisserenc clan, who had substantial investment in state bonds. All in all, the economic outlook of Barbot and Fournier was that of their heir-by-marriage and even more of the latter's son-in-law, Paul Leroy-Beaulieu.[35]

If Gaspard Barbot and the Fournier brothers made their way largely by their own efforts and one intelligent partnership, the bulk of the manufacturing elites of Lodève became intertwined by marriage and mutual obligation to such an extent that the competitive edge of capitalism within the city must have become considerably dulled, at least in comparison with the days of the Revolution and early Empire. Indeed, a fascinating hypothesis can be offered: that the very pressure toward large-scale, high-technology production in the name of efficiency and competitiveness had the opposite effect, making the major families increasingly intertwine themselves for the sake of security; virtually all the survivors sought to create an oligopolistic front to deal with both their chief customer and with their workers. The "masters' coalition" of 1845 was the clearest public expression of it, but a look behind the official record of government reports reveals a world that Balzac knew only too well: a labyrinth of interest and influence among a fairly circumscribed elite, all cemented by marriage and debt.

Although a full-scale study of the multiplying bonds of fabricant interdependency is beyond the scope of this study, let us journey as far as possible into the byways of their society. This was an elite, it must be remembered, many of whose ancestors were making cloth two or three hundred years before. It was a way of life and a source of social and cultural identity. To lose this status was to die. Cauvy the bankrupt actually expired only eighteen

Table 3–4   The Déclaration de mutation par dèces
of René Fournier, 27 August 1858

Mobile Wealth		
1. Personal property	13,600	francs
2. Credits		
a. Public Treasury (woolens)	103,415	
b. Private		
1. Loan, Fabry (Millau)	69,695	
2. Loan, Martin (Lodève)	1,810	
3. Loan, C. Bertrand (Béziers)	28,572	
4. Divers	17,508	
5. Current Accounts	70,700	
6. Customs surety-bonds	8,000	
3. Stocks and Bonds		
a. Government bonds	1,375	
b. 50 shares, Orléans RR	68,750	
c. 50 shares, PLM RR	40,812	
d. 100 shares, Austrian RR	73,500	
e. 4 shares, Lodève stockyards	800	
f. 1 share, Cercle (Lodève)	500	
4. Part interest in Olonzac (Hlt)		
Mining Company	2,000	
5. Patent on machine: "finisher"	600	
6. Stock:		
a. Forge and Woodshop equipment	6,760	
b. Merchandise		
1. Primary materials	277,536	
2. Dyes	41,050	
3. In process	2,000	
7. Price of a house in Bédarieux sold to		
Bonniol, weaver, by the Maison Barbot		
et Fournier	2.700	
		1,041,531
Real Estate and Fixed capital		
1. 11/16 of Domaine de Monplasir	104,680	francs
2. Meadows and fields (Canalets)	16,000	
3. 11/16 of Manufacturing Establishment		
Barbot et Fournier (Monplasir)	257,500	
4. Dyeworks (Alban)	20,000	
5. Dyeworks (La Barrierè)	50,000	
6. 1/3 Domaine de Cazilhac	70,000	
7. 1/3 industrial building "de Cazilhac"		
with hydraulic machinery and woolens		
production facilities	20,000	
		538,180
		1,579,711

Mandataire: Michel Chevalier en qualité de maître des biens dotaux de Emma Fournier, sa femme.

months after his business went under. Normally, however, people in or as close to the charmed circle of power as he did not go bankrupt. As Jean-Clément Martin has shown in detail for Niort, the elites rarely ended up before the Tribunaux de Commerce in the humiliating strip-search that nineteenth-century bankruptcy (especially before the law of 1838) amounted to. But the smaller fry who succumbed served, on one hand, as scapegoats before a public eager to believe in shady business practice while the "grands" escaped, but, on the other, as reminders to even the most secure industrial or commercial notables that such a fate might also be theirs.[36] This, of course, did not prevent the more substantial from circling the dying beast and then descending to pick away at his bones. Indeed it seemed almost the normal procedure for expansion of plant in Lodève. But who better to feel the cold fear of *faillite* than a judge at the Tribunal, a *syndic* in a case, or a participant in an auction. There but for the grace of . . . if not God, what?

Family connections, of course. Clearly important in creating partnerships and broader alliances, family also meant inheritance, and, with some luck, an industrial *appanage* might fall into your hands if you were widely enough connected. One can imagine how aghast the other great families were to see Emma Fournier slip away.

The best way to enter this labyrinth of family ties in Lodève is to attend the "breaking of the seals" after the death of Guillaume Rouaud in 1834. When a succession was contested, the Justice of the Peace put the possessions of the deceased literally under lock and key and sealed them with wax. A full inventory was then made of his assets by a notaire in the presence of the interested parties. In the case of Guillaume Rouaud, the numbers of the latter were legion, the product of an ever-widening network, reinforced at strategic points, of intermarrying fabricant families. Rouaud, eighty-seven at his death, never married. He lived with his sister Elizabeth, a widow, until her death in 1812. Shortly thereafter, he hired a young woman named Elizabeth Jullien, the daughter of a lawyer from Nîmes, to run his household and serve as hostess for the numerous affairs required of him as a great manufacturer and, after 1815, as mayor of Lodève. The city's leading citizen, a solid monarchist and traditional Catholic, appears to have had some Chateaubriand in him as well: romance bloomed in his home at Prémellet and Elizabeth Jullien bore him a child, a girl they called Marie Elizabeth Alexandrine, in 1823. She was legitimized and was the joy of his life.[37] This, of course, is why so many people showed up for the inventory, for he had left half of his considerable estate to his "natural" daughter and a trust for her mother.

If Guillaume bore no children in wedlock, his siblings certainly did, and, in view of the family's wealth and prestige (and Guillaume's resolutely celibate status until the "*troisième age*"), their flock became much sought after.

The key figures representing themselves as legitimate heirs or their representatives were Pierre Ménard for his wife Eulalie; Jules Calvet, the oldest Calvet brother, for his mother Anne; and Frédéric Martel for his sister-in-law Victoire, all nieces of Guillaume Rouaud by virtue of his oldest sister's marriage to Jean Fabreguettes, who died before the Revolution. The latter's brother, Augustin, with whom he had been partners, was one of the larger producers during the Revolution and Empire. This was the conservative Fabreguettes clan whose fortunes were not as great (or the fall so hard) as the liberals Michel and Pierre. Jean's only son, Jean-Pierre, had married the sister of Tribunal President Fulcran Faulquier and of Thérèse Hélène Faulquier Teisserenc. Though an active entrepreneur, his fortune, it will be remembered, was modest enough to require his mother-in-law's help to become a censitaire. Nephew Pierre Rouaud, Guillaume's closest male relative and virtually the only friend the old man's daughter and her mother had, was not a fabricant, but listed only as a propriétaire.

If these were the principals, the cast of characters spread across the elites of Lodève. Predictably, those left out were the circle of the "other" Rouauds and, of course, the Causses.[38] Even the Fourniers had an interest in the affair, although they and Barbot still qualified as outsiders compared to the rest. The Teisserencs, though mildly interested through their Calvet marriages, sent no representatives to witness the inventory. The gathering nonetheless read like a who's who of the woolens industry and of city politics. At one point or another, the following men, besides those mentioned above, put in an appearance: Augustin Vallat, J.B. Salze, Auguste Soudan, Joseph Rouaud, Fulcran Crouzet, Pierre Gauffre, Claude-Marie de Laurès, and Augustin Luchaire. The first three, like Ménard, Calvet, and Martel, were leading fabricants. Crouzet was the son of a bankrupt manufacturer and had a claim on the estate through his mother. Gauffre and de Laurès, a legitimist former noble with an estate in Gignac, though not relatives, were beneficiaries in Rouaud's will for personal and political reasons. Finally, Luchaire, the nephew of Bernard Luchaire and a knitwear manufacturer, represented the other end of the political spectrum.

The range of kinship was extraordinary, as illustrated by Pierre Ménard's network of family connections. Besides being the nephew by marriage of Guillaume Rouaud, he was the father-in-law of Auguste Soudan and Frédéric Martel (and their business partner), as well as Isadore Coulet, a prominent Montpellier banker; the brother-in-law of Louis Calvet (and "Uncle Pierre" to all the Calvet sons), of Frédéric Martel's older brother Jean-Jacques (they were first cousins of the mayor of Bédarieux, Jacques Martel-Laprade), and, of course, of Jean-Pierre Fabreguettes. Through the latter, he was connected by marriage to the Faulquier clan. Thus, when Zoë Teisserenc married Adrien Calvet *and* when Adolphe Teisserenc married Alexandrine Fabreguettes, Uncle Pierre Ménard was there.

Moving in the other direction, Ménard was related by marriage to the Lagare family through brother Maurice's wife (kindly Fulcran Lagare was his cousin by marriage) and to the Salzes through his niece, Virginie (again, Uncle Pierre to J.B. Salze, one of the most enterprising fabricants of the age). An even more important event than the Rouaud succession also occurred in 1834. This was the marriage of Pierre's eldest granddaughter, Victoire Martel (possibly named for Victoire Fabreguettes Martel who was both her genetic great-aunt and her aunt by marriage), to his nephew, Maurice Ménard. Such close marriages were not at all unusual in this tightly knit elite and precisely parallels the Prosper Teisserenc/Christine Calvet nuptuals discussed earlier. Such first-cousin-once-removed or second-cousin marriages (frowned upon by the church, but long supported in Occitan culture: "A cosina segonda tot loli afonsa," went the proverb)[39] seemed to be the norm.

But in the case of Lodève, the intertwining of the elite families appears all the more prevalent as the pressures of nineteenth-century competitive life worsened. The eighteenth-century pattern of bringing in new blood from elsewhere virtually disappeared. The only relatively important outsider who entered the Lodève industry in the boom years of the 1830s was Parisian Jean Marréaud, who formed a partnership with Louis Rouquet, the former paper mill owner, to create a spinning establishment that grew to 275 employees by 1845, but went bankrupt in 1849. The only other non-Lodévois to enter the industry in the nineteenth century were the Mellets, who came from Orléans during the Imperial boom. Father Pierre was a machine builder and his sons were engineers. François Mellet married the daughter of Joseph Gauffre, a middle-income master dyer, and with his brother and her dowry financed a small (forty-three employees, four of them adult males, in 1845) spinning mill using Gauffre's hydraulic system and his services for dying in the wool, but it failed in the early 1850s. The only Lodève fabricants seeking outside ties, neither Rouquet nor Joseph Gauffre were really part of Lodève's upper crust in any case. The old elite closed in on itself.[40]

This process, obvious enough in the intertwining family connections created by marriage, comes into sharp focus in examining the institutions of sociability among the bourgeoisie of the city. In 1807 an organization simply called le Circle had been formed, but not until the law of 1825 on associations did its statutes become known. The purpose of the club was purely social. It occupied a large house in the center of the city. Among its facilities were a banquet hall, a sitting/reading room, a game room, and various smaller chambers for private gatherings. Smoking was permitted only in the "gardens." On one point the Circle's founders were adamant: "Because peace and union should reign in our society, . . . all political discussion is forbidden." The club was limited to fifty members. To join, one had to be proposed by a current member and agree to purchase an existing share (five hundred-to-seven hundred francs, according to death declarations) owned by a retiring or deceased member. In addition, there was an annual fee of forty francs. One could will one's share, but the final decision on entrance into the exclusive circle depended on the vote of the members. Ten "black balls" would exclude a candidate. Since le Circle was formed in the first place by fifty leading members of Lodève's leading families—by their own estimation—the likelihood of contamination by the less worthy was slight.

The list of its members thus provides a rather remarkable profile of a social elite. Although the majority were manufacturers, money was certainly not the only criterion for membership. A combination of family name, wealth, and public service, especially in the commercial court, the chamber of commerce, and the conseil des prudhommes, provided the foundation for acceptability.

What makes the Cercle list so certain is that a second club, called *l'Union*, was formed in the mid-1820s for the express purpose of providing a haven for those bourgeois of Lodève snubbed by the original fifty. It was considerably cheaper (a 15-franc fee and 100-franc shares) and had unlimited membership. Its first list totalled 100, all men. Unlike the Circle, which allowed important widows to succeed their husbands until their sons could take their place (not exactly a feminist position in any case), l'Union was exclusively male. To join, one was again presented by a current member, but the vote was by simple majority. Thus an ordinary weaver or agriculteur might have little chance, but moyen bourgeois and wealthy parvenus could now sip brandy and play billiards just like the notables if they won the hearts of only half their compeers.

The two lists (both from 1825) are striking in their consistency.[41] Woolens manufacturers dominated le Circle with thirty members, followed by nine propriétaires, five men of the law, three public officials, a retired military officer, and a lone commission agent. L'Union was much more diverse, including only thirteen fabricants along with eleven propriétaires, four lawyers, three doctors, and six other professionals. Seven commission agents headed a long list of moyen bourgeois. But the most prominent element consisted of woolens master artisans (ten) and other master artisans and shopkeepers (twenty-two). The Cercle list also included thirty-two "subscribers," those waiting in the wings for a place who also paid their forty-franc annual fee. Many were simply the sons of members, usually without professions or designated propriétaires (ten), but there were a number of recently appointed officials and older proprietors from lesser families included (fourteen); there were also seven lawyers and a surveyor who sought entrance into the charmed circle.

The social distance between the two organizations is obvious enough from the professions listed, but when one examines the names and public roles of their numbers, an entire history is recapitulated. To begin with those involved in the woolens industry, everybody who was anybody (except, for reasons unknown, for Guillaume Rouaud and Pierre Ménard) was a member of le Cercle or hoping to be. Besides Gaspard Barbot, Eugène Brun, Louis Calvet, Jean-Pierre Fabreguettes, three Fourniers, two Lagares, Lugagne-Jourdan, four Martins, the two Martels, a Pascal, Pierre Rouaud, J.B. Salze, two Teisserencs (Thérèse-Hélène Faulquier was one), three Vallats, François Vinas, and J.A Visseq, several of the older and less fortunate manufacturing families were represented. These included Michel Arsson, the last of that ancient clan and now municipal treasurer, Jean Beaupillier, a fabricant most of whose kinsmen had gone into the priesthood, Fulcran Captier, fabricant, Jean Christol, now just a propriétaire, Raymond Costaing, whose family hung on through its association with the more enterprising Jourdan family,[42] Pierre Gauffre, whose woes were only beginning in 1825, Auguste Labranche, whose firm, in the hands of his prudent son, Martin, would remain in the game until the crisis of 1847–49, Auguste Lacas, the last in his line to make cloth, and old Raymond Valz, whose firm would reel toward oblivion in the late 1820s. But the up-and-coming, if properly connected, also joined the club—or were candidates. Mme André (née Vallat), whose husband had built a solid firm through her dowry, his energy, and a solid partnership with Joseph Puech, would soon be joined in the Cercle by the latter and a new third partner, Salaville, fils. Her son Jules, the lawyer, Saint-Simonian, and mayor and deputy in 1848, would take her place upon her death in 1833. This family's politics were leagues to the left of many Cercle members, but pedigree was more important than politics. Other acceptable newcomers included Auguste Deidier, négociant, who married into the Faulquier family, and Joseph Vitalis, a man of credentials similar to those of Barbot who would build one of the great firms in the city.

But the "excluded" are just as interesting. The list of l'Union reads like a catalogue of the industry's pariahs and middling entrepreneurs. (There are a few exceptions: two young Ménards, both fabricants, apparently were more interested in games, companionship, and good food than they were in social status, had joined l'Union rather than waiting in line down the street, and Etienne Vitalis, Joseph's father and founder of their then small firm, probably did not have the will or interest to break into town's upper stratum.)[43] Naturally there were the Causse brothers and Jacques Augustin Fabreguettes, the son of Pierre, the Imperial Sous-préfet, and his cousin Bruno. To complete the Bonapartist triumvirate, Jean Léotard, the former Procureur, was a Union man. The Restoration Prefect Creuzé noted that although there were "suspect" elements in the group, he was assured most were good royalists.[44] The Montbrun Rouaud brothers, however, did not join, at least in 1825, even though they were not welcome in le Cercle. Perhaps they were simply busy (or too "economical"). But they were virtually the only industrialists from the wrong side of town who did not. Joseph Gauffre and Pierre Mellet were members, as were Fulcran Hugounenq, also a struggling young filateur who borrowed heavily from the Teisserencs in the early 1830s, and his future partner Etienne Cauvy, then listed as a commis-négociant.[45]

Another Union member, Etienne Brunel, owned Lodève's only machine-building firm, but his German origins and poor education forever banned him from polite society. Nevertheless, he shared with better-placed entrepreneurs like Barbot, Fournier, and Vitalis a spirit of initiative that can be seen most clearly in his will made in 1835. He made sure to indicate that he was not only leaving his existing facilities to his son (and partner) Fulcran, but also "the augmentations, improvements, and construction that I intend to make on the said property" as well as on the "canal or ditch of M. Despons."

All this might not seem so unusual except for the fact that at that point Brunel was almost seventy. Also on the Union list were four members of the Grimal family, including Fulcran, the proud dye-master who succumbed to the pressures of large-scale industrialization in 1830.[46]

A number of commission agents in the woolens industry joined l'Union, while only one, Jean Martin of the wealthy branch of that family, was listed with le Cercle. An idea of the level and type of income, other than their salaries, that a typical commis commanded can be gained by looking at the 1830 settlement of the estate of the agent Fulcran Caisso, whose nephew, Augustin, also commis-négociant, was a member of l'Union. He and his brothers, Fulcran, a dyer, and Hippolyte, also a commis, split a fortune of Fr 27,900. It consisted of a substantial house worth Fr 6600 in the place de l'Abbaye, an acceptable, if not fashionable address in St. Fulcran parish, a piece of vine, olive, and almond land (Fr 3,600), Fr 4,344 in cash, and Fr 5,256 in credits, mostly real estate loans. This type of investment was typical of people in Caisso's social category.[47]

If le Cercle was nearly exclusively the domain of the city's woolens elite, l'Union attracted a wide range of its middling sort. Excluded from le Cercle, physicians and all but the best-connected lawyers in town were most welcome. Other manufacturers, such as wax producers Fulcran Benoît and Berthomieu, fils, soapmaker Martin Lashûtes, paper manufacturer Louis Rouquet, and the distiller Jean Portier, had no place to go but l'Union. Rouquet was certainly an energetic businessman. After trying to make a go of his paper mill, he finally sold out to Martel in 1830, and then went on to form his partnership with Jean Marréaud and operate a relatively successful spinnery. On the surface, Jean Portier appeared to be a likely candidate for the other club. As one of Lodève's chief fabricants of eau de vie, he was in a growth industry, and his transactions in land and construction appeared frequently in the notarial minutes of the 1820s and 1830s. He had enough available capital in 1825, for instance, to loan eight thousand francs to Jean-Antoine Visseq, a cloth manufacturer who came from the city's highest social level, but who did not fare very well during the Restoration. What is more, Portier's business was also considered a worthy object of investment by the Hector Teisserenc, who poured twelve thousand francs into its expansion in 1833. But Portier did not then—and never would, despite his growing wealth—enter Lodève's notability.

What was the problem? Why was it that enterprising, hardworking men such as the Causses, the Montbrun Rouauds, Brunel, Rouquet, Mellet, or Portier continued to be shunned, while a Fournier or a Barbot or a Vitalis might "make it?" A definitive answer cannot be given, but several things seemed to come into play. Obviously family reputation was extremely important. It was a reputation established over time through networks of relationships that went well beyond the region. Long-term connection with respectable commerce was important. Lodève's merchant families had ties in the major cities where they operated—Montpellier, Lyon, and Paris—as well as those where members emigrated, such as the Teisserencs of Louviers and Châteauroux. International connections existed as well—at least three wives of prominent fabricants were born "en Amerique."[48] Aristocratic blood provided an advantage as well. One branch of the Visseqs had been ennobled in the eighteenth century (becoming Visseq de Ginestout) and the Teisserencs were doubly tied to nobility—to the Count of nearby Fozières and to a Scottish/Aveyronnais family called Boisse de Black of Pegairolles. Moreover, both Pézenas and Gignac, residences for dozens of lesser noble families of ancient pedigree, yielded husbands and wives to Lodève, and many of the names (Perier of Gignac, Lavaur of Pézenas) bespoke aristocratic roots.

Education certainly made a great difference. Little direct information is available on elite education, but large numbers from the old families were sent to Paris or Lyon (or at least Montpellier) for higher education and several young men had attended the *grandes écoles*. Where the contrast becomes most obvious is in the handwriting on various documents—the high elites, including women, invariably sign with a practiced and flowing signature, and what private correspondence is available shows the same for ordinary communication. On the other hand, a Brunel or Grimal reveals a rough, blocky signature from a hand not used to such niceties. Madame Marguerite Portier, the sister of Jacques Augustin Fabreguettes, suspected Bonapartist and the President of l'Union, could barely sign her name to the document recording her husband's loan from Hector Teisserenc. Still, by contrast, education alone was not enough. Antoine Plus, a commis and accountant trained in Lyon, was trustworthy and intelligent enough to serve as the representative of Prosper Teisserenc's mother (a Visseq now married to a Montpellier Parmentier, a family with noble pretensions) in business deals, a function almost always given to a family member. But he too was merely a Unionist for he hailed from a family of substantial, but unremarkable, landholders.[49]

There was also simply tradition, for Lodève's elite was never really open from below. Names such as Balp, Caisso, Hugounenq (or its phononyms), Mercadier, Jeanjean (or any name derived from a first name), Albagnac, or Caldier, though among the most common in the city, were never preceded by "Monsieur" and rarely by "le sieur" in notarial or official (other than Revolutionary, when it was "citoyen") documents from 1700 to 1848. They were of the people, and although some might rise (in the late twentieth century they run the city), they were never admitted to the notability. Wealthy outsiders, as indicated above, had no problem; an occasional Lodévois of modest but respectable birth such as Barbot or Fournier might be ushered in, and a rare notable de clocher, if he came from far enough away, such as Vitalis from St. Jean de Fos, also could find a place. In the nineteenth century, however, these streams of renewal dried up, with the unique exception of the Emma Fournier-Michel Chevalier marriage. The protective layers of intertwining family relationships therefore multiplied. Kinship, bilateral but with strategic agnatic reinforcement, became more central to their lives. The impulse was not, however, simply defensive in face of declining fortunes. Rather it arose, it would appear, from the need to bring large amounts of capital together to form companies that could compete successfully for the huge army contracts. In Lodève, there was no niche for the small, independent clothmaker. A few small spinners and Brunel's machine-works managed to get by, but most business was of necessity large scale.

Family also meant protection if things went wrong. We can now appreciate with greater subtlety the turnaround of Pierre Ménard's fortunes in the later 1820s and early 1830s. The right combination was the *family* combination—Ménard, Martel, Soudan, a relationship reinforced with the marriage of 1834. A close look at Guillaume Rouaud's loans show on one hand general confidence in the industry—his investments in the big banking concerns of Montpellier and Paris (Tessier and Sarrus, Rey, Mourgue, and Durand) and in major rising firms (Zoë Granier of Montpellier, Barbot et Fournier, Jourdan, and Vitalis), but he also had done a great deal for his closest relative actively involved in the industry, Jean-Pierre Fabreguettes, who from all indications (including his 1837 probate evaluation of Fr 150,000) was no more than a middling fabricant. The latter only did weaving until 1833 and decided to develop spinning and fulling capacity. As we have seen, he completed a deal for the lease of a substantial mill from the Teisserencs in early 1834. Much of the money for this expansion came from his uncle Guillaume, Fr 25,420, or 10 percent of the latter's outstanding credits at his death. Rouaud also had money out to J.B. Salze and to Augustin Vallat, though in lesser amounts. Moreover, he had been deeply involved in trying to save as much as possible in the collapse of his nephew-in-law's small firm, Crouzet et Cie, which finally declared bankruptcy in 1829. Crouzet had contracted with Raymond Valz and Pierre Gauffre for army business, and their rejection in 1828 caused the doom of the first and the beginning of unending trials for the other two. Rouaud was loyal to both, absorbing considerable losses in buying some of their property. He also included Gauffre in his will in the amount of Fr 4,000 and chose him, along with legitimist friend de Laurès, as his executor. Both Valz and Gauffre, though unable to end their decline, at least avoided the shame that befell their associate (Crouzet died in 1830) due to the good offices of Guillaume Rouaud.[50]

On the other hand, he was not the "family player" that the world of the Lodève fabricant elites had come to expect. There was, after all, the matter of that child and her grasping mother. It takes little imagination to feel the frigid atmosphere in which the inventory of Guillaume Rouaud's worldly goods took place. The entire elite of the city was stacked against them. Yet they prevailed, first finding crucial support from a "family council" (a legal entity) of the executors and Pierre Rouaud and then, when taken to court by the rest of the potential heirs, brilliantly organizing a defense stressing testamentary liberty, thus appealing to older Languedoc legal tradition, that convinced a Lodève judge of the validity of their claims.[51]

In this case an individual won out against the dense kinship network of the city, but in general, layers of family ties increasingly characterized the world of the fabricant elites. These defenses should not be viewed as "traditional" or "routinière." In fact, reliance on elaborate marriage strategies and kin support seems to have become more prevalent in the nineteenth century as the pressures created by industrial capitalism mounted. Such a perspective runs against received wisdom on the history of the interplay between family and capitalist development, but makes considerable sense, at least as a step toward the creation of large, solid firms. Other avenues, such as the creation of sociétés en commandite, were available and utilized, but the first response, rather logically, was the securing of one's interests by widening a mutually supportive network of family ties. This did not mean that young men were not encouraged to strike out on their own, but they generally did so well-fortified with dowry and wedding gifts. And even so, a tie with their father-in-law was often the initial means to successful business. The cases of Adrien Calvet, René Fournier, Auguste Soudan, and Frédéric Martel suffice to render an idea of the process. In stressing "individualism," as have writers on the enterprises of the Nord and Alsace, one should also remember the importance of familial seed money and, in fact, the continuing confidence created by having well-established elders in one's bilateral kin network.[52]

From another vantage point, these observations help us appreciate mechanisms operating beneath the outward divisions of Lodève's upper bourgeoisie that were creating greater solidarity among them. The old tripartite socio-political segmentation that we have identified before 1830 progressively dissolved. By the time of the strike of 1845, the entire fabricant elite was willing to bury its differences and formally (and illegally) unite to crush the workers' movement. How easy it must have been for them to communicate! A family dinner could bring most of the key manufacturers together. And those that were a bit outside the circle of direct kin connection, such as André or Brun, could be talked with over billiards at the club. Politics and economic values no doubt continued to matter some. Jules André might feel twinges of Saint-Simonian sympathy for the workers, but cousin (by marriage) Eugène Fournier or his partner's brother-in-law, Félix Fournier (married to a Salaville), could remind him of his duty. A few, like Fulcran Lagare, with his soft spot for his men, might resist the pressure, but it should not be forgotten that he retired right after the great strike. His successors, tied as they were by kinship to the ruling class, were less principled.

It was also the case that a good number of the potentially recalcitrant fabricants were gone. With Valz, Gauffre, Crouzet, Beaupillier, and Guillaume Rouaud out of the picture, the Catholic royalist contingent had been much reduced. Their traditional ways (Guillaume excepted) had ended their families' long involvement in cloth making. Moreover, the Revolutionary upstarts, with the exception of Etienne Brun-Fabreguettes, had disappeared. By 1845, the Causses were out of the business in Lodève, although a son continued to make cloth in Bédarieux. The Montbrun

Rouauds, Jean-Baptiste and Joseph, had both died (1838 and 1844). Neither had married, and so their holdings were left to their more respectable, and less political, nephews François Vinas and Gabriel Fraisse. The Rouauds had long had a partnership with the Fraisses and Vinases (through their sister and mother, both of whom seem to have also been active in the business). Joseph left a substantial estate, totalling over Fr 400,000. Predictably, Fr 160,000 was in merchandise, movable machinery, money, and other mobiliers (but not a single piece of commercial paper, possibly meaning he operated only in cash) and another Fr 170,000 in industrial property. Vinas, who had taken over effective control of the 350-worker company, happily went along with the other manufacturers. Possibly the flattery of his recent initiation into le Cercle had something to do with his decision.[53]

The common front presented by the *patronat* of Lodève was thus essentially complete by 1845. Preexisting threads of social antagonism rooted in the bitter guild fights of the eighteenth century, the rapid emergence of a premachine factory system, the Revolutionary promise followed by widespread failure among small fabricants, and the battles over machines and over efforts to cut costs and enforce labor discipline and the social distance manifested in demographic, geographical, religious, and cultural differences between the two classes now came to complete rupture. Even during the hardest moments of conflict, some members of the manufacturing elite had sought to smooth things over, to compromise, to retain a working relation with the workers. But it was an imperious and haughty bloc of clearly defined enemies that sealed the workers' defeat in the strike of 1845. With its termination, after a traditional ritual symbolizing a mythical corporate equality, Lodève workers then swung to a thoroughly modern mode of action: an attack on the building that represented the new reality of massive social and economic inequality, the Maison du Cercle.

4

Workers' Lives

The sullen hostility of that night—and the prison sentence its leaders received—made the confrontation of 1834, with its charivari overtones and worker self-confidence, seem far in the past. Worker solidarity was now matched by the unity of a small, relatively homogeneous, and determined class of employers, who had been reluctantly supported by the state in blocking and severely punishing working-class economic resistance, until then a seemingly fruitful path. Grievances would not evaporate, however. As we have seen, the struggle for power on the shop floor had increasingly given way to the fight to maintain a decent level of income upon which, it was thought, a decent life might be built. This was a process to be repeated again and again in the history of capitalism. But this was the first round, and the bargain came nowhere close to being struck.

The process of proletarianization had largely been completed for Lodève woolens workers by the early 1830s. A working class had emerged. But its consciousness, despite willing agreement among various crafts to work together, remained corporative in the sense that most continued to assume that action in the economic realm would suffice to give them new forms of independence in their life beyond the job. Although they obviously did not use the term, they were thus evolving toward a trade-union consciousness in the 1830s and early 1840s. As we have seen, they in fact pioneered strategies in the trade-union struggle and had a strike-rate probably higher than any group in the industrializing world. Yet in the 1840s it became clear that such activities were not achieving even the limited goal of accommodation within the emerging industrial capitalist system. Indeed, they believed that their total life situation had deteriorated and would soon let the world know about it. The historical record supports their belief.

On the face of it, the workers of Lodève, of all the southern wool towns with the possible exception of Bédarieux, would appear to have enjoyed sufficient income, especially in view of their frequent efforts to forestall its erosion, to achieve a margin of security. The various measures of degradation and social pathology with which Louis-René Villermé titillated his bourgeois readers did not seem to apply in Lodève. Crime rates were low. Illegitimacy was virtually unknown, sobriety the rule. Family life flourished. Workers seemed to have access to land and a fourth (by Villermé's estimate) lived outside of town and sometimes farmed their own plots. Lodève was a mecca for woolens workers from depressed textile towns and villages in the region. Although health conditions were not particularly good, Villermé was unable to report on those slimy handloom weavers' caves that he and Ange Guépin described with such freak-show enthusiasm elsewhere. In fact, in the 1840s Lodève only had a handful of *tisserands à domicile* left. Moreover, according to the *Echo de Lodève*, efforts by Mayor Barbot and the municipal council were creating public social services that, as it said in 1844, would "create long-term social stability." These included the generation of substantial private contributions to the chronically underfunded bureau de bienfaisance and the use of municipal revenue in the creation of four day-care centers (salles d'asile) for small children.[1]

But "long-term social stability" was not to be. What was wrong? Why did Lodève explode in 1848? Should we talk of "rising expectations" and all that the term implies about a supposedly unappreciative poor? Or should we look beneath the rhetoric—and the rhetoric of statistics. If the "morality" of Lodévois and Lodévoises was "high," so high in fact that even Villermé could not fault it, was it because conditions of existence were so wonderful? The fallacy, in fact, is to attribute such failings *simply* to poverty. We already know of the moral rectitude of Lodévois. The city certainly had its wastrels, its sexual deviants, and its "loose women."[2] But the celebrants of the Pénitents bleu et blancs, the *dévots* at the reliquary of St. Fulcran and various other saints on display, and, above all, the practitioners of quotidian acts of devotion (nobody married and few had productive intercourse during Lent and Advent)[3] created an atmosphere that made good behavior the rule. Those who shunned it—repeaters before the lowest courts—were extraordinary. To be poor did not necessarily mean to be unusually disorderly.

It might mean, however, stoning fabricants. Let us now inquire into the conditions of life and work of Lodève workers. How much could they buy? How often did they not work? How did their pay come to them when they did? Who in the family worked? What were their houses like? Did they own them? How much personal property did they have? How many had to seek relief? How was their health? How did their babies fare? What did they do about their old folks? Above all, how had all this changed since we last looked at their lives under the Empire? Such questions may seem a bit old-fashioned as preoccupations with power, selfhood, dignity, and other psychological factors have nudged "standard of living" issues aside. But, without having reference to the Maslow needs scale, who can deny that these questions are important? As will shortly be apparent, they were very important to Lodève workers, important enough to put their lives on the line to seek positive answers to them.

It is possible to be relatively precise with regard to the degree of poverty of Lodève's woolens workers in the 1840s thanks to the twin documentation provided by the probate declarations and the tax rolls. Moreover, the use of the first in comparison with similar records of thirty years before can provide a rare look at one of the thorniest problems in the historiography of the early industrial period: did workers become poorer as the factory system progressed?[4]

Other indicators seem to point to a negative answer. As usual, wage and cost of living data are extremely spotty and difficult to compare from one point to another. The key problem with regard to income, of course, is that most workers were paid by the piece or task, while official estimates attempt to gauge daily rates. We have seen that the central issue for weavers, the most contentious of the woolens workers, revolved around attempts by fabricants to increase the size or quality of the cloth without changing the rates. Their successful defense of their scales then became a factor in the bosses' determination to introduce the power loom. We know, however, that there was virtually no change in weaver's rates (basically a franc per 100 warp threads for the standard démi-pièce) during the first half of the nineteenth century, save for a cut during the late Restoration that was restored with the strike of 1830. Rates for shearmen clearly changed, and from all indications, the operators of the power-driven devices made less than their handicraft predecessors despite efforts to shore them up. Spinners were paid a bulk rate for the amount of thread produced and compensated their assistants from it at day-rates established by the owners. If anything, their pay improved with the quality of the machinery they operated. Estimated day-rates of women and children remained stable, somewhat less than one franc and around sixty centimes respectively. Compared to elsewhere in Languedoc, Lodeve's wages were higher than anywhere except Villeneuvette, which had a special relationship with the government and a visionary employer in Paul Maistre. Villermé's figures for 1836 contrast Lodève, Bédarieux, and Carcassonne. All were caught at a quite prosperous time. The main body of adult male woolens workers in Lodève made between 2 and 3 francs per day, with dyers (who contracted on a monthly basis) at around 1.75. In Bédarieux, home-working weavers, he reported, averaged less than 2 francs as did fine spinners (jenny operators), while mule-jenny men made over 2.50. "Others," no doubt excepting the hand finishers, made less (1.50–1.65). Female averages were proportionately lower. (In Lodève, he found that a good tisserande or fileuse en fin could clear up to 1.50). All categories in Carcassonne fell a notch further: mule-jenny men at 2.25; jenny operators at 1.50; and weavers—still à domicile and using the old hand-shuttle loom—making 20 to 25 francs for eleven days work in the production of a piece, an operation requiring the constant participation of a helper and the half-time contribution of a reeler.[5] From a national vantage point, Languedoc wages were lower than average, but Lodève's were at least generally on a par with other urban woolens centers.[6]

Food costs in Lodève also hovered around or a bit below national averages. The 1863 *Statistique générale* study of "prices at various times" showed Lodève in 1844 at thirty-two centimes per kilogram for bread and ninety for beef of "second quality." (Little pork, the other food surveyed, was eaten there.) Wine was a bargain (as everywhere in the Midi), but its consumption low. Only in housing, at an estimated annual rent of fifty francs, did Lodève fall well below average. Compared to the rest of the Hérault, reported that food prices in Lodève slightly exceeded the average, no doubt due to transport costs. Clothing was rough, but most Lodévois owned a Sunday suit; all had at least sabots, and many sported umbrellas when it rained. Villermé put rent at a higher level than the later inquiry (as low as 50 per year but stretching up to 100 francs). Actual home ownership was another matter, as we shall see.

From all reports, it cannot be said that conditions in Lodève's factories were particularly oppressive or unhealthy. Villermé was positively rapturous. Unlike almost anywhere else in France, spinning factories kept windows open in the summertime without any increased incidence of thread-breaking. This was instituted during the cholera epidemic of 1832 and 1833. Weavers might work in cramped positions, but with 2 to 2½ hours of break time in a 12-hour day and housed in "spacious and well-ventilated" workshops, their factory work lives were better than those of most of their home-working brethren in France.

Such outward indications of relative ease, however, seem contradicted by information drawn from the probate records and the tax rolls. A careful study of all succession declarations for male deaths from 1839 to 1842 reveals that of those recorded at all,[7] (297 individuals) nearly half were listed as having "nothing" to declare and a third of these were "indigent," their heirs having produced a certificate in proof. If we make the same assumption as did Daumard for Paris, that those unrecorded are without assets of any sort, the figure rises to 52 percent but comes nowhere close to her figure of 73 percent for the capital in 1847. For the population at large then, access to property, as one might expect in a small town with large numbers of people working in agriculture, was better than in Paris.

But the percentages transform dramatically when we factor in occupation. Table 4–1, based only on recorded declarations, reveals a remarkably unequal hierarchy of wealth. Two-thirds of all deceased woolen workers thus possessed less than 100 francs in movable assets and no real estate. Twenty-three died officially "indigent" and, therefore, as recipients of public assistance. Looked at another way, woolens workers made up 41 percent of the total number of indigents in town, even though they comprised less than a third of the active male work force.

What wealth woolens workers did possess was insignificant. Only four

Table 4–1 Declarations of Assets at Death: Male Lodévois, 1839–1842

	"Rien"	*Movables Only*	*Real Estate*	*2000 F+*
Total (279)*	48% (135)	9% (25)	43% (119)	21% (59)
Bourgeois (41)†	17% (7)	15% (6)	68% (28)	61% (25)
Trades (84)‡	55% (46)	14% (11)	31% (27)	24% (20)
Agriculture (63)	38% (23)	2% (1)	63% (39)	16% (10)
Woolens (76)	68% (52)	5% (4)	26% (20)	5% (4)
No occ. (15)	47% (7)	20% (3)	33% (5)	0

*Eighteen entries provided occupation and no other information.
†Includes négociants, fabricants, propriétaires, religious, military, and civil officials, and liberal professionals.
‡Includes all non-woolens occupations—artisanal, clerical, retail sales and other service activities—except agricultural work and bourgeois categories.

out of seventy-six died with more than Fr 2,000 in capital, for Daumard, the line separating "le peuple" from the lowest echelons of the petite bourgeoisie.[8] Even so, that represented only Fr 100 in annual revenue, a sixth of what was needed to live. What did they own? The heirs of five declared mobile wealth only. Fulcan Crébassa, a pareur, had Fr 700 in cash, but the other four had much less, mainly in furniture and clothing. The owners of real property numbered twenty-one and deserve some detailed attention. Only six owned a house by themselves and another ten, anywhere from a sixth to a half of a house. Nine owned a piece of vine land, thus confirming Villermé's observation that woolens workers would try to get some land if they could. But obviously not many could.

Let us put their real property ownership in perspective. Table 4–2 is drawn directly from the probate records. It represents the twenty-four men (31 percent) who did own enough property to be taxed. What do "furniture" and "effects" actually mean? Pierre Arbouy, a fifty-two-year-old married weaver, died on 19 July 1840 and his estate was probated on 7 January 1841. His Fr 230 worth of movables were inventoried as follows: two beds and their bedding, Fr 50, bread cupboard, 15; kitchen utensils, 20; wine-making utensils, 40; one table, 5; chairs and armoire, 35; table and bed linens, 45; personal belongings, 20. These are the possessions—along with his thirty-two ares vineyard, no doubt his pride and joy—of the eleventh wealthiest woolens worker to die in the years 1839–1842. He figures toward the middle of those possessing enough to declare anything, but compared to the mass, was quite well off. Obviously, his furnishings are the bare minimum for a family, with no frills at all. His wine-making equipment, for that value, would have consisted of no more than a tub, a *cuve*, and an array of bottles and pitchers. He had no cave, in contrast to many of Lodève's better-off people, thus indicating that he sold the bulk of his wine, probably to a regular dealer, for immediate processing into eau de vie.

Table 4–2 Assets of Woolens Workers at Death, 1839–42

Occupation	Marital Status	Age	Mobile Wealth	Real Estate		Total
Tisserand	M	58	—	600	(partie maison)	600
Tisserand	M	52	230	800	(vigne)	1080
Ouvrier en laine	M	76	100 (meubles)	1000	(2e et 3e étage d'une maison)	1100
Ouvrier en laine	M	46	800 (meubles et créances)	400	(vigne)	1200
Tisserand	V	89	—	400	(3e étage d'une maison)	400
Fileur	M	60	20 (vestiaire)	400	(maison)	420
Tisserand	M	70	500	5200	(partie maison-3800) (vigne-800)	5700
Pareur	M	51	700 (argent)	—		
Pareur	M	39	—	500	(vigne, 40 ares)	500
Tisserand	M	78	60 (lit garni, effets)	300	(une chambre)	360
Ouvrier en laine	C	34	—	160	(un tiers d'une maison)	160
Tisserand	V	83	—	1200	(maison)	1200
Ouvrier en laine	M	31	—	500	(2 petites chambres)	500
Ouvrier en laine	M	59	20 (vestiaire)	200	(vigne et herme)	220
Pareur	M	61	200	6200	(maison, 3 chambres, vigne)	6400
Embaleur	M	63	200	2700	(maison, 3 vignes)	2700
Tisserand	M	78	200 (meubles)	—		200
Ouvrier en laine	V	75	100 (meubles)	—		100
Tisserand	M	74	—	1000	(petite maison)	1000
Pareur	M	59	78.50	800	(maison)	878.50
Pareur	M	51	—	600	(2 chambres)	600
Tisserand	V	84	—	1200	(partie maison-800) (vigne-400)	1200
Ouvrier en laine	M	69	276	1700	(partie maison-700) (vigne, 60 ares-1000)	1976
Tisserand	M	49	3600 (espèce)	—		3600
			(average 1308)			32,695

Gabriel Fulcran, a sixty-one-year-old married shearman, was the richest woolens worker in our sample at Fr 6,200. But his movable possessions were virtually the same as those of Arbouy. The basis of his wealth was his own rather substantial home (Fr 3,000), three rooms that he rented out for Fr 20 each,[9] and a large (more than two acres) vineyard.[10] Even the richest woolens workers, therefore, lived modestly and used their money to buy equally modest amounts of real property.

We already have an idea of the crushing difference between the wealth of the fabricants and woolens workers. The sample simply confirms it. The eight men listed as fabricants or négociants who died in 1839–42 had an average total assets of Fr 182,000 and, if one excludes two who had minimal movables only, the figure is an astronomical Fr 242,000. Among the manufacturers who died in this era were Jean Teisserenc, Louis Calvet, and Jacques Soudan, all of whom we have met. Although the "propriétaire" category varies, eleven out of fifteen exceeded the Fr 2,000 barrier and five topped Fr 100,000, Daumard's next plateau in the measurement of wealth. And on it goes. The only socio-occupational group that came remotely close to the woolens workers' record of indigence and low levels of property acquisition were wage workers in the artisan and service industries. The highest levels of "nothing to declare" were found among shoemakers, five of seven; tailors, five of eight; ironworkers (blacksmiths, locksmiths, and machinists), six of nine; and leatherworkers, five of five. The last reflects the collapse of this industry in the Hérault and doubtless more than one was a "master." The tailor and shoemaker totals mirror master-man ratios in their traditionally downtrodden trades. (Virtually all artisans in these crafts who died younger than forty were without worldly goods.) The weakness of the ironworkers (especially two *mécaniciens*) is surprising, but perhaps understandable since most of them, like the woolens workers, worked for the town's major industrialists. Building trades artisans, on the other hand, were rather well off, as only about a third of them declared nothing, and several master joiners, carpenters and masons were rather wealthy. Food industry artisans and service people were the best off of all. Every butcher (four) left some property, thus reflecting a universal avariciousness that got results,[11] and even a twenty-nine year-old bequeathed Fr 633 worth of goods and real estate. In general, seventeen out of seventy-two people strictly in the retail merchant or artisan category (or 24 percent) exceeded the Fr 2,000 line. Agriculturalists (cultivateur, agriculteur, jardinier, cerclier*) split, like the artisans, but with more property owners (64 percent) than not. Few of them had much land, however, as their low land values reveal. A handful owned only a house and were therefore simply better-off agricultural laborers. Of the forty who owned property, only ten exceeded a worth of Fr 2000, and their worth averaged Fr 920.

---

*This profession combines artisanal skills with cultivation of green-oak thickets. In Lodève, they were always real property owners.

In all regards, woolens workers appear at the bottom of the town's economic heap, sharing a place with certain wage-workers in artisan industry and agriculture. A look at the Lodève's deceased indigents and at the tax structure rounds out the picture. Twenty-three out of the town's indigents at death in 1839–42 (44 percent) were woolens workers, although as a group woolens workers comprised only 27 percent of the total sample of 279 men. Thirty-seven percent of the indigents were artisans, six percent failed commerçants, and the rest agricultural workers. There were no professionals or businessmen in the group. Age breakdown indicates the expected predominance of those over sixty-five, but the thirty-five-to-sixty-five-year-old group had an indigence ratio twice as high as the death rate for that age range generally.[12]

A reading of the tax rolls of 13 September 1846 reveals a similar picture of the structure of wealth and poverty in Lodève. If 68 percent of all woolens workers died in the early 1840s with no resources worth listing for inheritance purposes, similar numbers paid no taxes. Only sixty weavers, for example, appear on the tax rolls, although 160 are enumerated in the census of 1851 (that of 1846 is lost). Thus, the averages that follow are those of heads of household who actually paid taxes, leaving out the poorest altogether. Still, the differences are enormous. Sixty-nine négociants/fabricants paid an average of Fr 227, while weavers averaged 8; spinners and croppers, 13; agricultural workers, 12; tailors and shoemakers (masters and men are not differentiated), 12; joiners and masons, 13; foremen, 17; butchers and bakers, 23; "white collar" (employés), 25; commission agents, 35; liberal professionals, 107; and propriétaires, 133. A further measure of the material abyss between woolens workers and their employers is that the total tax paid by the 69 owners was over thirty times as great as that paid by the 107 weaver, spinner, and cropper heads of household wealthy enough to be taxed at all (Fr 15,631 to 509). But the same may also be said for any of the artisanal populations of Lodève. There were, quite simply, two worlds of wealth in the city, with a small and fragile layer in between.[13]

Villermé attributed woolens workers' paltry assets to a lack of "economy," failure to save. He noted that the institution of a savings bank (a *caisse d'épargne*) in the city in 1837 only attracted ten worker-depositers. This same situation continued in the 1840s and beyond. The implication of his argument is that they frittered their decent incomes away, and he gives the example of their Sunday feasts—male only, at the house of a friend where doubtless, in typical Mediterranean style, the women cooked and served—on which one could easily spend "a day's pay or more."[14] This is the *only* example he gives, however, and measured against those things on which we know they did *not* spend money, it pales in significance. Prostitution was virtually unknown (Villermé and the sous-préfets' reports agree) and gambling was among official concerns, but little actually occurred. Workers' taste for *luxe* was limited to a Sunday suit or dress, but Villermé admitted that "all the same, it is impossible to mistake them for their masters." They went to cabarets or cafes, but wine was cheap and they drank little. Talk (or plotting, depending on one's perspective), as we already know, was much more important to them. The few cases of carousing that make the lower court (*premier instance*) docket involved late-night noisemakers, youth on the prowl, and often the same persons were netted. The notorious Flour Py was brought to trial no less than five times from 1830 to 1835 for his raucous behavior. He was turned in by people in the working-class districts of Carmes or Montbrun who needed their sleep.[15] The fact is that Villermé simply contradicts himself. It is difficult to be sober, moral, laborious, and all the rest, while simultaneously squandering money on bad habits. The essential point is that workers did not have much money to squander.

Did they have less than before? This is extremely difficult to answer, but we can look at the amount of property that woolens workers died with during the Empire as opposed to the early 1840s, and we have census figures on home ownership from 1798. The changing composition of the work force certainly meant declining incomes for some. The pareur was dethroned, and machine work became the rule in the finishing processes. Female and child labor became increasingly prevalent in the lesser crafts. Proletarianization may involve severe psychological consequences, but these are accompanied by physical deprivation as well. And they all came to a head in the early 1840s. Let us look at this more closely.

A nine-year run (1806–1814 inclusive) from the period of the Empire in the succession registers contained information on 70 male woolens workers. Death certificates for the same period listed the occupations of 120 adult male woolen workers. The discrepancy is largely explained by the more relaxed recording procedures of the earlier period: people who obviously had no taxable property were simply left off the register. In addition, twelve men were subjects of "negative declaration," meaning that the inheritance tax collector had at least examined these effects and found them not worth declaring or that the workers were in debt. Finally, the tax floor on movables was lower in the earlier period, often going well below the 100-franc minimum of the July Monarchy. Those declared with "nothing" comprised 52 percent of the total during the Empire, increasing to 62 percent at the later date, while 18 percent declared movables of some value, which dropped to 5 percent in the early forties. Real estate owners comprised 31 percent of the earlier sample and 26 percent of the later. Those with assets exceeding 2000 F were at 9 percent before and 5 percent during the July Monarchy. The differences are not remarkable, but are nevertheless significant. They become more so with further refinement. Worker access to land seems to have declined significantly. During the Empire, of the thirty-seven with real property, twenty-seven (73 percent) owned land. As we saw above in Table 4–2, in 1839–42 only nine of twenty, or 45 percent did so. Compared to the total deaths in each era, the numbers of Imperial-period landowners are even more impressive, 23 percent vs. 12 percent. Land values in the city seem to have changed little in the ensuing forty years.[16] This simply means that fewer woolens workers could buy some land, despite Villermé's assertion that it continued to be a goal for many of them.[17]

With regard to home ownership, a major change occurred. In the earlier period, among the twenty-six men possessing living quarters (22 percent of all deceased woolens workers), sixteen owned entire houses. Of the ten who owned apartments or rooms in a house, eight also owned some land, suggesting that they had chosen to cut back on housing in preference to land. During the July Monarchy, sixteen men out of the seventy-six in the declarations owned living quarters, or 21 percent. It should be recalled, however, that seventy-six is well below the actual number of woolens workers who died. Four in the declaration records simply had no information recorded by their names, and if we assume the woolens workers made up 30 percent of the deaths in 1839–42 that were never entered in the succession registers (forty-one men over fifteen),[18] we should add another twelve, producing an N of ninety-two, and a figure of 17 percent for dwelling owners. (Up to this point, there has been no need to make these extrapolations, since the figures were strongly supportive of our impoverishment thesis without it.) But, in fact, only five owned an entire house, just about reversing the situation of thirty years before. Now this undoubtedly reflects some tightening of the housing market as the city grew (but again, there was little change in values), although new housing in Carmes and Montifort was opening up. Also, the general household to house ratios for the city went up, from about 2.4 to 1 to 3.5 to 1 from 1798 to 1851.

We have no global measure of home or apartment ownership for the July Monarchy, but the census of the Year VI showed that 180 male woolens workers owned a place to live, while 33 women with woolens occupations (mostly widows) did so. This meant that 20 percent of the houses, apartments, and chambres of the city were owned by woolens workers, for there were somewhat over 2,030 households in the city (in 855 occupied dwellings). Among woolens workers who were *chefs de menage*, a quite substantial 31 percent were owners. If women are excluded, the figure rises to fully one-third. This of course does not reflect the entire woolens worker population, since the census only recorded with care the occupations of chefs de menage, thereby overlooking many sons and brothers (and all daughters and wives). Adjustments made for this fact might take us closer to the property ownership percentages derived from the successions. The census does help to corroborate the Imperial succession percentages, though, thus supporting our assertion of impoverishment.

The final comparative figures, however, are the most important: how much did woolens workers whose successions were taxed under the Empire leave behind when compared to our list in Table 4–2? Because Imperial inheritance laws allowed taxation on virtually anything a person owned, one finds "inheritances" of twenty or fifty or eighty francs inmovables ("*son vestiaire*," "*les outils de son métier*," "*ses hardes*," and so forth). If the person had no real property, any evaluation of less than one hundred francs in the later period was not taxed. I have therefore made the two lists comparable by eliminating the five men whose mobile wealth totaled less than one hundred francs.[19] Simple averages of the wealth of woolens workers from one date to the next are: Fr 1,607 (53 men) and Fr 1,308 (24 men).

Those who left only movable property worth one hundred francs or more are listed in Table 4–3. The large cache of money in the possession of the weaver skews the later figures unnaturally, but the most interesting thing is the small number. Most woolens workers simply had very little of value. The minuscule mobilier of many of them who were taxed on real estate attests to it (see Table 4–2). Those taxed during the Empire had a variety of mobile wealth, including their own equipment and credits. It is likely that both the pareur (age fifty-one) and the weaver (forty-nine) who died with significant amounts of money in the early 1840s were on the verge of buying property.

But there, too, the men of the 1840s could not expect the levels of wealth of their fathers. If we chart the real property owners alone, the gap becomes quite staggering. Obviously some of them had significant mobile wealth in both periods and one complemented the other. Our totals are therefore for their general fortunes in each period. The average for the Empire is Fr 2,147, meaning that the nine individuals above the Fr 2,000 barrier offset the other twenty-seven below. For the July Monarchy group the average is 1,351. If one eliminates the top two among the thirty-six Empire people (a dyer at Fr 14,984, a packer at 13,000) and the highest of the twenty-one from the July Monarchy (a pareur at 6,400), the difference remains impressive, 1,513 to 1,098. Although the buying power of the franc

Table 4–3

1806–1814 (Mean = 341)		1839–1842 (Mean = 1150)	
Woolens worker (reserves)	120	Pareur (money)	700
Woolens worker	100	Weaver (furniture)	200
Pareur	100	Woolens worker (furniture)	100
Weaver (his loomand effects)	200	Weaver (money)	3600
Weaver	100		
Rough carder (life annuity)	800		
Pareur (clothing)	100		
Weaver (clothing)	100		
Weaver (movables and credits)	2060		
Carder (credits and cash)	700		
Winder	200		
Teaseler (clothing and tools)	200		
Carder ("a sum")	400		
Dyer (clothing)	100		
Rough carder (cash)	216		
Weaver	100		
Weaver (clothing)	200		

may have improved somewhat over the ensuing years, that was less true for basic necessities than for products out of reach for most workers. Land and housing values in the Lodève area remained stationary, with demographic pressure and deflation offsetting each other.

The decline was not spectacular. Lodève workers were not ground into hopeless poverty as industrialization proceeded. But things *were* worse, despite the rosy pictures painted by some. What were the causes of declining spendable income? Here, one must report back to the exigencies of developing industrial capitalism. The number of shearmen in the list of those dying with "nothing" in 1839–42 is remarkable. But few spinners are to be found. Spinning, totally mechanized, was one of the steadiest occupations in Lodève. Unemployment was minimal, except for times of low water levels in the summer, because of the city's role as thread supplier to fabriques elsewhere. On the other hand, weavers and finishers in army-cloth Lodève as in commercial-cloth Bédarieux, suffered long periods of layoff, and shearmen, at any rate, were being made redundant by machinery. Weavers had their problems with technology as well, given the painful transition to the fly-shuttle loom, but the key issue for them was competition of women and of migrant weavers from distraught woolens districts elsewhere in Languedoc. Fully half the weavers of Lodève recorded in the census of 1851 were women. This figure increased dramatically with the growth of power-weaving to 64 percent in 1872. The insecurity of employment for cloth workers was also visible in the quarterly prefectoral reports, which record cyclical and seasonal swings in the industry.[20] The mid-1840s saw severe problems not only in Lodève but throughout the cloth region. The public assistance offices were hard-pressed to keep up with demand. Lodève faced a crisis in late winter 1844 when the *Echo* reported the strain on the local bureau "where so many families go to get the bread that they look for in vain elsewhere . . . [I]t is sad to say that nearly 1500 persons have received aid . . . in the past month and one half."[21] Sheer misery was thus a periodic experience for many workers and had become a public issue by the mid-1840s.

Housing, even for better-off owners, was paltry. A random survey of notarial acts involving various transactions reveals that a woolens-worker family dwelling rarely consisted of more than three rooms, often shared with family members or boarders outside the nuclear unit. For example, a marriage contract of 1826 showed Louis Guivaudon, twenty, moving in with his wife's family (all *ouvriers en laine*) in return for her dowry of a bedroom, an attic above it for storage, and access to the kitchen (the total evaluated at ten francs per annum in equivalent potential revenue); this was *half* their dwelling in the rue Basse de la Triperie in St. Pierre parish. In another contract of 1830, Fulcran Sauvy, an old weaver born in St. Affrique, turned his worldly goods (an old bed and bedding, a cabinet and two chairs, a small copper stew pot and his clothes chest) over to his son-in-law and daughter in order to occupy part of one of their three rooms rent-free (a privilege evaluated at twenty-five francs per year) for the rest of his life, but with the proviso that he pay for his own food.[22]

Two sales made in 1816 symbolize, perhaps, the kinds of property transactions that weavers' children would remember at a later date. The first was the sale of their "part of a house," (three rooms and an attic) in the upper city on the "rue d'Alban across from the hospital" by Pierre Jeanjean, a weaver, and his two brothers-in-law, also weavers, who held their shares in the form of their wives' dowries, to an unspecified "trader" (trafiquant) for Fr 800. Where they would now live was unclear, but the Jeanjean family had been in that house at least since 1798, for their father owned half of it in that census year. One can imagine their emotions and the bitter anger they passed on to their own children. The second example was a purchase of sixty in vine and chestnut by another weaver, François Baumes—a proud moment, no doubt. But the cost was only Fr 200, an immense amount for him, perhaps, but a remarkably low price for the surface involved; we read on to discover that the land was in a "very bad state," with ancient and ill-kept vines and collapsed terracing.[23]

To discuss housing is to broach an issue that may well have been as important as threatened incomes and proletarianization as a cause of growing working-class discontent in Lodève. This was the abominable public health situation in the town. In a fascinating book that may well have been an answer to Villermé's rather rosy picture, Dr. Xavier Rame, a *chirugien* (surgeon) connected with the Hospice de Lodève and a correspondent of the Society of Practical Medicine of Montpellier, gave a full accounting of the problem. The work, published in 1841, was dedicated to Mayor Barbot. Rame, a strong proponent of industrialization and technical progress, characterized his town, "relative to its size," as "one of the most active manufacturing and commercial cities in France." Unlike an Ange Guépin or François-Vincent Raspail, his sympathies were frankly Orleanist, but he feared that without reforms, the town was doomed, either because of death due to disease or working-class revolt.

Lodève's setting, lovely as it might have been, was a natural amphitheatre, meaning that air movement, especially in the warmer months when prevailing southerly and westerly winds were blocked by the steep rise of the Escandorgue and Montbrun, was reduced. Still, the rich verdure of the immediate environment, up and down the Lergue and Solandres, freshened the air and created a beauty that "elevated the soul." But the town itself quickly sapped the feeling. "It diminishes a little when one reaches the outer boulevards; it ends and changes to a contrary sentiment when one penetrates the town's interior. How can one not despair at the sight of these somber, narrow, torturous, humid streets that make up the major part of this city?" This was the root of the "ill health of its inhabitants." The faubourg Montbrun was even worse. No town the size of Lodève had so many *impasses* (blind alleys); they were "veritable cesspools." This meant little air circulation and poor light.

There were no public sewers (though the wealthy in the newer quartiers often built private systems), so excrement was dumped in the streets or in courtyards where it would be mixed with straw or leaves for fertilizer. Only recently had Barbot instituted a system of water flow to flush out some of the streets. Presumably before, sewage was simply left for the rains to wash down to the rivers. One can imagine the infectious stench, especially during the long dry spells of the summer. Rame also noted—and it is much the same today—that many of the ground floors were actually below the surface of the streets. The damp and fetid air hung in the main living area— the kitchen—of most families. Moreover, Lodève had no public slaughter- house so that the butchers' quarter, located right in the center of town above the St. Pierre residential area, provided the daily spectacle of shrieking ani- mals, offal and blood running in the streets, and the emanation of unspeak- able odors.[24]

The consequence was poor health—at least for the working class. Rame noted that the bourgeois and peasants were much better off. "Like the sap of a plant [workers'] impoverished blood becomes watery; from this derives a harmful activation of the lymphatic system that rapidly leads to a thou- sand forms of scrofulous ailments." Young women were abnormally white (though generally attractive) and slow to reach puberty—he said fifteen or sixteen was usual. Their fecundity, however, seemed normal and they had few problems with lactation. Rame argued—without statistics—that they had greater than average difficulty in birth and that women went through menopause at an earlier date than normal. He did add some quantitative data to his analysis, but it is better to refer to the documentary record, which supports his argument rather well.

Despite its rapidly growing population (7,906 in 1796, 11,238 in 1851), birth/death ratios remained close to one. During the July Monar- chy and Second Republic (1831–1851), deaths exceeded births by a total of 133 despite a sharp downturn in the death rate in 1849–50. The overall population of the city grew during that same period from 9,919 to 11,238, or 1,319. Thus net migration amounted to 1,452 persons. This was not that unusual for industrial towns in the first half of the nineteenth century, but Lodève's failure even to renew its native population was atypical of the Hérault where, with the exception of towns undergoing significant out- migration (for example, Pézenas), births regularly exceeded deaths.[25] Nîmes, similar in its industrial history though less developed technologically, main- tained a modest excess of births over deaths during the same period. Break- ing the death figures down by age (possible from summary data only after 1839), it is clear that infant and child mortality maintained its grip on Lodève families and would do so well into the 1860s, when the first real break occurs. In the 1840s, infants less than one-year-old accounted for about 20 per- cent of all deaths and those one to five for another 25 percent.[26] This is high even for industrial settings.[27] Stillbirths were also significant, averag- ing twenty-three per year from 1837 to 1854 (range: fifteen to twenty-nine); this represented half the stillborn total for the arrondissement, even though

Lodève itself only accounted for one-fifth of the district's births. Causes of death were enumerated only after 1853, but the overwhelming presence of respiratory, tubercular, and digestive track diseases attests to the grave shortcomings of public hygiene even at that point. Infant and child deaths were heavily due to croup/bronchitis and, still, to small pox and the measles, while the leading killers among adults were scrofula, lung diseases, diarrhea, gastritis, and meningitis, all potential consequences of hygienic deficiencies. Finally, supporting Rame's claim, between six and twelve women's deaths per year were attributed to childbirth.[28]

Xavier Rame agreed with Villermé that the factories ("grands ateliers") were not the cause of ill-health, being "vast, well-ventilated, for the most part drier than private houses." *Progressiste* that he was, he could not help but add that "besides, the use of machines has greatly reduced workers' fatigue." Since almost no one worked at home anymore, factories, he argued, were if anything a positive influence on public health. Certainly their location on the outskirts of town up and down the valleys in the midst of irrigated meadows took workers out of the nasty environment of the town. The factories were often new or largely refurbished, and as Villermé noted, the natural humidity of the valleys allowed their windows to be open, weather permitting. Hours were long, 12 to 14 hours per day on a 6-day week, but breaks were often, totalling 2 to 2½ hours a day. Workers would usually trek home for the midday meal. Night shifts had been increasing, especially in the newer establishments. A glance at maps, plant-layouts, blueprints, and the few surviving buildings corroborates both Rame's and Villermé's estimates.[29] But workers, who clearly sensed their own health problems, tended to blame the factories for them. This fascinating point, stressed by Rame, underlines the psychological impact of proletarianization. Although the residential conditions of hygiene for workers had worsened because of population growth and their greater concentration in the poorer neighborhoods of the lower town as declining incomes banished them from the upper, they were unwilling to identify ill-health with where they lived. In reality, workers currently were getting out of town more and getting more exercise than they had as home workers, and it is even possible that they, if not their families, were less unhealthy than earlier generations *because* they worked in the factories. But they refused to blame the community of which they still felt themselves an integral part and focused instead on that which had changed, the industrial plants where they had to report to work.

At what point did they make the connection between power over the place of work and power over the city and its services? The wide boulevards of Recollets, La Bouquerie, and Villeneuve and the "domaines" where the bosses lived, the open square of St. Fulcran where social halls and public offices, clerics' quarters and bureaucrats' houses were to be found were just as real seats of authority as the factories.

The attack on le Cercle in 1845 symbolized a new awareness of the social and political authority possessed by the fabricants, even though the form of attack still smacked of older practices. Trade unionism had been maturing for fifteen years, and the tactics in that arena had moved from the older repertoire—to borrow Charles Tilly's terminology—that included charivaris, social/sexual inversion, and community turnouts to sophisticated union methods, equally premeditated employer responses, and long-term confrontation. But this form of worker resistance had been defeated by a capitalist class that drew together into a veritable cartel and manipulated the political arena, despite its own patently illegal "coalition," to the end of crushing a great strike. "Community" was no longer a world in which various elements held differing (though unequal) fields of power and used tolerated modes of protest behavior, as was the case in the 1834 upheaval. Pushed on by the logic of capitalist solidarity in face of mounting national and international competition (in a manner quite similar to the pressures that created the coal-mining combine called the Compagnie de la Loire in the same year), the woolens barons of Lodève smashed the earlier concept of community and thereby snipped the last thread of working-class deference. Never again would weavers deliver their morceau de pain. The class struggle would be *for* the community; it would be political.[30]

In Lodève, the Revolution of 1848 began in 1845. But before returning to that narrative, let us come closer to the men and women who would be the revolutionaries, to seek to understand their lives and links as we have those of the fabricants. They can be approached by using similar sources. Because of their lowly status, the *état civil* records have been more fruitful than the probate documents, and they figure hardly at all in the scratchings of the notaires. The group pursued is the logical one—those men who had the commitment and the daring to make the last stand of the 1848 era, the resistance to the coup d'etat of 1851. What can we find out about their lives that might help us to understand the sources of their militance?

Those Lodévois arrested in the wake of the coup d'état had not participated in any acts of violence at that time because, as we shall see, the city was already under virtual martial law with its garrison of regulars on ready alert. To have taken up arms would have been absurd. There was a general meeting of Lodève militants, however, at the nearby hamlet of Camplong and a "committee of five" was elected, apparently to make a call to arms if deemed reasonable. The government had a fairly complete list of those in attendance thanks to a spy. But more important, Louis Napoleon's officials drew up a longer list of individuals who were démoc-soc activists, especially those suspected of connections with the murder of Paul Adam, the Procureur de la République for the Lodève district, in 1849. A total of seventy-seven men were tried before the special Commission mixte. Information provided by the "Decisions de la Commission" is most useful, for it indicates age, birthplace, occupation, marital status, number of children, the charges (along with past criminal record, assorted assessments of character, and whether or not the accused was still at large), and the verdict.[31]

Several general features in the collective profile of these men (no women were arrested) emerge. Occupationally it was a working-class group, rather faithfully mirroring the city's worker population. Textile workers predominated, totaling thirty-three out of the sixty-seven whose occupations are known. These included seventeen weavers, eleven spinners, three dyers, one shearman, and one mechanic. The only unexpected result here was the virtual absence of cloth finishers (laineurs, tondeurs, "pareurs," presseurs). These formerly aristocratic crafts had been thoroughly proletarianized by this time, however, filled with unapprenticed machine tenders working closely under the eye of the boss. Spinners and weavers actually had more on-the-job autonomy, but the status of both had been severely threatened in 1845, and the spinners especially woke up to the fact. The other occupations of those arrested after the coup d'état generally fall into expected categories—five tailors (no shoemakers, however),[32] nine building trades workers, one tanner, and one miner (there was a tiny lignite mine in the canton). The service trades were little in evidence—save a lonely, but pivotal, barber, Jean Esprit Benoit, as all cabaret owners/wine merchants escaped the net. Agriculturalists numbered well below their proportions in the city, with four cultivateurs, two jardiniers, and one domestique (the Spaniard Fernando), or about 10 percent of the total; according to the census of 1851, tillers of the soil living in the commune constituted 28 percent of the active male population. Finally, a handful of lower-level businessmen and professionals filled out the group: Moïse Lyon, marchand des nouveautés and the leader of the Lodève démoc-soc movement, Stanislas Kawalerski, a Polish-born "doctor to the poor," a huissier, a lawyer, a jewelry store owner, and interestingly, Théodore Brunel, machine-builder, a younger son of the enterprising Etienne. The overwhelmingly proletarian cast of Lodève's activists underlines the high degree of politicization that had occurred among workers there and the level of class antagonism. Lyon, Kawalerski, and Charles Savy, the lawyer, were the only leaders who might be considered bourgeois. The other sixteen "*meneurs*" or "*chefs*," were, with the exception of the barber and a farmer, all workers. The first two "bourgeois" were outsiders in any case—Lyon, a Jew born in nearby Clermont with Montpellier family connections, and Kawalerski, a Polish leftist exile—and Savy, though born in Lodève, was very young, twenty-seven at the time of his arrest in 1852, meaning that he was little more than a law student when the Revolution began.

The age of most of those tried, however, belies any notion that this was merely a group of young hotheads. The average age was thirty-six and the median thirty-five. Although only three were over fifty, only another five were Savy's age or younger, and just one was under twenty-five—the eighteen-year-old Emile Boudou, an "affilié" to the "plot" to join the resistance whose sentence was the lightest—"put under surveillance." (Only four men, incidentally, were acquitted.) The great majority were born in Lodève (forty-six of sixty-seven), its tributary villages (another eight), or cloth-working towns and villages that traditionally sent migrants to the city (five). Two Spaniards and Kawalerski made up a tiny foreign contingent. The only figure who might be regarded as an "outside agitator," Godefroy

Siadoux, came from Paulhan, a démoc-soc hotbed. He was accused of "provocation of civil war and convoking a secret society" and was arrested armed at a meeting at the café Audemar. The settled, localized nature of Lodève radicalism is further shown by the number of married men (fifty-two of sixty-seven) and among them only eight were childless. Naturally, most of the single men and those without children were fairly young. These percentages correspond to averages among the general population.

Overall, then, the militants of Lodève were decidedly working-class with roots in the city, mature men with interests and families to defend. In this, with the exception of the clearly proletarian character of leadership, they were not that different from urban démoc-soc populations elsewhere or from the parade of protesters and rebels who cross the pages of July Monarchy history. These were men whose jobs and incomes had been altered by emergent industrial capitalism, who had fought wars in the industrial battlefield but who rallied to a democratic-socialist political agenda before and during the Revolution and then moved toward resistance in 1851. But we know a good deal more about some of these men, and this knowledge corroborates the earlier stress on poverty and its attendant health hazards. The primordial threats of sheer misery, death, and family tragedy stalked many of them, a reality that carries this study beyond correlation and into the lives of those who rebelled.[33]

We have probate and birth, death, and marriage information on thirty-eight men and their families out of the list compiled by the Commission mixte. Twelve men were tried in absentia, and we therefore have no record other than their names, the charges against them, and their sentences. Of these only Lyon and Jean-Baptiste Fraisse were located in other documentation. Thus, of the sixty-seven arrested portrayed in general above, 57 percent figure in the following more detailed analysis. Since we were interested in events that occurred before the time of their arrest and in particular in their fairly recent past, systematic examination of records began with the marriages of those wed in Lodève (all in the 1830–51 period). Marriage documents provide a great deal of basic information (social milieu, ability to sign, existence of contract, parents' geographical origin and occupation, and so forth). Also included are, if applicable, parents' and parents-in-law's dates of death. From there one may go to probate records for income information on the individual's or his bride's family. Next, one may pursue the records of birth of children and deaths of family members, including those children. A much deeper appreciation of these people's world thus emerges. Witnesses at these various critical life events also help to identify a circle of friendship cementing many of these men together.

Information on the single men is harder to find and less valuable because their immediate family life is less visible. Therefore, no systematic attempt to follow up on them was made. Moreover, those not married in Lodève naturally have thinner dossiers, although birth and death records for their families, if located, are useful. The greatest problem here of course is that one is working with last names only in the indexes because the records list the names of those born or deceased, not the individual in question. Thus, sadly, the famous Balp brothers, arguably the most violent of Lodève's militants, escape us entirely. Because they were contumacious, all we have are their names and approximate ages, and they do not appear to have been born or married in Lodève. Trying to trace their children among Lodève's dozens of Balp families was an impossible task. Moïse Lyon was also difficult to trace, but other information yielded a biographical portrait of Lodève's "chef de la démagogie," as the Commission mixte described him.

In many respects, this profile of Lodève's militants again mirrors the city's working class as a whole. Most were poor or at least "lacking ease." Although we were only able to trace the inheritance of fifteen of the men and five of their wives, of this group only seven received anything at all. Of those from clearly working-class backgrounds, only three inherited something from his or her parents—Fulcran Roux Fr 150 in cash from his mother, Jean Rouble a tiny vineyard worth Fr 160 (8 francs annual revenue) and his wife some cash and a house from their fathers (a mule driver and a spinner) — while Marie Vaillé brought her first husband's twelve ares of vine (18 francs in revenue) into her 1835 marriage with the journeyman dyer and strike leader, Pierre Cabot. The others whose inheritances have been traced came from nonworking-class home environments, but they hardly commanded great fortunes. Frédéric Benoit, whose presence on the list at all troubled officials, was far and away the wealthiest man arrested; he had inherited real property worth Fr 4,000 and some Fr 1400 in mobile capital from his fabricant father. J.B. Fraise, the son of an innkeeper, and Antoine Mallet, whose father had farmed in Soubès, complete the group. Moïse Lyon's widowed mother was forced to declare bankruptcy in 1844,[34] so it is unlikely that he had much money. In May 1852, on the birth certificate of Lyon's son, we discover that his wife—he was still at large—was living in a house owned by a butcher on the place au Blé. There is no evidence that he ever owned a home. Doctor Kawalerski, on the other hand, seems to have had some money. His family possessed a house at the time of his death in 1879, and his marriage to the daughter of Jean Faulquier (witnessed by Dr. Teisserenc and other "progressive" types among Lodève's elite) brought in 2,000 and some land.[35]

In general, home ownership, another variable that can be picked up in the death notices, was low among these men. Of the twenty for whom we have information, eight owned a house or apartment at some time before 1851. Two of these appear to have lost their home; when friends reported the death of spinner Pierre Balp's ten-month-old daughter in 1850, they noted that she died in the "maison paternelle," rue du Collège, but his three-year-old son died in 1851 in a house rented from Joseph Solandre in Montbrun; Pierre Sauvayre seems to have experienced similar downward mobility from 1840 to 1847. If we count only workers on the list, only Fulcran Roux, Louis Montel, Noël Maizou, and the tailor Antoine Liquier owned a place in 1851. Obviously, given the nature of the source used, this indicator is skewed, since all the group did not lose children. Overall, however, the poverty of the militants of 1851 cannot be doubted and appears to be about "average" for the Lodève working class as a whole.

Average also was the grim toll that the city's public health conditions took on their children. Thirty-seven percent of the children born to these men died. Our "sample" overwhelmingly consists of men married in the city whose wives were residents. The great majority of both had also been born there and thus experienced life-long exposure to its noxious atmosphere. Most striking here is the fact that only eight couples who had children at all did not lose at least one child; these included Benoit, the merchant jeweler, Moïse Lyon, Morant, the Spanish immigrant, and three others from rural origins. Virtually all Lodévois de souche faced the tragedy of child death.

A few had a history of grief that alone would have been sufficient to make them permanent revolutionaries. Witness Fulcran Roux and his wife, Marie Sophie Hortolan, who like her husband, came from a thoroughly woolens-industry background. The Roux were not as badly off as many of their neighbors. They lived with her parents (both weavers and relatively young—Marie Sophie was only nineteen when she married Roux in 1832), who owned a house in St. Pierre parish, until the early 1840s. Roux was listed on his marriage document as an ouvrier en laine, which usually meant work in preparation of the wool, but by 1841 he had become a journeyman dyer, a better job but still part of the early stages of woolens production. The increased income probably was the basis for the purchase of a house close by a year or so later. Fellow activist Joseph Albagnac was renting a portion of it when his own eleven-month-old daughter died there in 1844. (The Albagnacs also had a disastrous time with the loss of their young, although by 1847 they had bought a house or apartment on the rue Gazillier.)

For the Roux, the 1840s seemed like a long procession of death. They had three children when, in January 1840, their four-year-old son died. A year later, as if to repair the loss, a daughter was born—only to die before the year was out. After their move and a respite from tragedy, Marie Sophie's sixth pregnancy ended with a stillbirth on 28 September 1845. This, of course, occurred shortly after the great strike in which Roux had been prominent enough to be singled out by the authorities.[36] Could the deprivation and the anxiety of the long strike have been a factor weakening the thirty-two-year-old mother's constitution? Eighteen months later, in March 1847, their daughter born in 1844 succumbed. Her mother had shortly before given birth to a son, conceived immediately after the stillbirth, so the blow was softened somewhat. But this same boy, having survived the ravages of infant disease and learned to talk and play as the Revolution of 1848 unfolded, died on 24 January 1851. By that time, Roux had moved to a lower paying factory job, but the multiple tragedies besetting the family surely loomed larger than this in his life.

Roux was a foot soldier in the démoc-soc movement, listed only as an "affiliate" by the Mixed Commission. But his involvement with others in the movement went deep. Pierre Antoine Jourdan, a joiner whose brother Jean worked at the city excise-tax station (*l'octroi*) during the July Monarchy and served on the municipal council in 1848–49, and himself was called a "démagogue exalté" by the 1852 tribunal, had twice (in 1840 and 1841), declared the deaths of Roux children as a "friend of the family; Sauvayre, *dit* Collet, had done the same in 1845. The charge in 1851 against Roux was a simple one: he was a member of a secret society. But—and should we be surprised?—the Commission added that he was "very dangerous." He was "transported" to Algeria, his still young wife and her remaining teenage children left to make their own way in the chilling climate of the early Second Empire.

There were many similar stories. Perhaps saddest of all are of those, like Pierre Balp, Pierre Boyrat, Jean Maury, and Hippolyte Paulier, who had yet to see a child of theirs live beyond three years. Then there was Pierre Gros, whose wife of nineteen years died in childbirth—along with the baby. It might be argued—and has been—that working people were inured to such tragic circumstances and lived wooden lives where love was in short supply. Such a view does not hold water when put under close scrutiny, especially through the use of the documentation of working-class culture and court records. For all the sensationalism of a Pierre Rivière case (the 1834 parricide made famous by Michel Foucault), the level of domestic violence among the "people" was rather low in nineteenth-century France, and in Lodève it was virtually nonexistent, if the absence of prosecution in the First Instance Court means anything. Obviously, the brutality implicit in wet-nursing and the treatment of foundlings shows some level of disregard for small children's tender lives, and the situation of domestics qua prostitutes reveals a similar callousness toward female children at a later age. Apprentices were often harshly treated. But evidence of caring, if not always harmonious, family life among working people abounds. The work of Pierre Pierrard and William Reddy on the Nord, Laurence Fontaine on Alpine artisans, Elinor Accampo on St. Chamond, and Joan Scott and Louise Tilly more generally emphasize a humane family universe in an often oppressive and inhumane society. The family wage economy forced cooperation for survival, and wives' and children's labor was exploited due to this necessity; but the evidence on intrafamily hatred is largely limited to sensational cases. And most of those, like the Rivière murders, arose in contexts where property conflict was central. For working people—and the evidence for Lodève is incontrovertible—property, its inheritance and contractual exchange, was of little relevance. Drawing up a marriage contract, for instance, became less and less the practice for woolens workers. While this need not imply marriage for love, in all circumstances where wage-work became the central source of income (the pioneering study of Rudolph Braun remains the most interesting), the intricate game of marriage as a strategy of property enhancement declines, clearing the way for more open sexual mores and marriage based on some sort of attraction. Parental disapproval certainly has less impact.

The cooperation among family members in strike situations, the wide participation of women in collective action, and, in general, the broad work force participation of all family members over the age of twelve, and the rarity of single young people living "on their own" all indicate an interdependence that could only enhance the appreciation of a child's (or a wife's) value. This need not imply any sort of devaluation of traditional patriarchal practices in Languedocian families. But it does mean that the loss of a child, and more rarely a wife in her prime, would be a matter of deep sorrow. That such sorrow might translate into anger and a desire to seek social redress seems thoroughly plausible.[37]

There was one way in which the group of militants analyzed was not at all typical of Lodève's working class as a whole, and this was in their level of literacy, or, at least, in their ability to sign marriage and other ètat civil documents. Only ten of thirty-nine were unable to sign their names. One, Basile Barthe, learned to do so from the time of his marriage and the birth of his first child in 1834 to that of his second in 1845. (He and his wife also learned about birth control as well, since no births or deaths of children were recorded in the interim.) This 26-percent illiteracy rate (1827–32) is far lower than that among the general male population of military recruits (41 percent) and the general Hérault average (49 percent).[38] A more refined analysis of the signatures divided them roughly into three categories— S_1 (practiced, flowery, "bourgeois"), S_2 (cursive, but without the same indications of constant writing activity and extensive training), and S_3 (printed in block letters without any semblance of style). The last is typical of individuals—often women—who only learned to sign their name and might or might not be able to read. The vast majority of the militants fall into the middle category and none into the last. It is interesting that a number of workers revealed quite "learned" hands, an indication of extensive training and/or use: Pierre Balp, weaver and son of a spinner; André Escudier, weaver, son of a trader; his brother Pierre, mason; Noël Maïzou, weaver and son of one; Louis Montel, spinner and son of a cultivateur; Hippolyte Paulier, a dyer and son of an ironworker (*fournier*); our friend Fulcran Roux; and Joseph Vaillé, a weaver and son of a baker. These men share no particular characteristics, although a disproportionate number are weavers and all are native Lodévois, and are no more likely to be "leaders" than men in the next group. But their sizeable presence—and the unpleasant social and economic circumstances surrounding most of their lives—gives pause to any tendency to stereotype proletarians in this day and age. Probably worker-intellectuals, if they entertained notions of becoming the latter instead of the former (à la Jacques Rancière), they failed to make it and instead fought to transform society as workers.[39]

The relative homogeneity of the militants of Lodève goes beyond occupational and income similarity and commonality of life experiences. It may also be glimpsed as a series of human links. They are not links forged to any significant extent by family. To be sure, there were several sets of brothers among those arrested: the Barthes, the Escudiers, and possibly the

Pauliers (though we have no information on Fulcran save general similarity of Mixed-Commission information about him and Hippolyte) from the detailed list and the contumacious Balp brothers (Bernard, Didier, and Hippolyte). Moreover, Pierre Balp and A.F. Alinat married sisters, daughters of the iron worker Jean Cadilhac, a known militant who escaped the net. But family ties are not the most visible here, rather it is friendship—the place of comrades rather than family in life-crisis situations. We looked for individuals from the list who turn up as witnesses to others' marriages and/or those who gave their time at the moment of a friend's child's death to report it to the authorities. Twelve men were connected to others on the list. The ties show up more in birth and death declarations than in marriages, since family members were usually the witnessing parties there (along with city officials). Jean "Esprit" Benoit, a barber whose shop was no doubt a center of union talk and political discussion, Louis Montel, a spinner, Pierre Antoine Jourdan, a joiner, and Fulcran Vallié were the busiest witnesses. Montel's friendship network included Albagnac, Cabot, Liquier, A.F. Alinat, and Roux; the last two lived in the same house. Liquier also signed for the 1851 death of an Albagnac child. Benoit witnessed for the Barthe brothers; P.A. Jourdan was tied to Lyon, Hippolyte Paulier, and Roux, and Fulcran Vallié, to Maizou and Basile Barthe. Obviously we are only looking at the tip of an iceberg here, but it is a rarity to attach names and events to working class links of solidarity, and these few—retrieved with difficulty—relationships must be recorded. They imply a whole world.

This examination of the working class of Lodève and its most militant members brings us to some rather striking conclusions. First, misery made a difference. Whether viewed from a global, correlational perspective or from that of individual activists, poverty and pathogenic conditions of health figured prominently in the growth of resistance. Second, ties to and in the community remained central as native Lodévois, with the exception of a few middle-class leaders like Lyon and Kawalerski, dominated the movement. Figures unknown to July Monarchy officials such as Benoit, Montel, and Jourdan emerge as the human network-builders, the men who could be counted on in life as well as politics. Third, how working-class this revolutionary vanguard was! If the list of arrested men represented "the Party" in Lodève, workers, not an intellectual elite, ran it. And even the worker-intellectuals, if our means of identifying them comes close to the truth, were not necessarily the key figures. Finally, what of work and work life in all this? It was important to be sure, but as the 1840s wore on, the older process of proletarianization was largely complete. Workers were smashed in their workplace struggle in 1845. The town, the larger community, increasingly seemed to be the problem—it was killing them and their young, and the traditional leadership seemed unwilling to respond with concrete, positive action any more than it had to the grievances surrounding the strike. So let the community be the prize. The next step might be the state.

5

1848

The Second Republic marked the turning point in the industrial history of lower Languedoc. But the reversal arose less from forces inherent in the regional economy itself or in its relationship with national and international markets than from the political consequences of class conflict. Unlike much of the rest of the nation, the economy of the coastal departments, and the Hérault in particular, did not suffer significantly from the Revolution itself. But welling antagonisms formed in the battles of the 1840s found expression in political radicalism that took a violent turn when met with the repression of 1849–51. The Hérault emerged in 1851 as the nation's most active department in Montagnard secret-society organization and, as is well known, one of the main bastions of resistance to the coup d'ètat. It paid dearly for its heroism.

A Plebeian Public Sphere

In the immediate prerevolutionary years, there was little forewarning of the upheaval to come. As everywhere in France, the subsistence crisis of 1846–47 took its toll. "It has been a long time since we have seen so many petty crimes as have occurred in the last two months," noted the *Echo de Lodève* in February 1847; the high case load of the local lower court corroborated this opinion. Grain-poor areas were the hardest hit, but urban areas paid as well with skyrocketing bread prices.[1] Comparatively speaking, however, lower Languedoc remained immune to the violent upheavals that tortured so much of the rest of the nation in 1847.[2] Textile manufacturing even experienced a minor boom late in the year. The cantonal reports for Enquête of 1848, undertaken by the Luxembourg Commission, present a retrospective picture of stability. St. Chinian appeared to be in the worst shape, but the vine was emerging there as an alternative source of wealth and employment. St. Pons's decline had bottomed out, and Riols actually prospered with a small, efficient operation. Both Bédarieux and Lodève filed generally optimistic reports. In Bédarieux, despite subpar woolen sales after February, the cantonal commission, appropriately balanced between employers and employees, seemed confident that the industry would rebuild to its twenty-five million franc annual average. Employment was down somewhat, but in general, "the hard-working worker is never indigent." The town's four mutual aid societies, whose adherents also received unemployment payments, boasted a membership of seven hundred men, or about one-third of the adult male work force. And Bédarieux still attracted immigrants from the "less favored" nearby villages. As for Lodève, where workers in fact dominated the commission, National Guard demand compensated for cuts in army orders, and indeed the commission wondered what areas might be expanded since things were "going so well in woolens." Eight mutual aid societies, including a rare organization of women, comprised a majority of the woolens workers.[3]

Lodève's Enquête report and related correspondence provide a good picture of workers' chief concerns.[4] The strike of 1845 still hung heavy over the town, especially since the key manufacturers had indeed established their joint mechanical weaving factory. It was "destroying hand weaving," replacing men with lower-paid women, and degrading quality, "threatening the future" of the city. Moreover, mechanization in weaving hit the building trades, where unemployed weavers and their sons sought work. Hand-shearmen continued to protest the shearing-machinery revolution. The crisis of mechanization had reached a fever pitch by 1848. Only three woolens operations still relied largely on human power—forty sorting and cloth-repairing workshops, twenty-one hand-weaving sheds, and sixteen dye-works. Low-paying women's occupations alone seemed immune to *les mécaniques.* Altogether, then, besides the new weaving establishment, nineteen spinneries in the commune and four more in nearby villages, twenty fulling mills and two elsewhere, and fifteen finishing shops made use of 190 different sets of textile machinery. Steam power was not yet widespread (though at least twelve small engines were in use), as hydraulic drive-trains remained sufficient.[5] The workers' solution to all this was disarmingly simple: "The weavers wish to work at home as in the past without being subjected to the rules and surveillance of the factories," and "the shearmen request the suppression of the shearing frames." They were joined in this sentiment by nonwoolens artisans worried about the labor market glut produced by technological redundancy.

In 1848, Lodève thus found itself at the final crossroads in its long history of industrial capitalist development. The great strike of 1845, capped as it was by capitalists' determination to forge ahead with their (less than competitive!) program of modernization, on one hand, and the workers' recourse to frustrated violence on the other, set the framework. For the workers, the Republic now appeared as their lifeline to a new world. And at its outset, Lodève weavers saw the return to home work as a panacea to reverse an entire process of proletarianization. Machines robbed their jobs, but the fact that they were also being replaced by women in operating the new devices implied a double degradation, also threatening their role as principal breadwinner and chef de ménage.[6] Moreover, if they pursued another job, it would be at the lowest ranks of the alternative trade. They would also risk antagonizing neighbors established in those crafts whom they previously counted as their friends and allies. Home handloom weaving thus represented to them a way of life in which "proper" familial relations would obtain: the husband-father head of household directing a family operation. And perhaps Year II dreams of weavers-become-fabricants still floated in their heads. Thus, their initial revolutionary demand was to leap back into a world of restored autonomy. Weavers found support among the joiners of the city, who had long done contract work for the fabricants, but were now being replaced by unapprenticed employees of the firms. They argued that this was a direct violation of the law, because the fabricants paid patentes "for their business in woolens, not woodworking," akin to using "prison" labor.[7] "Fair competition," guaranteed by the Republic, lay at the core of the initial demands of Lodève's workers, just as it did, along with concepts of autonomy and dignity in work, for most workers in France. It was when it became clear there was nothing the least fair about the Republic itself that a new, more specifically socialist orientation became evident.

What was remarkable was how rapidly it occurred. By June of 1849, the Sub-Prefect of the city assured his supervisors that "all the factory workers belong to the Socialist Party."[8] As elsewhere, a history of high expectations, patience in the beginning, and a growing sense of betrayal led to this consequence. The rapid transformation of opinion, most basically, was rooted in the solidarity of Lodève's workers. We have seen how shop-floor conflict and material circumstances pulled them together. But we must also recall the cultural nexus of their unity.

Their highly concentrated living circumstances meant constant interaction. Most went back and forth to work four times a day, walking and talking in groups and "dropping off" friends and relatives at one plant and the next before going on to their own. (Strikes unfolded in the same manner.)[9] Regular intercourse in the workplace itself was relatively easy, save perhaps in the spinneries because of noise. Weavers in their sheds worked on a piece-rate basis, thus allowing break times, but they could also converse while at their looms. The number of contre-maîtres in the entire Lodève industry was small, meaning that their presence was only an occasional hindrance to shoptalk.[10] Communication among women workers went on unhindered in their two primary occupations, wool-sorting and burling, both of which involved group activities in a quiet environment.

Oversight was minimal and their main contacts were with other workers, carders and cloth finishers.[11]

Worker interaction off the job was as natural as it was in the shop. The Lodève workday amounted to around ten hours divided into two phases with a long main meal break at midday. This appears to have been largely family time, although observers remarked on the many cafés dotting the workers' quartiers and on the roads leading to the mills. It is quite probable that many lunches, especially for "business" purposes, were taken there. Lodève's cafés hosted deliberations of all sorts, including mutual-aid society meetings. Such gatherings more likely occurred on work-shortened Saturdays or Sundays after church, but less formal get-togethers could take place any evening.[12] Women's contacts outside their workplace were more casual, usually in the context of their unpaid work—marketing, washing clothes, at the wells scattered throughout the town.[13]

As everywhere in the Mediterranean world, a great deal of leisure time was spent out-of-doors. The promenades along the rivers, on the esplanade, and into the nearby countryside provided much-needed open space away from the air-deprived and malodorous neighborhoods where workers resided. Sundays and *jours de fête* were the special days for outings, and reference to well-dressed working people's families gathering with relatives and friends for strolls, games, and picnics is sprinkled across the official reports and observers' comments of the era. *Boules* matches—men only—punctuated the afternoon air with clicks of metal balls and guffaws of combatants. But also there was the buzz of talk—like a low whir of an enormous engine—in every public spot. For talking itself, again mainly among men, was a pastime almost as interesting as boules. Another sacred pastime—which went well beyond mere sport as it contributed to the family's well-being—was hunting. The wild boar was the game of choice. The boar hunt is preeminently a group affair resulting, if successful, in the parceling out of the succulent meat among the participants. Wolf control was also a task undertaken by hunters not only to clear the land of the majestic boar's chief predator and the scourge of shepherds, but also to collect bounties offered by the state. The seriousness of the problem may be understood by a merchant butcher's encounter with a pack of wolves in the well-traveled road to Clermont when they massacred his herd of swine as he was driving them to market in 1816.[14] Hunting thus brought Lodévois into regular contact with the state both as foe and friend, but the good turn done the government by killing wolves all the more increased their resentment toward it for restricting their perceived *droit de l'homme* to hunt when and what they pleased. The sport thus had a clear political impact, one that would flare during the Second Republic—quite literally in the case of Bédarieux.

All these networks of solidarity could easily mobilize people for political action. There existed an anti-Orleanist political atmosphere that had been heated from time to time with outbursts of republican sentiment nurtured by positive memories of the First Republic mixed with snippets of Bonapartism. But unlike Bédarieux, where a worker republicanism encouraged by bourgeois democrats had to struggle to displace popular legitimism, the politicization of Lodève workers had evolved incrementally and, for the most part, invisibly to ever-vigilant July Monarchy officials.

What was not invisible was the alternative Catholicism of a majority of the city's workers. And in 1848, it would mix immediately with politics. We have already noted the significance of the lay piety organizations in the city. Moreover, workers' mutual aid societies bore religious names and were undergirded by Christian ritual. The basic Christian morality of Lodève workers was legendary. As the Enquête of 1848 reiterated, "moral and religious *éducation* among the inhabitants of this canton leaves little to be desired. Everywhere the churches are regularly attended and holy places respected; but what best demonstrates the morality *du peuple* is the rarity of crimes against property, especially in a manufacturing district where it is so easy to make off with materials."[15] Throughout the 1840s, a number of itinerant preachers, part of an understudied French Catholic "great awakening," visited Lodève and spoke at both St. Fulcran and St. Pierre. Hawkers of devotional tracts and icons crisscrossed the nation.[16] Some, such as Emile Brée in his *Almanach-Catechisme*, tied Christ's message and social redemption together.[17]

The most significant evidence, however, of a social-Christian political base in Lodève's working class was the immense popularity of Abbé Jean-Etienne Valibouze, who ran for election to the Constituent Assembly on 23 April 1848, finishing a resounding first in the city, though twenty-third in the department. Valibouze was born in Ceyras in 1806. In the early 1830s, he became a professor of ethics at Montpellier's Grand Séminaire, very likely having the future novelist Ferdinand Fabre as a student.[18] In 1845, he received an appointment as curé in Paulhan, a town with a developing radical reputation. Two years later, the conservative bishop of Montpellier, Alexandre Thibault, demoted him to the village parish of Soumont, near Lodève.[19] There he joined forces with Pierre Nougaret, another populist curé in nearby St. Etienne de Gourgas, who also had been "exiled" by Thibault after serving as curé of St. Pierre in Lodève from 1843 to 1845 and likely acting as the go-between in strike negotiations in 1845.[20] Tension ran high within the Hérault church during the 1840s between Thibault and several theologically and politically adventurous priests. An 1845 article in *L'Indépendant* by "X . . . prêtre" entitled "Du despotisme épiscopal" condemned the arbitrary powers of bishops to reassign priests at will. He defended theological liberty and stressed the practical damage done to both the old and new parishes.[21] The banishment of Valibouze and Nougaret did little to cure them of their idiosyncrasies or to reduce their interaction with the city workers. Another key Christian leader was Anatole Roussac. In 1844, he became the *aumonier* of Lodève's hospital, which put him in daily contact with the workers whose loved ones faced the disease and death that stalked the city's poor. He also worked on behalf of Lodève's domestic servants, founding a lay sisterhood called *Les Servantes de Marie*, which functioned as a haven for the unemployed, the abused, and the pregnant, as well as a mutual aid society and possibly a placement agency.[22] In 1848, Roussac spoke out for democracy and Valibouze, concluding a preelection oration:

Jésus, la justice et la république!
Vive la religion! Vive la liberté![23]

If the political consciousness of Lodève workers seemed amorphous on the eve of 1848, it nevertheless had strong roots. They had undoubtedly absorbed elements of the Jacobin tradition, although it is difficult to prove it. They endorsed a Catholicism that rejected hierarchy and social dominion, one thus compatible with social republicanism. They had created a sophisticated trade unionism that made them the marvel of worker France and the bane of the government. What the first three months of the Second Republic revealed, therefore, was a working-class political world that had existed largely beyond the vision of official France. Its rapid evolution in 1848–1849 was then carried forward by the political dynamics of the revolution itself. It was not preordained by economic structures, but it would not have been possible without them either.

Even under the July Monarchy, there existed therefore a submerged world of working-class public activity and participation in a discourse that stood apart from the bourgeois public sphere. Jürgen Habermas adumbrates the concept of such a "plebeian public sphere," which he associates with the more obvious manifestations of the Year II, Chartism, and the "anarchist tradition in the worker movement on the continent," but stresses its inability to retain its functional autonomy and provide a meaningful challenge to the bourgeois public sphere because it "was oriented to the intentions of the bourgeois public sphere" by virtue of their common intellectual roots in eighteenth-century rationalism.[24] But, in fact, the materials of working-class political discourse in Lodève only marginally drew on these roots and, indeed, the same may be said for worker France generally. Autonomy, dignity, and the right to work; Christian visions of brotherhood and social justice; and solidarity as workers against bourgeois exploitation: these elements owed little to the bourgeois public sphere as articulated in the eighteenth century and constructed, however flimsily, since the Revolution. Jacobinism of course did, but it only indirectly informed these workers' outlook. A plebeian public sphere *was* advanced in the Second Republic and possessed a vitality that should not be underestimated. It was an alternative, a "path not taken," to use Habermas's own words, and not an unwitting dupe, as he seems to imply, of "bourgeois intentions."

Revolutionary Politics

The proclamation of the Republic was "warmly received everywhere in Mediterranean France."[25] The July Monarchy had been more tolerated than supported, and political enthusiasm tended to be located both to the left and to the right of the *juste milieu*, with legitimism more feared by officials than republicanism.[26] But the left, as in Lodève, existed, a fact made clear by the jubilant acceptance of the new regime. How republicanism had evolved is understood only for a few pockets of the entire area, notably the Var, and our sense of it in the Hérault is particularly deficient.[27]

Montpellier had a relatively strong history of left-of-center politics during the July Monarchy. Its base was located in the professional and commercial business community, particularly among Protestants and Jews. Legitimism had been blunted by the political chameleon, wealthy business-man Zoé Granier, who wore the Bourbon hat long enough to insert him-self, as Mayor and Deputy, as the broker between the Carlist notables of Montpellier and the Orleanist regime. In the mid-forties a Girondist, con-stitutional left reasserted itself, bolstered by the threat "from below," and elected two moderate republicans, lawyer Gustave Laissac and merchant Jacques Brives, on the Municipal Council and the "dynastic left" politician Charamaule in the Chamber. Also, in 1844 *L'Independant* became a forum for left opinion, countering the journalistic success of the legitimist sheet, *L'Echo du Midi*. Republicans sponsored a successful reformist banquet on 5 December 1847, helped force Granier's resignation from the Chamber, and had assembled to select his replacement on 24 February 1848, when word of the revolution arrived. A republican ambiance, though not always genuine, quickly arose.[28]

A popular movement in the Hérault occurred, but mostly in the form of peaceful demonstrations. Exceptionally, at Lodève after "groups spread throughout the city singing La Marseillaise and La Parisienne," in the wee hours of 26 February, "young people" tried to force the door of a "leading citizen" with a beam,[29] while another crowd "pillaged the tobacco and powder warehouse." Several people attempted "to set fire to manufactur-ing establishments."[30] Clearly resentments of the past remained alive. At Lunel, a wine bourg in the east, the tollhouse and its registers were burned, as were the indirect tax records for the town, attacks reflecting discontent over high wine prices.[31] In Bédarieux, a large crowd first invaded the indi-rect tax office and burned its records in the streets, then looted the collector's dwelling, adding furniture to the burning records, and moved on to take "all the lead, powder, and caps" from the *bureau de tabac*. After the police held them off at the mortgage record office, they surged through the streets threatening bystanders and went on to sack the office and house of the direct tax collector.[32]

But these were the only violent incidents recorded. The Procureur at Montpellier contrasted his jurisdiction with much of the rest of the nation.[33] And despite the effervescence of 26 March, most of Lodève's workers seemed willing to use the promised instruments of the Republic—manhood suffrage, a guaranteed "right to work," the unencumbered freedom to form associations, and a forum, in the Luxembourg Commission, to which to address the specific problems of craft and locale. In all, these were the well-springs of hope to transform their lives.

Initially, their activity focused on Abbé Valibouze's election. His vision was simple enough: "Abbé Valibouze wants to transform the three great verities that we have taken as our motto—liberty, equality, and fraternity—into natural elements of French life. This is the most noble task a priest can undertake."[34] To this end, he campaigned vigorously, seconded by fellow clerics Nougaret and Roussac. Rejected by legitimists and mistrusted by mainstream republicans, he had little chance to win a place on the major lists circulating the department. They therefore concentrated on the upper Hérault Valley, heading lists that included left-wing republicans known locally. Nougaret seemed a man possessed. Opponents reported that he neglected his appointed duties and preached politics from the pulpit when he was there.[35] More important was worker support. In Lodève Valibouze appeared on electoral lists of the two people's clubs in the city, the woolens workers' *Comité électoral républicain des travailleurs*, and the artisans' *Société des artistes réunis*, but also benefited from growing pressure from the streets. According to the conservative *Echo du Midi*, "the workers declare that if Valibouze is not elected deputy, they will throw the city into upheaval . . . and install him as curé of Saint Fulcran." He also made the lists of the bourgeois *Société des amis de l'ordre* and the conservative Catholic club and won the endorsement of the *Echo de Lodève*. Discretion thus seemed to do its part.[36]

Inevitably, Valibouze lost the department-wide election. But he was overwhelmingly supported in Lodève, outdistancing the moderate republican Mayor Jules André (who was elected, having appeared on all the major lists) by several hundred votes. He also did well throughout the Lergue and upper Hérault valleys, a region corresponding narrowly to the matrix of the strongest démoc-soc presence in the Hérault later on.

Despite his defeat, Valibouze remained a hero. When he decided not to run again in the by-election of 4 June, he threw his weight behind the straight republican candidate, Gustave Laissac, against de Genoude, the legitimist editor of the *Gazette de France*, running with the blessing of Bishop Thibault; Lodève's workers followed his lead. Lodève's *Comité électoral des travailleurs* replied to an entreaty to support Laissac, despite his moderate reputation, with enthusiasm, for he would stand against those who "conspire to tear away from France the freedoms that she had conquered in her first revolution." This communication was signed by five men whose titles indicate the organization of Lodève's principal workers' club, soon to be called simply *le Club*: "Gelly, le président des Tisserands, Louis Montel, le président des Fileurs, Pierre Créuzet, le président des Cultivateurs, L. Viguier, le vice-président des Tisserands, and Louis Devic, secrétaire." They spoke, they said, for the "Lodève working class."[37]

Religion largely defined the initial context of working-class political culture in Lodève. The Republic would be a new moral world in which the conflicts in the workshop and the degradation of existence in one's social space would come to an end. Valibouze spoke a language of hope and harmony. And so indeed did the new city administration. Jules André was a manufacturer and former Saint-Simonian, chosen as mayor by Ledru-Rollin's hand-picked commissaire of the Hérault, Oscar Gervais. The municipality negotiated directly with the woolens fabricants for an increase in the schedule of piece rates paid to their workers and augmented public assistance allocations.[38] It also revitalized the slaughterhouse project, which became a symbol of political change, urban renewal, and social reconciliation. The local government issued 100-franc twenty-year bond shares and encouraged the rich to buy them. In the atmosphere of March 1848, scores of industrialists subscribed and the project flourished.[39]

Claims for other civic improvements arrived in the mayor's office. One petition "from the inhabitants of the faubourg Montbrun" breathed the conciliatory spirit of March. Noting the slaughterhouse project, it called for the same sacrifices in the reconstruction of a bridge over the Soulandres connecting their neighborhood with the city. The better-off of Montbrun were willing to get the ball rolling financially. At the head of the signatures at the end we find Hippolyte Calvet and Philippe Rouaud, two of a handful of fabricants still living in the faubourg and both nephews (Calvet by marriage) of the Jacobin Rouaud brothers of Revolutionary fame. Speaking for all the ordinary folk of the faubourg, the letter invoked the highest republican virtues. Besides improving the movement of people and goods, the new bridge will "unite" them "in work," carrying them up "the gentle slope of Fraternity." The petition was presented by a "numerous gathering" at the mairie. The signatures that followed became less and less practiced, finally reaching that arduous stick-printing that signified functional illiteracy. The goodhearted Jacobins among the affluent were underpinned (and overseen) by the vigilant sans-culottes of Montbrun.[40]

As it turned out, this project met with delay after delay, never reaching fruition during Second Republic. Its form and its outcome symbolize the politics that unfolded during that era. A written, formal proposal with a concrete, problem-solving goal spearheaded by men of property, education, and good will was placed on the political agenda for consideration by representatives. But its impetus arose from the lifeworld problems of a mass of ordinary people who assembled to sign and then to deliver it en masse, announcing with these acts a politics that extended well beyond the formal, written, focused, ordered, and compromising politics of elections and representative institutions. It was a politics of public demonstration, of *manifestations*, of direct pressure undergirded by the threat of violence. The Valibouze campaign possessed the same elements. It was in fact a revolutionary politics with a pedigree not only dating back to the journées of 1789–93 and 1830–34, but to multiple occurrences of upheaval during the July Monarchy. While many were met with repression, others in fact were taken for what they were: political expression by those who could express themselves in no other way and treated by electors, candidates, representatives, and officials as "votes" demanding responses. "Demonstrative politics" or "revolutionary democracy" could not help but have a role in defining the nature of the Second Republic, especially as it became increasingly

The Montbrun bridge over the Soulondres

clear that having the formal right to petition and to vote—particularly when mediated through representatives who did not have to respond—meant a good deal less than one might have imagined. This our Montbrun petitioners learned as they continued to trudge hundreds of meters up the river to the nearest bridge for the next three years—and in dozens of other lessons about the nature of power in their society.

Although hardly unique, lower Languedoc turns out to be an excellent laboratory in which to examine the workings of the plebeian public sphere and the dialectic of conflict leading to its suppression during the Second Republic. Working people, Michelet's *peuple*, defined politics differently—or more broadly—from the notability who had constituted the *pays légal* of the July Monarchy and their bourgeois successors who dominated the assemblies of the Second Republic. Although electoral politics under manhood suffrage certainly had meaning, the arena and the agenda of plebeian political life went far beyond the ballot box. Indeed, the exercise of the vote turned out to be less significant than the public manifestations, peaceful and violent, supportive and hostile, that accompanied elections. Voter turnout varied considerably from election to election, but virtually all elections were accompanied by a flurry of demonstrations, some of quite serious proportions. Political organization—formally m clubs and more fleetingly in issue-specific activities—did not take on political party structures for the purpose of electing officials. Rather people petitioned and demonstrated to show their concerns to those officials, while also working to determine who the officials

By 1848, France had reached a point where "colonization of the life-world" by a host of disruptive elements spawned by the inherent mechanisms of national state formation as it intermeshed with the dynamics of capitalism had struck deeply into the body social. Habermas likens the process of cultural, social, and personal disorientation arising from perceived loss of power and material deprivation among Western workers to the impact of colonial conquest.[41] What was being "violated" and what people responded to often had to do with a sense of loss to be countered by a restoration of power, position, or material status. This, then, was what a good deal of the popular politics of 1848 was about: efforts at lifeworld "decolonization." As it related to state police authority, such politics was basically negative: keep it out of our lives—the republic means self-regulation. But as it related to capitalism, such politics was positive: the society must reinvigorate autonomy over one's working life by eliminating through legislation the unfair advantages of accumulated capital—in short, make capitalism fair. If it meant restricting technological development, so be it. Thus, what was asked of the arbiter, politics, was to some degree contradictory, but in both cases, the goal was similar—cultural, social, and personal autonomy, ultimately rooted in the unifying catchword of the day, "the right to work."

If the practice of this politics was demonstrative and its content lifeworld decolonization, what was its form? Was it a "class politics"? The answer is located in its dynamics as it faced the realization that it could not be integrated in the bourgeois public sphere. It moved from populist/Jacobin alliances with the notability, largely moderate republican, increasingly to plebeian exclusivism. Its practice then changed too. As the open contexts of debate and demonstration were systematically repressed under General Cavaignac and then Louis Napoleon, conspiratorial activity interacted with heightened confrontationist electoral politics. Thus a plebeian "party," the démoc-socs, emerged side by side with necessarily secret revolutionary societies. The content also shifted dramatically, although it lost its precision. The democratic and social Republic would *replace* the bourgeois public sphere. Visions of modified social ownership or significant regulation of the means of production with cooperative units of output commingled with those of a *fraternal* state where regional, local, and craft rivalries would be harmonized by a central government operating in the interests of all because elected by all. Thus, the essentials of a yet unrealized democratic-socialist society glimmered in the besieged and isolated plebeian public sphere by 1851. To crush it, the custodians of the bourgeois public sphere abandoned all pretense of enlightened universalism, opting for a manipulative, bureaucratic, and propagandistic format that was the harbinger of the contemporary neocorporatist state. Its first victim was the region where the plebeian public sphere had achieved, perhaps, its deepest roots in France: lower Languedoc.

Let us now document the process. Across the Hérault, dozens of incidents involving public demonstrations and occasional violence occurred in the wake of the February revolution, including the antitax riots already noted, a variety of family/neighborhood rivalries "released" into political conflict by the revolution, and widespread rural-urban conflicts especially in the Orb-Jaur corridor.[42] An atmosphere of demonstrative politics was thus established by the revolution itself. Our concern now is to see how it played off against electoral politics.

The first elections of the Second Republic, those for the Constitutent Assembly (23 April) provided the context, according to Commissaire Gervais, for a "contagion of lawless acts," including the work of gangs of "marauders and thieves" such as those camped in the marshy thickets near Aigues Mortes. "Forest incursions," however, captured center stage. A telling upheaval occurred in La Salvatat, a commune in the high plateau above St. Pons. Just before the polls were to close, "two or three hundred people invaded" the voting hall of the mairie. The president of the municipal council, M. de Raymond told them that he would stay open late so that they might cast their ballots. But that was not what they came for. Instead, they presented a petition for "le partage des biens communaux." When he tried to put them off, "a unanimous cry went up from the crowd: '*aro, aro*! sign it now or no one leaves this room.'" Raymond, a well-respected figure, was able calm them and lead many outside, though the demand rang out again. No violence occurred, but for several days thereafter similar incidents took place. What was happening? A number of pieces of communal land had been sold recently to private, and well-off, purchasers. This led to fears among smallholders and semilandless artisans that traditional access to public lands would be increasingly restricted. Outright sales now signaled a final and potentially devastating phase. Hence the drive for equitable division. The petition, of course, was not taken seriously, and so people took to direct action in the woods only to be arrested—and martyred.[43]

Two fundamental points arise from these details. The first is the commitment of the ordinary folk of La Salvatat to demonstrative democracy and their mistrust of the parliamentary option. Theirs was obviously a politics in the public sphere, but one at variance with acceptable standards of bourgeois representative politics and property law. Thus the second point: in steadfastly rejecting the claims of revolutionary democracy as practiced in the plebeian version of the public sphere, the largely bourgeois officials of the new Second Republic were already defining its politics in the restricted field of parliamentary, representative democracy.

The assumption by Raymond that the crowd had come to vote counterposed to the people's assumption that the revolutionary circumstances meant that a petition radically altering the law of property was in order delineates the coexistence of two distinct political realms. If voter turnout was low and/or traditional elites got elected, it did not necessarily mean that the masses were indifferent and/or deferential. They often had their own agenda and their own mechanisms for communicating it in public, one in which demonstration, the threat of concerted power, and the expression of their written will on a petition, a collective document, were deemed more meaningful than casting a ballot, an individual, isolated experience. Citizenship signified much more than the occasional act of voting for representatives. Indeed, the very concept of representation was problematic, possibly counterproductive, but at best inadequate as an expression of people's desires. Moreover, this demonstrative politics could also include (and did at La Salvatat) a voice for women and even children, thus expressing the will of the community in ways clearly not communicated through parliamentary politics.

Still, such demonstrations tended to cluster around election days. Public attention became focused on political questions by campaign posters, newspaper hawking, speeches, and endless discussions in a contentious atmosphere. The festivals and the games of vote-getting politics provided an arena of legitimacy for those ordinary people who wished to speak and act on behalf of multiple, often quotidian concerns. The actual vote might seem almost incidental in the wider public space opened by the days or weeks of electoral combat.

The newly anointed citizens of lower Languedoc did not hesitate to utilize that space. Agricultural workers, until 1848 notably quiescent, mounted a campaign of their own for higher wages in the Lunel region after the 23 April election: "the grades champêtres, trembling before assemblies that sometimes reached 400 persons, did not even prepare a report" on them. After the by-election in June, harvest workers in the Aude, many of them women and children, fomented an "uprising" against the scythe, recently required by many farmers in place of the sickle and thus reducing the work force largely to men. City workers, hard hit by unemployment in May and June, took to the streets and highways in a variety of causes. In Montpellier, distraught journeymen mounted a protest before the Hôtel de Ville and finally invaded it, making off with several dozen rifles belonging to the National Guard. Following a *fête national* in the textile town of St. Hilaire (Aude), where many cloth workers were already in the Guard, gendarmes, who had earlier arrested some weavers in a protest for the right to work, found themselves besieged by a troop of "fifty or sixty" guardsmen led by a physician and club president named Bonnafous. The *chef de logis* of the gendarmerie was injured in a confrontation. Bonnafous was arrested and jailed for six days, sealing his popularity, for he was later elected mayor. In Carcassonne four to five hundred workers on relief paraded through town demanding a raise in pay. An "invasion" of the mairie resulted in two arrests. Unpaid railway navvies combined with teamsters to tear up railroad track between Nîmes and Montpellier.

But it was the fishermen of Cette who perhaps expressed most vividly the spirit of revolutionary democracy in the early days of the Second Republic. The situation was this: for many years Sardinian fishermen had had the right to fish the waters off the French coast between Port Vendres and Aigues Mortes, but not those on the Marseille side of the Rhône; Cettois were fed up with this injustice. Thus on 11 May, they massed their boats in large numbers to prevent the landing of a Sardinian fishing vessel for supplies. To reprimands from the port authorities, their spokesman responded: "We now have a Republic. The people are sovereign and we will make justice ourselves." It quickly became clear that this was not to be the case, as the navy of their Republic escorted the Sardinian boat into port.[44]

Such incidents—and their unsuccessful outcomes—had a dual effect. On one hand, they heightened the political awareness not only of participants, but of wider segments of the population. On the other, in demonstrating that representives of the new regime seemed as unresponsive as the old to many grievances that people brought before it in the streets, they made the parliamentary option more appealing as a route to reform. This was clearly a double-edged sword. For while greater electoral participation among a population radicalized by the failure of the regime to meet demands made via demonstrative politics could translate into broader mobilization and positive legislative results, it also meant being drawn into the parliamentary game and relying on men (only) who possessed the skills specific to that type of politics: educated individuals largely of bourgeois and notable backgrounds with legal training or "political" experience. As the situation existed in May-June 1848, this did not need to be an enormous problem. Although a mistrustful and tax-shy peasantry had assured a rather conservative Constituent Assembly in its first incarnation, the nation was rife with effervescence and disappointment similar to that which occurred in the lower Languedoc, and the elections of June swept a number of radicals and socialists into office, auguring positive possibilities for the electoral route.

Above all, however, there existed a political phenomenon that *bridged* electoral politics and demostrative politics in a most elegant manner: the hundreds of clubs created everywhere in France whose membership, activity, and political clout were in full flower by early June (though they peaked earlier in Paris). Clubs served as the perfect intersection between the bourgeois public sphere and its plebeian counterpart. Speaking of the Parisian clubs, Peter Amann summed up their functions: "As long as they remained a vital force, the popular societies pursued three main goals: first, to educate and indoctrinate the lower-class electorate of Paris, whom the clubs considered their natural constituency; second, to force lower-class aspirations on the attention of the authorities—first the Provisional Government, later the National Assembly—by means of pressure ranging from petitions and delegations to mass demonstrations; third, to organize the revolutionaries' political campaign in successive Parisian elections."[45] Where the lines between these roles should be drawn is impossible to say, for in the minds of leaders and participants, all were part of the same revolutionary process: the remaking of France by "the people" who sought to bring their interests fully into the arenas of public debate and have them addressed seriously by the bourgeois notability.

Early on in lower Languedoc, activity focused on electoral preparation but was immediately linked to direct action of various sorts. Officials, even the most radical, were dismayed. The Sous-Préfet Marcel Atger of Lodève:

> The Republic will tolerate neither anarchy nor disorder: it ordains respect for the law and commends concord and fraternity to all.
>
> Honest discussion and reciprocal concessions will alone lead to the fusion of all interests. The National Assembly will soon decide the great questions of our future organization. We should await, with calmness and confidence, its *sovereign decision*.[46]

This obviously connoted a rather different concept of citizenship and a different vision of sovereignty from those voiced by the fisherman of Cette when they spoke of the "sovereign people." Atger nevertheless encouraged the clubs in Lodève and won the thanks of workers, only to find how deep— and impossible to bridge—was the class division in the city. The fabricants' intransigence caused him to resign.[47] His was an enlightened vision of harmony through rational debate that would *culminate* in electoral politics. But the bourgeoisie quickly rejected it when the clubs also became conduits for the expression of the demonstrative politics of the people. The smashing of the clubs thus became the most prominent symptom of the disease that overtook the Enlightenment political project.

While in the Hérault, as elsewhere, the 4 June elections lent some credibility to Atger's vision (the Laissac victory was touted as one of class harmony),[48] the rest of the month recorded the completion of the dragnet against those alleged conspirators of 15 May, the dismantling of the National Workshops, the institutional isolation of Louis Blanc and the Luxembourg Commission, and, in response, the great Parisian insurrection. And in its aftermath, the gulf between bourgeois republicanism and plebeian republicanism widened dramatically. The immediate popular response in lower Languedoc seemed relatively mild. "Anxiety" without violence was reported in Montpellier; Lodève saw "an assembly of two to three hundred people gather at the post office to seize dispatches as they arrived," while in Bédarieux "workers were in ferment, and placards were posted to call for revolt." Nothing came of these (and three or four other) incidents.[49] But the breach became evident from the other side. The editorial policies of *L'Indépendant*, which had so warmly welcomed working-class club formation and politicization, condemned the Parisian violence and concluded on 29 June that "with universal [sic] suffrage, freedom of the press, and the right of association, insurrection for any reason is nonsense." And how the hotheads had hurt the cause! "Order will be reestablished, but we shall pay dearly for it." Who were "we" and what was the cause? *L'Indépendant* gave its full support to Cavaignac and argued that the National Workshops had been a mistake, for the surest way "to create work" was "through business confidence and credit." Specifically, it lamented the failure to move forward with a Comptoir national d'escompte in Montpellier to replace the branch of the Banque de France that had been closed by the revolution. Although it scolded capitalists for their timidity, *L'Indépendant* attributed their hesitation to public disorder. The newspaper thus was forced to clarify its economic program, since the insurrection brought the problem of "revolutionary politics" to a head.[50] The restrictive character of the bourgeois public sphere was beginning to emerge. Workers certainly sensed it. The atmosphere of harmony began to evaporate as summer gave way to autumn.

In general, the dialectic between electoral politics and demonstrative politics continued, with the former serving as a stimulus for the latter. The municipal elections in July and August kindled antagonisms. The first documented conflict between miners and the coal company in Graissessac/ Camplong surfaced at this point. With elections approaching, a road official came with a crew from Bédarieux to widen a chemin vicinal in Graissessac. A wall belonging to Abbé Granier, a priest known for both his strict Catholicism[51] and his sympathy for the miners, was slated for removal. An angry crowd blocked the work, vowing to "kill the first person who touches M. le Curé's wall." Granier had got the mayor to join the resistance. On 27 July, the Prefect replaced the mayor with Prosper Moulinier, the works manager of the mining company. Backed by the current municipal council, the deputy of the former mayor refused to give Moulinier the keys to the Hôtel de Ville, while "large groups" heckled the appointee with "cries of *à bas*," though an understanding was later reached.[52] This incident underlines the complexity of post-June politics. Granier was considered a "legitimist," but defended the mining proletariat. The Republic took its stand with the local capitalists. But orderly republicanism had its supporters among Protestant mule drivers and the nailmakers who hated the company more than the miners did.[53] Class factors began to modulate religious antagonism in 1848, but definitive change remained in the future.

Elsewhere, the elections of 2 August crystalized antagonisms of diverse sorts. The official report for the Montpellier district listed physical confrontations in eight communes.[54] Reporting on them, the *Echo de Lodève* now attacked manhood suffrage, because it lit "a torch of discord tossed among the citizens," eliciting "the most narrow and mean-spirited of ambitions."[55] Lodève witnessed a curious combination of results: a 62 percent abstention rate, a wholesale rejection of incumbents, and the election of Club leader Noël Maisou (a weaver) and a dozen other workers, artisans, and farmers from families never associated with Lodève's power elite. Significantly, none of the paternalist petition leaders on the Montbrun bridge question was to be found among the electees from the faubourgs.[56]

The shift in Bédarieux occurred somewhat more slowly. Its municipal elections were equally marked by high levels of abstention, but the old elites held on. Hortala, a woolens worker, had lamented to the Prefect in mid-July that "the workers are so intimidated by their superiors that they dare not make the least complaint."[57] Only six republicans were elected out of twenty-three members of the council. Among these, however, was Paul Belagou, the "intrepid" leader of Bédarieux republicanism.[58] In the course of August and September, "extreme republicanism" rapidly ascended. Belagou ran for the departmental council on 27 August, and handily defeated Mayor Sicard after having made a deal with Martel-Laprade, a legitimist, thus marking "a major turning point in the political history of the canton."[59] Unfortunately, only tantalizing snippets of the process of republicanism's emergence can be gleaned from the available evidence. As early as 27 July "threats of disorder coming from the workers' club presided over by citizen Belagou" concerned Mayor Sicard.[60] Republican confidence grew with the election of Belagou, and demonstrative politics in September and October took on an even sharper class character. In response, the Prefect ordered "the immediate dispatch of two hundred troops of the line to this city,"[61] heightening tensions. On 19 October, a group of some two hundred hardy republican workers "coursed through the city in the evening crying 'down with the rats, collaborators with repression, down with the drink tax, down with the Municipal Council, down with the frock coats.'"[62] This slogan summed up an ideology tying the bourgeoisie ("frock coat" was its universal symbol in working-class parlance) and its political arm (the council) to military and fiscal oppression. We have some sense of who the radical republican leaders in Bédarieux were by virtue of an application for official recognition of their club, the Club du Château. Besides Belagou, the list included the secretary, Joseph Maillac, a salesman, three of the six republican municipal councilors, and sixteen others. Occupations are not listed, but by family name, religious composition can be estimated. Interestingly, only Antoine Ricateau and Belagou himself were from Protestant backgrounds.[63] This percentage is in fact precisely that of the city itself (in 1851 there were 9,136 Catholics and 823 Protestants in Bédarieux). We may surmise that little religious prejudice entered into montagnard politics here, nor did the kind of Protestant Jacobinism that Margadant stressed in examining Gard and Ardèche towns and villages factor out as a base of radicalism in Bédarieux. Protestants here tended to be professionals and artisans, as we have seen, while Catholics dominated the woolens-worker milieu. But intermarriage was widespread. In effect, class, not religion, seemed to be sorting out in late 1848 as the chief foundation of political radicalism and, as in Graissessac, would become more so as the Napoleonic republic emerged.[64] Bédarieux (like Graissessac) may have followed the "Cholvy rule" in that a Protestant presence heightened its Catholic sentiments, but this did not prevent Catholic workers from rejecting legitimism for the democratic and social republic, nor from joining hands with Protestants in their quest for a new life.

The elections for the presidency in December showed how far they had come. Although turnout (51 percent) indicated that electoral politics still did not yet hold sway over demonstrative (and there was an active abstentionist campaign), the results were astounding; in the city of Bédarieux, Alexandre Ledru-Rollin actually won, with 659 votes to Bonaparte's 617 (Cavaignac had but 212), thus capturing 44 percent of the vote. The rural communes of the canton, including Graissessac/Camplong, gave Bonaparte a majority, but even there the montagnard standard-bearer managed 16 percent of the vote, exactly the Hérault average, which was fifth in the nation. Bédarieux's vocation as one of the most radical cities in all France had begun. Mayor Sicard knew it and was dismayed that demonstrations ensued as soon as troops pulled out after the election. "Our city possesses now and forever the most significant elements for upheaval. . . . [It] is composed of a worker population very difficult to satisfy."[65]

Elsewhere in industrial Languedoc, to a greater or lesser degree, a similar process ensued. Movement politics both eschewed and were emboldened by electoral political activity. Local "success" was stifled by national defeat, thus stimulating a tendency to take again to the streets. Ledru did well in Pézenas (40 percent), Béziers (43 percent and 36 percent in the most popular quartiers), Clermont (28 percent), Paulhan (37 percent), Agde (31 percent), Cette (32 percent), Montpellier (25 percent but approaching half in working-class areas), several important wine bourgs (28–43 percent) and, Lodève, where he won 35 percent of the vote in the canton (though losing to Bonaparte) and 43 in the city itself.[66] But increasingly, demonstrative politics would not be tolerated. As it was driven from the public sphere, a new vision began to dominate Republican politics: that of a second revolution to create a republic that would be both democratic and social, thus abandoning hope that compromise with liberal constitutionalism and laissez-faire capitalism was possible.

Repression

The first half of 1849 saw ever-mounting political ferment as radical activism was met with repression that in turn fueled heightened radicalism.[67] In the heart of industrial Languedoc, repression led to acts of political violence without precedent in the region and with few contemporary parallels elsewhere. As the Bonapartist republic moved rapidly to regulate the public sphere on behalf of the "honnêtes gens,"[68] whatever hope there had been for genuine democracy disappeared. Whereas the north of France and selected pockets of the Midi could at least be compensated by economic progress, no such payoff occurred in industrial Languedoc. Thus, the Second Republic in the Lodévois and the upper Orb wrote the epilogue to a century and one-half of industrial growth, class formation, and democratic genesis, and the prologue to deindustrialization, political manipulation, and blighted lifeworlds.

Lodève workers radicalized rapidly during the summer of 1848. First, in August, their "worker-priests" were banned from the district. Abbé Valibouze had worked on behalf of the popular candidates for the city council and was summarily suspended by Bishop Thibault. Pierre Nougaret paid for his republicanism in the same fashion, sent off to La Caunette above Olonzac. But Nougaret kept returning to Lodève anyway, assuring his friends "that this cruel disgrace [his transfer] will in [no] way diminish the ardor of my dedication to the holy cause of the people."[69] The promised changes in urban infrastructure moved glacially. In early September, an exasperated Moïse Lyon, a slaughterhouse shareholder, complained: "what occult power thus paralyzes the execution of a project the urgency of which nobody denies?" Might it be, perhaps, due to those who seek to discredit the Republic's social mission?"[70] In general, due to regular military and National

Guard demand, Lodève's work force did not face the unemployment that ravaged textile workers elsewhere. But this did not lessen the tensions. The Enquête hearings in July exploded: "Due to long-standing disagreements between the workers and the fabricants, it was impossible to reach agreement between them . . . on several of the questions. Comprising a majority, the workers prevailed in their opinions."[71] Judge de Paix Damian prudently submitted the report intact. Lodève's demonstrative politics motivated the Cavaignac Republic to take precautionary measures. On 2 November, the Sub-prefect authorized a grant of Fr 1,541 to cover the costs of an already-constructed powder magazine, explicitly "for public security." The irony of such rapid action, when compared to work on the abattoir, surely was not lost on many Lodévois.[72]

As the December election campaign heated up, so did temperatures in the workshops. Three days before the election, young women and boys who prepared slubs for the spinners went out on strike. Although they had grievances of their own concerning the pace of work, the new Procureur, Paul Adam, quickly discovered that the "shrewd" spinners had urged the stoppage to air their own demand: pay equalization between 60 and 120-spindle loom operators. The latter received four francs, while the former got two francs fifty, on the average, per day. Though paid the same piece rates and requiring similar skills, the small loom spinners had to push even harder to make much less. The hierarchy of work ran from slubbing to small machine to large, and therefore considerable camaraderie existed between workers at the first levels, especially since a number of the 60-spindle jenny operators were women recruited from among the slubbers. But men working the large looms also supported the strike, understanding the wage-drag created by the other category of spinner. The obvious solution was expanded investment in larger equipment by the fabricants (the current ratio was about fifty-fifty), but of course the workers demanded higher pay for the jenny spinners. The upshot, however, was repression: a dozen women were arrested for illegal coalition and six received jail sentences.[73]

This blunt and uncompromising approach to popular collective action may have found favor with his superiors, but Paul Adam shocked Lodève workers, who routinely expected officials to make some effort to find compromises with their bosses. But those who heard his installation address on election eve should have known better. Seeing revolution as a "social crisis" rather than a time of creation, Adam assailed those "subversive and evil doctrines [that] produce . . . the worst passions . . . of the heart: envy, which engenders hatred; illegitimate ambition, which gives birth to envy and impotence." The role of the magistrate was not just to "keep peace in the streets, but to reestablish moral and intellectual order. . . . Defender of property and the family and . . . protector of individuals, he guarantees to all liberty and security, inseparable one from the other." The law, he swore, would "retake its force." Finally, as if searching for yet one more way to outrage Lodève's working people, he condemned strikes, noting that "freedom of work . . . exists as much for the masters as for the workers."[74]

Adam was the son of a small proprietor and the brother of a pharmacist from the *bourgade* of Illiers, near Chartres. A figure from Balzac (or Simenon), at thirty-three he was unmarried, with a widowed mother "of mediocre fortune" to support, a lawyer who had done well in school only to fail in a competition for a position in Roman Law at Paris. He owed his career to a relative on the Cour de Cassation. The most generous thing that his superior could say about him was that he was "laborious," someone who "liked to take difficulties head on, particularly those that aroused political passions."[75]

Perhaps no official could have been less suitably placed than this rigid, narrow northerner. Lodève's history of class violence, its workers' passionate embrace of the Revolution, and the political juices excited by the election and subsequent repression placed him in a milieu that he neither understood nor cared to understand. Although radical political consciousness had already reached a high level in the area, during the winter of 1848–49, it went much farther—every bourg and village seemed infected. Both grain and wine harvests had been mediocre and, except for army production (but even that was beginning to decline in view of the many dissolutions of local and regional National Guard units),[76] the textile crisis deepened, and propagandists proliferated everywhere, despite growing legal restrictions on political activity. Villages that had voted overwhelmingly for Bonaparte suddenly became objects of concern. For example, poor peasants of remote Ceilhès, urged on by two "socialist agents," "repossessed" former communal lands that had been sold cheap to a few local notables in 1816. Adam saw to their return, but Ceilhès would give the montagnard list strong support in the 13 May, 1849 elections.[77] Small towns and villages where woolens outworking and vine-tending combined proved to be fertile ground for montagnard cultivation. For example, Prémian and St. Etienne, Orb villages that worked for Bédarieux and had mills of their own, voted overwhelmingly for the left.[78] Such gains were hard won, for even before the December election, the Club du Château of Bédarieux was shaken by the arrest of Paul Belagou under the charge of "gross violation of public morality, exciting disorder, insults to several honorable men." He was still in jail when the commissaire de police reported on 23 January 1849 that, happily, the "dispersed" character of political activity in Bédarieux made it impossible for radicals there to affiliate with *La Solidarité républicaine*, the montagnard national network aimed at the rural masses.[79]

The tensions in the expanding world of the left seen in the Orb valley were typical of the Hérault generally. The Eighth Army commander felt troops were needed everywhere "in this country where anything, a quarrel between madcaps, a fight between drunks, often leads to a political affair, the consequences of which have no relationship to the point of departure."[80] The tinderbox was particularly dry in the Lodévois, where propagandists such as Moïse Lyon tirelessly worked their region. Lyon was a traveling yard-goods merchant, born and raised in Clermont and, since the early 1840s, a resident of Lodève. Married, with young family, he was one of the few Jews living in this part of the Hérault, though religion seemed unimportant to him. Lyon, and others, did their work well, for by the time of Adam's arrival in the district, a corridor of démoc-soc strongholds had been established, stretching from Soubès in the north to Paulhan in the south, shading from wool-dominant to wine-dominant economies, but all encompassing a mixture of both. It was a classic setting for the urban-rural nexus established by the montagnard movement.[81]

Lodève and Clermont were the principal centers. In a long report dated 18 January 1849, L. Raynaud, the new commissaire de police, seemed bemused by the fact that Lodève's workers, although "tied to family and place" and currently "fully employed," should be so susceptible to "agitation" by preachers of "violence and sedition" who seek to bring "power and wealth . . . to the working class." The *Club de Lodève* was a "school of disorder where the chiefs of riot and coalition can come to learn and carry thereafter the fruit of these lessons into the workshops." The Club brought together various formations of earlier 1848, and Raynaud's list of twenty-two leaders included many of the names encountered in radical and trade-union activity in the past and at least eight who would be arrested after the coup d'état. It possessed a "secret society" component connected to "Paris, Lyon, Montpellier, and so forth." Most important, "cafés, inns, and cabarets," like so many "branches" of the club, "are every evening full of workers. . . ."[82] Adam faced a formidable opposition.

On 31 January, the order abolishing unauthorized political organizations arrived in Lodève. The next morning the new Sub-prefect, N. Alazard, upon consultation with Adam, rejected the Club's application for authorization. At dusk, in a hall in the hamlet of Soulatges on the outskirts of town, some sixty members met anyway and were surprised by police around 8 P.M. Efforts to disperse the meeting met with physical resistance. The police called for help from the Lodève National Guard, which gave "the worst example of indiscipline and insubordination." A riot ensued outside the hall and soon spread into town. Although no one was seriously injured, six arrests were made, and the upheaval wound down around midnight. Alazard the next day requested that the garrison of troops of the line stationed in the city be increased by 50 to 144 men. On the morning of the trial of those arrested, 13 February, *bonnets rouges* appeared on trees of liberty in Lodève, Soubès, Gignac, and St. Etienne de Gourgas, as well as in Avène and Truscas, up-country villages that had long sent migrants to Lodève. The jury acquitted all six.[83]

The next big worry was what to do about 24 February, the first anniversary of the Second Republic. Alazard recommended skipping any official celebration and even "adjourned" a flag ceremony involving the National Guard scheduled for the sixteenth "to avoid any occasion that might stir up trouble." He had also got wind of a "Socialist Banquet" planned for the 24th and requested another 50 troops to prevent "a demonstration." To salt the wounds, somebody, probably legitimists, cut down Lodève's Liberty Tree in the wee hours of the 20th. As it turned out, the banquet—

well-attended—took place without incident. Commissaire Raynaud even went.

Things did not turn out so happily in Clermont. There, authorities allowed an official ceremony, with a mass, no less, to occur. This naturally challenged the imagination of the montagnards, whose club activity and political organization had equaled or bettered Lodève's. All groups were officially dissolved, as was the entire National Guard of the city. As in Lodève, a small garrison was in place. Nevertheless, on the 24th, some one hundred démoc-soc demonstrators first went to the guard's ex-commandant's house and picked up the battalion flag and paraded through the official city, donning red cocardes, and then headed for church, making a noisy entrance. Paul Adam described the scene: "The honorable citizens were insulted and jostled. Cries of 'Vive la République démocratique et sociale! Vive Ledru-Rollin!' had accompanied these gestures, and I found in the local authorities either weakness and foolishness or connivance and complicity. I was surrounded by a crowd of respectable and notable people who told me that their position is no longer tenable and that a hundred *miserables* agitate and cause trouble incessantly." Adam complied by making several arrests and taking his prisoners back to Lodève.

The young magistrate had full support all the way up the line. Having held four men in jail for nearly a month, he let them go after their bail was met. Upon receiving this information from Procureur Général A. Gilardin, Léon Faucher himself berated Odilon Barrot, the Justice Minister, for having allowed the release to occur, and so came the word down the chain of command. Well, said Gilardin in a measured response, it *is* the "gist of the law" to free people charged with a *délit de coalition* if bail is met. "Individual liberty" rather demands it. But he did understand the Minister's concern: the "drawback" is that "the influence of the persons [probably Moïse Lyon] who advanced the bail money naturally increases in a harmful manner; such an act of patronage elevates confidence in their party." Next time, he implied, greater circumspection will be practiced.[84] This small incident serves as a metaphor for the structure and ideology of the Bonapartist repression: the law, already stringent, was increasingly bent to suit the purposes of the state in its defense of the "respectable and notable."

Adam thus undertook an uncompromising course. His next case was a complicated conflict that arose in Paulhan around the anniversary issue. This wine bourg of 1500 people had been ignored by previous authorities, but Adam suspected that because of its central location between Montpellier, Lodève, Bédarieux, Pézènas, and Béziers, it might well be serving as a center of communications for the now illegal *Solidarité républicaine* and other "red" groups. César Azémar had founded a socialist monthly called *Le Peuple* there, and its government, Adam wrote, was "une petite république de '93." A majority of its municipal councillors were agricultural laborers who showed up at meetings "with clubs, threatening all those who are not with them." The "notables and the rich" were afraid to walk the streets at night. Montagnards paraded after club meetings offering "long lives" to "Raspail,

Barbès, Blanqui, Proudhon, Ledru-Rollin, and the Guillotine," followed by a chorus of "Down with God and the rich." Some hearsay no doubt informed Adam's perception, but it was clear that this was an uncontroled left-wing town.

His crackdown followed a series of incidents from Carnival (17–20 February) to the anniversary, with a range of crimes from costumes looking like phrygian caps (now banned) to harassment and assault of political opponents. In mid-March, Adam led an armed force to round up several Paulhan montagnard leaders, perhaps motivated by a report of secret society missions from Lyon. Five, finally, were jailed. The town was invested with a permanent force of gendarmes whom he authorized to make house-to-house searches. In effect, martial law was established: "Montagnards have been forbidden to meet, and we have made it clear to *ces Messieurs* that their reign has come to an end."[85] When the leaders were finally tried in Lodève on 18 April, two were sentenced to seven months, two to five, and one found not guilty.[86]

The spectacle of this "show trial" undoubtedly had its effects in Lodève. Certainly montagnard leadership there was mortified to see their friends and comrades crushed so brutally. But Lodévois were next in line. On 18 March, Mayor Jourdan posted a placard banning all "tumultuous songs, outcries, and assemblies in the streets and other public places." Reading it, several activists took to the workshops to spread the news and plan a response. It occurred the following day—Sunday—as 200 "former clubistes" gathered in their old meeting hall. Adam immediately called out a contingent of fifteen troops to join gendarmes converging on the hall. The Guard was not called. When the militants emerged, they were entreated by the armed force to disperse. Insults flew, then fists, and swords were drawn. In the melee, one of the soldiers was beaten to the ground and took a boot heel to the eye. The "rioters" then took flight, heading home without pursuit. Eight men were finally arrested. Adam concluded his report: "Since the closing of the club, its former members have seized every opportunity to appear united in public," including funerals and other ordinary events. "Repression will not be long in coming and I hope it will be severe: there is need of it."[87] As the various trials ensued in April, Adam called in more troops and responded to any incident instantaneously. Thus Abbé Nougaret, after giving a speech, was formally escorted from the city, and Alazard implored his superior to tell Bishop Thibault to keep him away given "all the trouble he causes."[88]

Then came the May elections. The démoc-soc effort, despite nationwide repression similar to that in the Lodévois, was remarkable. Although it came nowhere close to capturing a majority and although the ill-conceived Parisian rising in June decapitated the movement, the efflorescence of a plebeian vision of the good society, of a democratic and socialist republic in which humane and interactive relationships among people would prevail, seems breathtaking in retrospect. And so in Lodève and Bédarieux, in Clermont and Paulhan—as well as countless other cities, towns, and villages where

working people defended their right to be human—the left won. The liste
de Pézenas (Jacques Brives, Ledru-Rollin, Alfred Sabatier de Pézenas,
Ronzier-Joly, Lombard, Medecin, Marcel Atger, Joseph Pellet and César
Azémar of Paulhan) crushed both right and center. Their totals in Lodève,
where the turnout this time was 76 percent, ranged from 1,611 for Pellet,
locally unknown (thus showing considerable "party" discipline) to 1,701 for
Brives. The "moderates," led by Michel Chevalier, gathered from 425 to 900
votes, while the right won 265 to 900 (Charamaule). In total, the left had a
remarkable (61 percent) majority. Clermont and Bédarieux followed suit. In
Paulhan, smashed as its left was, the race was closer, but the left list prevailed.[89]
In the department, which the left hardly swept, two candidates, Brives and
Ledru-Rollin, were elected along with six official candidates.

Clearly Adam—and all the Hérault officialdom—had failed. It is not
clear precisely what occurred as results were announced in the red cities,
for it was not reported, but unquestionably a certain sense of satisfaction
had to exist.

On the evening of 19 May, a point at which electoral victory locally
and defeat nationwide would have been known, groups of young people
marched through the streets of Lodève singing "patriotic songs" and making a great deal of noise. Adam left his house near St. Fulcran square a little
after ten, rounded up two gendarmes, and caught up with a crowd of rev-
elers on a neighboring street. Adam ordered them to disperse and they
refused. He then decided to go for reinforcements at the Mairie, sending
the two gendarmes to the Post Office where they would meet the others.
Alone, "M. Adam entered the Broussonnelle Square by the rue du Parc. . . .
At this moment, an assassin, lying in wait in one of the two pockets in the
rue du Parc near the Square, discharged a firearm at M. le Procureur de la
République at a distance of ten to twelve paces. The explosion was heard
throughout the neighborhood. Shot from behind, in the middle of the back,
he was heard to cry out: 'au secours, au secours, je suis mort.' A pool of
blood spread quickly beneath the still body."[90]

The officers, joined by Commissaire Raynaud, rushed back to the
square, but saw no one run away. It was soon determined that a hunting
shotgun was the murder weapon. Two hundred more troops were immediately called to town, and as dawn broke, Lodève was placed under martial law. Systematic house-to-house searches began.

The commissaire reflected universal opinion when he identified the
cause of the attack: "it is to be found in the furor of political passions." In
his report of 22 May, he reflected on the past six months of Adam's tenure,
noting that he "exercised his functions in the firmest, most resolute manner. This brought him implacable enmity. And it is said that other victims
are targeted, [including] the investigating judge and the sous-préfet."
Lodève had been "profoundly overtaken by the contagion of socialist ideas,"
made obvious by the election results. Raynaud therefore assumed that the
killer came from among "the men of the secret societies or the clubs, where
political fanaticism so easily combines with a proclivity toward vengeance."

Now it so happened that that very day, one of the leaders of the Club, Didier Balp, an insurance agent, had been paroled from prison for his involvement in the 19 February affair. His brother Hippolyte, a pareur, under indictment for the same offense, had long eluded police. And indeed it was a "party" for Didier in a country house called the "arch-deaconry" that began the march on the fateful night. Didier Balp lived near the Broussonnelle Square and could have reached the spot easily by an alleyway. *And* police found a two-barreled shotgun at his home (two days later), one barrel of which had "recently" been fired. Never mind that he had gone hunting —or so he said—the morning after the killing. Didier was arrested and so too was his brother, who was located in the house-to-house search of the area. They were charged with the crime and taken to jail in Montpellier.

Adam's funeral ceremony in Lodève, with Procureur Gilardin delivering the eulogy, drew few mourners from the people. Meanwhile, one of the Lodève's mutual aid societies went ahead with its annual festival as planned. Gilardin reported later that "ill-concealed signs of triumph were evident. [A]ny number of people saw . . . blood spilled for politics as a kind of propitiation. A workers' society . . . sang the Marseillaise on the very spot where M. le Procureur had been killed!" Dismayed at the "savage joy" expressed, he wondered "how *moeurs françaises*. . . could have been so altered."[91] And indeed the signs of quiet solidarity (the procureur called it "the terror of public opinion") were everywhere. No one would testify about the night of the murder, and prosecutors had to admit that all their evidence against the Balps was circumstantial. The murderer, it was thought, had tried to fool the investigators into thinking that he had been hurt by the shot's recoil and left a trail of "blood"—thought to be red dye but it was washed away by rain before it could be analyzed—leading out of the city. "No means to deceive justice and opinion is neglected," said Gilardin, who personally spent six days in Lodève investigating. "Clearly people are acting on behalf of the killer and have cultivated a kind of *solidarité du crime*."[92] He advised letting the matter rest for a while, replacing the police chief with someone more in touch with "what is being said in the factories," and creating a secret fund to finance spies.

Although a spy sent in from Paris (did he know Occitan?) was found out and nearly killed, this plan finally bore some fruit. Gilardin was in fact replaced by a more reliable Bonapartist career man, A. Sénéca; whether this case had anything to do with it is unknown. By August, some evidence against the Balps had been assembled. The spy had learned from Curé Beaupillier that a street sweeper, Molinier, had confessed to him that he witnessed the crime: two men were involved, and the one who did not shoot checked the body to make sure Adam was dead. Was it the Balps? Molinier dared not say. Moreover, he would not testify nor of course would Beaupillier because of the confidentiality of the confession. Also one of the convives at Balp's release party, Joseph Guiral, a clockmaker, city-councilman, and leader of the Club, had loosened his tongue over drinks with the *mouchard*. Guiral allegedly said that the affaire was planned at the banquet and that Balp *aîné* (Hippolyte) had actually done the shooting, showing him the gun (and two pistols, just in case!) before Adam came out. So the government moved: at 4 A.M. on 27 August, police agents simultaneously arrested nine of the banqueteers (the Balps were still in jail). They were questioned for two days, and all, especially Guiral, denied all the allegations of the spy. Moreover, Hippolyte Balp, who was wanted at the time for the risings of February 1 and 19, said that he would have to be crazy to come to town with the group, so he stayed at the country place; the proprietor there provided his alibi. He later snuck home (after 1:30) to get his gun to go hunting next morning. All nine joined the Balps in the maison d'arrêt in Montpellier.[93]

On 14 September, the "very reluctant" mouchard (whose name is never given) was brought to Montpellier to confront Guiral. The latter "denied all with great assurance," wrote Sénéca, who witnessed the whole interrogation. Moreover, more people who watched or participated in the parade had come forward to testify that they had not seen Hippolyte Balp in town that night. Sénéca concluded: "I regret most deeply, M. le garde des Sceaux, that all efforts of justice have failed up to this point to discover with certainty the odious author . . . of a crime that has moved all France"; nonetheless, he felt he had to seek an indictment. And, with the same grinding inevitability that led to the assassination, the Chambre d'Accusation (the French equivalent of a grand jury) determined, on 8 October 1849, that there was "insufficient evidence to hold the prisoners and that all must be put at liberty." Although no police report tells us about it, one can imagine the reaction in working-class Lodève.[94]

There was a final possibility—to get Molinier to talk. Officially, justice did not even know his name. The only path was through the curé Beaupillier. Finally, after months and months of further investigation that led to one dead end after another, an exasperated Sénéca asked for authorization from his new boss, Eugène Rouher, whose career of quietly disdaining Languedoc —and the law—was just beginning, to allow him to "try to convince the bishop to take the necessary steps to obtain from the curé precious indications." Rouher's response: go right ahead. As it turned out, nothing came of this either.[95] And while the Balps and all the others would be special targets after the coup d'état, the assassination of Paul Adam remained an unsolved mystery. The democratic socialist working class of Lodève had proved its solidarity, had manifested its revolutionary consciousness *in extremis*.

And it paid dearly for it, not only under the Second Republic, but in the longer run: Rouher and his cohort of the Second Empire would not forget that the plebeian world of Lodève had been out of control, that for a brief moment it cemented itself in unity to proclaim the justice of the ultimate revolutionary act, the execution of the oppressor.[96]

The action of the state, however, could not be in doubt. Gravely concerned about not only Lodève but the rash of demonstrations and other indications of the power of a left more and more deeply rooted in the popular classes of town and country,[97] it responded with armed force. Garrisons were created or strengthened everywhere. In Lodève, 500 troops of the line were now in permanent residence.

This occupation became the central focus of demonstrative politics over the next two years, but at the same time it is clear that démoc-soc leaders there remained in contact with electoral and secret society networks throughout France. As elsewhere, the mutual aid societies became legal mechanisms for organizing political activity and were regularly investigated. "Seditious cries," "tapages nocturnes," "disorders," "charivaris," and "outrages against soldiers" punctuate the logs of the Prefecture. One example suffices to reveal the level of tension always just under the surface. On 30 June 1850, a child harassed a dog belonging to an officer of the detachment, a Lt. Veuillot, a northerner who likely spoke only French. He chased the boy into a stable and gave him a whipping. Another boy tried to stop the lieutenant and was cuffed as well. Then came the people's response: "Workers were on their way to the shops" and a number of them stopped and "defended the children," chasing the officer away. He soon returned with several of his soldiers, but the police commissioner had also arrived and managed to forestall violence. The officer was suspended for fifteen days by his superior. The sub-prefect thought they were lucky that this occurred in the daytime. This incident came on the heels of a much more serious confrontation in April in which stones were hailed on the troops. During the later trial of several attackers, a large crowd successfully intimidated the jury decision. The acquittal was finally overruled, but not before much nervous judicial correspondence about the impact had been exchanged. Lodève was a tinderbox and remained so.[98]

Things remained stable economically, though several workplace conflicts occurred. On 18 June 1850, fifty power-loom weavers, "tisseurs," urged on by "agitators," walked out for higher wages. There are no details about this tantalizing incident, because they were quickly mollified. But the interface between workshop grievances and politics is fairly clear even from this brief report. Later in the year, an unemployed worker threatened a fabricant with death if he did not call him back from a layoff.[99]

It is appropriate to close the tale of the Second Republic at Lodève with this incident. For all the brave class struggle and all the judicial and military oppression that can be recorded, the life line of the city and of all industrial Languedoc was the vigor of the woolens industry, with defense contracts remaining the catalyst of its peculiar chemistry. And this small notice of a desperate act documents a reality that would soon engulf the entire region: Languedoc's dosage of its catalytic elixir was being reduced—not by much, but it was an omen. Although no one mentioned it, Lodève's prominent, indeed unique, place on the radical map of France no doubt crossed the minds of the War and Interior officials responsible for army orders. The *lots* of 1851 were halved in size, although the number of lots was doubled from twelve to twenty-four. But, despite the Minister of War's protest that nothing had changed, Lodève's share was raised from five lots to only nine, amounting to a production decrease of 20 percent.[100] Moreover, Lodève had already received a shock when a new and thoroughly modernized spinning company, Griolet and Mazade, closed down in February 1850.[101] The inexorable process of decline had begun. Plebeian Lodève's dramatic and concerted challenge to bourgeois dominance had unquestionably something to do with it.

Across the Escandorgue a similar kettle was boiling. Thanks to Ted Margadant, the coming crisis in Bédarieux has become rather famous, and we may be brief.[102] After the abolition of the clubs in January 1849, Bédarieux radicals transformed the Société de secours St. Paul into a démoc-soc campaign organization. Headed by an old and revered (and deaf) artisan named Gaston, the notability had no idea of its new purposes, nor, went the story, did Gaston. Throughout 1849, "socialism was discussed at every meeting." Late in the year, several alarming public demonstrations of démoc-soc sentiment surfaced, including calls to violence.[103] Finally on 14 February 1850, the gendarme commandant, Liotard (also spelled Léotard), led a raid on the mutual society. "When the agents arrived in the hall," he wrote, "they noted that the meeting was presided over by the famous Maillac, Joseph, salesman, and secretary of the former club, which was headed then by the intrepid Belagou, Paul." To his dismay, since the meeting itself seemed to be about problems of aid to members and discussions of Bédarieux's on-going economic crisis, no action was taken.[104]

As in Lodève, a quiet period ensued in later 1850; but in the spring, political juices flowed again as nocturnal meetings of the "parti rouge" were reported in March, and a "secret society" assembly of some 150, representing a "committed" left of 600, supposedly declared itself ready to "rise up." Seditious songs were sung in cabarets and a funeral mass was postponed for fear of upheaval.[105] Also noteworthy was the growing anticlerical tone of the occasional montagnard pronouncements that were monitored. And in July 1851, a cross at an intersection was overturned. Police reported that colporteurs of republican propaganda found easy haven in Bédarieux. In July a huge cortege accompanied the body of socialist leader Paul Miquel, a migrant from Clermont and a member of the mutual society of the spinners.[106]

All of this transpired without violence or arrests, and thus the parti rouge kept its organization, through the mutuels, intact. The sub-prefect in Bèziers repeatedly pressed the municipality to authorize the installation of a garrison, like the Lodévois towns, but the municipal council, led by Belagou, repeatedly rejected it. In September, the mayor, who wanted troops, stepped aside due to public outcry, and Belagou, as the leading council vote getter, became acting mayor, thus further frustrating the Bonapartists' plans for a crackdown. Although arrangements were made for a compromise mayor by early November 1851, other events, responding to a growing nationwide fear of the full establishment of Louis-Napoleon's authority, heightened political tensions dramatically. A huge turnout of workers, some fifteen

hundred strong, accompanied the funeral of a baker, who, although a legitimist, had long opposed current hunting laws. The crowd protested recent
arrests made by gendarmes of citizens violating these laws, an ominous sign
in view of the cries that arose on the explosive night of 4 December. Then
on 11 November, the Protestant socialist Paul Ricateau, a longtime ally of
Belagou, was buried, again with hue and cry against the gendarmerie. Alexandre Vernazobres-Lavit, a "liberal" now in the mayor's seat, vowed to create
a barracks for 200 troops after the tensions of that day. But it was too late.

Word of the coup d'état reached Bédarieux on 3 December, but unlike
in Béziers and Pézenas, no action was taken immediately. Only late the
following afternoon did a mass of workers leave their shops as if on cue and
march, unarmed, on the Mairie to demand the installation of a "revolutionary" government. The gendarmerie, the only armed force in town, had
moved to the mayor's headquarters; initially Vernazobres-Lavit, a man of
considerable stature and backed by the handful of gendarmes with guns
cocked, was able to convince the popular forces to disperse. But soon they
reassembled, *armed*. Belagou, it turned out, was out of town on a business
trip, and thus two relatively inexperienced figures (many of the other leaders having recently died), Pierre Borinal, a clockmaker, and Victor Caux,
stepped forward to call for a revolutionary government. To the wonder-
ment of all, the gendarmes had, under orders from Vernazobres, retired to
their caserne on the right bank of the Orb across from the heart of the city.
The mairie fell without a shot. The République rouge de Bédarieux began
its brief existence. The password in town was "Montagne."

But then, who knows from where, came the word that a worker had
been killed by the gendarmes. Suddenly, all the anxiety and hatred of
decades, heightened so greatly in the past three years when fear succeeded
hope, exploded in a fury that would shake all France. Carrying torches into
the chill night, the crowd, urged on by municipal councillor Jean Mercadier,
surged across the bridge, hunting rifles in hand, and simply devastated the
caserne. They set fire to it, and as the hapless policemen fled and tried to
hide in nearby buildings, they were gunned down. Before being executed,
Lamm, an Alsatian, received this indictment: "So coquin, you're the one
who fined us for hunting." The gendarmes' families were shot at as well,
and one worker, who sought to help one of the more sympathetic gendarmes, was mistaken for the enemy and killed. The smoldering bodies of
the three gendarmes who died were left in the street. Liotard, the hated
brigadier, came in for a special revenge. Several men urinated on his corpse
"to cool him off"; later in the night, someone returned and castrated this
symbol of the state's unyielding power.

There was no repentance the following day. One worker, Etienne
Cabrol, *had* been killed in the battle and Combes was the one shot mistak-
enly by the insurgents. Both received hero's funerals (2,000 came out for
Cabrol), while the three gendarmes, outsiders all, were buried quietly with
few in attendance.

The main business of the fifth was the establishment of a new government. Emile Appolis has provided a thorough analysis of the acts of Bédarieux's "Commune."[107] The workers of the city really did take over. They first sought to reassure the rich that the violence was over. Nevertheless, they thought immediately about means of income redistribution. Access to marriage contracts and inheritance tax records in the Mairie stimulated various plans to reorient these sources of ready wealth to "necessities." One worker proposed that a childless fabricant's assets be turned over to the children of his employees. Another proposed that Sicard's wife's château be given to his workers, because it "belongs to us, for it is we who have bought it for her, we will set her right." On the 6th, the new government convoked a meeting with fabricants about "wage augmentations." Certainly a sense of social justice—rather specific in its character—dominated the people's minds, if not clear notions of socialist reorganization. The acts carried out by the provisional government, though few, showed a similar spirit: generosity and specificity. Thus, one of the first proclamations was to order bakers to bring bread to the mairie for distribution to the needy, especially those who had "suffered" for "the revolution." But also the maintenance of order was essential. One decree regreted the loss of life the previous day and called for an end to further attacks on property: "Mort au voleurs." Another also guaranteed respect for the family and religion. But make no mistake: the main proclamation was the following.

> Citizens:
> Be not afraid; under the government of the sovereign people each will find the safeguard of all interests, all rights, all liberties.
> The people, in whom repose all powers, will be worthy of its responsibility and of its mission, and its efforts will make certain that no further accident shall occur.
> Citizens, an era, a new era has arrived.
>
> Vive la République
(Signed) Le Peuple[108]

In these simple words, the decades of working people's struggles for a place in the public sphere seemed summarized. Let there be a chance for all to participate, let the universal claims of the enlightenment tradition come to realization. Socialism meant, essentially, fairness in the economic realm. Gendarmes might die, but they represented an evil past. The fabricants must pay—literally—for what they have taken unjustly by the sweat of their workers' brows, but there is a place for them and their "interests" in the new society.

This democratic moment lasted but five days. On 10 December, General de Rostolan entered the city at the head of his conquering army. Much of the Hérault had already fallen and Bédarieux capitulated without a shot. One of the main reasons was that most of its workers were busy at work in their factories and workshops.

The aftermath of the resistance needs no rehearsing. The revenge of the state was thorough and uncompromising. Bédarieux, along with Béziers and several smaller towns and villages, was in a tiny minority of places where revolutionary governments were actually established. Virtually everywhere that garrisons existed saw little or paltry efforts at resistance—thus, in the Lodévois, though meetings occurred, few shots were fired. Nevertheless, arrests were rampant, and the new, illegal state made certain that social-democratic republicanism was purged from the land. Those arrested (including contumacious), 166 from Bédarieux, 77 from Lodève, 26 from Clermont and the thousands upon thousands of others across Languedoc (2,663 in Hérault alone), the Midi, all France, were just ordinary people reflecting the lower orders of their locales. Thus 80 percent in the three woolens cites at the core of industrial Languedoc were working class, 63 percent from the woolens industry. Most of the rest were peasants. Those who were neither, the Lyons and the Atgers, the Mercadiers and the Bélagous (though he was not prosecuted), were in touch with another version of the bourgeois public sphere than the one that had prevailed—a world where "bourgeois" connected with its original meaning, where it merged with "commune" and "citoyen" and "civil" in the struggle against feudal tyranny and obscurantism.

But in official France and the new bureaucratic, deformed public sphere, their vision was not forgotten. Bédarieux became a symbol of the evil pathways of democracy. The editor of the *Echo* (now also *de Bédarieux, Clermont et Gignac*, Henri Grillères, provided copy for its detractors when he wrote on 11 January 1852:

> One cannot go to Bédarieux without returning with a saddened soul. The agony of three days spent in anxiety and the cruelest apprehension [he is here speaking for the *honnêtes gens*], the multitude mistress [note gender usage here] of the city at all points, flames glowing in the faubourg, the pavement red with blood, infinite horrors of which a French pen dare not write, a mairie transformed into a *château-fort comme au temps du moyen age*, projects of the most appalling sort made public, above all the sounds of arms and the cries of insurgents: such was for several days the aspect of Bédarieux, of this city, so industrious, so proud of its renown, whose glory and advantages were shared so peacefully between the workers and the masters.[109]

II

DEINDUSTRIALIZATION, 1851–1920

As the smoke cleared after the horrors of those December days, it became increasingly evident that the terms of the relationship between Paris and the rebellious areas of Languedoc had changed dramatically. Whereas before there had been no particular shortcoming on which to hang unfavorable governmental policy, under the Second Empire the specter of 1851 set the region apart. Louis Napoleon had to search long and hard for loyal supporters, and official correspondence revealed an arms-length mentality.[1]

In Languedoc, the general trends may be easily discerned. Bédarieux never recovered its former economic vitality. One may cite certain difficulties in the late 1840s, but the rapid turnaround after the coup d'état places popular resistance to oppression at the root of its economic decline. Lodève, as usual, stolidly plugged on because of its competence at making sturdy cloth and cajoling governments. But the road was now rougher, and Sedan and low-wage towns like Châteauroux, peaceful islets in 1851, were attracting the attention of the Emperor's men in the provisioning business. And then there was poor Montpellier and its would-be port at Cette. Whatever promise existed in the 1840s evaporated. Zoë Granier went bankrupt in 1851 (although he resurfaced later)—a staggering event that had reverberations across the financial landscape. The ball quickly moved to Lyon's court, and its emergence as the banking capital of the south was assured; the Crédit Lyonnais was established in this atmosphere.[2] What a magnificent dream! Montpellier-Cette, a great metropolis that would not be.

What occurred instead was the triumph of the Paris-Lyon-Méditerranée railroad conglomerate (PLM), of Parisian capital, with its loyal vassals at

Nîmes, Alais, and Marseille—the Rhône valley yoyo—obediently, and profitably, taking the field in full battle array. But the *maudits* of the Hérault did not simply capitulate. Despite the previous setbacks and the new disasters, it still might have been possible to bounce back. Two possibilities held great promise: the development of the coal field at Graissessac, which might fuel commercial and military steamboats, as well as the engines increasingly needed in the textile centers; and the creation of a second major Parisian rail connection originating in Montpellier-Cette, traversing the Hérault, and serving its industrial cities, especially Lodève. A positive resolution of these two great questions preoccupied the progressive minds in the Languedoc business world throughout the Second Empire. They found themselves locked in battle not only with the knights of the Rhône Valley but the *rois de Paris* themselves, the great financial empire of the Rothschilds and their ubiquitous alliance systems within the government. Not surprisingly, despite a powerful alliance of their own with the brilliant (and mercurial) Pereire brothers, they lost.

As seems universally the case, regions facing deindustrialization play out their last act largely on the political stage. The Languedoc situation, the first in the history of industrial capitalism, is illuminating. The central concern of the French state in the months following the coup d'état was to consolidate its political authority. The new Prefect in the Hérault, Durand St. Amand, summed things up neatly in his report to Interior Minister Fialin de Persigny, late in 1852: "The extreme party, whose power had become formidable under the influence of a constitution that promoted excess, has today been crushed by the force of authority."[3] These early reports provide remarkable documentation of a style of rule new to European politics. Unable to retain power under the aegis of representative government with either highly restricted suffrage and a constitutional monarch or manhood suffrage and a republic, the increasingly bourgeois-dominated notability of France opted for naked physical force, which did indeed "crush the extreme party." The relative weakness of the French bourgeoisie in face of both the popular classes and the older elites made force an inviting avenue; the nephew of Napoleon certainly had nothing against it either, and his prefects happily resorted to it. But there was also the carrot, the promise of the extinction of poverty through cheap credit for the micropeasant, mutual aid, and cooperatives. Above all, however, the Empire meant peace with a small *p*: the calm pursuit of profitable enterprise with strong state encouragement. What the French bourgeoisie achieved with the advent of Napoleon III was a situation of *dominio*, as Gramsci would put it, a rather precarious authority rooted in military might, not hegemonic control.[4] Many of them would abandon the Emperor as their economic and social power became more secure—ironically due in large measure to his policies—calling for direct political representation of their interests.[5]

The tragedy for lower Languedoc, however, was that while the bourgeoisie rallied, they got little for their loyalty, somehow remaining sullied by an experience of radicalism that they may have caused, but that they certainly disavowed. Economic growth rates in France during the 1850s were as high as in any decade until after World War II, but the Hérault did not share in it. Although Prefectoral reports indicate brief periods of hope, the situation of the woolens industry, despite Armand Audiganne's optimism about the ongoing potential of the region, had moved in fits and starts. The crisis of 1858 capped off a decade of disappointment. It came at a particularly tragic moment. Revival seemed in store. Lodève was diversifying beyond military cloth. Bédarieux was finding new markets in the Mediterranean and regaining domestic customers. But by mid-1859, with the momentary exception of Lodève, which had new orders from both the Piedmontese and French armies due to Louis Napoleon's new adventure in Italy, the woolens industry was again in deep trouble. As if to symbolize the entire decade, thirty-seven-year-old Pierre Eugène Nougaret, director of the Banque Nougaret et Cie of Montpellier, which had many accounts in the woolens district, committed suicide because of his "embarras financier."[6]

Yet the social impact of the troubled era does not appear to have been severe. In the Lodévois and Bédarieux, owners reduced hours and laid off as few workers as possible without shutting down. The mutual aid program had experienced a "progressive extension" in the 1850s, and workers found alternative employment in public works, especially the construction of local roads and the railroad. Overall, officials congratulated themselves that they had survived the decade in one of the nation's most rebellious regions despite important economic difficulties. They knew that the "parti socialiste" was still out there, especially as more and more amnestied rebels returned to their towns, but "repression" kept it quiet.

Let prosperity return, reasoned local officials, and socialism would disappear. In the Lodévois, this meant above all the railroad. Wrote Sub-prefect Nicolas de Vésins: "the arrondissement is waiting with great impatience for the work on the rail line in its area to begin, and deprived to this point of any rapid means of communication with the departmental capital and the sea, it would be most grateful if your Excellency should wish to hasten the coming of this important progress by your *haute intervention*."[7] The time had come when the role of the state meant everything. It was not a question of asking for favors, but to be provided with the essential infrastructure for the development of a modern industrial economy that would give the region a competitive chance. In the complex history of rail construction (or nonconstruction) can be located much of the explanation of why that chance disappeared. The problem evolved in two interconnected stages, the troubled opening of the mines of Graissessac to the world in the later 1850s and the failure to concede the rail connection through Lodève that would have realized the Pereires's great dream of providing a competitive alternative route to Paris from the south.

6

A Mining Empire
That Might Have Been

In general, the extractive industries of the south showed great promise during the earlier phases of French industrialization. The upper Loire and Gier valleys, the wild country above Alès, Grand'Combe and Bessèges, the group of villages that became known as Decazeville, and the hills of Carmaux developed coal mining and its attendant industries (metallurgy or glassmaking) at a rapid pace during the first half of the nineteenth century. It is important to underline the fact that the industrialists involved went far beyond the mere exploitation of raw materials to be utilized elsewhere. Moreover, local and regional capital (and capitalists) played a crucial role in the growth process. In the Loire, an entire economy of ironwares production blossomed, and while the main coal-mining complex became the monopolistic Compagnie de la Loire with significant outside financing (it was the favorite target for 1840s socialists), local interests remained prominent. Decazeville and Carmaux had similar early histories in which both coal mines and the industries they fueled (iron and glass) were owned by the same man (Elie Decazes and the Marquis de Solages, respectively). The situation in the Alès basin was more complex, and indeed an outsider, the Saint-Simonian entrepreneur Paulin Talabot, played the key part in its emergence, having pushed through the concessions for its rail connections and organized its financing with significant input from his influential friends in Paris. But even here, as Robert Locke has shown, regional capital was quite important in the early growth of its metallurgical industry.[1] Overall, then, significant amounts of risk capital for rapid development of modern industry came from local and regional businessmen. The southern tradition of enterprise continued in the industrial era. As these businesses grew, however, they attracted national, particularly Parisian, attention. In one case after the other, beginning with the major modernization of 1836 in Alais, the proportion of northern money and influence became dominant. Only Solages held out, but even he sold off his glassworks in 1862 to Fernand Rességuier, an entrepreneur from Toulouse; this was the prelude—as were similar earlier changes in control elsewhere—to tightened management and eventual worker upheaval.[2]

The coal basin of Graissessac languished in mismanagement and petty squabbles during the Restoration. As with all previous changes in régime, the Revolution of 1830 once again provided the opportunity for surface proprietors to reopen their little caves (no doubt simply boarded over and hidden under rocks and brush in any case), but they were reeducated by the new commissaire de police.[3] The July Monarchy, in fact, augured a new day for Graissessac, as it did for so many parts of the country. The transformation of the Ministry of Public Works, which promoted the vigorous B.A.V. Legrand to reign over the development of the early French rail system, produced the same orientation toward combining a traditional focus on technical excellence with a much more powerful concern for stimulating economic advancement in the mining section as well.[4] This was reflected in the quality of engineering expertise and an interest in discovering new areas for exploration and development in the extractive industries. The first thorough analysis of the promise of the Graissessac basin arose from competitive bidding among several local groups of capitalists for a concession or concessions in the far western part of this region, St. Geniès and Castenet-le-Haut. The report made by the regional mining engineer, R. Thibaud, and annotated by his superior, A.H. Bonnard, Inspector General of Mines for the Southeastern Division, contained not only a positive assessment of the basin, but also provided a fascinating glimpse of the new régime's perspective.

The chief bidders were groups organized by Louis Jourfier, the mayor of St. Geniès, and Joseph Bayle, like the mayor, a large property-owner who lived in a hamlet in the same commune. Jourfier chose for partners mostly men whose most notable quality was their function as public officials, although all had business experience. They included no less than four mayors (including Bédarieux's loyal Orleanist, Jacques Prades), a tax official, and an infantry captain. The seventh, however, was a banker, Silhol of Alais (Alès), who had investments in mines there and paid a substantial 816-franc direct tax. The total tax paid by these men was Fr 5,757—an average of above Fr 600; they were grands notables to be sure. The Bayle group was more modest (without titles and barely censitaires), but included Jacques Martel-Laprade, the cloth manufacturer of Bédarieux (cens Fr 609), who, despite his known legitimist leanings, was described as "one of the most commendable manufacturers of the district." Bayle and especially a young geologist-proprietor from nearby Clairac (whose brother, also in the group, was an homme de lettres in Paris), had presented a masterly analysis of the technical problems and the expected yields of these new areas. Thibaud recommended the latter in arguing for entrepreneurship over position and was backed by Bonnard, who remarked, "a mining concession is not a prize given to wealth; it suffices that a concessionaire have enough capital and ability to make productive the mineral wealth that the government puts in his hands." They did their research well and, besides, applied first. As it turned out, after repeated appeals, the Jourfier group managed to get the less-promising Castenet area, but the point was clear.[5] It was significant also that both groups included prominent woolens fabricants of Bédarieux, who found diversified industrial investment inviting.[6]

The report itself, over one hundred pages long, sang the praises of the basin's deposits for a variety of uses, but argued that transport difficulties— especially after the opening of the already-conceded rail connection between Alais and Beaucaire and the existing ease of transport from the Rive-de-Gier mines—might well doom Graissessac to permanent second rank. Thibaud hoped that enterprising types like those involved in the current bidding might find ways to overcome these problems, but the very best deposits— in the Devois and Boussagues concessions—were also the most inaccessible. In general, all movement of coal down to La Tour or Villemagne, like nails or scrap iron (going the other way), was by pack mule. Ferdinand Fabre, a regional novelist who achieved some fame later in the century, remembered that during a trip in the early 1830s when as a boy he was taken to Graissessac so the fervent priest there could "knock some sense into him," after St. Xist (see map on page 156) "only one noise reached us: the ringing crack of the relentless whip on some beast hauling his load of coal along the terrible *chemin des mines* on the other side of l'Aire Raymonde." The only things of interest in La Tour, which he had just left, were "several inns for the teamsters who came up from the low country to load coal from the Graissessac mines and three or four woolens mills whose enormous wheels turned in the river."[7]

The most promising development in recent years had been the appearance in the basin of Philippe Usquin, whose company had a variety of interests in Montpellier and contacts in Parisian financial circles. He purchased the Le Bousquet mine with an eye toward reopening the glassworks and the Devois concession, which had rarely turned a profit due to the high cost of transport.[8] This placed Usquin on either side of Giral et Moulinier concessions in Boussagues. Moulinier, who also managed the St. Gervais concession, and had achieved virtual ownership of it from the genteel Delzeuzes family, was Usquin's major rival. Usquin, meanwhile, had in 1834 sued for a fourth of the Delzeuzes inheritance there and won. The point was that two enterprising concerns ran the older part of the bassin. Engineer Thibaud seemed to feel, however, that making rail service viable for the area would be so difficult that it would not pay to attempt it.[9]

The Usquin Company was not convinced of this and had dreams that went beyond the imaginations of most in the region. Philippe-Francois-Dédier Usquin, former Napoleonic officer and Chevalier de la Légion

GRAISSESSAC
COAL DEPOSIT

Graissessac Coal Basin

Drawn By: Bonnie S. Talaga

d'honneur, came from Montpellier but lived most of the time in Paris. He was fascinated with the possibilities of developing the mineral resources of the entire upper Orb/Mare area. The Compagnie Usquin was originally formed in 1825 for the purpose of gaining the concession to the iron mines of Maurian, located in the Graissessac area. The development was opposed by Giral and Moulinier because Usquin wanted to install charcoal-burning Catalan forges. Since they were upheld by the administration (which accepted their deforestation argument), he decided to go for coal, which he hoped could be converted to coke. All this explains both his purchases and his antipathy toward Moulinier. Unfortunately, technology had not yet advanced sufficiently to convert any of the coals in Graissessac to coke, because they had too little oil in them for viable compression. Usquin also promoted copper mining, revitalized the glassworks in Le Bousquet, and would be a partner in a zinc-products factory there. In the 1830s he joined forces with a young man who would become a central figure in the history of Graissessac, Aaron B. Simon, son of a Montpellier merchant and a member of its old and distinguished Jewish community. Simon, an engineer with legal training, had little money, but much enthusiasm and intelligence. His first successful effort on behalf of the Compagnie Usquin was to chart and plan its purchase of the moribund Le Bousquet glassworks in 1845. The Giral enterprise in Hérépian had failed largely because of the cost of transport of coal to it.[10]

From the *plaintes* of the old régime to the petitions of the Revolution and engineers reports of the nineteenth century, the central issue in the lives of these hillfolk was the miserable state of roads (if the term can be used) until one reached the Béziers plain. The cost of improvement never seemed worth it either economically or politically.[11] As a result, Graissessac coal, when it finally reached a destination (usually Béziers) where further transhipment would be on a par with its competitors, already cost almost three times the price of its extraction. At twenty-seven francs per ton for ordinary qualities in the early 1840s, it would sometimes be undersold even in Béziers itself by similar coal from Alais. Its better quality combustible (used widely in distillation) could count on sales only up to about the Hérault river to the east but considerably further, via the canal du Midi, to the west. At Toulouse it encountered the competition of Carmaux and did not spread beyond. It was obvious that a rail line to Béziers was critical if Graissessac were to have a future.

This had been a subject of intense discussion during the "rail fever" era from 1837 to 1842. In that year, in one of the hundreds of requests and petitions following the passage of the fundamental law that would govern French rail construction thereafter, the deputies from the Hérault clamored for such a line.[12] Also in 1842, Usquin, no doubt anticipating a rail concession, made his move. Although the details escape us, he brought about a merger of his coal company with that of Moulinier. The concession names remained separate, but from 1842 on, a sophisticated and cosmopolitan businessman controled the destiny of the mines. Management arrangements left Moulinier in place as works director, but installed Aaron Simon as the chief operating officer under the title Ingénieur-Directeur. Usquin initiated the first official request for a rail concession on 21 April 1845. It was for a narrow-gauge track that would replace the mule trail from the mines to la Tour and be built entirely at the company's expense. The Prefect enthusiastically endorsed the proposal, and it passed Ponts et Chaussées the following year. The company faced no obstacle to its rapid completion, wrote Usquin, "other than the avidity of several isolated proprietors." None of the local bitterness toward the mine company had disappeared, but obviously the new owner's verve and willingness to proceed without a definitive judgement on the main rail line impressed Orleanist officials.[13]

In the interim, however, the most important event in the early history of the Graissessac mines had occurred. Napoleon Garella, an ingénieur ordinaire in the service of the Division des Mines, had made a remarkably complete study of the basin, published in 1843. Above all, he demonstrated how regular and thick were the seams in the central part of the coal field, the Devois and Boussagues, proving ancient local knowledge correct. He also stressed that removal from the deposits themselves was not a difficult task—most cuts were into the mountainside and, in fact, slightly uphill.[14] Embranchements were then cut in parallel lines also at an incline. All movement of coal could therefore be effected by relatively easy movement, increasingly by "cheins," wheeled carts on plank rails let down by winches placed near the top of the advancing corridors. The seams were generally one and one-half-to-two meters high and quite wide. Schists were there, but would pose no great problems with proper geological analysis. Although wherever possible, existing rock served as pillars, the volume of coal per area meant considerable timbering was necessary—and costly. In compensation, aeration, in view of the relative closeness of much of the activity to the surface, was easy and cheap.

The big problems, of course, were on the outside. Le Bousquet, though it produced the lowest quality coal, was the most developed area simply because of access. Its "mixed coals, large and small, of second quality" provided the energy for the company's glassworks, now booming. Even so, much of the haulage was by pack mule or small carts. Only in 1858 would a ramp from the pithead of Le Bousquet's most productive mine down to the glassworks be built.[15]

Garella's study of the current (1838) markets for Graissessac's coal made fascinating reading, for it underlined how important the mine was for the future of the region. The total output for that year was 16,353 metric tons (T), a small amount when compared with the big fields. Twenty percent (but only 10 percent of the value) was *menu*, or very small pieces, of the second quality supplying the local nail industry, which remained wedded to its old ways but provided a livelihood for four or five dozen households. Menu of the first quality—hard coal similar to American anthracite—was used in forges and smithies in the Hérault and nearby areas of the Tarn,

Aveyron, and Gard (8 percent of the volume and 13 percent of the value). Lime and roof-tile ovens in Lodève and Béziers, along with the glassworks, consumed the small/large mixture, which had considerable amounts of earth in it (*mélange terreux*) and accounted for 22 percent of the total product and 16 percent of the value. Distilleries throughout the region used first quality large—the finest grade produced—mixed with some menu, absorbing one-fourth of the four mines' total output and providing a third of its products' worth. Finally, the woolens industry made important use of number-two quality large and the large/small mixture favored by the distillers. For dyeing wool and steaming and lustering finished cloth, Lodève and Bédarieux used 2,420 T at a value of Fr 26,550, and, not to be ignored, 225 T of second-quality large fueled steam engines in both fabriques and was worth Fr 2700. The rest was used for home heating and other "domestic" purposes.[16]

The "value" here referred to the price of extraction—the cost price (prix de revient)—which Garella calculated with great care. It was nowhere close to what users actually paid for the coal. Profits were only around ten percent of production costs. The vast increases in cost to the consumer derived from transport. Even in Bédarieux, prices were double the cost price. At Lodève, reached only by the difficult, though improved, road across the Escandorgue, it was not unusual to pay thirty-five or forty francs per ton, three or more times the cost price. This city was, after the glassworks, Graissessac's "principal market." Despite their own distance from rail or main highway connections, Lodève manufacturers also imported coal from Alais, especially for rush orders that could come from the canal port in Agde fairly quickly.[17]

Curiously, Garella gave more emphasis to the need for good roads rather than for rail. Moreover, he tended to think largely in terms of regional—though thoroughly industrial—use. Both points were somewhat surprising because he estimated that the mines could easily produce 400,000 T per year "for several centuries." Its finest hard coal could outcompete anyone with some reduction in transport costs. Mine owners were also beginning, during the Second Republic, to experiment with compressing machinery and coke production. For the Usquin Company, a rail line to Béziers was an absolute necessity if their goals were to be met.[18]

The decisive factor in developing the momentum toward a railroad, however, was the definitive proof that Graissessac's best coal was a perfect fuel for marine steam engines. In July 1850, the French navy carried out a series of experiments using Graissessac coal. They fully corroborated estimates of chemists hired by the company that this short-flame, slow-burning hard was the "best French coal" and "has its greatest analogue in the English coal *Cardiff*; it is superior to any coal from Grand'Combe . . . and when mixed with live-flame Blue Rock, provides sufficient pressure. . . ." The Maritime Prefect at Toulon felt that if this coal could achieve a delivered price in the high twenties, Graissessac coal might substantially reduce the troubling dependency of the emerging French steamship fleet on coal from a foreign power.[19] More fundamentally, the use of steamships obviously was not limited to the military. If Graissessac could exploit its special advantage, one might turn the tables on the virtual monopoly held by British products in the hard-coal market, at least in the Mediterranean. Another critical issue was the potential impact of Graissessac's development on the future of Cette. Perhaps a second Marseille could yet be created, not only as a coaling station and transhipment port for the mineral, but as the outlet for all the products (woolens and eaux de vie to be sure, but also bottles, lime and other chemicals, zinc products, tiles, and yet unimagined industrial goods) that cheap and appropriate quality coal might produce. A railroad from Graissessac (the closest mine to the sea in France—one of Wales's great advantages, after all) to Cette via Béziers might just be the stimulus needed to turn lower Languedoc around.

A former conseiller d'etat named Nicolas-Félix Carteret was present at the Toulon experiments. At Usquin's urging, he had already been making the rounds in government and Parisian financial circles and had found a willing supporter in the banker Joseph Orsi. The Graniers of Montpellier, despite their recent difficulties, were also enthusiastic, especially Henry, Zoë's nephew. Michel Chevalier, a conseiller général in the Hérault and soon to be a conseiller d'état for the illustrious Saint-Simonian on horseback, was mentioned as an important friend. Orsi and Carteret established the rail company definitively (siège social, 3, rue de l'Isly, Paris) on 15 March 1852, and the concession was granted two weeks later.

This, however, was not the key issue. The united mine company, directed by Simon and Moulinier, promised to increase production to 200,000 T in "several years" and, with appropriate transportation, predicted that the price of their marine coal would be twenty-seven francs per ton in Toulon, Port Vendres, or Algeria when shipped via Cette.[20] This optimistic appraisal was written to support the rail company's major objective, to gain a government guarantee of 4.5 percent annual interest on shares sold on the market. The Caen-Cherbourg and Bordeaux-Cette lines had recently received this benefit. But the Graissessac group failed. Public Works Minister Pierre Magne refused without explanation, although the company was allowed to bypass the usual caution money by way of compensation. This was the first setback in a series that ensued with pathetic consistency thereafter.

Company organizers nevertheless pushed forward. The promise of Graissessac was great enough to offset the absence of guarantees. On 26 February 1853 it was granted limited liability status and published its statutes and the amount of stock owned by its shareholders. It was not a group to inspire confidence. There was not a single figure from the mainstream financial establishment of Paris, with the possible exception of Edgar Aimé. Comparing this list, for example, with the contemporaneous Bordeaux-Cette group, it is obvious that the "rois de la Bourse," especially its Jewish contingent (Eichthal, the Pereires, the Rothschilds, Ezpeleta, the Solomons, Bischoffsheim), and the grand promoters of French rail development such as Thurneyssen, stayed away in droves.[21] No doubt the failure to procure guaranteed interest was a factor in this, but there seems almost a conspiracy of silence surrounding the Graissessac from the beginning. As a consequence, it was necessary to beat the bushes for small investors and seek out English capital in a major way. Theodosius Uzielli, with an office in Paris, was the principal go-between. He represented a group of forty-six individuals holding 6,870 shares, which like all French railroad shares at the time were Fr 500 a piece. Victor Monteaux, a French financier, acted for another twenty-eight London capitalists holding 6,125 shares; another twenty-one (2,415 shares) were represented by one Frédéric Toché. In all, British capital accounted for over 15,000 shares, or 7.5 million of the 18 million total capital for the railroad, a substantial, if not controlling amount. The fourteen major French shareholders who possessed more than 500 shares each, however, totaled slightly less (14,560), meaning that in any fight, the huge number of French small holders who reached into their savings to support this venture would play an important role, although for the most part, they grouped around key figures at the top.

The notarial act that created the company was included in the dossier retained by the Prefect in Montpellier, so we may see rather precisely the constellations that made up its shareholders.[22]

The most important characteristics of this structure, the unusually large number of small shareholders both in London and Paris and the absence of important financial figures, gave the Graissessac a "popular" cast, but this image in fact made it a subject of derision from insiders and suspect in the Hérault. Orsi possessed a reputation for shady dealings, and de l'Espine, a vain and pretentious man, was apparently something of a joke in Parisian circles.[23] His group of shareholders, in particular, would later be held up as an example of how *petits gens* could be misled. Few of their addresses were prestigious. A majority were hard-working petit bourgeois. Eleven of the twenty-eight were clerks, one of them a cashier at John B. Greene's bank (25 shares). A horse merchant, a painter, a furniture maker, and a bookseller rounded out the lesser professions. The "bourgeois" in this group included eight rentiers or propriétaires, who bought anywhere from 5 to 260 shares, Amédée Achard, homme de lettres (300 shares), a more prudent engineer (10), and the Monteaux banking clan—Victor, (who separately represented his brother Prosper and a London contingent), Nathan, and "la Maison de commerce Monteaux et fils, gallerie Montpensier, Palais Royal" accounted for 450 shares. They were Jews with links in Montpellier and correspondents of Aaron Simon.[24] Definitely not in the top Jewish financial circles of Paris,[25] their activities appeared to have been limited to loans to small businessmen and small-scale stock brokerage. It was they who probably found many of the individuals on the list, especially those who names indicate likely Jewish or Languedocian origins. Georges Kugelmann, printer, and Léopold Wintersinger, clerk, for example (5 shares each) both lived at 7, rue Feydeau in the heart of the Marais Jewish quarter.[26] Léon Crémieux, the horse dealer, was doubtless a member of the large Crémieux

Table 6–1

Principal Representatives	Shares	Representing	Shares	Total
Joseph Orsi, Négociant, Paris	2000	Himself	—	2000
François Charles Clinquet, prop. Paris	300	(1) G. Henri Granier, prop. Montpellier and Paris (2) F.G. Sabatier de l'Espéran, prop., Montpellier	2000 200	2500
Max. Fr. J. Delfosse, prop., Paris	2000	Himself	—	2000
Auguste Coulet, prop., Paris	2000	Himself	—	2000
Edgar Aimé, Banquier, Paris	800	(1) Th. Uzielli, agent de change, London (2) 46 Agents de change, props., and négoc. of London (City, Stock Exchange, Old Broad Street), no. shares from 660 to 25	500 6370	7670
Victor Monteaux, Banquier, Paris	—	(I) Prosper Monteaux (brother), Banquier, Paris (2) 28 London capitalists, no. shares from 500 to 25	800 6125	6925
Louis Honoré David, fils, Banquier, Poitiers	800	Himself	—	800
Etienne Roualle, vicomte de Rouville, Banquier, Paris	100	(1) Joseph Marie Arbel, Dr. en médecine, Paris (2) Raoul, comte de La Châtre, prop., Paris (3) 16 Parisians, diverse occupations, no. shares 125 to 5	750 1450 920	3220
James Leray de Chaumont, Marquis de St. Paul, prop., St. Paul (Hérault) and Paris	500	Himself	500	
Nicolas-Félix Carteret, ancien Conseiller d'état, Paris	900	11 Parisians, diverse occupations, 100 to 5	500	1400
Alexandre Emile, vicomte de l'Espine, prop., Montpellier and Paris	820	29 Frenchmen, all living in Paris but several natives of the Hérault, diverse occupations	2590	3410

(continued)

Table 6–1 (*continued*)

Frédéric-François Toché, prop., Paris	210	(1) Achille Pinta Reutier, London	500	
		(2) 21 London capitalists, no. of shares from 150 to 25	1915	2625
John Buckley Greene, Banquier, Paris	—	His bank	600	600
Guillaume and François	350	Themselves		350
Vandenbrock, props., Paris				36,000
				@ 500F = 18,000,000 F

family of Montpellier, and thus qualified on both counts, and Léopold Lunel's people likely hailed from that *bourg de vin*.

The amount of money invested by Héraultais overall was fairly significant, but their influence on the company's policies was minimal. Granier and Sabatier represented the very heart of the Montpellier business establishment, coming from the great mercantile families of the city. Clinquet was a relative of Granier. De l'Espine and St. Paul were large landowners in the Hérault with investments in a variety of southern business activities. The Monteaux and their clients represent lesser forces, but had Hérault connections. Mine company shareholders did not buy stock in the railroad because of conflict of interest, but family ties cemented the two firms together. Graniers (Théodore and Zoë) and Félix Sabatier were, with Usquin, the Quatres Mines réunies' principal shareholders. The commitment of Hérault big business to the entire enterprise was obviously great. Carteret did not come from the south, but he articulated the connections between the Hérault group and the Parisian crowd. He also was the main tie to the Ministry of Public Works. He and Orsi were the principal voices of the company as it got off the ground and chose its director of operations, a lesser Jewish financier in Paris, with training as an engineer, named Isadore Boucaruc.

There can be no doubt that this railroad's success was critical to the industrial future of lower Languedoc. Besides the obvious profits to be reaped from coal sales in the Mediterranean and the stimulation rendered to Cette, the predicted development of the mines would have reverberations across the region, increasing the potential of both old and new industries, as well as the will to improve its grid of communications. But it was not to be. The Compagnie de chemin de fer de Béziers à Graissessac recorded perhaps the most disastrous history in the entire annals of French railroad building (at least for those lines actually completed). The story reads like a Laurel and Hardy movie, but with none of the redeeming warmth that their bumbling evokes.

This was because the failure had to do with far more than bumbling. Quite simply, the company fell victim to criminal fraud perpetrated by members of its board of directors and its chief administrative officer. Orsi, Delfosse, and Boucaruc would actually be tried and convicted for illegal acts (though overturned on appeal), and most of the major shareholders would be driven from the Bourse.

From the beginning, rumors circulated about the ethics of some of the administrators and the competence of the engineering studies of the route, nowhere more persistently than in the Hérault. Cartaret wrote the Prefect in 25 June 1853 urging him to contact Public Works in order to expedite approval of the plans for the first twenty kilometers of the railroad. It was "critical above all to respond with positive action to the persistent allegations in your department that throw doubt upon the possibility of execution of the railroad. . . ."[27] Then it was again rumored that the line would not be built because the Compagnie du Midi preferred to link up with a line from Graissessac that would run to Lodève and thence to Agde and the Midi's main line from Bordeaux to Cette. This supposedly had the support of Michel Chevalier, a close friend of the Pereires.[28] These came to naught, and work got under way early in 1854.[29] Then, quite suddenly in November 1854, the Company was making headlines in the press and headaches for officials. The contractors were not paying their workers. As in any railroad project, the employment of hundreds of men, from common laborers to highly skilled artisans, provided a boon for the area and drew people from a wide radius (including those who simply followed the lines).[30] Not to be paid was a problem for anyone, but itinerants could not easily get credit from local innkeepers and grocers. Naturally, they quickly became unruly.

At the center of the controversy was a hapless subcontractor named Boyle, an Englishman whose French was terrible. He was the overseer for the work on the 2500-meter Faugères tunnel, the project that would make or break the financial viability of the line. But Boyle—and his superiors in the general contracting company, Gandell Brothers, a huge concern with current contracts in four European states—soon realized that money allocated for work on the entire line, Fr 12.3 million, came nowhere near the actual costs, the tunnel alone requiring four times the manpower that they had estimated. After trying to pay only when they had been paid (in three-month installments) and meeting resistance, they moved to an irregular schedule that proved even more explosive. On 25 November workers who had not been paid since 21 October besieged Boyle's office in Bédarieux demanding their wages. He put them off with a promise to pay the following Tuesday, but in fact had no money. While officials debated the propriety of government intervention in light of "the drawback of undermining the freedom of transactions," some two hundred workers at another site closer to Béziers, Laurens, went on strike and marched on Béziers. Fortunately, they arrived at about the same time as a rail company representative from Paris with eighteen thousand francs to distribute. The company thus made a de facto decision that it was ultimately responsible for the wages of the employees of its subcontractors.

But new problems arose the following February. Faugères workers were on the "verge of revolt" not only because of pay shortages but because they could not get their medical bills paid by the company, despite the fact that 2 percent of their pay was routinely retained for medical insurance. A few days later, François Combes, a Bédarieux explosives dealer, wrote Prefect Costa that Boyle had owed him Fr 1,150 for months; it was "toute ma fortune," and he was preparing to declare bankruptcy. The Prefect filed it with the other complaints pouring in from suppliers. Finally, authorized by Public Works Chief Engineer Léon, he issued a decree of "mise en demeure" (summons) against the company to pay workers and creditors in lieu of payment by its subcontractor. While this made Boyle happy, it did not help Grandell Brothers: on 30 June 1855, it filed for bankruptcy in Béziers. Moreover, in the intervening months both the Company and Gandell had neglected various payments because they were in court against each other. Now, however, the Company had no option but to pay— Fr 120,000 was the figure—but they would remunerate (mostly French) manual workers only, leaving the sixteen clerical and technical employees, all English, to fend for themselves.

By mid-July 1855 work on the Graissessac-Béziers came to a total standstill, the company was in disarray, and (the only real loser besides the "Béziers sixteen") the regional economy once again faced an uncertain future.[31]

What was going on? Several things at once, all symptomatic of the serious contradictions of a political economy that simultaneously trumpeted "freedom of transactions" and nurtured state favoritism toward the already-powerful. In the first place, we discover that Gandell, a true multinational before the word, had taken the ridiculously low contract to prevent several lesser competitors from getting it. As a foreign operator, its assets outside France could not be touched in bankruptcy proceedings, and its *passif* in the affair would simply have to be absorbed by the railroad company. Gandell Brothers marched on to a happy future.

But this was not the real story. How had it happened that "the Company" had contracted the work at such an unrealistic level in the first place? At its first stockholders' meeting on 14 March 1853, Fr 16.3 million had been allocated for the building of the road, the purchase of rolling stock, and the construction of stations, and so forth. (The rest would finance central administrative activities.) This amount was then awarded—*pour exécution à forfait* (contracted out)—to none other than Orsi and Delfosse, two of the biggest shareholders of the Company. They in fact had never lifted— or directed the lifting of—a pick in their entire lives. What next? Let M. le Ministre des Travaux Publics Magne, who had assembled the evidence by early 1855, explain as he did to Orsi before requesting his arrest warrant:

I have reason to believe that this contract was not at all executed by you and that you immediately ceded it to les Srs Briau et Daviot at the price of 14,300,000 francs, thus realizing without the risk of any work at all, a profit of 2,500,000 francs and that les Srs Briau et Daviot have, for their part, ceded this contract to the current entrepreneurs, les Srs Gandell, at the price of 12,300,000 francs.

According to this [calculation], therefore, while the real price of execution is 12,300,000, the limited liability railroad company would have paid and will be obliged to pay 16,800,000 francs for the same objective.

These payments were well underway: between August 1853 and October 1854, the Minister discovered that Fr 1,350,321.65 had been paid out under the heading "Orsi et Briau, à compte sur leur bénéfice." Magne then politely pointed out that this was all illegal by virtue of the Law of 15 July 1845, article 11, and asked him for an explanation. A thick dossier had been assembled by this time and certain other facts emerged. First of all, although Gandell was hardly blameless, it had put out Fr 2.5 million of its own money for materiel, wages, and so forth, without recompense from the company. In fact, the only payments being made promptly were those to Orsi, who at the time also remained the titular Chairman of the Board. At a certain point, these amounts were a full 60 percent of those made to the actual builder, Gandell. Meanwhile, however, one other group of people was receiving regular compensation—the shareholders, who for three years straight got their 4.5 percent, despite the fact, remarked the new chairman, Vte de l'Espine, in February 1856, that we "never received a state subvention of guarantee of interest."[32]

A complicating factor was Napoleon Garella's study of the route in which he estimated the cost at a mere Fr 10.6 million. This figure was no doubt used by everyone (though kept quiet until the first shareholders meeting of March 1853!) in making their calculations. Why it came out so low is not clear, for the report itself has disappeared. Garella had been locked in battle with a fellow engineer, Dupont of Alais, over the route the railroad should take. The latter recommended the Orb valley, while Garella argued for the shorter but more difficult line via Faugères.[33] It would appear that Garella gave as optimistic an appraisal as possible in order to help assure the future of "his" coalfield, in which, by then, a mine had been named for him and he owned a considerable personal interest.

A further element in the story, perhaps the most decisive for the future of Graissessac, began to emerge in 1855. Gandell, hamstrung by lack of money, worried about where it would come from, knowing there would never be enough, and rarely sending its own managers to the place,[34] cut corners on quality wherever possible. The totally disgusted state engineer N. Kauffman wrote Boucaruc as early as April 1855 that much would have to be redone: "The obligations and traditions of the Corps to which I have the honor of belonging oblige me to have all works executed with all the care and soundness desirable." His earlier letter to his superiors is lost, but Magne accused the company's entrepreneurs of "criminal negligence," not only in having done poor work, but in "endanger[ing] the lives of their workers" in the process of digging tunnels.[35] After the collapse of Gandell, a variety of entrepreneurs bid for the work and multiple contracts were awarded. One company in particular was handsomely endowed and would grow and grow. It was simply called Soubaigné et Associés. A few others, especially Roblin et Jeanty, seemed to be doing quite well, while most were always having problems keeping up with their payments to workers. Equally important, Engineer Kauffman was now filing almost monthly reports on this or that ill-made piece of work, until finally, on 11 June 1857, he was forced to resign by Boucaruc. Tragically, the toll taken on workers began to mount. No less than eighteen men were killed in the building of this road; another forty-three were injured. The official position was that most died through negligence on their own part (falls from viaducts, and so forth), but "flood in tunnel" (2), "cave-ins" (3), "tunnel explosion" (1), "rock on head" (1), look suspiciously like negligence at least by another worker, but likely due to bad management.[36] The one detailed accident report that has survived, indeed, makes one wonder about the rest. Two young navvies, a seventeen-year-old from Faugères and an eighteen-year-old from the Ariège (a typical mix), were removing rocks in a deep trench shortly after work began 12 January 1857. They apparently dislodged a major support stone and were crushed by rocks that tumbled from the side of the trench above them. No supervisor was present. The reporter blandly noted that "the engineers have written a report on the precautions to be taken in such situations." This was of little use to boys who probably could not read at all and certainly not a treatise in formal French. It was obviously up to the works manager to inform them of the danger they faced. The report does allow that "greater precaution might have been taken."[37] The speed-up by that time (the whole project was supposed to be finished by mid-July 1856) was tremendous and the sloppiness in work completed egregious. That neglect of safety existed seems incontestable.

In March 1857, it began again: strikes at Camplong—construction had progressed almost to the mines themselves—and at Faugères, where the tunnel was nearing completion, over delays in pay. It was the nineteenth of the month and workers were still awaiting February's wages. The contractor, L'Abbé, whose record seems spotless (we shall get to the others shortly), was "owed a great deal by the company"' and simply could not meet his payroll. Kauffmann got this situation resolved, but three months later, L'Abbé declared bankruptcy, leaving further disarray and seventeen thousand francs in wages owed. In the summer of 1857, a Béziers banker, Lagarrigue, who was chosen by Henry Granier to handle the Company's payments locally, began to suspect that the payments being made to some contractors were not consistent with the amount of work being done. It was common knowledge that the costs of Graissessac were wildly beyond the original estimates, but Parisians and others assumed that the terrain matched the "savages" (a term used by a state inspector for the local inhabitants) who lived there and thus presented natural obstacles unknown to the civilized world. Another five million had been raised through loans to cover mounting costs. In July 1857, (after Kauffmann's departure), Lagarrigue began sending reports to the sub-prefect in Béziers, in particular wondering why some entrepreneurs always seemed to have full and even lavish payments from the Company and others did not. Several of the latter were in court against the Company.[38]

Late 1857 should have been a time of joy because most of the work was finished and the first runs on the track were being scheduled. At its end, the mine company was building roads and track to connect with the main line. But a judicial investigation, rooted in Lagarrigue's suspicions, was turning up answers to his questions. The Procureur Imperial for the Seine, Cordoën, wrote the new Minister of Public Works, Eugène Rouher, a long letter on 23 December apprising him in advance that certain "grave facts" "compromising" the rail company's director, Isadore Boucaruc, and possibly members of the board had been discovered.

The story was a simple one—it involved massive kickbacks and straight embezzlement, although with a twist. The first benefited "notably" the entrepreneurs Roblin et Jeanty, who got the jobs they wanted and paid their workers on time, having received prices for their contracts "inflated so considerably that one must assume the existence of enormous *pots de vin* [fraudulent commissions] demanded of the entrepreneurs." This "fraud" operated in all sorts of contracts, "whether for earthworks, rail placement, or installation of equipment." This, according to an unnamed engineer fired with Kauffmann, was widely suspected in Béziers and had recently been confirmed by Kauffmann, whose "resignation" related in part to his unwillingness to tolerate such abuses. These suspicions were later confirmed through interviews with the entrepreneurs who, in effect, turned state's evidence to save their skins. Boucaruc was the main offender, but Carteret had profited as well.

But kickbacks of this sort were nothing compared to the scheme Isadore and his brother Eugène cooked up to bilk the shareholders. The latter and his friend Soubaigné were, before the collapse of Gandell, "simple employees in the wholesale dry goods business in Paris" and were "without capital or credit, and lacked even the first indispensable notion of how to direct a public works enterprise." But no matter. They scurried off to Béziers and set up shop as Soubaigné et Associés, having received Fr 120 to 140,000 from Company funds to start up. With Eugène "governing from below" and "holding the pursestrings," they concluded contracts with the Company for Fr 4,795,128.97. Experts established, however, that the work actually done, at current rates, and so forth, would have cost Fr 3,772,811.29 at the most, thus leaving over a million unaccounted for. Later investigations were unable to trace the whereabouts of that money, which remained Boucaruc's main basis for appeals from one court to the next over the years that followed. At his final civil court judgement in 1867, Boucaruc was required to pay Fr 95,000 to the state, which ended up in possession of the railroad. Neither he, his brother, nor Soubaigné spent a minute in jail.[39]

The Boucaruc scandal was the climax of the Graissessac railroad debacle. Everyone associated with the direction of the company—at least, the Parisians—had their reputations destroyed. Shortly after the stormy stockholders meeting on 26 March 1858 when Boucaruc's suspension was announced, the troubled company, which had now gone through a second Fr 5 million loan and still could not meet its bills, was placed "under sequestration" by the Ministry of Public Works (12 May 1858). This meant that while it would still have a private Board of Directors, retain its name, and (hopefully) pay dividends, its management and financial operations would be monitored daily by government officials. A. Thouret, the financial inspector assigned to the project did a thorough, professional job, returning some degree of respect to the company. Almost unnoticed in these dramatic events was the "grand opening" of the line to passenger traffic "to the acclamations of a bedazzled crowd,"[40] on 24 March 1858—two years behind schedule.

It *was* an impressive railway. The Faugères tunnel and the Bédarieux viaduct were important engineering feats. But Héraultais, by now used to bad news and expecting the worst (recall that this was a troubled time for woolens and the vine, too), even as they rode in the shiny new passenger wagons, had to be asking: how much will the coal cost? This would depend on a number of factors. Obviously, the monumental cost overruns of the previous years were going to have to be made up—how the state now managed the affair would be crucial in their impact on freight rates. Then there were the nagging technical questions—what would be the impact of the many imperfections and unresolved problems on cost and volume? Finally, the mine company's response to the route billed as its salvation was critical—and related to these questions as well. To be sure, transport still would account for more than half the cost of coal when it reached the consumer. But economies at the point of production—including those of scale—would also significantly affect it. A more general issue was the impact of the Béziers-Graissessac fiasco on the capitalist mind of the Hérault. Two of the major business families of lower Languedoc had been victims of the incredible maneuvers of Parisian *escrocs* and had vainly watched the company's collapse. The man who emerged as the strongest voice for regional interests was the Comte de St. Paul, but he was more personally concerned about how the general rail system of the Hérault would assist the export of wine than about its significance for industry.

As of the end of 1857—before the revelations and the *mise en sequestre*—the Company had spent Fr 27,030,000 and would have to put out another 3 million to finish, the total of which, a disgruntled (but unidentified) shareholder noted, was almost Fr 600,000 a kilometer for "a single-track spur line!" The average cost for other lines through similar terrain elsewhere in France was 350 to 400 thousand. The tragedy was that "Because of those successive issues of debentures, . . . the Company finds itself with a mortgage of Fr 16,150,000, an amount equaling the real value of the road if it were put up at auction." He also stressed the unknown costs of repairing the many technical faults in the railway. Finally, he fumed, there is talk of "floating another six million franc loan for branch track!"[41]

After the state began investigating the Company in 1858, it became clear that such assessments were absolutely correct. The reports of two thoroughly competent state inspectors, Izonard and Thouret, trace the continuing destiny of the company. Immediately after the sequestration (12 May 1858), state officials demanded a complete change of the Board of Directors. Only St. Paul and Uzielli held on. The key figures were Bénat, President, Chaper, and de Bousquet, all three relatively unimportant shareholders but experienced Board members, being also on the Board of the Compagnie d'Orleans; two others were former high government officials—a Procureur general and a Prefect. They cracked down on expenses, cutting staff while employing more outsiders with railroad experience (undoubtedly causing further unpopularity among the locals), improved the ordering processes, and by September of 1859 were shipping coal. They also initiated the civil suit against Boucaruc, who miraculously escaped criminal conviction on appeal. The sequester agent in Béziers, Campaing, was said to be quite popular with the business community and the mine owners.

Meanwhile, the feeder roads to the railroad were being completed. One from Castan, where coal and coke were produced, to Estrechoux, the actual endpoint of the railroad, was finished in 1858. Typically, mine boss Moulinier took the uncertainty with the rail company as an opportunity to delay payments worth Fr 3,842 to the "masons, stonecutters, and road workers of Camplong," who had to petition the Prefect for help.[42] The long highway from St. Gervais to Estrechoux was opened the following year. Unfortunately, after successful activity in 1859, coal movement ground to a snail's pace the following year—despite its increasing availability—because of major problems with the descent from the Faugères tunnel, which was assisted by a fixed cable mechanism. The cost of installing sufficient machinery and sidings that would allow large numbers of coal cars to be assembled and then taken on to Béziers was exorbitant, given the financial state of the company. Thus, although a trickle of coal continued, revenues were largely in passenger and light freight receipts. At the same time, the company was having increasingly bad luck in the courts of Béziers and Montpellier, where subcontractors by the dozen lined up to sue the company.[43]

Despite the government's austerity measures, the Company was fast becoming insolvent and desperately needed another loan. The problem was that although its reputation improved with the departure of Boucaruc and the old Board, its shares languished at around 45 francs and its bonds of the previous emissions, supposed to sell at 200 with a 250 franc maturity (6 year) tag, were well below their face value as well. What was needed was a legislative guarantee of the next loan (Fr 10 million was the goal) and all would be turned around. This was the central drama of 1860, with Thouret continually urging Rouher to "intervene" with his friends in the Assembly, even with Napoleon III himself, to obtain such a law. But it failed in committee on 9 June 1860. There is no way of knowing what Rouher did or did not do, but as we shall examine in detail in the contemporaneous Lodève railroad case, the Minister of Public Works was no friend of the Hérault. The *haut du pavé* of the PLM and Paulin Talabot was more to his taste.[44]

The company was now at the end of its rope. State support had not worked. It had Fr 150,000 on hand and Fr 300 to 400,000 in immediately payable debts and Fr 18 million in bonds, the collateral of which, of course, was the railroad, which most analysts argued was not currently worth that much. Its shares, though they still had some market value, were virtually worthless. On the Bourse, they were simply subjects of day-to-day agiotage. Bankruptcy was the only solution. This would mean that the bondholders were largely protected (though they might not get all their money back); the stockholders would lose everything.

The *procès verbal* for the general assembly of shareholders of the company that took place on 11 June 1860 reveals, not surprisingly, a "scene of inexpressible disorder." Bénat and the Board took the responsible position that they proceed to bankruptcy without being forced into it by the courts, carry out an orderly dissolution, regroup, and start anew. This had the support of the sequester committee and the Ministry of Public Works. It did not have the support of a majority of the *actionnaires*, who followed a team, led by de l'Espine, more or less made up of the old guard. A man only identified as Martin (100 shares) was the voice of the opposition. The current Board recommended they choose a committee to examine the books of the company (to prepare for bankruptcy) while Martin, supported by Bazille (this may well have been the artist Frédéric, whose wealthy family were prominent Montpellierians), cried out for new entreaties to Rouher, with whom he had "relations fréquentes." Neither side seemed assured of victory, but Bénat probably had more votes. The session descended to a shouting match, then to pushing and shoving at the podium, at which point Bénat walked out, closing the meeting "shortly before 6 P.M."

A series of assemblies followed, complete with petitioners from bondholders—who could vote only by proxy and found few "tuteurs"—milling about outside and besieging Public Works with paper and the shareholders ready to commit mayhem. Finally, on 28 September, the latter overthrew Bénat and Co. and installed a group of nonentities, though one was a general and three were civil engineers. They decided to keep up the fight for survival by floating a new loan.

But the end was near. On 8 October 1860, a process server, with moving van and men, arrived at the rue d'Isly headquarters with an order from the Tribunal de Commerce de Paris authorizing him to carry off the furniture as partial payment of the Fr 30,000 debt still owed to Hérault contractor Fassino. Only with seconds to spare did the "Director," Mauger, return with a delaying order. Such events became commonplace over the next several weeks. On 14 December 1860, nine well-known figures of Paris and Enghein des Bains who held 884 debentures among them wrote a carefully reasoned petition to Rouher, arguing that the state had an obligation to protect bondholders because it was at its authorization that they were put on public sale. The Graissessac, they knew, was finished. By not proceeding to bankruptcy, the government was destroying whatever value the bonds had left. His effort, they said, would help alleviate the current fear of rail investment in France. They hoped that he would intervene in an "efficacious manner to resolve a question the solution of which will serve as a precedent and is of interest to all *porteurs des titres des sociétés anonymes.*" Rouher marked "conf." in pencil on the document and scrawled a note at the top: "The state will not intervene. It is up to the judicial authorities."

And act they did. Against the will of the Board, the Tribunal de Commerce de Paris issued a judgment of *mise en faillite* on 27 February 1861. It then went to trial, and the Directors finally lost an appeal in the Cour Royale on 21 July. The struggle was over. The railroad line itself actually benefited from all this. The competing elements in the Company made every effort to make it run, and the new Board even found a cheap solution to the Faugères descent problem. In his next to last report, Thouret noted that there had been a doubling of the gross product in the first nine months of 1861 compared with the same period of 1860 (408,849 vs. 214,695). The coal company was putting out some 120 T of marine coal per day, 90 T to the Compagnie du Midi for sale along its lines, and 300 T for regional consumption. If such production continued, it appeared that the predicted goals might be possible. The total since the previous year was around 120,000 T.[45]

The mine company, despite all the uncertainties caused by the railroad, had in fact doubled its output since 1855. It had built access roads and rails, created an excellent ramp at Le Bousquet, begun to work on the problem of producing coke, and, in general, made "several significant improvements in the various mines."[46] Nevertheless, there was deep dissatisfaction with the works manager, Bartholémy Moulinier, not only because he seemed willing to sell out at a moment's notice, but, above all, because of his remarkable inability to get along with his workers and with the local population in general.

The Mouliniers, as we have seen, were the driving force in the mines earlier in the century, supplanting the Giral family, but carried themselves with the same notable-de-clocher hauteur of their predecessors. For all that, Bartholémy was hardly a fabulously wealthy person, barely joining the censitaires of the July Monarchy with a tax of Fr 254.[47] The Revolution of 1848 brought on a new explosion of illegal mining and considerable open conflict with Moulinier because of the past record of his company in failing to deliver coal to the nailmakers and for domestic uses at cost. Oscar Gervais, the first Prefect of the Second Republic, calmed things a bit by an arrêté setting the price at .62 francs per quintal for the low quality menus they used.[48] Although there was little to attract officials' attention to the mining district during the Revolution, immediately after the coup d'état, the first recorded strike occurred at the Ste. Barbe mine and spread to two others. It began in the wake of the fête à Ste. Barbe. The miners sought twenty-five centimes per cubic meter of coalface extraction, not sorted, which was the current standard and obviously one abused by the management. Significantly, with the assistance of "a band of *mauvais sujets* from the village of Graissessac,"[49] they also stopped the loaders and the carters from moving coal out. These would likely be Protestant nail makers showing solidarity with Catholic miners: no one, whether they worked for or against the mine, liked its management and, in particular, M. Moulinier.

Everything they did was suspect. A major conflict arose over the Company's move to dump waste into the Clédou stream. The main concern among residents to begin with was the probable effect of the sludge on the water level and the threat to the nail makers' mule track by its side. The government approved the dump on the condition that the company raise and reinforce the road. In March 1853 the mayor of Camplong informed the Sub-Prefect in Béziers that the road was under water and being destroyed because the company never fulfilled its obligations. Although the Company finally complied, hatred toward it did not abate.[50] By the later 1850s, excessive dumping had created ecological hazards, and the government ordered the company to dig a well at Estrechoux because of the filth in the Clédou. At Castan, the gunk in the water was so high that it literally stopped the flow of water in the ruisseau there. Downstream—at Villemagne on the Mare—the issue was a familiar one to twentieth-century big-city residents: all the fish were dying. But in an economy where trout might be the only meat you eat for months on end, it had more than cosmetic significance.[51]

Although it is quite possible that the real mastermind of these sorts of money-saving atrocities was Aaron Simon,[52] Moulinier, because of his proximity to the work force and community, usually took the blame. And he *must* have been unpleasant. Bédarieux's Commissaire de Police described him as a man "devoid of all sentiments of humanity. It is said that he once remarked that workers ought to be happy with a piece of dry bread." The man to whom the remark was made was later fired because he repeated it to others. A confidential report (for a nationwide survey) from the canton of Bédarieux on the status of industrial relations in 1858 gave pride of place to Graissessac/Camplong over Bédarieux as a scene of "antagonism"— Moulinier had recently laid off 350 of his 500 workers and had, in general, lost all regard "by the brutality that the workers attribute to him, manifested by his cutbacks in work and pay, and by the laughable accident benefits provided by the Company." He also tried to capitalize on the rivalry between Catholic Camplong, where his chief master-miner lived, and heavily Protestant Graissessac by encouraging the straw-boss's favoritism toward his countrymen in the mines. Rail Inspector Thouret added to the chorus, calling Moulinier "bullheaded" and "unintelligent."[53]

But in fact, as an outstanding report by Carrière, the Inspector of Mines for the Montpellier region, argued, Moulinier emerges as a scapegoat for efforts by the company to keep pace with rapidly changing market conditions in the 1850s. The early 1850s' demand for coal made it a time of special promise for the miners. Carrière said that they had been making 2.50 to 3 francs for a 7 A.M. to 3 P.M. day, "having the rest of the day to cultivate their *petit coin de terre*. There were no mine workers better paid than they."

Then came the 1853–44 agricultural crisis, which drove food prices up. And the company "spontaneously" increased wages when food prices rose in 1853–54. Alternative railroad employment in the mid-1850s also stimulated mine wages, while the new St. Geniès mine offered very high rates to lure experienced workers there. Increases at Graissessac were naturally accompained by speed-up tactics. The later 1850s saw some of these conditions reversed and the company cut wages, creating new antagonism. The approach of the rail line stimulated production, but sales actually lagged in 1857–58 due to the recession and dumping practices by rivals at Bessèges. Then came the new crisis in the rail company and the sequestration. At that point, layoffs began and continued at the time of Carrière's writing.[54]

But still, workers held Moulinier personally responsible. Increasingly the control of company affairs fell into the hands of the quieter and more competent Simon who, despite priestly denunciation of his religion, remained more popular than the Bounderby from St. Gervais. After carrying through a bond issue to increase liquidity and new works to expand operations to full capacity, Simon and Usquin won governmental approval to convert the Quatre mines réunies de Graissessac into a *société anonyme* in 1862. The head office would be in Montpellier, and its twelve-member board was dominated by Héraultais. The government report supporting the recommendation for a limited liability charter emphasized the importance of the railroad in the competitive potential of the mine company.[55] It also remarked on the need for more competent direction. The first general assembly of the company's shareholders overthrew Moulinier. Usquin, the Kuhnholtz family, the Bazilles, and a new and potent force, the Leenhardt brothers, led the move. The new Board of directors appointed Simon as the sole Director of the company's operations.

Improvements followed in rapid succession: a new coal-flake briquette facility at Estrachoux in 1863; new pits at Ste. Barbe mine in 1865; covering the loading docks at Estrechoux the same year; a good dozen new roads and ramps at various sites on the coal field in the mid-1860s; and the completion, by 1870, of a narrow-gauge rail from Alzon to Cap Negre in the Graissessac section of the basin.[56] Production followed suit. By the end of the decade, output topped 200,000 T; by 1875, Graissessac ranked eighth among French coal producers with 269,054 T.

As can be seen at a glance in Table 6-2, that was the peak year in the company's history. Dedicated to modern methods as the new Board may have been, Graissessac never lived up to its potential. The reason was not at all hard to locate. The ill-starred railroad that was supposed to serve it assured that the price of coal on delivery remained too high to compete at nearly the level one had hoped. In 1866, the bankrupt rail company had been virtually forced on the Compagnie du Midi by the government. The coal company's long-held dream that this connection would lower shipping costs did not come to pass. The Midi, itself facing rocky times as the Pereires began experiencing the shock waves from their collapsing Crédit Mobilier, sought to squeeze profits out wherever possible and would not think of lowering rates on a line

Table 6–2

1830	12,154 T.	
1847	43,143	
1853	41,870	
1856	54,431	
1859	79,891	
1862	124,682	
1866	172,593	
1869	188,398	
1872	215,985	
1875	269,054	(ranked 8th)
1880	243,857	
1885	222,629	
1890	261,898	
1891	248,679	(ranked 10th)

Source: Adapted from E. Gruner.[57]

it did not want in the first place.[58] The upshot was predictable. The price of five-centimes per tonne-kilometer meant that upon arrival at Cette, more than ten francs was added to the price of the coal because of railroad transport costs alone. Coal from Alais (150 kilometers distant), enjoying lower rates, could compete with Graissessac coal at its own port.

But cost was not even the main problem. Jules Maistre, the owner of Villeneutette and a key figure in Languedoc business life, wrote the main report on coal in the Hérault for the national Enquête sur les houilles of 1874. His remarks sum up the tragedy of the history recounted here. The Béziers-Graissessac "is a line of one track only and it is constructed in the most deplorable manner. While on the main lines of the Midi, one may pull fifty to sixty coal cars, on the Graissessac line it is impossible to attach more than twenty." The volume in any day thus had to remain low, and the problem was exacerbated by a lack of sidings, making passing difficult, while the cable at Faugères added even more time. Speeds were much reduced as well because of the poor construction in general. Thus, there was never enough Graissessac coal at Cette even to load the three ships that could currently dock there simultaneously (this low number was another complaint, of course). The consequence was obvious—a vast potential was lost. "It is not enough to have coal at low prices at a port to attract ships; we must above all assure ships that there will be coal in abundance so that they will not have to wait a long time in port. Under current conditions, nothing is certain." And what a sad thing it was, for "nowhere in France," concluded Maîstre, "does there exist a better location [for coals of such excellent quality], but we do not even have enough for our navy because the railroad is defective."[59]

7

A Railroad That Never Was

In this same 1874 inquiry, an unnamed correspondent from Lodève complained bitterly about the price of coal, which he attributed entirely to high freight rates. But underproduction due to the Graissessac railroad's technical bottlenecks clearly had an impact as well. In the last five years, the cost of steam-engine coal in Lodève had risen from Fr 26.75 to Fr 33 per tonne. Surprisingly, this was almost the same price industrialists were paying in Montpellier. How was this possible? By road, Montpellier was 85 kilometers from Graissessac while Lodève was less than 25. By rail, Montpellier was a good 130 kilometers via Cette. But, amazingly, Lodève was even farther: the city had a rail line, but it came from Agde. A glance at the map and some simple addition renders a total of 134 kilometers for the voyage of a load of Graissessac coal to what was formerly the Hérault's most industrial city. The correspondent pointed out, not without irony, that it was almost as cheap to import coal from Graissessac by the old way—*au dos de mulet*—and emphasized that they still used considerable quantities of coal from the Alais (Alès) basin.

There was, in this mid-1870s report, an air of resignation. By then, the Lodévois seemed beaten, whipped. But let us turn the clock back again to the 1850s. Despite the ups and downs, despite the doldrums of certain cities, the shot in the arm that the railroad might bring seemed enough to keep optimism afloat. As the Graissessac tale unfolded, an equally significant drama was played out on the other side of the Escandorgue.

Simply put, the future of Lodève and much of the Hérault became bound up in the international struggle for economic supremacy between the networks of financial interests led by the Pereire brothers on one hand and James de Rothschild on the other.[1] The Pereires were remarkably dynamic and persuasive entrepreneurs whose Crédit Mobilier sought to mobilize and deploy capital in ways never before imagined. Of all the disciples of Saint-Simon, they came the closest in the capitalist lineage to realizing his vision of limitless economic possibility. That they flew too close to the sun detracts little from the luster of their example. The more workmanlike (and far better heeled) world of Baron Rothschild also included its share of former Saint-Simonians, but having gained the high ground in France early on, many of their efforts—as the southern situation would reveal— were defensive, antiproductive, and smacked of old-regime influence peddling. Paulin Talabot, certainly in his youth a visionary worthy of Père Enfantin's praise, was the key player in Rothschild's southern strategy. He had pioneered railroad development and mining in the Gard and emerged quickly as its most illustrious citizen. He served as a deputy from the department during the July Monarchy. By the 1850s, he had become one of the half-dozen or so kingpins of French capitalism and a man as comfortable in the corridors of political power as in the boardroom.[2]

Talabot was the architect of the broad program, crystalizing in the formation of the Paris-Lyon-Méditerranée railroad in 1857, that gave the Rhône valley, the Gard, and the Bouches-du-Rhône their privileged, but Paris-dependent, position. As we have seen, Marseille and far eastern Languedoc cemented their dominant place in the south against the claims of Cette and Montpellier in the 1840s. Despite the nasty turn of political events in 1851, there still was reason to believe that the stranglehold might be broken, however. For one thing, Louis Napoleon himself had promised to promote enterprise and encourage local capital investment with a favorable state policy toward the rest of Languedoc.[3] More important, the Pereires conceived of a program by which they hoped to crack the power of their rivals in the south, one in which lower Languedoc, specifically the Hérault, held center stage. This was the famous "Cette-Marseille par la littoral" plan by which three objectives would be realized: 1) a second competitive route from Paris through the center of France to the great Mediterranean port would be created; 2) the Compagnie du Midi, already ceded Bordeaux-Toulouse-Cette, would have a smooth continuation on to Marseille from the west, and 3) Cette's role as a major rival to Marseille would be much enhanced, especially for western Mediterranean and Algerian traffic.[4] How Montpellier fit into all this was problematic, as we shall see, but Lodève's place was to be a central one because however the route from the north might run through the Hérault, the city would be the gateway into the department.

Emile Pereire laid out the essential vision for the shareholders of the Midi: "Marseille and Languedoc and by consequence the southwest of the Empire are freed [with the building of the Cette-Marseille], from the exigencies and the constraints on service of the Compagnie de Lyon à la Méditerranée, a company whose entire energy is focused on the main artery of its system and thus has no interest in developing east-west communication." And with a second north-south connection as well, "these beautiful provinces, having fallen little by little into a decline [*langueur*] due to the political development that has led to the preponderance of the north of France over the south, . . . will be reborn to a new life under the influence of our railroads." Finally, history would be vindicated: "An irresistible force once again leads civilization toward the Mediterranean basin: it pursues from shore to shore the barbarism that had taken possession of it on the ruins of ancient civilization."[5]

One should not imagine, however, that all barbarians would be treated equally. Or that, specifically, the potential benefits of this plan for industrial Languedoc were uppermost in Pereire's mind. Although the brothers' closeness to Michel Chevalier no doubt made them more aware of Lodève and the cloth district than otherwise would have been the case, they would happily sacrifice (as events would prove) the interests of a particular area in the pursuit of their larger competitive ambitions. This was especially unfortunate in light of their mode of operation in seeking railroad concessions. They counted on general support from the top, for it was no secret that Louis Napoleon admired their verve and their almost populist approach to capitalist development, but their essential tactic "consisted in bringing to life a global vision in the imagination" of the public, which meant activating local publicity, speaking before municipal councils, organizing mass meetings, and the like.[6] Not only did this approach irritate steadfast and cautious ministers like Eugene Rouher, but it created often unrealistic expectations locally, making failure to achieve a particular program all the more difficult to swallow.

If saving the industrial piedmont of Languedoc was rather an accidental aspect of the Pereires' grand design, so, too, was the enormous potential that it promised for Cette. The reason that the Hérault port seemed the keystone of the structure began with the simple fact that the easily built Montpellier-Cette railroad (in place by 1839) was the western end of the line for the Talabot rail empire. This made Cette, rather than the department capital, the natural depot for a line coming from the west. But in the general scheme of the Pereires, although it was nice that Cette would benefit, the real point remained the creation of a rival line to Marseille. Their plan for the littoral route in fact even bypassed Montpellier to the south, although a connector would be laid (see map on p. 179). The problem, of course, was that in order to include Montpellier on an all-Midi route from Bordeaux to Marseille, PLM track would have to be used, and the antagonism between the two groups made negotiating that unlikely. Currently, goods had to be transferred from Midi to PLM rolling stock at Cette, a costly and time-consuming operation.

The concept of a second route from Paris was what brought Montpellier back into the Midi picture. The littoral idea, although not formally proposed until 1860, was already suggested by the 1852 concession for the Bordeaux-Toulouse-Cette and much discussed thereafter. Included in the

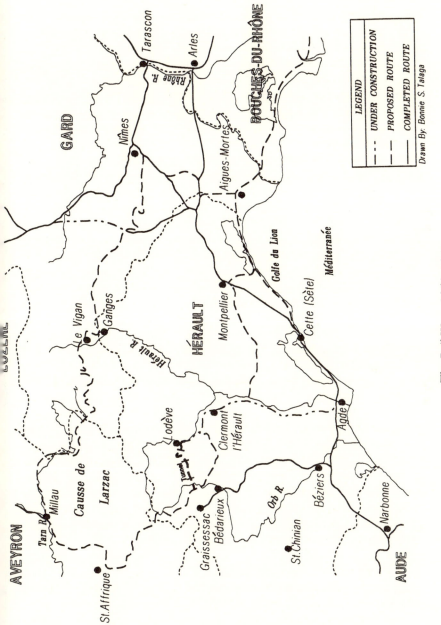

The Rail Wars, 1858–1866

LEGEND
-·-·- UNDER CONSTRUCTION
----- PROPOSED ROUTE
········· COMPLETED ROUTE

Drawn By: Bonnie S. Talaga

1852 concession was a line from Agde to Lodève, thus providing an outlet for not only the woolens industry and the growing Hérault valley wine output, but also for products from the Aveyron (then coming to Lodève by road), especially the rapidly developing Roquefort cheese industry. But by any reckoning, to bring a transnational line straight down to this little fishing town, on to Cette and thence to the east (possibly skipping Montpellier altogether) was patently absurd. Thus, in 1855, emerged a Pereire proposal to build a line from Rodez to Montpellier that would connect up with the Grand Central tracks from Clermont-Ferrand and go to Lodève, connect with the Lodève-Agde, and then fairly quickly branch off toward Montpellier, either at Cartels or at Paulhan. The former made more sense for industrial purposes, the latter for the transport of wine.

Determination of the route through the Hérault, however, quickly took a back seat to the main event: the decision by the Lyon-Méditerranée to bid for a concession that would allow it to complete a second axis and thus retain a monopoly over north-south traffic. It sought a line from Rodez to Nîmes via Le Vigan, thus by-passing the Hérault altogether. The occasion for this bid, made on 25 November 1856, was the impending bankruptcy of the Grand Central, which held the concessions through the Auvergne and down to Rodez. Talabot and François Bartholony, director of Paris-Orléans, had already made the decision to pick up the pieces of this over-extended firm. From the point of view of the government this rail purchase was a godsend. It was part of a complex move by which the PO and the Lyon-Méditerranée, in threatening to create a second line to the south that would outflank the Paris-Lyon, forced the latter fully into the Talabot orbit. The wheels were greased by Rothschild, a major stockholder in both, but it was a grand coup for Bartholony and Talabot. A merged company, Paris-Lyon-Méditerranée (PLM), was the consequence, and the PO and the PLM cemented their connection even further. About the same time, Talabot was completing the creation of the massive Compagnie des Docks de Marseille, which gave his group control of much of the port-side shipping operations in Marseille. "In 1857 [when the operation was carried out] the Orléans and the PLM saved the entire system by assuming the burden of the Grand-Central, too heavy for the Midi."[7] Besides official good will, the companies won a logical claim to operate the new Paris-Marseille connection, thus retaining monopoly control. Later on, the PLM also agreed to take over the troubled Algerian rail system, winning again the gratitude of Rouher, the Minister of Public Works, and his loyal assistant who oversaw the rail system, Louis de Franqueville.

The warmth of this relationship was enhanced by several factors. Bartholony, Talabot, and Charles Didion (Talabot's closest friend and a director of both the Orléans and the PLM) and Franqueville were all Polytechniciens and engineers, whose links the Pereires habitually decried. Rouher generally did his best to stay above personal relations and hence accusations of favoritism. He was reeling at the time over charges that he had conceded the Pyrénées network to the Compagnie du Midi before any adjudication had taken place.[8] But his decisions regarding the great war for "Rodez to the sea" reveal a studied neutrality that only reluctantly gave way to support for the PLM.

There was much dispute over who made the first claim for this line, but it was obviously critical for the Midi to secure it if it were to ever be in a position to realize its dream of total control of an entirely separate line from Paris to Marseille. Together with Bordeaux-Languedoc, the Pereires' power position versus their rivals would be significant indeed. Thus, as a first step, the Rodez-Montpellier was absolutely critical. PLM knew it and fought like a tiger.

The key moment in the conflict did not arrive until 1861–62, but the battle raged publicly for four years beforehand. Naturally, with so much riding on the outcome, armies of publicists supported by local officials, took to the field. There is no need to review all the arguments, and there were few surprises in the positions taken. The Hérault, especially the city fathers of and Montpellier, waged a ferocious battle. Mayor Jules Pégazy of Montpellier and Michel Chevalier, president of the Conseil général of the Department mobilized forces and subsidized publicity in an unprecedented fashion. Petitions from all over the department poured in to the Ministry in Paris. The most striking came from Lodève. It was covered with over 400 signatures from woolens workers and the names of 200 more who could not sign. Everyone knew that the future of the city depended on the outcome of this struggle.[9]

An early blow had already been sustained. Contrary to his own earlier estimate, Duponchel, Chief railroad engineer for the Department, had produced a report in late 1856 claiming that it would be virtually impossible to take a railroad out of Lodève to the north. Everyone knew that the Escalette was impassable. Route 9, an old Roman road, went by St. Etienne de Gourgas and up to the Causse de Larzac along the gentler easterly slope before turning north toward Millau.[10] But it had been assumed that a tunnel through the Escandorgue to the west or northwest of the city could be cut and thereby open the way for a line up the Orb river valley to Roquefort and Millau. Duponchel believed that not only would any tunnel have to be incredibly long and costly, but because it would have to start so low on the mountainside to keep the grade within legal (and physical) limits, spring waters above it would pose intolerable dangers. He therefore argued for a railroad that would skirt Lodève to the south, with a major station at Cartels and a five-kilometer branch to the city itself, and go on to join an extension of the Béziers-Graissessac that would then follow the same route to the north (see map on p. 179).

Lodève's Municipal Council, naturally alarmed by this report, decided to seek a second opinion and hired another state engineer, Duviol, to study the matter further. The chief technical problem was to find a route that would allow for a more gradual assent on the Lodève side and a higher tunnel. He discovered a route that would place the station on the east side of the city above the faubourg des Carmes, traverse the Lergue by a viaduct, thus maintaining elevation, and then proceed up the more gradual ruisseau des Plans, then loop below that village and on around the hillside to the valley of the ruisseau du Mas de Merou, and thereafter following the road to Lunas until it began to mount quickly by switchbacks. At that point (394 meters) the tunnel would begin and emerge at Vasplonges 2700 meters away. The rock through which the tunnel would be cut was generally easier to pierce (or so it appeared) than the series of strata facing builders in the monstrous seven-kilometer tunnel criticized by Duponchel. The descent toward Lunas was straight along the hillside paralleling the road. All grades were well within limits. The Duviol plan seemed to solve the technical problem and had the strong support of the General Council of the department, which pledged to award a million-franc subvention for the construction of the Rodez-Montpellier if (but only if) the line passed through Lodève.[11]

But, in fact, this conflict had little to do with technical issues, as became obvious when the war of words heated up. It was clear early on that the PLM was not serious in its desire to build anything through the center. Why should it compete with itself? The company had already exploited its monopoly shamelessly, charging more for carrying Loire coal than for coal from Alais. When a rival company set up shop at Bessèges (Robiac et Bessèges), Talabot and the rail company did all they could to prevent it from acquiring a rail concession and then engineered what would be called today an unfriendly takeover after the new coal company built its own track without subvention and began shipping.[12] Moreover, PLM had already been awarded (as of 1858) the concession of a line from Brioude to Alais, which in effect completed a second route from the north via Alais. But its construction plans satisfied only "local use" specifications, thus making any national routing through it precarious. (This was the same problem limiting the Bèziers-Graissessac as a through route.)

Monopoly conditions assured that rates remained outrageously high wherever rails were laid. Hippolyte Peut, one of the most ardent promoters of Languedoc rail development, wrote an excellent brochure on the general problem. He found it ironic that the rail companies had such marvelous support from the state and such careful technical assistance and regulation, but when it came to pricing policy, they claimed and gained the right "to use and abuse their rates *selon leur bon plaisir* even though these rates crush those industries . . . most useful and worthy of public encouragement." One of their most unsettling tactics was to charge low rates where rival transport facilities (road or canal) remained competitive and, after driving the latter out of business, sharply increasing them.[13] This form of "dumping" was not needed by the Companie du Midi over much of its east-west route because it also owned the Canal du Midi and could keep rates up on both!

There were no heroes and villains among the great capitalists involved in the disastrous history of rail construction in the Hérault. If they were not out-and-out criminals, as with Béziers-Graissessac, they used their great wealth and their influence to gain profit and advantage whether or not they violated the canons of laissez-faire. While the Pereires sang the virtues of competitive entrepreneurship in promoting the second route to Paris and the littoral line, they proved no more generous than the PLM when they possessed the monopoly.

Nevertheless, the circumstances of the present situation assured that if a truly rival route were created, lower rates throughout Languedoc would result. Indeed, one of PLM's goals in this fight was the termination of the Midi Company's ownership of the Bordeaux-Cette Canal. Whatever the outcome for Lodève, the key issue was the creation of a viable rail system through the heart of the Hérault owned by a company other than the PLM. A July 1858 report from M. Tardy, the Engineer in chief of the Hérault, was greeted with an enthusiastic "bon" scrawled across the top by Rouher and seemed to wrap up the question of viably passing through Lodève. It further proposed a line to the west (in addition to going north to Rodez) that promised to integrate the entire southern cloth district into the national rail network. Tardy found an important error in Duviol's study (nine meters too low at the entrance point for the tunnel on the Lodève side), but made a new proposal that would lengthen the tunnel but reduce the overall length of the route by shortening the loop at Le Plans. On a positive note, he found that while the tunnel would have to be lined with masonry, the basaltic rock would be even easier to move than Duviol thought, and that water damage posed no problem. He also favored the more direct route through Gignac to Montpellier, noting that the southern tier of wine villages only needed secondary track to serve their export needs. But more fundamentally, Tardy proposed a line that would link all the main cloth towns of the piedmont from Lodève in the east to Castres in the west. His justification:

> From Lodève to Lavaur, a distance of 160 kilometers, the total population of the communes traversed would be 112,455 inhabitants; [by way of comparison] the number of people from Lunas to Rodez is 51,107, smaller by more than half.
>
> The industrial significance of these populations is much greater still than their numbers. At Lodève in 1856, 8000 workers toiled in its factories. Bédarieux, Riols, and St. Pons together have more than Lodève. St. Amans and Mazamet produce more than Lodève, Bédarieux, and St. Pons together. Castres and Lavaur also have their specialties. In order to find an industrial presence as great and in the midst of this industry a coal basin as rich, there are, perhaps, south of Paris only two comparable points, St. Etienne to Lyon and Alais to Nîmes to Beaucaire.[14]

One could not ask for clearer vision of the continuing significance of industrial Languedoc. That it was so well received in Paris testifies to the relative impartiality of Rouher—as of 1858. Everyone sensed the urgency of the situation in southern industry. At this moment, the Graissessac rail catastrophe was producing glaring headlines, the crisis of 1857–58 had overtaken southern woolens, and the Montpellier financial community faced serious problems. A letter from one Pierre Soulages, neither a fabricant nor a worker, but a "small landowner of Lodève," spoke for everyone across the district: "The railroad . . . will be the radical remedy for all the recurrent ills that weigh upon our current situation in bringing to our worker population further resources capable of renewing the face of Lodève.[15]

Unfortunately, 1858 marked only the beginning, and the dreary controversy slogged on. The declining silk region around Le Vigan naturally jumped at the opportunity to try to recoup its losses. Marseille was the main commercial outlet for Millau, and, unlike much of the Aveyron, its municipal council, through vacillating, sided with the Rodez-Nîmes line. Decazeville, already connected with Rodez, would have been happy with either line, though generally favored the more direct route to Marseille via Nîmes. Roquefort was adamant about the Millau-Montpellier for its southern markets were all via Montpellier. Another interesting point made, not only by Pégazy, Peut, and their Montpellier juggernaught, but by many Aveyron petitioners, was the historic human connections between the Hérault capital and the uplands to its northwest. It was estimated that 10 percent of the people of Montpellier had been born in the Aveyron. Temporary migration brought an even higher percentage there on an itinerant basis. Goods and people cemented the endpoints of the proposed line.[16]

The populations actually served by the two proposed routes and the technical difficulties of construction (save for the Lodève tunnel) should have made the Hérault route the overwhelming choice. The land between Millau and Le Vigan was perhaps the most sterile in France with tiny clusters of sheep and goat herders eking out a living in the midst of breathtaking peaks, mesas, and vertiginous valleys. The wild beauty of this terrain was matched by the difficulty of traversing it. No less than forty-three tunnels and countless viaducts dotted the maps for the proposal. Even though Le Vigan-Nîmes made sense in all respects (and was an easy shot technically a few kilometers out of Le Vigan), the forgotten lands of the Gard-Aveyron border seemed to pose an insurmountable barrier.[17]

But this did not by any means assure the victory of the Rodez-Montpellier (nor certainly of Tardy's vision). The central problem in fact turned out to be a paralytic indecision about the route to follow in the Hérault itself. First of all, the Hérault's Prefect Gavrini thought of Montpellier as a "second order" city not worthy of having multiple lines radiating "like chemins vicinaux" from it. Throughout the controversy, he seemed less than excited about an Hérault victory and was in fact finally replaced by a somewhat more supportive bureaucrat, P.M. Piétri.[18] More important, because of earlier concessions, how precisely to connect everything up without too much overlap presented perplexing problems. As already noted, Cette, not Montpellier, had by default become the fulcrum of larger systems. The Béziers-Graissessac seemed useless as anything but a coal-feeder. The Agde-Lodève, though largely welcome when conceded in 1852, now appeared as a stumbling block. It was senseless not to try to use part of it in the proposed national network. But to go to Agde, thence to Cette and onward (to where? Montpellier? Palavas-Aigues-Mortes?) was ridiculous. Now there were the two proposals for crossing the Hérault. Gignac and

Paulhan, traditional rivals anyway and politically night and day, were at each others' throats over the issue. Clermont naturally supported Paulhan and was still plugging for a route going west up the Salagou to Valquières that would by-pass *both* Bédarieux and Lodève (Duponchel's proposal) and thus make *it* the key larger town in that part of the Hérault. Lies about population, production, and land under cultivation, and fantasmagoric visions of the future of the world (the-great-leather-boom from Aniane, alcohol-the-foundation-of-the-chemical-industry from St. Pargoire) punctuated the north-south debate. Tardy, though favoring the industrial north, had the bright, and immensely complicating, idea of scrapping the Agde-Lodève and creating two other lines: one from Lodève to Gignac to Cournonterral and then down to Cette, the other from Béziers to Pézenas-Montagnac and on to Cournonterral and Montpellier with the windswept little village of Cournonterral serving as an unlikely crossroad. Naturally, every time a town or village saw itself on a railroad map, a hundred newspaper articles, brochures, broadsides, and poems were written, and a thousand speeches were made to whatever body or public meeting would listen. With the Hérault criss-crossed by half a dozen proposals, hardly anyone was left out. The noise was deafening, the archives filled, officials tore their hair—and the peaceful route through inanimate rock in the Aveyron and Gard to Le Vigan regained its appeal.

In all this, of course, the Hérault's squabbles were not that unusual. Indeed, geographer Michel Chanais makes local particularism the central theme of his call to action for historical and contemporary study in his discipline of transport rationalization (in both senses of the word) in France.[19] But it would be wrong to blame the victim (once again) in this matter. The desperate struggle for rail service reflected the desperate economic situation of the late 1850s; even the wine industry was suffering. All the conflicts and recriminations (along with the odors from the Graissessac railroad affair), however, served above all as an excuse for officials to procrastinate. The most serious problem in the department was the growing acrimony between Montpellier and Cette, regarded at one time as potential twin cities. Montpellier already feared that Cette's place in the Algerian traffic might hurt its own commercial role, but the rail situation exacerbated things, especially after the Pereire's littoral plan was formally submitted in 1860. Referring to an earlier audience with the Emperor, the Cette municipal council addressed a position paper to Rouher in September 1861 arguing for their city's preeminent role: "You are aware of course that after an examination of the various plans, his majesty the Emperor recognized and announced that in the general interest, the route to adopt for the railroad through the center of France to the Mediterranean was the direct line from Rodez to Cette," which would branch off the Lodève-Agde at Paulhan and come to Cette via the east shore of the Etang de Thau. For its part, Montpellier had already launched a Port-Palavas study that would counter Cette's ascendancy.[20]

Such internecine bloodletting in the Hérault made the Gard's straight-

forward appeal for aid to its hard-hit silk area and the clear line of its uni-
tary proposal look very good indeed (see map on p. 179 for the only line
ever proposed). As if to paint in the details of this untroubled picture, an
engineer in the service at Avignon, Moriceau, presented a "definitive" report
on 21 October 1861, that gave the nod in all respects to Millau-Nîmes,
arguing that it served more people and more significant economic purposes.
The only trouble was that he was comparing it with only the first step of
the other route, the region from Millau to Lodève! The assumption,
although nowhere specified in the text, seemed to be that the Lodève-Agde-
Cette (and so forth) route could suffice for the rest. There was nothing at
all on a Lodève-Montpellier connection. Nor did he comment on the details
supplied by Hérault officials regarding the current freight (above all, wools
and woolens) moving by wagon between the two cities. The report did
everything possible to inflate the potential income from the Gard route and
even went so far as to say that virtually all traffic currently passing from the
Aveyron through Lodève and Montpellier was on its way to Nîmes and
Marseille anyway.

The response, as can be imagined, was immediate and vehement. The
most salient fact—which does not appear on the report itself—is Moriceau's
exact official title: "Principal Inspector for commercial operations of the
line from Lyon to the Mediterranean." This meant that, even though he
was a state official, three-fourths of his salary came from the PLM. The new
Prefect of the Hérault, Piétri (previously at Bordeaux and quite knowledgeable about the affairs of the south), wrote his superiors that the report, "filled
with errors" and in fact comparing apples with oranges, had to be "redone,"
put in the hands of someone "as honorable and capable" as Moriceau but
in a position to have "a more perfect independence."[21]

The Moriceau report created the moment of truth in the whole affair.
On 30 January 1862, Michel Chevalier wrote Rouher a letter pointing out
the absurdities of the report and also explicitly accused Moriceau and his
immediate superior, Teulon (who was a native of Le Vigan), of deliberate
misrepresentation. He wondered how Barreau, the chief engineer for the
southern system, could appoint so prejudiced an observer. In his response,
Rouher icily noted that the assignment was made by the "superior administration." Emile Periere had also written Rouher, saying that it all seemed
odder still as the little connection from Millau to Lodève was the only part
of this proposal that would cost the administration any money. The Midi
Company was on record that it would pay all costs of the Lodève-Montpellier line *and* the Cette-Marseille. In effect, he was saying that the Company would work out the needed refinements for integrating Cette-Mont-
pellier relations and interests. A huge petition from notables and deputies
from both the Hérault and Aveyron appeared in Rouher's desk on 5 February. It contained more than 2000 signatures, all in educated hands.

Rouher's response—not until 28 February—was hardly encouraging.
Simply ignoring both the Perieres's magnanimity and the departmental
Council's pledge of one million, he said that the Lodève-Montpellier con-

nection—"still very much alive"—needed further study (it had been six years now), and that the errors would be rectified by Barreau. As for the Cette-Marseille, he felt it "raised very delicate questions" and that he had appointed a "special committee of the Inspecteurs générals des Ponts et Chaussees to investigate it." And—whatever the outcome—there is no reason [beyond correcting the apparent errors] to change anything in the dispositions of the current inquiry."

When Rouher wrote this letter—with a copy to Periere—he had finally heard from Barreau. The latter said that they had not included any discussion of Lodève-Montpellier or Cette-Marseille because that was not their charge. Naturally, he was "shocked" that people would doubt Moriceau's objectivity. After all, "you appointed him." Thus, Rouher was directly responsible for the two central issues in the report. Had he set it up that way? Amazingly, he continued to defend Moriceau and accepted his "revised" report of 24 April 1862 without comment. On 24 May, Ernest Leenhardt, a key Board member of Graissessac mines and a "member of the Central Committee of the Hérault for the Rodez-Mediterranean Railroad," published an article in the *Journal de Montpellier* summing up the flagrant abuses that seemed to be occurring and challenging the Ponts et Chausées to return "to balance and objectivity." This prompted Rouher to order his Prefect there to explore "the situation of the *Journal de Montpellier* from the government's point of view" and "to inform the editor-in-chief of my observations" regarding the "exaggerated" and "inflammatory" perspective offered in Leenhardt's piece. Was he threatening censorship? Whatever the answer (and it seems quite obvious), Rouher had clearly decided that he would not bow to pressure.

The entire tale was soon to end, for he would officially refuse to authorize the Cette-Marseille line before the spring was out and simply leave the Rodez to the Mediterranean rivalry dangling—both projects were authorized, but both companies gave them low priority. Neither line was ever built according to the original designs, and a "national" line that would rival the Rhône corridor never came to pass. The 1866 Railroad Act, opening the way for local lines, would bring about, years later, one-track feeders for Le Vigan, Lodève-Montpellier (a horrible little line laid out like a class-C road that figures on no map today, but whose ill-made bridges and viaducts can be made out among the gorse and broom off route 9 to the north), a central line from Paulhan serving the wine villages toward Montpellier (today a very slow SNCF bus more or less follows the route), and toward the Béziers-Graissessac, connecting at Roquessels (the same slow bus takes one that direction too), and, finally, Tardy's dream on to the west was fulfilled in the same burst of Third Republic politically motivated public works enthusiasm (reaching Mazamet in 1890). By that time, the only town worth serving from an industrial point of view was the little capital of délainage.[22] The "center" route to Paris would finally be pieced together connecting up with the Béziers-Graissessac. It still runs today but takes twice as long as even non-TGV trains from Paris to Béziers by Lyon.

Thus the fate of industrial Languedoc was sealed in 1862. Obviously, it was merely the final blow, perhaps no more than the flick of a finger. But it was at least that. And Eugène Rouher did it. Neither the powers that be in the Hérault nor the Pereires hid their disgust. Said the Committee for the Rodez-Mediterranean (Hérault): The people of our department, "devoted to the Emperor . . . , had hoped from him the righting of the wrongs done to it in the past through the adoption of the defective lines that cross their land [the reference to Graissessac and Lodève-Agde is clear] and in that hope are deceived again; the sense of their rights is so great that this negative decision will disaffect them entirely." Emile Pereire was even more pointed: "I swear, to my great regret, that in the thirty years that I have been involved with railroad issues and about which I have earned the right to speak, never have I seen anything more extraordinary." The reference was to the entire development that at each step seemed to benefit the PLM. The greatest tragedy was that PLM had entered the fight only for the purpose of offsetting the initiative of the Midi Company. Even should their line have been accorded, a blue-ribbon committee in the Aveyron had no doubt that PLM, "being the proprietor of the mines at Grande-Combe, would not hesitate to do to the coal of the Aveyron [Decazeville] what it had already done to that of the Loire, that is establish rates that would prevent it from appearing on the markets of the littoral." The final issue, stressed by all advocates of the second competitive route, from Chevalier to the most trenchant analyst of the situation, Hippolyte Peut, was "the tremendous congestion," the "piling up of goods," and "the long delays in delivery," which have "given rise to commercial disasters" throughout the Midi.[23]

For its part, the PLM continued to trumpet its "right" to control the key north-south connection. To read their position provides fascinating insight into its directors' conception of capitalism. The Midi's move to build a rival line to Marseille "constituted a grave infraction of the principles that have served as the basis for the great systems (*grands reseaux*). If in 1857 the companies accepted the heavy burden of a large number of costly and more or less unproductive lines, they did so in order to assure a clearly determined zone where they might develop their activities protected from the aggression of an adventurous competitor. Until recently the companies appeared to have understood that their enterprises rested on the absolute respect for the specified systems. The Midi Company, the first and alone, takes a different attitude today and endeavors to penetrate a region that was the cradle of the Méditerranée road, the one whose *possession, if we may be permitted this expression*, is the oldest and least debatable. The cause that we defend in this circumstance is not only ours, it is that of all the railroad companies."[24] Inasmuch as the Rothschild group already controled virtually everything *but* the Compagnie du Midi (the Lyon-Geneva had just been taken over by the PLM), the last was a rather gratuitous comment!

The tension inherent in this statement is revealed in the italicized words. Clearly embarrassed by the use of such language in a supposedly competitive capitalist system, Talabot nevertheless did not edit it out. On the other hand, it should be remembered that the Midi did not hesitate to use its position to gain easy control of the Pyrenees network, nor did it fail to argue that Rodez to the Mediterranean fell into *its* national network. Still, there was no question that PLM *did* represent northern interests at the expense of much of the south, whereas the Midi group, despite their *mission civilisatrice* mentality, was more a friend of south, at least by default.

How far this commitment went, however, would soon be revealed. The key decision that Rouher had to make related to the Cette-Marseille, for, despite all the Pereires' cries of the public good and love for Languedoc, he knew that their interest in the Rodez-Montpellier would flag if the littoral route were not conceded. From both technical and commercial viewpoints, there were reasonable arguments against the latter, which would pass through the marshy, sandy, shifting terrain of the Camargue and require many bridges and trestles through the *étangs* and across the canals and natural mouths of the Rhône (see map on p. 179) and serve virtually no economically important center en route. (The Grand Rhône remains today unbridged below Arles, although the region between Port St. Louis and Fos-sur-mer has recently become a major industrial park and port.) Nevertheless, such impediments were usually grist for the Saint-Simonian mill, and, obviously, the brash offer by the Midi Company to foot the bill itself put incredible pressure on the Administration.

But Rouher said no anyway. His public rationale stressed the technical difficulties and the commercial barrenness of the route. But the most serious aspect of the Pereires' arguments of late had been the question of making coal competitive and hence conquering the Mediterranean market from England. Rouher's (or very likely Franqueville's) response was nonsense, although it provided some interesting figures. The report said that English competition at Marseille was already eliminated. Of 470,000 tons exported, 100,000 came from Bouches de Rhône lignite mines, 30,000 from the Loire, and 298,000 from the Gard. And "only" 44,000 tons was English coal. Therefore, English competition was "conquered." For Marseille, yes, and this was an improvement, for one of the port's main roles in the past was the re-export of English coal to more distant foreign markets. But of course this does not in the least address direct English competition everywhere else. Most obviously, the Gard *did* have a virtual monopoly. Not a lump of Graissessac coal came through Marseille. Rouher (Franqueville) said this was because of the high price of its coal at the pit-head; he gave no source, but undoubtedly it was some ancient statistic, probably from Napoleon Garella, for it simply was not true. Clearly one of the key fears of PLM was the competition from Graissessac (*and* Decazeville). And with such competition—out of Cette and out of Marseille—French coal export just might have beaten out the Welsh in the Mediterranean.

Rouher, obviously aware of the anti-laissez-faire position he was taking in all this, provided a classic rationale: with "further industrialization," competition "will be most desirable, but it is my most profound conviction that the moment has not yet come" because it would "frighten potential investors and panic those already holding titles."[25] This lesson in the contradictions of developing capitalism was complemented by a sweetening of the pill. The decision ordered an end to transbordement at Cette, imposing a *tarif* for Montpellier to Marseille equal to the 160-kilometer rate that would have been created with the littoral route (it was 200 via Arles, a track under construction) and awarding the Midi a station in Marseille. Indeed, as a friend of Aaron Simon's, the Parisian businessman N. Lataud, remarked in a letter, although "La Méditerranée seems to have won a victory, I think that Le Midi gained all the real profit. This company, with [these concessions], has all it needs for the organization of its route from Marseille to Bordeaux and it saved itself at least fifty to sixty millions."[26] Finally, by the same decision, the Midi was given the Graissessac-Béziers railroad and a concession for a Rodez-Montpellier route without specifying its exact trajectory.[27] The PLM magnanimously gave up all claims to a Millau-to-the-sea, although it retained control of Rodez-Millau, which it had already been conceded.[28]

So what motivated Rouher? This is a difficult question. In many respects the entire situation takes us to the heart of the political economy of the modern capitalist world. Rouher had not been "bought." He believed in a system in which state and private interests could work together as much as possible while still retaining a modified competitive framework. This was not markedly different from states, such as England and the United States, that seemed to give greater license to competitive forces and entrepreneurial verve.[29] France was at a point—one that England happily passed through in the Napoleonic Wars and the United States would reach in the post-Civil War years—where considerable state input into economic growth was needed, but giant private interests had to be simultaneously satisfied. It was a state capitalism, a "loaded" laissez-faire that had the consequence of concurrently enhancing the power of the great (and not necessarily the daring) in the private sphere and the power of the holders of the decision-making mechanisms in the public sphere. Generally, the latter were not for sale (although this was not always the case in the U.S. experience), but held a "professional" viewpoint that just happened to satisfy their desire for orderly progress, while benefiting the state and the economically powerful.

There is no smoking gun, no evidence that Talabot marched into Rouher's office with a bribe or with stories about his wife or daughter. Rouher was an immensely competent career bureaucrat. He served in various high capacities during the Second Empire, including that of Minister of Finance after 1865. His key function seems to have been to put the brakes on the overenthusiastic—Baron Haussmann's grand designs for Paris more than once faced the budgetary ax of Rouher. On the other hand, while personally mistrustful of Haussmann, he also supported him when he thought the Prefect to be right.[30] Rouher was not a member of Louis Napoleon's inner circle and people like Persigny disliked him. As we have seen, they were in fact more taken with the audacity of a Pereire. But Rouher's stability and good sense could not be dispensed with; it served as a constant check on potential "excesses." The Cette-Marseille was apparently in his mind as such a problem. On the other hand, Rouher had the reputation of being a free trader and was a close friend of Michel Chevalier, whose commercial treaty with England he had steered through the channels of government. In this, of course, he had the support of the Emperor's inner circle and won their respect for his work.[31] Chevalier corresponded regularly with Rouher, although rarely did he use this mode of communication to try to influence him. His terse note of 4 May 1862, reveals a world of past social encounters and an almost for-the-record account of what must have been for him a personal betrayal:

> Dear Minister and friend,
>   I was so sorry, last night, not to see Madame Rouher to offer her my regards before my departure to London.
>   I dined with a number of people interested in the Cette to Marseille railroad. They said with deep concern [on disait fort] that it would go before the Conseil [d'Etat] with the Emperor present this morning and that, personally, you had announced yourself to be in favor of the Cie de la Méditerranée and against competition.
>
> Tout à vous
M.C.
>
> M. Pégazy has been advised to write to you from Montpellier.[32]

If Rouher thus went against a personal conviction favoring competitive capitalism, and against the Emperor, was there something beyond his renowned probity at work?

Perhaps. For Rouher did not write the report condemning the Cette-Marseille, nor did he write the agreement among the state, the PLM, and the Midi that finalized the situation. That was the work of his director for Chemins de fer in the Ministry, Louis de Franqueville. His influence with Rouher was immense. Franqueville could well claim to be the architect of the French rail system's development under the Second Empire. His technical expertise and his sense of the railroad's significance for economic development matched those of any of the great pioneers who actually built the system. But his entire career unfolded within the state bureaucracy. A letter to his son, written in 26 May 1862, allows us to pinpoint the circumstances of the final decision:

> My correspondence right now, my dear Charles, leaves something to be desired. This accursed Cette-Marseille affair [*affaire maudite*] has absorbed me totally of late; I locked myself in the house all day Friday and Saturday morning to write a long and difficult report on the question that the minister had requested of me, and, yesterday morning, Sunday, I went to read it to him in his quarters. He listened very attentively and was kind enough to tell me that he had nothing but praise and thanks to give me.

Young Franqueville, a government representative (chosen by Le Play) at the London Exposition, went on to say in his memoir that "my father had to cope with the heaviest of attacks. He did not hesitate for a moment to do what he considered his duty in defending the Compagnie de Lyon. M. Rouher, it must be said, supported him fully, but the triumph was difficult to obtain." The language of the son no doubt reflected the attitudes of father. He also spoke of the "rights" of the PLM in a manner reminiscent of Talabot.[33]

And there was every reason for him to do so. He and Talabot were the closest of friends and had been since they were classmates at the Ecole polytechnique. François Bartholony and Charles Didion, Talabot's closest collaborators in his various projects and board members of both the Paris-Orléans and PLM (Bartholony was director of the PO and, with Didion, the architect of the Lyon-Geneva buyout), formed the rest of Franqueville's clique. There is no question about the closeness of these relationships nor of Franqueville's favorable disposition toward their companies and against the Pereires. Certainly the latter were aware of this direct pipeline to the heart of the government and fought to counter it.[34] Talabot's easy access to the levers of power was legendary, but most of the evidence for it is indirect (recall for example, the stalling of the Bessèges line).[35] Young Franqueville, however, in all innocence, tells the following story, which he witnessed first-hand:

> It was precisely at that moment (March 1863) that [my father] received a visit one evening from his friend, M. Talabot, who came to tell him that the portfolio of public works had been offered by the Emperor to M. Béhic, and that the latter was counting on the collaboration of M. de Franqueville.
>
> My father was naturally very upset to think that he was going to have to educate [faire l'éducation de] a new minister at a time when he so much needed rest.

But he said he would remain at his post if Talabot could arrange time for him to take the waters and have Béhic take steps to reduce the arrogant use of power within the administration by the director of personnel, de Boureville, a man kept under control by Rouher, but whose ambition needed to know about.[36] That a man in charge of what arguably was the most important department from an economic point of view in the French government should be informed that he had a new superior not by his old one, not by another minister, not by a direct representative of the Emperor (or the Emperor himself), but by a man whose only governmental role at the time was that of an elected official (member of the Conseil général of the Gard) was amazing. But obviously someone (presumably Rouher) assumed that Talabot was the man to break the news most effectively. He was regarded as a more pivotal figure within the informal network of connections as they related to railroads than, indeed, anyone. This was the power, then, that Rouher would not buck. It is not clear exactly why he resigned, but it appears that the stress of the great struggle may have got to him. He had a new post—as a member of the Counseil d'Etat—and would soon move on to become Minister of Finance, so he retained his prominence.

As for Franqueville, it is possible that he and Rouher had also had a falling out over the affair, because Rouher, early in 1863, had personally removed his son from a list of individuals slated to receive, upon the nomination of Frédéric Le Play, decoration for their work with the Imperial Committee of the London Exposition. The elder Franqueville wrote his son: "to think that it is M. Rouher, whose devoted collaborator I have been for eight years, who would take this initiative against you deeply grieves and irritates me."[37]

It might well be that Rouher made the move out of spite because of the pressure he felt from the Talabot-Franqueville circle of power and then resigned once he had seen the awful affair through. Still, honorable to the end, he asked Franqueville if he would like to join him on the Conseil d'Etat (obviously an invitation having the Emperor's approval), but the latter refused.

These details allow us to observe some of the nuances of how history happens. It is all very well to talk of "northern power" or the "great interests" or "political disfavor" with regard to the decline of industrial Languedoc. But the actual explanation of how the national rail system by-passed the region and ended up mainly serving the vine is complex indeed. We cannot cite a master plan or evil conspiracy to relegate Languedoc to the status of a mono-agricultural dependency of Paris any more than we can speak of a *bourgeoisie fainéante* meekly accepting this fate. But Languedoc *was* grievously injured—in an atmosphere of unpleasant political relations rooted in its past radicalism (or barbarism, as some would have it)—by economic powers with massive influence in the state over which the region had little control. It is simply pathetic to sift through the thousands of documents relating to these affairs and come across one petition filled with the familiar names of hundreds of workers, who once, however briefly, dominated a city, and another filled with those scores of notables against whom they struggled—both groups now pleading with someone of whom few had ever heard and fewer still had ever seen to save their city from death by allowing a railroad to come through it. But Rouher was not listening to them in any case. His world was that of Talabots and Pereires and concerns about "investment climate" and "orderly economic progress." All of which added up to satisfying the most elaborate and well-connected financial-industrial combine in France. The next chapter reviews the dreary aftermath of this decision in Languedoc, but the essentials were well understood: Languedoc had been sacrificed to what Michel Chevalier called "that mysterious influence" within the Ministry of Public Works, an agency which also was "avid for domination on its own account."[38]

Although the local and regional response to the 1862–63 decision was one of shock and disgust,[39] Lodève at least could welcome the railroad that *had* been conceded, the line from Agde. The Midi opened the line with normal fanfare in July and August 1863, and the region had benefited from associated employment opportunities for the three previous years. Both Clermont and Lodève were provided with well-equipped stations. Lodève had two long (400 meters) passing tracks, four freight sidings, and one 150 meter track especially equipped with ten large bins for unloading coal. The "first class" station had a covered quai for passengers and an interior waiting room, later outfitted with a *buvette* (refreshment bar). The merchandise station was equipped with three wagon turntables and several storage halls. As a terminus, the station was also equipped with an engine turntable and provided locomotive service and repair. In short, any Lodévois who took the time to walk up to the station (for it was about 600 meters to the south and east of Carmes) would have been impressed. The blow thus may have been softened at the time by the novelty and the inspiration of new and shiny buildings and trains rolling.[40]

In fact, however, the realization that Lodève was only a terminus did not take long to sink in. Plans for a tunnel had been scrapped officially in the concession of the Rodez-Montpellier (however it might go). An embranchement at Cartels toward the Orb valley seemed the way that the route to the north would follow. That it too would need a major station had already raised official eyebrows. Meanwhiles, Lodève got its coal from Graissessac via Béziers and Agde. Clermont luminaries, for their part, sought to take the embranchement up the Salagou, thus making their city the hub.

As it turned out, none of these plans came to pass. A petition to the Senate late in 1868 from the municipal councils of several towns in the Lodévois revealed a sordid tale that explodes whatever hope one might have had regarding the good intentions of the brothers Pereire. To everyone's shock, a new law, carried in *Le Moniteur* on 2 October 1868, conceded a westward embranchement that began in Paulhan and joined the Béziers-Graissessac at Roquessels, below the notorious tunnel at Faugères. A glance at the map shows what a disaster this was for Lodève and the northern tier of towns and villages so in need of coal and rapid access to Montpellier for their goods. Even Clermont and Villeneuvette were now left in the lurch. There had been talk of providing goods shipped from Lodève (but not the other towns)—specifically its woolens—with a special state rate-subvention, but even this disappeared from the final draft.

Why had this happened? The petition offered an opinion (challenged by no one) that amounted to an indictment of the Midi Company. The Cartels branch would have gone to Le Bousquet via Valquières and been joined to the Béziers-Graissessac line by a branch. Even if the northern route to Montpellier via Gignac were to be abandoned, this would still put Lodève and the other communes of the Lodévois more or less on a main route north. The conceded route, however, seemed to have but one purpose: the easy, direct shipment of coal from Neffiès and Roujan, never a significant basin, but recently adjudged to have some potential. The reason: these were "mines in which everyone knows MM Pereire have controlling interest, the same Pereires who dominate the Midi Company." But the plans of the department for "lines of local interest" already included a branch to these mines from Pézenas; ownership was to be departmental, leased to local operators. "But the Midi Company, or its directors, did not find this to be enough. They wanted the line that carried the coal of Neffiès and Roujan to be in their own hands. By means of the plan to which the administration has now lent its authority, without suspecting its true end, the directors of the Midi Company want to render themselves masters of the conditions of transport of coal for all the mines in the department. By this, they count on having the ability to influence the respective prices and markets of the coals." Hence the Midi would be in a position to manipulate rates in ways to out-"compete" the Graissessac Mines Company, which it was gouging outrageously in any case to the tune of eight centimes per T/kilometer, at least in certain markets, notably Montpellier.

The petitioners also noted the counterargument of the Midi Co., namely that the Lodève market for rail-shipped freight and passengers was insignificant, amounting to a total gross revenue of only Fr 80,000 in 1867. The implication was that Lodève just was not worth serving. The response demonstrated how specious this argument was. To go to Montpellier, the main destination of goods and travellers from Lodève, all one had to do was to compare the time and price of using the diligence or road-freight (*roulage*) (a 54-kilometer trip) to the train (a 110-kilometer trip). Table 7–1 demonstrates why virtually none of Lodève's cloth went by train and why a passenger's main reason for taking to the rails would be largely for the thrill of it. Clearly the main sources of what revenue there was came from imports (coal, wool, wine) via Agde from the south, and exports (spirits, leather, some cloth) to Cette or local Hérault or Aude markets. To say that the reason for the low revenue figure given by the Midi Company—that Lodève had little to sell—was absurd: it could still put out 300,000 meters of cloth annually. "Why don't you find out from Elbeuf or Sedan whether

Table 7–1

	Rail (Lodève-Agde-Cette-Montpellier)		Diligence (Lodève-Montpellier)	
Hours of departure	6:20 A.M., 2:00, 5:40 P.M.		5 to 8 trips daily, 6:00 A.M. 4:00 p.m.	
Changes	At Agde, 2:00 at Cette also.		None.	
Elapsed time	5 or 7 hours.		5 to 8 hours depending on number of stops.	
Rates	1st class	12.75 F	Coupe	5.60
	2nd class	9.50	Interieur	4.60
	3rd class	6.95	Rotunde	3.60

Freight
(100 kg draps, loading incl.)

	Rail	Roulage
Rates	1.25 F	1.25
Delivery	4–5 days	next day

that is significant!" Obviously Lodève was taking a terrible beating because of the rail situation, and now it was going to be put further *"à l'écart."* The Senate did not even debate the issue. This setback proved definitive.[41]

Even though the Paulhan connection finally made both Montpellier and Graissessac a little closer, Lodève (and its region) remained a balloon on the map of the Midi system, floating above the main currents of commerce. By the mid-1870s even Clermont ended up with more rail traffic, ranking a rather dismal thirty-seventh in volume among the Midi stations, while Lodève languished at a distant forty-ninth.[42] The old woolens towns of the Lergue/Hérault area were not the only losers in this process, for the entire piedmont region had to wait long years even for local-interest roads to be built. Although the Graissessac basin and Bédarieux were somewhat better situated (and as we shall see benefited from it), the absence of a cheap main road to Montpellier injured the upper Orb area as well. And the capital itself remained the second-rate rail center Prefect Gavini had labled it, losing more ground to Nîmes and Béziers and thus adding, perhaps decisively, to its troubled situation. In general, the heart of old industrial Languedoc, the department of the Hérault, had been dealt a heavy, indeed fatal, blow.

8

Deindustrialization

The attentive reader might have wondered what happened to Michel Chevalier in the course of the 1867–68 round of discussions about the rail future
of the arrondissement of Lodève. If he did not possess quite the stature of
Cardinal Fleury, Chevalier was undoubtedly the most powerful defender
Lodève had had for a very long time. But, despite his later grousing about
"mysterious influences," he was remarkably silent—at least with his pen—
through these last trials. The answer is rather simple: Chevalier had by then
lost interest personally and, one may suppose, his individualist/libertarian
principles (or naked self-interest as others might put it) permitted him to
stop banging his head against the walls of northern power. Indeed, what
he had done was to submit to northern power. On 5 May 1865, Mayor
Jules Teisserenc discovered that Chevalier, through his wife Emma Fournier,
sole owner of the largest and most progressive firm in Lodève, had sold
out to one of the great textile magnates in France, Baron Sellière of Sedan.
The name of the firm would be retained, but thereafter would contribute
to the reputation of Sedan, not Lodève. Chevalier would continue to occupy
Monplaisir, but only the great house and its lands. The factory, so lovingly
constructed by Gaspard Barbot and the Fournier brothers, was closed and
later largely dismantled. The economist, living up finally to his surname,
became a country gentleman.

Lodève's first major plant-closing was a shattering event at the time
and remained a symbol of the road to industrial oblivion long thereafter.
Today, however, it seems blotted from popular memory.[1] Chevalier and
his wife had taken full control of Barbot et Fournier when René Fournier

died in 1858. The Company employed between 500 and 700 workers, depending on demand, mostly in or near its large factory complex on the Soulandares, also called "Monplaisir" because of its proximity to the estate. Its productive capacity was estimated to be one-quarter of the city's total and its equipment, including two steam engines, among the most up-to-date. It regularly garnered two to three lots in army orders, meaning that it could be called upon to put out as much as 198,000 meters of cloth per year. It had gained two of the fourteen *lots* accorded to Lodève in 1864.

Chevalier, an economist and senator as close to the heart of power as anyone in France (Talabot excepted), undoubtedly read the message sent by the outcome of the rail conflict of 1863 as a warning sign. Clearer still, however, were the signals from the War Ministry regarding open competition for army orders and its encouragement of Lodève to expand its commercial cloth production. As the Minister of War, Jacques-Louis Randon, wrote to Prefect Piétri in 1863, Lodève and Clermont should no longer expect to benefit from their past "privileges," for that "is to deny justice to the other manufacturing cities of France. . . ."[2] Lodève also irritated the ministry by delays in delivery. For example, large portions of the 1861 order remained undelivered in Paris, and manufacturers requested a one-month delay until 31 January 1862. Part of the problem were the bottlenecks in the PLM system out of Montpellier, so they further asked that final deliveries be deposited only in the Magasin de Montpellier. But another part was timeworn hydraulic equipment. Rouquet, Marréaud et Devaux, for instance, had to halt all operations at their Bellerive plant because "the lynch pin of the vertical shaft that transmits movement to our [equipment] gave way suddenly. . . ." The company sent to Montpellier for an "engineer-mechanic" who had to transport the gear-shaft and gears back to the capital to repair them in his shop, thus making "us late in delivering our order to his Excellency the Minister of War. . . ."[3]

A larger issue, the use of waterpower, presented ongoing difficulties that were not unique to Lodève, but were perhaps more pronounced there than in many centers where water flow was steadier and better regulated.[4] The problem of overuse was reaching crisis proportions by the Second Empire. It is exemplified by a huge fight in 1855 between Ménard, fils et Soudan Frères and Bézard et Jules Teisserenc that arose when the former sought to expand its operations by building an additional factory and dam that threatened to disrupt the flow into the latters' channel and, hence, their total motive force. Settlement came only with a detailed plan drawn up by the central state in which the height and location of the dam, the structure of the intake channels, and the emplacement of the outflow channels were specified to the centimeter.[5] The proper response to such problems was the adoption of steam power, if not totally, at least for adjunct, backup, and partial purposes.[6] As we shall soon see, Lodève's manufacturers did indeed adapt significantly to steam in the late 1850s and early 1860s, but the problem of the high price of coal cut into the cost-effectiveness of such a development. Hopes for cheaper coal prices with better rail services no doubt caused companies to put off major renewal projects on their hydraulic works, assuming that they would soon be able to go to steam. Government officials, nevertheless, regularly chastised Lodève manufacturers for not making the transition to "modern" ways in an intensive enough fashion. As frustrated Lodévois pointed out, the failures of one agency of the state, Public Works, harmed their relationship with others (War, Interior), but they, the victims, took the bulk of the blame.[7]

Chevalier himself had said as much, but obviously he was not as willing to continue the fight as were most of the other fabricants, despite the fact that he was best placed to publicize this contradiction in the halls of power. Instead, he used information regarding Lodève's declining image to get the jump on the others. The affair, however, was more complicated and Chevalier's bad faith more serious than first meets the eye.

Jules Teisserenc was then mayor of Lodève and as usual had made the annual pilgrimage to Paris in the spring of 1865 to lobby for the army contracts. He and other Lodève fabricants were simultaneously constructing business alliances that would maximize their bidding power. Deeply involved, he wrote a privately circulated "mémoire" shortly after the affair.[8] Teisserenc served as "an intermediary between the house of Puech, Fournier et Vallat and that of M. Michel Chevalier. . . ." The former was a relatively small company, but two of its owners were cousins of Emma Fournier. Their only hope of gaining military contract work was by associating with a large company, and Barbot et Fournier had contracted with them the past. Emile Fournier and Joseph Peuch met, along with Teisserenc, with Chevalier in his Paris office and, "having consented to all the conditions that he imposed, thought the affair to be definitively concluded. One of them proposed that they sign a provisional agreement on the spot," pending new ministerial requirements. "M. Chevalier said to us, 'between people like us, our word will suffice'" and promised to set a date to finalize things. Three days later, Chevalier informed Emile Fournier, "without further explanation, that there was no further reason to pursue the affair." Shortly thereafter, while Teisserenc was attempting to repair whatever the damage was—for they all assumed that this was simply a negotiating tactic on Chevalier's part—he received a telegram from "my first deputy-mayor apprising me that the plant manager at Barbot et Fournier had informed the workers that the factory would be closed starting the following Monday." Workers from the plant, joined by others, took to the streets in protest. Officials feared the worst.[9] No reason for the closure was given, but Teisserenc got an immediate invitation to meet with the Minister of the Interior, De la Valette, who told him that "the government would do all in its power" to help the laid-off workers. Teisserenc *still* did not know what had happened, but it is obvious that some high government officials did, because what Chevalier had been doing while stalling with his relatives' company was negotiating with the government to assure that the 1865 order would be transferred to the account of Sellière, as the latter demanded. Had authorization been denied, Chevalier could have returned to the other engagement, and no one would have been the wiser. Chevalier obviously wanted to move carefully in order to avoid a concerted effort by Teisserenc, legislators, and other notables to stop the process.

The workers' response—the first threatened violence of any magnitude in Lodève since 1851—was a fly in the ointment, and the government was concerned. When, on 7 May, Teisserenc finally found out that Barbot et Fournier had been sold, he stormed into the Interior Minister's office and warned of upheaval in Lodève. "Not to worry," said de la Valette "for just this afternoon M. Michel Chevalier was sitting in [that] armchair while I wrote [this] dispatch—of which he fully approved: 'I have examined the affair: it is clear the work will remain in Lodève.'"[10] The reopening was set for 4 June. The only person who could have made it "clear," however, was Baron Sellière, the new owner of Barbot et Fournier. And the plant did not reopen at all. Equipment was removed during the summer slack season when many Lodévois were working (or even relaxing) elsewhere, and the building was put up for sale or lease. Early in 1866, having failed to achieve its needed association with a larger company, Puech, Fournier et Vallat, a one-lot company, sold out to Sellière as well, and another 200 full-time jobs were lost.[11]

What was the upshot of all this for the seigneur of Monplaisir? No doubt a few cold shoulders at le Circle and perhaps an occasional *menace* as his carriage passed by on the way to the club, but how often, in any case, was the Senator and Conseiller d'Etat actually chez lui? Mainly, the sixty-year-old Chevalier could count on another 100 thousand francs per year for twenty years—for those were the terms of the sale.

A later life of opulent gentility thus awaited France's most prominent political economist. Revenues from the Monplaisir estate, estimated at Fr 7,500 per annum, in 1858, were also on the rise. By the later 1860s, not only were its hillsides redolent with vines, but its valuable irrigated meadows on the left bank of the Soulandres were producing fodder-grasses as never before. This was because not one, but two dams, now operating full-time, were diverting huge quantities of water to these sixteen hectares of prime land. Chevalier's father-in-law, who bought the meadows in the 1830s, had contented himself with the 1806 regulation that allowed irrigation during the spring and summer months only from 6 P.M. on Saturday to 6 A.M. on Monday. Otherwise, water flowed downstream during industrial working hours. Early in 1866, Chevalier sought to deregulate the water flow. Using an earlier victory over Jules Teisserenc, who owned some land on the other side of the stream, as precedent (it had been decided finally by the Conseil d'Etat, of which Chevalier was a member), Chevalier was now awarded, by the same body, a free hand in the use of his dams. He, of course, was less interested in what happened downstream since he sold his textile mills. Others faced disaster. Because of water shortage, wrote the complainants, "six tanneries, two mills, and one dyeworks are forced to halve their operations. The undersigned employ 130 workers altogether . . . and seek justice . . . ." The petitioners were unsuccessful in their bid to reverse the situation.[12]

Thus did one of France's great proponents of free enterprise use the state to help him pocket an extra hundred francs annually. This achievement did not perhaps have the same significance in the city as his success in the sale of Barbot et Fournier—where he cajoled one minister and lied to another to gain his ends—but the pettiness of hogging water while gutting a half-dozen small industrial firms bordered on criminal behavior.

In many respects, the sage Chevalier's voyage to gentrydom serves as a metaphor for the final stage of deindustrialization in Languedoc. He *did* fight very hard for the region during the rail wars, as did the vast majority of the industrial, commercial, and political leaders of the area. He did modernize his own establishment as much as possible, not fearing extensive investment in industry. But when the odds became too great, he bailed out and invested in land, while continuing his career as an academic in the Collège de France. If his *fashion* of getting from one place to the other was rather specially unseemly and if his personal importance in contributing to the general process was greater than others, his path and the fate of those who suffered in its wake were not at all untypical. For the bourgeoisie of Languedoc survived handily, while small businessmen (and not just those in industry) and the working class did not. But did that bourgeoisie simply "accept, indeed invite, its defeat in advance?" This is the thesis of Raymond Dugrand, who writes of two historical bourgeoisies, divided by the Revolutionary era: "On one side, in the eighteenth century, the merchant manufacturers with accounts in Odessa and Constantinople, in Cadiz and Amsterdam; on the other, in the middle of the nineteenth century, shrivelled industrial *rentiers.*" The reason for this remarkable shift in attitudes, which he thinks preceded "external factors" (he mentions geography, market access, and Marseille's competition), was the easy placement of capital made possible by the rise of the vine, thus echoing Fohlen's 1949 article.[13] Dugrand marshals much documentation demonstrating the massive shift of investment to viticulture in the later nineteenth century and shows how the old urban bourgeoisie came to dominate the wine industry in lower Languedoc. There is no question that this was as true as The United States Steel Company's shift to the insurance business and other tertiary activities in the 1970s. And no doubt the opprobrium that believers in justice heaped upon each was to some degree deserved.

But as an historical explanation, the answer is surely too simple. Much space in the preceding chapters has been devoted to analyzing the range of forces that undermined the industrial potential of the region. Like Dugrand, while recognizing the significance of larger factors at work in the economic geography of the West, I have focused on flesh-and-blood human beings and the decisions that they have made within the constraints of those factors. Unlike Dugrand, however, I have examined the two worlds that most consistently affected the behavior of Languedoc businessmen: the state and its policy makers, and the regional working class. It is symptomatic that Dugrand hardly mentions the deep history of social conflict in the precocious Languedoc textile industry and the upheavals of the Second Repub-

lic. Nor do the rail wars of the Second Empire and their disastrous outcome for the industrial and extractive industries beyond the well-connected
industrial seats in the Gard receive much attention. More concretely, however, it is obvious that the Languedoc bourgeoisie did not give up without
a fight, as Dugrand implies. Only when it became clear that the battle was
lost can one discern an air of resignation regarding the region's industrial
future setting in. That the bourgeoisie should use its means to cover its losses
and redeploy its capital at that point should come as no surprise. That they
would do so in ways that would scandalize public opinion and leave many
believing in their treason toward the region should come as no surprise
either. The 1860s were the time of escape; Chevalier's case was only the
most striking. But even so, some businessmen in the Hérault, despite the
appeal of investment in the vine, did not give up on industry, and, indeed,
the area that seemed most destined for industrial oblivion, the district of
Bédarieux, if not the city itself, came back to life despite the array of cards
stacked against it. And it did so under the leadership of successive generations of hardheaded Montpellier businessmen, first Usquin, Simon, and their
associates, and then the Leenhardt family, which at that time began its long
climb toward becoming one of France's leading business dynasties, currently
claiming Arnaud Leenhardt, the PDG of Valourec, a metallurgical firm and
the fifty-first largest company in France.[14]

Dugrand also made a number of important factual errors with regard
to Lodève. This would not be so critical were it not for his use of Lodève as
the prime example of his lackluster nineteenth-century Languedocian bourgeoisie. The central accusation is technological backwardness, an unwillingness to invest capital to enhance productivity. It is true that Lodève's
bosses were wary of wholesale technological changes, but this had practical foundations, as we have seen on several occasions. Fear, of worker re-
prisals or poor workmanship, was obviously one of them, and concern about
fuel costs was another. Nevertheless, by the mid-1860s, in the words of
Camille St. Pierre, "among the manufacturing cities of the department,
Lodève occupies first place and is distinguished by the general solidity of
its industry and the organization of its factories." The town's industrialists
"have always followed a progressive path, and [their] industrial equipment
has undergone a remarkable development during the last ten years." The
pressure from the government for competitive bids was obviously a factor,
especially in the total conversation to "mechanical looms, which have entirely replaced hand looms for all military production." St. Pierre noted that
twelve of the seventeen houses were nearly entirely devoted to military production, but that finer hand-loom work for export and internal commerce
continued to occupy a "good number" of workers. The machinery level
was most impressive: besides 800 power looms, Lodève housed 400 power
carding machines, 150 mechanical fulling rigs, and spinning machinery
totalling 35,000 spindles. He did not provide information on the exact
number of these machines, but states that nearly all carried 200 and 240
spindles. This was an important advance from the 1850s, when many smaller

shops still had old machines of 60 or 120 spindles.[15] All in all, Lodève did not compare badly with France's most vital wool town, Reims, which, with a population more than six times a large, counted 76,000 spindles in 1866.[16] There is thus no basis for Dugrand's claims of technological inadequacy. He cites St. Pierre, but largely for his opening statement that viticulture was becoming the department's main economic activity; misleadingly, Dugrand fails to note the author's following line in which he says he hopes that his study "will help to stimulate industry."[17] In general, then, St. Pierre's careful analysis, which can be partially validated from existing official statistics,[18] demonstrates how biased Dugrand's influential study was. A final, and telling point: Dugrand cities Audiganne's remark that of the thirteen firms in Lodève, only one relied on steam power. This, of course, was from Audiganne's quite positive general assessment of the Hérault's textile future made in 1854, but it referred to operations where steam was the main *power* source, not mentioning the use of steam engines in back-up and task-specific work (for example, for fulling rigs or carding machines).[19] More important, there had obviously been some vast changes since the early 1850s, for as St. Pierre put it in bold print on page 187, the "force motrice" in Lodève totalled 2,000 horsepower of which "nearly half is furnished today [1865] by steam." Dugrand notes only St. Pierre's general estimate that of the motors in the entire department, 441 are hydraulic and "only" 121 are steam. In that day and age, this was a healthy percentage in any case. It is likely, although St. Pierre does not provide a figure, that a majority of these engines by that time were located in Lodève. It had an outlet for a steam engine company and, since 1862, however circuitously, could bring in heavy machinery by train.[20]

To be sure, all this does not gainsay the fact that the costs of energy—both in terms of the increasing expenses and losses incurred due to the overutilization of hydraulic power and the high price of coal—were fundamentally detrimental to Lodève's competitive position, a reality finally faced by many industrialists who reoriented their capital. It remained a central fact of industrial life throughout the city's painful decline. Hector Teisserenc's 1908 study of the industry echoed the same theme, and Paul Marres's outstanding survey of 1924 rehearsed the tragic history of rail service to the city, but concluded that now perhaps sufficient hydroelectric power could be provided by damming the Lergue as had been done on the Vis for Ganges.[21]

In light of St. Pierre's careful analysis and corroborative official statistics, it can hardly be said that industrialists during the Second Empire, at least in Lodève, were not "trying." Evidence from elsewhere is mixed. St. Pons and Riols, especially, made significant efforts in the area of technical improvements, and languished some in the 1860s, although they both by-passed rival Bédarieux. St. Chinian, however, was on its last legs.[22]

The happiest stories were Villeneuvette and Mazamet, though for quite different reasons. The former royal manufactory had been progressively transformed by its owner, Jules Maistre, into a model community, a paternalist utopia similar to Godin's famous experiment at Guise.[23] Maistre furnished his "family of workers" individual row houses with playing fields between them or apartments in large buildings on the village's central square.[24] St. Pierre found Villeneuvette fascinating. He noted that some worker families had been there for two centuries. Their dedication to clothmaking was remarkable: "Ici point d'oisifs." Impressed also by the large number of old people, he found that the company/community maintained a retirement program relieving families of heavy obligations toward their older members. This and a community health system were financed by wage deductions matched by employer contributions, but "administered by the workers themselves." Consumer cooperatives were formed under workers' control as well. Education of the young was obligatory until age fourteen, and the company provided assistance for promising young people to go on to the lycée level. Adult education programs flourished. Although we should withhold judgment until a full study of Villeneuvette is undertaken, contemporaries were certainly impressed. "Honor to Work," inscribed over the gate to the village (and still there), seemed to pay off: Maistre regularly garnered one lot of army orders.[25] Clermont's otherwise desultory economic life was enlivened by Villeneuvette's nearby presence.

Mazamet experienced a more "normal" development, though it, too, became a kind of company town. In 1851, Pierre Elie Houlès, director of the leading firm of the prosperous little city in the Tarn, "possibly imitating what he had seen in Bédarieux, . . . imported two bales of sheepskins from Buenos Aires." He had them stripped of their wool at a washing house in nearby Ausillon under the direction of a foreman named Joseph Poursines. This was perhaps the most famous moment in the town's history, for on the basis of "*délainage*"—by which wool and skin from animals dead from epidemics or (less often) butchering were separated by a combination of chemical and mechanical means and then sold on the market—that Mazamet's future would be built. The wool, though less resilient than live-shorn, was adequate for lower-grade products, and the skins were readily sold in an already active regional circuit. Only after 1856, with the establishment of permanent representatives in South America, would this processing industry begin to boom, but low prices of materials that otherwise were a glut on the market meant huge profits for the entrepreneurs involved. It also further stimulated the quite successful low-cost woolens industry built by Houlès and other pioneers in the first half of the century. Thus, at the very moment much of Languedoc woolens faced extreme problems, Mazamet manufacturers, essentially using its traditional means of production—the clean and powerful streams from the Montagne Noire, plentiful, cheap, unskilled labor from the same area, and existing woolens production facilities—carried out a revolution. The smelly and insalubrious operation of délainage itself went through several improvements, so the special labor and water supply situation was apparently the key factor limiting imitation elsewhere. The wool itself was marketed, but special advantages went to those, above all the Cormouls-Houlès firm, who integrated vertically, from purchasing at "the origin" to the sale of woolen cloth. Without a remotely close parallel anywhere else in southern textiles, sales of Mazamet woolens leapt from twelve million (already higher than any Hérault center) in 1860 to twenty-five million in 1877. Similar levels were achieved in the sale of wool.[26]

Although the délainage "miracle" was critical to Mazamet's distinctive success, its deeper history contrasted sharply with most Languedocian cloth towns, including its neighbor in the Tarn, Castres. The tiny town had an industrial history that stretched back into the sixteenth century, one that Rémy Cazals lovingly reconstructs in his delightful book. But, in fact, Mazamet was a mushroom city of the nineteenth-century industrial revolution. It had no corporative history among the producing crafts at all, in that sense more like an Hérault village than a wool town. Bédarieux alone among the old Languedoc textile centers approached Mazamet's record, but it, as we have seen, was prominent enough to inspire the envy of rivals in the eighteenth century. Mazamet inspired disdain. It was hardly involved even in the finishing of its own petites étoffes, largely sending off "an unfinished product" to Bordeaux for finishing there before being shipped to English possessions in North America—undoubtedly for the clothing of slaves. Similarities with the vast cheap-cloth outworking world of the up-country Gévaudan are obvious. As it boomed in the nineteenth century, the collapsing woodlands industries of the Black Mountain fed the city's woolens industry cheap labor in village and town. The Mazamet working class formed from this human base and shared similarities with burgeoning factory towns elsewhere: a significant number of industrial workers still rural in both orientation and values whose deep connection with their roots was manifested in urban settlement patterns, dwelling structures, and land use. Village life—to which many returned regularly in any case—was reconstituted in town (or its faubourgs), in stark contrast to "urbanized" Lodève, or even Bédarieux.

Compliance to the authority of paternalistic management was a corollary. Mazamet's indigenous worker population, especially the weavers and finishing craftsmen, were little troubled in the first half of the nineteenth century by significant technological threats. The Jacquard loom, indeed, only came into use in the 1840s. The only major disturbance of a Luddite character was the reaction by jenny spinners and others to the introduction of mule-jennies early in 1848. Mazamet's one important worker uprising before the late nineteenth century occurred in 1845, a classic case of a response to cuts in the tarif of weavers that led to major demonstrations, arrests, and a raid on the local jail, followed by occupation by a few troops. Mayor Houlès (one and the same as the town's leading fabricant) refused to consider encouragement of compromises on pay, but declared an "amnesty" that returning employees seemed gratefully to accept. Audiganne's general assessment is largely supported by Cazals' research: "Like the woodsmen and herdsmen of the neighboring mountains, the workers of Mazamet are generally moderate in their demands and easy to satisfy." Despite a significant religious split between the *patronat* (75 percent Protestant) and the largely Catholic working class, Mazamet workers, unlike those of Nîmes or Bédarieux, contented themselves with regular church attendance and simple Sunday pleasures. Some slight *prise de conscience* occurred among more rooted woolens workers during the Second Republic, and twenty-nine were condemned (though to light sentences) in the wake of the coup d'état, but militant radicalism there was a pale reflection of the Hérault.[27] With délainage, if anything, the worker movement became more quiescent as relative prosperity combined with a major new influx of unskilled labor-ers from the declining up-country, further accentuating the urban village character of the rapidly growing city. Only toward the end of the century does a modern worker movement in Mazamet emerge, one which finally exploded in the great strike of 1909, though politically, the clerical and conservative weight of the past continued to have a deep influence.[28]

Clearly, there remained considerable vitality to the spirit of industry in Languedoc, but it was not reckless. Successful businessmen for centuries, Languedocian bourgeois followed the logic of their particular situations in the search for productive investment. Clermont might be seen as exceptional in this regard and is worth considering. It is the one town among the Hérault woolens centers that seems to validate fully the Dugrand thesis, and it also provided the basic evidence for James Thomson's preindustrial deindustrial-ization cycle. In 1871, as if to shake an almost embarrassed fist at a century of disappointment, the Clermont Chamber of Commerce attributed the success of English business to "continuity," to reinvestment from genera-tion to generation, whereas "we" (they grandly generalize to "the French," but are obviously talking about Clermontois) "retire after having made our fortune. *Chez nous* each generation thus has to undertake a long and costly apprenticeship." We have seen in detail how untrue this was at Lodève and Bédarieux. But it was also not the case at Mazamet, the Jaur valley towns, and St. Chainian.[29] Clermont businessmen did indeed invest early and ex-tensively in the vine, contributing to the rapid growth of middle-Hérault wine and table-grape viticulture.[30] Even so, there were a number of cloth-making families who preferred to abandon Clermont rather than the wool-ens industry. If the Flottes family's investments in St. Chinian, including the purchase of the royal manufactory there in 1784, are the most famous, sev-eral of Lodève's industrial families also originated in Clermont.[31] Whatever the case, it was obvious that with the exception of Maistre's flourishing estab-lishment at Villeneuvette, Clermont's industry had long been in decay. The basic cause? Said the Chamber: "The worker all too often regards his boss as an enemy—and it must be said that the boss does not do what he could to preserve good relations with those he employs." Beneath this conflict lay constant political upheaval and "new and false ideas." Only a return to "true Christian principles" would reestablish "good harmony" and the social peace necessary for a flourishing and competitive commerce. Although projected again on all France, this view captured both the hopelessness of the region's oldest troublespot and the atmosphere of social tension that *did* have some-thing to do with bosses' ideas about how to invest their capital.[32]

Bédarieux's collapse was swift and decisive. It was as if the town's will had been broken. It is possible that the tragicomedy of the Graissessac rail line, which was largely played out in the little city, served as a final reminder of the corrupt nature of capitalist society. Bédarician bosses got out in a hurry and, with some reservation, also gave some credence to the Dugrand thesis.

C.H. Refrégier has documented the tale of woe.[33] From 1851 to 1872, the total population dropped from 9,921 to 7,818 (18.5 percent). Emigration played an important role. After 1856, the city experienced the departure of 1,385 individuals. Natural decrease also contributed as fewer marriages and fewer births occurred, while the death rate remained high. The age structure of the city lost its pyramid appearance, with the twenty-to-thirty-year-old male population particularly restricted in 1872. The loss of work in the woolens industry was the critical factor. Official figures for the period 1856 to 1866 show a drop from 2,706 men, women, and children workers in the industry to 1,600 (41 percent) and census calculations trace a decline from 1045 men at all levels of the textile industry to 653 (38 percent). Service artisan and building trades employment suffered as well.[34]

Bédarieux's fabricants, Protestant or Catholic,[35] very quickly gave up the struggle for viability in the world of textiles. They repeatedly demanded a greater share of the army cloth business and trumpeted full "deregulation"—that is, straight bid-based awards—against Lodève's "privileged" status.[36] Tragically, however, such rhetoric was overshadowed by attitudes of fear and even indifference. The post-December 1851 shock waves seemed to leave them paralyzed. In 1858, the Prefect of the Hérault simply accused Bédarieux's manufacturers of giving up. City revenue was in decline, and the promise of that rapidly growing "model city" praised so highly in the 1820s by Vilbeck waned rapidly. Audiganne was appalled by conditions and, in contrast with Lodève, thought that Bédarieux had little hope of recovery. Pressure from the authorities to clean up disastrous conditions of health, which had grown in part due to official tolerance rooted in the desire "to favor the creation of industrial establishments in an area where agriculture is nearly nil," underlined the negligence that had become part of Bédarieux's existence. The Vebre, the key stream for washing, fulling, and power, had, in the words of a health officer, become a "true dump."[37] If declining respect for public health standards was one indication of industrialists' attempts to cut costs, another was wage levels, which declined by 20 percent from 1851 to 1866 in an era when wages generally rose.

Curiously, at a time when overall employment in the industry was falling off, the number of small concerns actually increased as large manufacturers leased parts of their operations to individuals who, perhaps unwisely, attempted to stay in the hunt.[38] We can take a close look at the type of small entrepreneur involved by examining the bankruptcy proceedings against one of them, the wife of Gaston, Cadet, in 1859. Amedée-Laurent-Auguste Gaston, who ran a small spinning firm, changed its *raison sociale* to Femme

N⁰ 5. — Bédarieux. — Vue sur Vèbre

The Vèbre, Bédarieux's main mill stream, with the Béziers-Graissessac rail
viaduct in the background

Gaston, Cadet, in 1857, thereby officially turning responsibility for the affair
to his wife, Françoise, née Cavaillé. Neither family had been listed among
the fabricants in the 1851 census. The move was described as a legal "pal-
liative" by the executor of the bankruptcy, for M. Gaston continued "to
do the books and carry out the correspondence of the firm." Obviously, it
was a deeply troubled activity, for in February 1858, Gaston "disappeared."
His wife struggled on, but finally in April 1859, she "abandoned her remaining assets to her creditors and joined her husband elsewhere." It turned
out, however, that she did not own much of what she claimed, having sold
"verbally" to one M. Cau, "a Bédarician rope maker become thread manufacturer (*filateur*)," her firm's "movable property, industrial equipment,
and merchandise in March 1851." The total sale was Fr 14,000, but of this
the purchaser was to pay some Fr 3,300 to free property already under
attachment and, most interestingly, "3000 francs for factory rent for 18
months," a sum long overdue to Antoine Causse, a major fabricant of
Bédarieux (and the descendent of the famous Causses of Lodève). Cau had
met many of these debts but remained delinquent on some Fr 10,700 at
the time the Gastons' creditors forced them into bankruptcy. Much of the
bankruptcy proceeding, in fact, evolved around attempting to collect from
Cau, who tried various maneuvers to avoid paying. He obviously had no
money and went so far as to offer the executor of the bankruptcy (Birot,
apparently) wool he had on consignment from a creditor elsewhere! Causse,
in better straits only because of extensive real property ownership and investments elsewhere, sought to squeeze every sou he could out of Gaston/
Cau—and the other creditors. Cau claimed that he sold a mule-jenny machine outright to Causse as part of the rent payment. But Causse said that

was not true; he was holding it as collateral against rents owned by the Gastons. As it turned out, the executor was able legally to turn aside this claim and "put an end to this imbroglio."

What is important in this sorry tale is the extralegality and viciousness to which the panicky state of business affairs in Bédarieux gave rise in the late 1850s. It symbolizes the enormous tragedy then unfolding. The small operators, especially the eager newcomers like Cau who were still trying to make a killing, obviously suffered most. But bigger manufacturers whose business sense, connections, and capital allowed them to salvage something by sucking the blood of these lesser folk, clearly faced frightening circumstances. Bédaricians were not alone, either. A glance at Gaston's creditor list (Table 8–1) demonstrates the extent of deindustrialization's web.[39]

The textile industry in Bédarieux succumbed quickly, carrying with it the inevitable trail of unpaid debts and acrimony. But other forces were at work in its region. In the first place, the 1840s and 1850s saw a substantial increase in the vine. In the commune of Bédarieux itself, terraced land on the hillsides previously used for hay or grazing was heavily converted to vines, with vinyards increasing from 27 percent of arable in 1836 to

Table 8–1

Name	Probable Nature of Debt	Amount
Viel et Cie, négociant à Montpellier	Wool	16,910
Laurac, négociant a Nîmes	Wool	8,257
J. Melon et Cie, banquier à Montpellier	Credits	5,191
Pinchinat et Gros, négociants à Marseille	Wool	5,030
Crozals frères, négociants à Béziers	Wool	4,264
Sabatier frères, de Bédarieux	Wool?	3,422
Tiffy et Richard, tanneurs de Bédarieux	Equipment? Water use rights?	2,937
Antoine Causse, négociant de Bédarieux*	Various claims	2,589
Bellotiny et Cie, Banquier à Béziers	Credits	2,563
"Acheteur," Bd Bonne Nouvelle, Paris	Advance	1,525
Birot frères, négociants de Bordeaux	Loan	989
Benj. Dellassus de Bédarieux	Wool	648
A. Villemagne, coutre-maître-mécanicien	Wages	400
Mirande, fabricant de cardes à Rouen	Carding brushes	259

*Causse's claims were "sent before the Tribunal" de Commerce. In a judgment in 1861 he was awarded only 37 francs.

59 percent in 1857. Bédarieux was joined by the nearby communes of Faugères and Hérépian as important piedmont centers of wine production. Although a thorough survey has not been undertaken, an examination of inheritance tax declarations in the 1850s and 1860s reveals that fabricants continued to invest in land, as they had in the previous generation, but now vines, rather than pastureland, came to dominate. But nothing like a wholesale transfer of capital can be discerned.

A typical example is the breakdown of the holdings at the death of seventy-seven-year-old Jacques Martel-Laprade (who was mayor of Bédarieux during the Restoration) and his wife Marguerite née Martel (daughter of the great Pierre Martel, she was born in 1777).[40] They died within a year of each other in 1857–58. The picture is mixed and quite instructive. Their combined landed holdings, including industrial fixed capital, was evaluated at Fr 132,100. Of this, 100,000 was sunk in land, buildings, and machinery related to their woolens company, most located in the Vignal and La Prade districts. The remaining property included the following: a garden worth Fr 600, pastureland and cultivated land near Boussagues (Pradel) worth 1,800, their house and surrounding lands worth 22,000, a few other scraps of land, and finally three vineyards, all in Bédarieux, evaluated at 4,500. Thus, only 3.4 percent of their fixed capital was tied up in vines, an amount dwarfed even by their own dwelling. They were still, despite everything, a manufacturing family. Beyond their real property, both had considerable incomes in credits and bonds and, in this regard, were more conservative than some of their counterparts in Bédarieux and especially Lodève. Jacques Martel-Laprade possessed nearly Fr 50,000 in state 4½ percent bonds, and his wife held a variety of mortgages and bonds on lands she had sold worth Fr 23,000. She also had her huge dowry—its form, probably in rentes, was not specified—of Fr 64,098.

The central question is what happened and *had* happened to their family's money as it was passed along? Jacques and Marguerite had no children themselves. To examine to whom they bequeathed money (besides considerable amounts—a total of Fr 20,000—to local charitable institutions) gives an inkling of capital migration that might otherwise go unnoticed. The principal beneficiary of Jacques Martel-Laprade was his great-nephew, the grandson of his wife's brother and namesake of her father, Marie-Pierre Martel. The latter was still a minor whose father, Emilien, was dead and whose mother was Caroline Causse, sister of the money-grubbing Antoine. The point was to keep the business going and in the hands of a Bédarician, despite the storm clouds over the industry. Those also figuring in their wills appear in Table 8–2. Giret was the son of Marguerite's cousin-german, Marie Martel (Marguerite was old Pierre's only surviving daughter), who went off to the wine country near Béziers to marry a major proprietor there, no doubt bringing with her a sizeable dowry and gifts. The Pouget men were sons of Jacques' sister, who had followed a similar route. This subtle movement of capital on the wings of marriage would be a process worth following in detail, but is beyond the scope of this study. These details,

Table 8–2

Relationship	Beneficiary	Occupation/ Title	Commune	Amount
Second cousin of Marguerite	Emilien Giret	Proprietor and mayor	Bassan (Béziers)	8,000
Grandnephews and nieces of Jacques	Décamp children	Father a lawyer	Bédarieux	2,000
Niece	Elisa Martel	Unmarried, proprietaire	Bédarieux	10,000
Nephews of Jacques	Camille and Jules Pouget	Proprietors	Nizas (Roujan)	4,000

however, suggest that the process of capital reallocation in Languedoc was highly complex.

To this complexity must be added the fact that Bédarician textile magnates also invested heavily in industry—to wit, the Graissessac mines. Going back to the 1830s, Martel-Laprade himself was a major actor in concession bids. Several of the inheritance declarations from Bédarieux (Bompaire, Cruvellé, Vernezobres, Sicard, Lapierre, Moulinier, Sabotier) record shares in the Quatre mines.[41] The Sabatier and Moulinier families were long the principal shareholders in the mines. And a list of major actionnaires of 15 January 1894 lists the following known Bédaricians among them:

Veuve Arnaud née Moulinier	550 shares
Veuve Pietre, née Moulinier	295 shares
Guillaume Sabatier de l'Esperan	855 shares
Mme Sabatier de l'Esperan	281 shares
Veuve Farjon de Besson, née Moulinier	767 shares
Mme Kuhnholtz-Lordat, née Vernazobres	1429 shares
Prosper Moulinier	1200 shares
Félix Sabatier	385 shares
Joseph Sicard (rep. née Usquin)	298 shares
	6060

The Moulinier family was originally from St. Gervais, of course, and their money was in mining from the beginning. The Sabatiers were ubiquitous Hérault capitalists who had made considerable money in wool and woolens while also involved in mining and the vine. Vernazobres and Sicard were full "woolens-origin" capitalists. But Bédarieux people accounted for more than half of the 11,849 shares owned by "major shareholders" in the mine company, one of the few viable industries in the Hérault at that time.[42]

Lodève's history of deindustrialization is more typical and contrasts sharply with the bailout mentality of its former sister city. In the later 1860s, the fear of permanent economic decline, made palpable by the railroad defeats and the departure of Barbot-Fournier, seemed to be creating a kind of social harmony rooted in desperation. As noted in the Lodève City Council deliberations of 19 June 1868: "For almost four years our worker population has borne with courage and resignation crises occurring nearly without interruption." Four more houses had "closed down their factories" and three more *lots* were lost since 1865. "More than 2000 workers have left their *pays natal* to go elsewhere in search of bread for their children." But the crisis situation was more severe than that. In order to meet the increasing pressure from the War Administration to cut costs and to find ways to compete in the commercial market, several firms had already switched over to a sulfuric acid-bath process that would eliminate the need for *époutoyage à la main*, the work performed by women straightening the weave or removing knots and stray matter from cloth before it was fulled. The quality of the cloth was somewhat undermined, but the savings in labor was considerable. Estimates put the number of women affected at 1,500. Although this was only one of three duties most performed (along with washing and wool-sorting), it was the most important. The rapid elimination of this job cut deeply into family wages and sent single women off in search of work as well.

The larger impact of all the developments, so familiar to towns wherever plant closings occur, was predictable:

> The Municipal Council knows better than anyone the consequences of this emigration: depreciation of housing values, the reduction of local commerce, the diminution of municipal revenues; and all this occurs just at the moment when the city Administration was undertaking significant material improvements, so needed in our old town.

Lodève had shared in the civic-improvement movement characteristic of the Second Empire and, as we have seen, was in dire need of public health measures. The abbatoir had been an important step, and gas lighting was introduced in the early 1860s. The train station, despite its distance from town and its sad use-rate, symbolized progress. Bridges and streets needed work, however, and plans for street widening, a sewer system, and improved water service were on the board. The municipal council now included individuals like the author of this report, entrepreneur Jean Hugounenq, and the accountant Hippolyte Plus, who were not directly involved in the woolens industry. The mayor, Jules Teisserenc, in his efforts to organize assistance—including small municipal travel grants for the unemployed—seemed closer to the old Saint-Simonian ideals than did his adversary at Montplasir.

The purpose of the report, however, was yet again to seek aid from the government—for the creation of a tobacco manufactory in Lodève. Tobacco processing was a lucrative government monopoly, and contracts were awarded based on need and capabilities. Lodève seemed to have both. Its several "idle factories were perfectly adaptable and the State could acquire or rent them at very low prices," but, above all, the town had a work force that was perfect: "1,500 women, young, intelligent, respectable, would be delighted to put at the disposal of a tobacco manufactory the dexterity and the habits of discipline acquired in the practice of a craft [*époutoyage*] that calls for the highest degrees of these qualities."

This was absolutely true, and the answer was absolutely *no*. The next several months witnessed a brutal correspondence with Interior, Public Works, and War in which each ministry outdid the other in trumpeting "free enterprise." It was as if once the state had done its work in shoving this forgotten (or too-well remembered) corner of France to the wall, it would now let it collapse without firing a shot. The problem with the tobacco contract was, of course, that Lodève was not centrally located from the point of view of communications. The basic indicator? The low volume of traffic at its train station!

Simultaneously, the city fathers asked for a restoration of some lost army orders. The desire to strangle someone was undoubtedly enhanced by War Minister Adolphe Niel's latest lesson in laissez-faire, preached on New Year's Eve 1868:

> If one always stops due to the fear of injuring certain interests, of destroying certain acquired positions, of upsetting the lives of certain people, industry would be condemned to immobility and would have to renounce progress of any sort; for it cannot make a single step forward without some individuals finding themselves struck down and *declassé*. I do not need to insist on this point.

A bit later, both Niel and his colleague in Public Works returned to their *leit motif*, the failure to convert more to draps de commerce. Lodève manufacturers had been in a rut for "two hundred years; they are convinced that the administration is in some way obliged to provide for their factories and create work."[43]

The tragedy was that Lodève had done everything it could to perfect its specialty, which was, after all, military cloth, in an age where specialization, not diversification, was the key to success. Mazamet was proving it at that moment. Even so, Lodève had tried—and was still trying in the most demeaning manner. If begging for a tobacco plant had required fortitude, several of the town's manufacturers were experimenting with an even more degrading alternative: *effilochage*. What was that? In English, the term was "shoddy." Rather in the manner of the ancient nailmakers of Graissessac who melted down rusty old iron, practitioners of this art brought old wool scraps from rag pickers, shredded it in giant machines, and with the fluff spun rough thread that would be woven into rougher cloth for capes and blankets and the like. The thread was also (and increasingly) used for the warp of heavy, cheap woolens for clothing. Lodève itself did not produce much of the latter, but sold thread to other struggling Languedoc centers (for example, Riols and St. Chinian) and to textile towns in the Center and North.[44] Whatever one might say about the greed or hard-heartedness of

Teisserencs past, it is impossible not to sympathize with the disgust of the present scion of the family as he felt the scratchy, limp fabric that he now tried to sell in "commerce."

But did he, or the workers who had to breathe the dust and *produce* this stuff, have any choice in the matter? Of course, they could all "vote with their feet," as a later head of state would so eloquently put it, and go elsewhere; the capitalists could also redeploy their money into other forms of investment. In the end, this is what happened. But if anything proves the determination of Lodévois to keep up the struggle for the industrial viability of their region, these efforts of the late 1860s provide the evidence.

For Lodève's proud working class these were years of unrelieved heartbreak. Although army orders rose along with the war clouds of 1870, and further, no less dishonorable attempts to "diversify" (such as cloth for prison uniforms)[45] averted total collapse, employment in the city's woolens industry was in a state of permanent decline. With it, all of the basic demographic indicators followed suit. Despite brief periods of revitalization as early Third Republic ministries proved somewhat more generous in 1873–75 and sales to foreign armies boomed around 1880, employment, census, and état civil statistics chart the descent. General population growth and the marriage figures follow the peaks and troughs of Lodève's industrial history very closely. Birth statistics are less clear indicators because they are complicated by deliberate family limitation, especially after infant mortality begins to decline in the 1860s.[46]

Specific employment figures are obviously less reliable, as are occupational totals derived from censuses. However, the latter for 1851 and 1872, both of which gave careful attention to female employment, show a global decline of all those in textile production from 3,573 to 2,344, or a drop of 34 percent. As a percentage of the total population, the fall was less drastic, from 31.8 percent to 24.7 percent (a 22.5 percent drop). This is a good indicator that new jobs in other sectors were not easily found in Lodève itself. The concern over the collapse of époutoyage à la main reflected another reality visible in occupational statistics: women's employment opportunities had held on better than men's in the period of decline. Although there was a decline from 1851 to 1872 in both categories, the percentage of women in the textile work force increased from 63.7 percent to 71.7 percent. The percentage was probably even higher in the mid-1860s, before the impact of chemical processing. The main change occurred in weaving, where women almost doubled the number of men in 1872 (423 to 236) because of the transition to female-tended power looms. In view of the substantial difference in male-female wage levels, the entire process, even for those retaining employment, meant declining family incomes.

As in most monoindustrial settings, alternative employment could not easily be found for either men or women. Retail commerce and service industries in Lodève were intimately tied to the success of woolens and transferring to jobs in that sector was most unlikely. The city's other "grande industry" was machine construction, which, although generating a gross product-value of Fr 200,000, comprised only two shops for steam engines and two for drive-trains (manèges) employing a total of 24 men. Naturally, these small operations were also beset with difficulty because their customers were woolens firms. Agriculture undoubtedly absorbed a few hands, but the number of males listing agriculture jobs in 1851 and 1872, (647 and 562) roughly parallels the overall population decline. As for women in these categories, they are too rare to be meaningful, although grape-harvest work undoubtedly occupied both women and men in the Lodévois and elsewhere for a month or so in the autumn.

Neither did the surrounding communes provide significant employment opportunities. In this region, rural industry had long been virtually nonexistent and, while the vine had made important strides, the peasant-proprietor largely relied on familial labor or local wage-workers. The best measure of the situation is the fact that every commune in the canton, with the exception of Soumont (1,876) and Le Bosc (1,866), reached its population peak in 1856 or earlier. The peak for the entire canton occurred, not surprisingly, in the same year as Lodève, 1856. Emigration was the rule, therefore, for the entire area.

Depopulation of the city in the period 1861–72 was of alarming proportions, with a net loss due to out-migration totalling 1,650 or a good 15 percent of the population. The plummeting marriage and birth rates during the same period suggest that most of these emigrants were young. Many, of course, had been short-term residents in any case, coming to the city in the boom years of the mid-1850s, for the net migration loss from the 1851 census to that of 1872 was much lower, 740. But by whatever measure one uses, people were abandoning the old woolens town. It would appear that earlier migrants to the city, in general, predominated among those who left, as only 10 percent of those listed in the detailed census of 1872 were not born in Lodève. Our only other comparable measure is the census of the Year VI (1798–99), according to which, it will be recalled, 31 percent of the population was born in other communes. Logically, people with deeper roots in the city would have a greater tendency to stay because of both sentiment and material circumstances, including family and friendship support networks.[47]

Where did Lodève's emigrants go? Although this question cannot be answered for the 1860s and 1870s, some indications can be gleaned by virtue of the legal requirement instituted in France after 1892 to record the date and place of marriage(s) alongside the birth entry in the état civil records in the commune of an individual's birth. Birth certification before marriage had long been required, but had not been recorded in such an easily accessible manner. Thus, it becomes possible to trace those people born in Lodève (mostly after 1870) who married either there or elsewhere by an examination of birth records. I chose two cuts: all birth records 1873–1875 and 1885–1887. It is understood that this procedure does not capture a large contingent of out-migrants from Lodève, those who were not born there but came there in better days. Still, the sample provides a sense of deindustrialization's most profound effect on human beings—the necessity of seeking their livelihood elsewhere in the absence of life chances in their native habitat. If we cannot reconstruct the emotional content of that wrenching experience, we can document the outward circumstances by means of this source.

Most marriages in the samples took place between 1892 and 1925; the numbers are not large enough to identify any chronological trend, so all have been lumped together. Information on date and place of death was also recorded by virtue of legislation in 1945, so for those who lived long enough, whether or not their marriage was recorded, we can know where they died. A few may have succumbed in Montpellier only because they had been taken there for specialized medical care, but the number is too small to be statistically significant. Overall, then, we have 471 entries out of 1,178 births in these six years. Of these, 361 provide marriage information and 110 death information only. This does not necessarily mean that they all never married, for certainly failure to report could occur, and a handful were likely married before 1892.[48] A majority (198) of those for whom we do have marriage information died before 1945, or for some reason their deaths were not recorded; thus, place of both marriage and death is available for only 163 individuals. Only eight of those who were married elsewhere died in Lodève, so the marriage records, at least for those who lived to old age, provide a good indication of definitive migration. Let us begin our analysis with them.

Out of a total of 361 individuals in our samples (people born in Lodève 1873–75 and 1885–87 whose marriages were recorded on their birth entries), 55 percent married in the city and 45 percent elsewhere, with men more than doubling the number of women leaving. Still, it should be remembered that even if a woman had already migrated or intended to, she would be much more likely to marry in her hometown than would a man in similar circumstances. This is proved by the post-1945 place-of-death statistics. Of thirty-five individuals who were married in Lodève but died at advanced ages elsewhere, 22 (69 percent) were women.[49] Moreover, among those who apparently never married but whose post-1945 deaths occurred elsewhere, 40 were women and 23 were men. Hence, men and women left the city in roughly equal numbers, with the latter more likely to leave after marriage or as singles unlikely to marry (at least officially). A majority of those who remained lifetime singles and who died after 1945, 61 of 110 (55 percent), left the city. A much smaller number of people married in the city also left (28 women and 15 men), meaning, rather obviously, that marriage usually meant settling down, especially for men, while out-migration was a decision undertaken mainly by single people, whether or not they would marry later on.

If one takes the entire sample of those of both sexes born in the city who married and/or died after 1945, whether married or "single" (471), out-migrants totalled 265, or 56 percent, with 8 of the post-1945 deceased returning home at some point after marriage elsewhere. This leaves a picture of very high definitive migration, and is surely too low since the place of death for the entire cohort has not been recorded. The key information to be drawn from this material, of course, concerns where people decided to move. There are several logical choices: 1) to the "wine belt" in search of jobs (or spouses with jobs) in growing, processing, distributing, or supplying lower Languedoc's new staple; 2) to Algeria; and 3) to the industrially vital areas of the country. Decisions should also logically vary with one's background and circumstances; the only information of significance in this regard is the occupation of the migrants' parents at their time of birth. What do we find?

To begin with, the attraction of the lower Languedoc wine villages was low, at least for this generation. Twenty-three (twelve men, eleven women), 9 percent of the out-migrants, married and/or died in villages where the vine dominated. Of course, the villages of Lodève's canton increasingly converted to the vine as well, but their attraction was slight, only eight Lodévois settled in these communes. Somewhat stronger poles of attraction were the towns and villages of the highlands, causses, the Sorgue valley, and the upper Orb valley that had long provided the bulk of the migrants to the city. But there was a major difference between the two cohorts, with twenty-three, or almost a fifth, of the 1873–75 group going to Cornus, Ceilès, Caylar, and so forth, and only seven of the later group doing so, with four of these ending up in Le Bousquet, probably to work in the mines. It appears, then, that the return to ancestral turf exercised a pull as long as such a move was economically feasible. For those marrying in their teens and twenties, these depressed areas could no longer absorb people.[50] A similar problem obtained in the wine villages. As Harvey Smith and others have shown, the postphylloxera reconstitution process, especially heavy in the 1890s, did attract uplanders—but generally from the Aveyron. Later on, new job opportunities declined.[51]

Surprisingly, few Lodévois went to North Africa. In this sample, indeed, only three did so. All were of middle-class backgrounds and married in urban areas. This tends to corroborate the view that migration to Algeria came from rural southern France and from the port cities. Industrial skills that Lodève people might bring with them were in little demand in France's colony, where most settlers replaced forcibly expropriated Algerians on the land.[52]

Thus, it is not at all surprising that the major flow of migration from Lodève was toward urban centers, above all in the Midi, but Paris and its region as well. There was virtually no statistically significant difference between male and female maps of migration; thus the totals in Table 8–3 aggregate all migrants and include both marriage and death indicators.

We have no way of knowing, from this data, the sorts of jobs out-migrants were able to find. Montpellier and other towns of the wine region of lower Languedoc, if not booming, did well enough as a consequence of the viticultural transformation. Machinery, chemical, and commercial firms serving the vine grew and stimulated typical urban development with its

Table 8–3   Urban Destinations of Lodève Immigrants by Birth Cohort

	1873–1875	1885–1887	Total (%)
Montpellier	26	29	55 (35%)
Béziers, Sète, Carcassonne, Nîmes, Narbonne	10	16	26 (17%)
Marseille	8	2	10 (6%)
Other Midi cities*	20	19	39 (25%)
Paris and suburbs	17	8	25 (16%)
Other large northern cities†	1	1	2 (1%)
Total	82	75	157 (100%)

*Limoges, Perpignan, Tarbes, Castres, Montauban, Brive, Romans, Bayonne, Toulouse, Bordeaux, Auch, Aix-en-Provence, Riom, Grenoble, Toulon, Cannes, Orange, Lyon, Clermont-F, Limoges, Nice, Vienne.
†Tours, Reims.

accompanying employment opportunities.[53] But the attraction of cities elsewhere was also strong. If nearly one-third of all emigrants married and/ or died in the larger wine centers of Languedoc, another 30 percent went to cities elsewhere, though heavily to those where a southern accent of some sort would still be heard. Paris, however, showed its exceptional drawing power, even on those from the far south.

For several, a pattern of multiple movement can be discerned. Twenty-nine people whose deaths are recorded were married somewhere significantly distant from the place where they ended their days. Another thirty-seven moved to a different commune in the same general area. A few (a guess is four only) seem to have retired to a resort residence, but the vast majority no doubt moved again to find employment. There is no particular pattern in the resettlement process. Montpellier, Cette, and Nîmes were the starting point for nine, but they went in all directions (Paris, Le Bous-quet, Gignac, Castelnandary, the Pyrenees, etc.). The numbers are too small, in any case, to make meaningful assertions. The Lodève diaspora, in sum, saw well over half its natives depart, and a good number of those were unable to find satisfactory work in their first place of settlement.

If one examines the socio-occupational milieu from which migrants sprang, at least as indicated by their fathers' occupations at the time of their birth, the difference between those who left and those who stayed behind is not particularly striking save, perhaps, in one respect (Table 8–4).

As a percentage of each respective population, the numbers of children from woolens families more or less reflects the percentage of male woolens workers in Lodève in 1872 (12 percent), and, indeed, such is the case for most of the sample. The central fact remains the sheer overall volume of departures. But the more one moves from the working-class milieu, the more discrepancies appear. Logically those whose fathers were involved in agri-

Table 8–4 Father's Occupation in 1873–75/1885–1887

	Migrant		Life-long Lodévois	
Woolens worker	43	16%	46	22%
Machinists	9	3%	5	2%
Other industries	13	5%	14	7%
Service artisans/shopkeepers	77	29%	64	31%
Agriculture	42	16%	41	20%
"White collar"	38	14%	10	5%
Bourgeois—	31	12%	10	5%
manuf./com.	18		3	
prof./property owners	13		7	
Common laborer	8	3%	7	3%
No profession	3	1%	3	1%
Illegitimate	1	0%	6	3%
Total	265		206	

culture were more likely to remain—but only if they had property. Children of wage-working *domestiques* (seven) and *journaliers* (twenty-three) make up the bulk of the migrants in this category.

But access to property ownership did little to hold the children of the educated middling classes and the bourgeoisie to Lodève. Here is the only clear variation from random expectancy: 26 percent of the migrant group were the offspring of the *classe moyenne* (clerks, salesmen, public employees, and teachers) and the bourgeoisie (officials, doctors, lawyers, architects, and the city's business elite). Among the business class in this sample, only three children (all daughters) stayed on in the city, while the rest (eighteen) located elsewhere. Several daughters married landed proprietors or men in the wine business. Honoré Teisserenc's daughter Fulcrande celebrated her wedding in 1908 with Jean François Boisse de Black at the latter's parish church in Villerombel in the Aveyron, the location of the estate granted to his Scottish ancestors by Louis XV after the collapse of Bonnie Prince Charlie's forces in 1745.[54] Another, Marie Camaret, was the daughter of a wine and eau de vie shipper headquartered in Cette who had married into the Ollier family of dyers and wool merchants. She ended her days on an estate in Vinas, having married a négociant en vins in Lodève. Sons of the bourgeoisie went to Paris, Lyon, Toulouse, Riom, and other cities where their money might be profitably invested. From this sample, at least, there is very little indication of marriages by fabricant's sons taking them directly into the lower Languedoc vineyards. The children of the *classe moyenne* abandoned Lodève with equal alacrity. Their dispersal patterns generally mirrored that of the town as a whole, although places of marriage were more diverse. The offspring of employés and police ranged farther, dotted from the Pyrenees to Paris, while those of postmen stayed closer to home. In general, one can discern a pattern where those with financial and educational advantage found it possible to escape the depressed environment of industrial Languedoc with relative ease, while the workers and the tradespeople who depended on them found movement, unless forced by dire necessity, more difficult.

This was particularly true of the children of woolens workers. Although not spectacularly higher numbers stayed, they are clearly the most "stable" group in the sample. This is all the more striking if one examines the occupations of the mothers, an operation conducted only for the 1873–75 birth records. Employment opportunities of women, despite the collapse of époutoyage à main, were greater than for men in the woolens industry. What was being established, in fact, was what labor economists today would call a dual *internal* labor market in an industry where "out-sourcing" of elements in the manufacturing process was less feasible.[55] A female labor force gaining lower wages and exhibiting higher rates of turnover, often working part-time or at various jobs seasonally, numerically comprised about two-thirds of the employment in the constricting industry. The big change in the 1860s had been the rapid advance of power-loom weaving, which drastically increased the demand for women workers, while killing off the more heavily male domain of the hand loom. We have already seen the impact of this process on the total population of Lodève. But for many of those who stayed into the 1870s, the secret of survival in their native town was a dual income situation, with the mother working in woolens and the father working either there, if he could, or in other occupations. Such family management, then, seems to have been an ongoing factor in decisions of both sons and daughters to remain in Lodève.

Let us examine the figures more closely.

The central point is that the out-migration rates from families where the mother worked was decidedly lower than from those where she did not. Two factors are operating here. The first and obvious one is that life styles of bourgeois and those attempting to emulate them dictated that the wife, certainly the expectant mother, not work. The remarkable fact about Lodève is how high the number of working mothers was in the middle 1870s—51 percent. Those who did not work out of choice are hard to calculate, but only one woman whose husband reported a profession for her (a "marchande") was married to a bourgeois (a propriétaire), and only six wives of "white collar" workers worked, one *époutieuse* married to a postman and five *modistes* or *couturières* married to employés and other office workers. For the 1873–75 sample, this left the vast majority among the gentlefolk (twenty-four bourgeoises and thirteen of the classe moyenne) as "ladies of leisure." As we know, their children emigrated in large numbers. At the other end of the scale are those families whose circumstances were such that women could not find jobs. The figures in Table 8–5 demonstrate how important married women's contribution to the family income was in allowing—and encouraging—their children to stay at home. Unquestion-

Table 8-5

Mother's Occupation		Children Migrants?		Husband's Occupation (Migrant/Non-Migrant)					
		Yes	No	Woolens	Trades	Agriculture	Other Workers	White Collar	Bourgeois
Weaver (*tisseuse*)*	45								
Wool worker (*ouvrière en laine*)	28								
Burler (*épouilleuse*)	20								
Woolens	93	37 (40%)	56 (60%)	12/18	6/14	11/10	7/14	1/0	0/0
Service	6								
Needle Trades	14								
Silk Worker	1								
Agricultural Worker	5								
Trades Women	2								
Other occupations	28	14 (50%)	14 (50%)	2/0	1/5	1/5	5/3	4/1	1/0
Total working mothers	121	51 (42%)	70 (58%)	14/18	7/19	12/15	12/17	5/1	1/0
Nonworking mothers	114	72 (70%)	42 (30%)	9/5	24/18	10/5	5/3	9/4	15/7
Total mothers	235	123 (52%)	112 (48%)	23/23	31/37	22/20	17/20	14/5	16/7

*Includes 2 unmarried mothers whose work—both in woolens—provides the child's social milieu. Both children (2 girls) married in Lodève.

ably, they established examples for their children to follow; this helps to explain further why daughters, especially, even though they might ultimately leave, stayed (and worked) at least until they married.

Thus, even in economically depressed Lodève, France's tighter labor market allowed native workers in the traditional industry to stay put in greater numbers than one might expect—as long as the family could piece together a living income. Alain Cottereau has generalized this argument in a brilliant article,[56] and Tessie Liu and Whitney Walton, analyzing Choletais textiles and Lorraine embroidery industries, found a similar determination to remain in one's pays natal in contexts where low-paying women's work provided the most stable element in the job market.[57]

The "stability" achieved in Lodève represented a new equilibrium at a much lower level of employment in general and a transformed structure of work in which women's jobs became the critical element in the viability of both firms and worker families. Survival meant cost-cutting, and the obvious path had been in the area of disguised wage concessions rooted in increasing lower-paid female employment. Still, a certain degree of company-worker harmony had also emerged for those (both companies and workers) who continued to operate. This meant paternalism on the part of the companies and a "cooperative attitude" on the part of the workers. In the mid-1860s, as the first ravages of deindustrialization were being felt, all reports agreed that Lodève's "worker population endured the crises that have occurred nearly without interruption with courage and resignation."[58] Although 1870–71 brought brief strikes by époutieuses and by machinists, none of the vaunted militance of old was evident.[59] Politically, the Lodève working class reacted not at all to the examples of the siege and the Paris Commune. A correspondent of Jules Guesde wrote from Lodève that the republicans were "completely certain of defeat [in the approaching elections] here," for both "peasants and workers are without energy."[60] This lassitude continued. There are repeated comments by political observers about the lost luster of Lodève's labor movement over the next thirty years. The city's politics gradually shifted leftward again, particularly with the emergence of démoc-soc Paul Vigné d'Octon and his heated campaigns against Paul Leroy-Beaulieu in the 1880s,[61] but those workers who remained behind as Lodève shriveled exhibited a cautious and fearful moderation in all things, a mindset obviously bred of experience. This phenomenon has continued to be an almost inevitable consequence in deindustrializing regions. Far from sharpening class conflict, deindustrialization, a constant aspect of global economic change, creates, on one hand, enormous pockets of working-class conservatism and, on the other, migrants to more prosperous regions, who may bring a militant tradition with them, but who find themselves at the low end of labor market competition and are often regarded as a threat to those in entrenched positions.

In 1903–04, in response to a general nationwide crisis in textiles, a detailed survey of the industry was undertaken by the Chamber of Deputies. It was indicative of the depths to which Languedoc had fallen that the

Lodévois was among the "régions non-visitées" by the blue-ribbon commission created to carry out the inquiry. Nevertheless, the report to the Commission filed by the Chamber of Commerce of Montpellier and authored by Vincent Vitalis of Lodève, provides a remarkable picture of a once-great industrial region in its twilight.

The worst of the cutbacks had by then taken place. Only five companies still produced in Lodève. There were two in Clermont, including Maistre at nearby Villeneuvette. Together they were capable of putting out 900,000 meters (700,000 at Lodève) of cloth, but even in good years sold half that much. True to their heritage, "all the progress achieved over the last 20 years in industrial equipment has been adopted by the fabricants," including the latest carding equipment, self-acting spinning machines, and new mechanical weaving looms, "equipped with the latest improvements with several shuttles and faster action, thus realizing a 15 to 20 percent increase in productivity and better quality" when compared to the previous generation of "already very good" power looms. The work force at Lodève totalled about 1,300, with another 450 or 500 in Clermont/Villeneuvette. Only 550 to 600 adult men were required; women (900) and teenagers (250–300) provided the main component. Male carders, spinners, finishers, and mechanics, all working at piece-rates, pulled down the best pay, five to six francs per day, while the large force of women weavers could make up to three francs for piece work. The report, written by a fabricant, of course, stresses that these were competitive wages. As always, although the wage share in the cost price had declined from close to 50 percent in premachine days to 25 percent in 1903, the cost of wool and its fluctuations still remained the central concern of the manufacturers.

Nevertheless, labor peace, hard work, and as low a wage package as technology would allow remained the key to survival, for only there would continued savings be realized. Transport costs and the "price of coal and iron" gave a permanent advantage to northern competitors. The decision made by the remaining firms marked a retreat from the stern, confrontationist orientation of the earlier years into a frankly articulated paternalism. This trend was hardly limited to the declining industries of the south, of course, but it was all the more crucial for them.

For those who remained employed in Lodève, a framework of health and old-age protection was provided largely by the companies with pensions of Fr 200 to 300 per year for men and mutual-aid based health care, including medicines, supplemented when needed from company funds. It seems clear that other firms took their cue from Villeneuvette, for its program of "familial" industrial relations pervades Vitalis's report. Woolens work was a family question as well. Firms did not really recruit, but counted on sons and daughters to follow in their parents' footsteps. In discussing "apprenticeship," Vitalis puts it this way: "the piecers, in growing up, learn how to operate the spinning machine and become spinners. The winders and the knotters are in general daughters and sisters of the weavers and learn naturally on their looms. The industrialists obviously benefit from this and

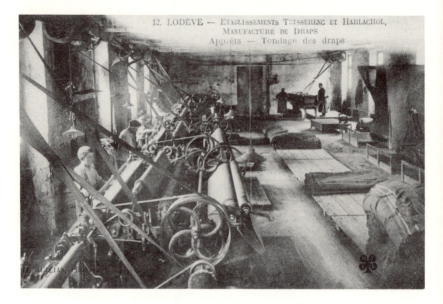

Lodève's last woolens firm

do everything they can to encourage it." Companies had succeeded in creating long-term work-force stability. Workers rarely changed companies and many "worked for 35 to 40 years" for the same firm. Health and safety conditions within the plants passed the increased vigilance of government inspectors after the Law of 1898 with flying colors; only seven industrial accidents serious enough to warrant disability pay had occurred since 1898, and the only worker death was the result of an insect bite. (The family was compensated anyway.)

The consequences of such programs—for the vastly reduced work force and their employers—were obvious. There had not been a strike in thirty years. No unions were necessary and none existed. Workshop discipline was light, at most. No fines were levied for ill-made work. Virtually no one was fired except for total incompetence, and temporary layoffs were avoided if at all possible; instead, firms reduced hours by closing down one day a week in slack periods. Women workers "generally return to work three weeks after giving birth [there was apparently no birth benefit, however]; the greatest felicity is accorded them in this regard; their place at their loom is always reserved for them and when they breast-feed, they are authorized to go to their babies during rest periods to feed them." These lines make clear how important married women were in the new work structure of the threatened industry.

Obviously then, as the report reiterates, relations at the point of production were "good." But, in return for this high quality of work life (as one might put it), there were a couple of expectations that workers dutifully fulfilled. One, complementing the absence of union agitation, was that the employees "are never inspired by political or civic preoccupations, which never cross the threshold of the factories." And the second? It was that without which all the rest would not make any business sense: "Most of the operations are done by the task and the wage usually depends on the skill and the assiduity of the worker, male and female." Although there is no mention of a bonus system, productivity rooted in differential rewards of piecework lay at the heart of the system. A submissive, temperate, "family" of workers had become the face of deindustrialized Lodève.[62] Gone were the days when brothers conspired in class warfare, and the entire family of a different working class kept their secret.

The multiple parallels with the experiences of contemporary deindustrialization must await this book's general conclusion, but the reference to the Balp brothers' infamous deed underlines the central argument of this part of it. The very struggle that so precociously erupted in Lodève and other parts of old industrial Languedoc tended to isolate the region in the mind's eye of bourgeois France. The Second Empire in virtually every respect could not have been a worse regime for Languedoc to relate to, for image increasingly became a reality of official disfavor. Theoretical geographer Paul Clavel has stressed the positive importance of image: "Dynamism depends in large part on the transparency of a region, on the manner in which it is known in other parts of the country. Theoreticians of the firm have insisted on what they call the prestige of an enterprise."[63] So too with a region, though in the case of nineteenth-century Languedoc, it was notoriety rather than prestige. Much like Detroit in the post-1967 riot period, this center of social upheaval with a discredited past faced overwhelming negative odds in the new political dynamic that emerged under Napoleon III. It was a dynamic geared to the economic interests of ascendant dynasties of capital located elsewhere. Rail policy was where this showed up most clearly, though obviously as a seat of the "defense" industry, Lodève was a perfect laboratory for examining the changing winds of state policy toward the South. Only when reduced to an industrial shell with a quiescent working class and market-controled microfarmers would Languedoc again be worthy of sympathy from state and society.

9

La Défense Viticole and the Politics of Deindustrialization, 1880–1920

A people that entrusts its subsistence to one product alone commits sui-cide. . . . The nation that buys, commands. . . .

José Marti

During the Third Republic, Languedoc completed its transformation into an agrarian region sustained by a single cash corp. The vine proved to be an unreliable friend even for those who lived from it, as the phylloxera, then overproduction took disastrous tolls. But for the people of the piedmont the vine was almost a vexatious intrusion. Having offered some hope (though hardly stemming the tide of emigration), it then betrayed them cruelly. Good wines had long come from the band of hill country stretching from the Minervois through the middle Orb and the upper Hérault valleys and on to the "Costières" du Gard. Yields were low, but good drainage, chalky soil, and careful vinification assured (as they do once again today) a sought-after product. Vine work intermingled with rural industry in the villages, male weavers often made the transition to full-time employment (or partial ownership) in wine-making, but their daughters led the *exode rural* during the 1860s and 1870s.[1] With the phylloxera, however, the vine was effectively removed as a factor in the piedmont's collective life for a generation. Unlike the plains and the coastal area of Languedoc, none of the methods of combating the dreaded American mite could be used precisely because of its uneven terrain and calcareous soil. Only with the development of calcium carbonate resistant rootstock in the 1920s did wine production revive.[2] The economic shift to the flatlands of lower Languedoc thus seemed definitive as the natural history of the vine conspired with the very human history of deindustrialization to doom the old cloth district.

The political implications of the dramatic alteration of Languedoc's economy in the later nineteenth century were profound. It is well known that the region, and the Hérault in particular, came to be a stronghold of the political left, first in the triumph of Radicalism and then, especially after the betrayal by Clemenceau, "briseur des grèves," in 1907, in the advance of socialism. In many respects, the emergence of the "Midi rouge" makes sense simply in light of its deeper history, one laden with class conflict and the constant threat of a violently counterrevolutionary Catholic right, which polarized political life virtually everywhere, thus fanning the flames of left radicalism. The inheritance of the liberating atmosphere of the Second Republic and its deep penetration into rural society when coupled with an Imperial regime that seemed to reserve its harshest treatment for Languedoc certainly predicted a left politics.

Leo Loubère, in a careful quantitative study of the changing political geography of lower Languedoc, stresses the centrality of the rise of the vine and the numerical preponderance of those perfect representatives of Léon Gambetta's *nouvelles couches sociales*, the *petits vignerons*, as the force propelling Radicalism to the fore in the region. There is much to be said for this argument, although as Raymond Huard has shown, it does not work for the Gard. There the greatest strength of republicanism lay in the nonviticultural (and heavily Protestant) Cevennes and its greatest weakness in the vineyard cantons. Catholic-populist legitimism long provided the political home for workers in Nîmes and elsewhere against their Protestant, and often Republican, bosses. Republicanism emerged more slowly in the Gard than elsewhere, with the final breakthrough coming only in 1881–82 as Catholic workers, spearheaded by miners in the Alès basin, went over in large numbers.[3] It should also not be forgotten that the Gard had been favored commercially and financially by virtue of its relationship with the power elite in Paris. Despite severe problems in the silk industry, due the *pébrine* disease, Nîmes continued to be the key pole of attraction in the area for migrants from the mountains.[4] But as the city and the mining district faced growing hardships in the late 1880s, both Radicalism and Socialism, propagated by Eugène Fournière and Jules Guesde, made headway.[5]

The example of the Gard is important because it underlines the politically radicalizing effects of economic distress. In the Hérault, however, the impact of deindustrialization and the shift to a precarious single-product economy was already well underway by 1870. Its politics had long been Left, despite pockets of monarchism, and would continue to move leftward, becoming one of the strongholds of socialism in the years before the war. Its practice, however, was a far cry from the class struggles of the past. The objective for the vast majority of vine workers and industrial workers alike was not the transfer of ownership, the reconstruction of the social order, or even necessarily a higher wage. Rather it was "justice" from the state in the form of legal changes and subsidies that would combat the *mévente* or protect withering industries. What emerged was politics of regional defense. Socialism leapt successfully into the combat, but its primary function was to take the most radical position in demanding Languedoc's "rights"—namely, positive governmental action to shore up the vine, the region's only viable resource. Basically, this meant two things: toning down the rhetoric of class and embracing a kind of regional nationalism. Thus, the very character of capitalist development, wildly uneven not just between large areas of the world, but on regional, interindustry and intraindustry levels as well, cut to the very heart of the socialist project as workers in troubled regions and industries found themselves in too precarious a situation to opt for anything beyond a class-collaborationist clamoring for protection within the bourgeois state.[6]

The Last Struggle: The Upper Orb Industrial Region

By the early twentieth century, the demise of manufacturing in lower Languedoc was obvious to one and all. Although statistics precisely measuring the changing work force structures are lacking for the pre-World War I era, general demographic shifts within Mediterranean Languedoc render a sufficient indication of the dramatic change occurring.[7] The collapse of the textile areas—in both woolens and silk—and the remarkable growth of wine production are clear. The cities that benefited the most were those at the heart of the lowland vine revolution, Béziers and Narbonne. Both Nîmes and Montpellier continued to grow as well, but, larger to begin with and less influenced by the dizzying expansion of the new staple, their percentage of growth over these sixty years was more modest. Sète shared in the process too, but it actually declined in population from 1886 to 1906, due to the changing direction of Languedoc wine sales, the decline in coastal trade, the collapse of its barrel industry, and the 1890s falloff in coal exports.[8]

Two other points may be made from Table 9–1. One of the piedmont towns, Saint Chinian, had, by the 1880s, become a fairly important wine center. Its population decline from 1846 to 1886 was only 11 percent. But the inability to replant clearly had major effects, and a good number of its inhabitants had to find work elsewhere.[9] Second, the second half of the nineteenth century witnessed a significant expansion of employment in the extractive "industries," as population figures for the major coal basins indicate. But just as obviously, the greatest growth occurred in the 1846–86 period. Thereafter, severe problems began to mount.

Vine and mine, which became Languedoc's potential saviors, share an important characteristic: the greatest proportion of labor and fixed capital costs are absorbed by the process of making a natural product available for consumption, not in its transformation, as in manufacturing.[10] But if wine production stimulated local chemical and machinery firms, its secondary sectoral impact paled in comparison with the potential of coal mining, which routinely gave rise to massive industrial growth, especially in metallurgy. Many great industrial regions around the world grew because of their proximity to coal deposits. Even where iron was not naturally available in large amounts, coal attracted it and huge iron and steel industries blossomed.[11]

Table 9-1   Population of Selected Communes, 1846–1906

	1846	1866	1886	1906	Change, 1846–1906	
Textile Centers						
Lodève	10718	10571	9532	7895	−	26%
Bédarieux	9369	8985	7320	6131	−	35%
Clermont l'Hérault	6134	6050	5191	5140	−	16%
Saint-Chinian	3973	4284	3572	3037	−	24%
Ganges	4658	4121	4369	4582	−	6%
Le Vigan	5789	5104	5353	4595	−	21%
Saint-Jean du Gard	4193	3957	3712	3582	−	15%
Mining Centers						
Alès	17838	19964	22514	27435	+	54%
La Grand'Combe	4011	9367	11341	11292	+	182%
Graissessac	1209	2311	2738	2092	+	73%
Plain cities						
Nîmes	53497	60240	69898	80184	+	50%
Montpellier	45828	55606	56765	77114	+	68%
Sète	19041	24177	37058	33005	+	68%
Béziers	19596	27722	42785	52268	+	167%
Narbonne	11427	16037	29702	27039	+	137%
Wine Villages (Canton de Capestang, Hérault)						
Capestang	2039	2999	3519	4012	+	97%
Maureilhan	615	903	1007	1261	+	94%
Montady	320	366	515	660	+	106%
Montels	64	63	125	247	+	286%
Nissan	1658	2019	2296	2608	+	57%
Poilhes	219	230	309	624	+	185%

In Languedoc this was not long the case. Lorraine iron, once dephosphorization was perfected, combined with coal from the Pas-de-Calais and the Nord to shift cheap steel production northward. Decazeville effectively abandoned its iron production in the seventies and the various companies of the northern Gard followed the 1874 lead of the Compagnie d'Alais and either leased or otherwise withdrew from their iron and steel operations. Both technical factors and market geography contributed, but the fact was that in the later nineteenth century, the two most important centers of heavy industry in the south reverted to the production of raw materials.[12] Interestingly, the smaller coal basins of Carmaux and Graissessac, whose coals proved unresponsive to coking, had retained and were expanding their off-shoot industry, the production of bottle glass, which in both cases was stimulated by the general growth of wine production in France and was only moderately affected by the phylloxera because most Algerian and Spanish imports were bottled in France.[13]

Thus, there seemed to exist in these corners of the deep south some hope for a continued industrial presence. In the Hérault, Graissessac and the upper Orb industrial region had in fact rivaled the vine elsewhere in the department as a growth factor compensating for the decline of textiles in the decade after 1865. Despite the impediments resulting from an inadequate rail connection, the production of the Quatre mines réunies de Graissessac mounted steadily, reaching 269,000 metric tons in 1875. The glassworks at Le Bousquet also prospered, while various other industries benefiting from the presence of abundant coal, such as zinc founding and distilling, expanded. Employment opportunities arose not in Bédarieux, but in the small towns stretching up and down the Orb, Hérépian, La Tour, Le Bousquet, and Lunas, and in the mining villages of Estrechoux, Graissessac, and Camplong. As we have seen, steady, if not always satisfactory, improvements in road and rail communications made this subregion accessible. The Graissessac mine company was the flagship of the region. From the 1870s through the early 1890s, it appeared that it could stay the course. Its owners, largely supported by Hérault capital, certainly tried.

Henri Rascle, a product of the Ecole des Mines, was appointed works director in 1872. Usquin remained the kingpin of the operation, but had considerably broadened the financial base of the company and, specifically, had drawn enterprising men from the Protestant business community of Montpellier into it. Aaron Simon remained the chief executive officer of the limited liability company and simultaneously served as director of the profitable Le Bousquet glassworks. Simon recognized that in both firms, to overcome the multiple disadvantages of location, freight costs. and a checkered history of industrial relations, cost-effectiveness depended on a disciplined work force. Rascle seemed just the man for the job. Besides increasing efficiency through new technology and encouraging greater professionalism among employees, he became deeply involved in local affairs and gathered enough support to be elected mayor of Graissessac in 1880.[14]

These efforts, however, largely served to shore up an enterprise still facing difficulty. As it turned out, Graissessac reached its production peak in 1875. Thereafter, the production of the Company stagnated, remaining between 220,000 and 250,000 tons. The late 1880s then witnessed a crisis in southern French coal mining. The Bessèges company went bankrupt and Grand'Combe reeled, while Decazeville failed to pay a divided of more than 1 percent in the four years following its strike of 1886. Carmaux remained viable, largely due to profitable sales of low-quality fuel to the Rességuier glassworks, recently converted to the Siemens continuous flow system. Graissessac held its own because of the steadiness of marine engine coal demand and the growing importance of the Spanish market. Moreover, in 1889, Simon signed a lease agreement with Rességuier for the construction of Siemens ovens in the Le Bousquet glassworks.[15] Hope remained alive.

But in 1891 the coal company experienced a sudden decline. Net production fell from 254,000 T to 237,000 T, while inventories mounted. It was at this point that company officials began to examine carefully their productivity figures. The board hired a young engineer/accountant "to assist" the aging Simon.[16] Analysis revealed that since 1888 production costs in wages per ton had risen 17 percent. Historically, the company had never paid high dividends, averaging 5.43 percent from 1854 to 1891. But the bottom fell out in 1892. Profits collapsed and the company paid no dividends at all for two years. Spanish retaliation against the Méline tariff was the principal reason, but a further increase in production costs contributed as well.[17] This situation triggered a series of events that amounted to a revolution in company management and stimulated a massive upheaval among the mine workers. I have described this process in detail elsewhere and will only recall the main points here.[18]

Under the leadership of Charles Leenhardt, a group within the Board, mostly younger Hérault-born Protestant bourgeois, carried out a takeover that removed Simon and his allies. They instituted a series of financial measures, but, above all, sought to enhance productivity at the mines. Since technological advances, except in the area of worker safety,[19] had been steady and up-to-date under Simon, there existed little choice but to attack labor costs, beginning with a rollback on certain "welfare" provisions. The same no-nonsense attitude also came to Decazeville and Carmaux at about the same time. Overall, then, Graissessac participated in the arrival of the "drive system," the prototype for the labor methodologies of mass production.[20] Although the new regime did everything it could to speed up production, its primary concern was to take charge of the labor market, with a special interest in breaking the traditional patterns of recruitment and coal-face decision making controlled by the largely home-grown labor force. These moves, in turn, generated trade unionism.

The organized labor movement in the Hérault made rapid strides in the early 1890s, as it did everywhere in France. The miners, however, were well behind their brethren in other parts of the country—the Loire, where the miners' federation originated, was organized in the late 1870s, the Alès basin in 1881, Carmaux in 1883 and Décazeville in 1884.[21] Only in the spring of 1891, did Le Bousquet and Graissessac miners respond to the personal appeal of Miners Federation President Michel Rondet to participate as local unions in May Day demonstrations. As in so many other localities, the massacre that day of marchers at Fourmies in the Nord dramatized for them the character of class conflict in France.[22] Moreover, the influence of the organized glassworkers at Le Bousquet, who were affiliated with the Carmaux union, spurred miners to action. By mid-1893, some 800 people had signed up.

It would be incorrect, however, to attribute this development to the transmutation of "peasant-miners" into "worker-miners," as was the case in Rollande Trempé's Carmaux. Graissessac had *always* been an industrial area. In 1851, less than 22 percent of the heads of household in the commune classified themselves as working in agriculture. This was a lower percentage than one finds in the *cities* of Lodève in Bédarieux.[23] Historically, many nailmakers, the largest group, with 30 percent in 1851, had dug their own coal or bought it from small-scale "artisan" miners who operated their own mines despite the government's concessions to major companies. Only during the Consulat did officials begin to clamp down, causing bitter fights that left scars of hatred lasting throughout the century. This did not translate automatically into boss-worker antagonism in the mines however, because many members of nailmaker families, despite pressures on their declining craft, refused to work for the Company. It is also important that many of them were Protestants, while miners were heavily Catholic. This split was apparently manipulated by the mine supervisors, who were all Catholic and thus could count on some sympathy from their coreligionists. However mitigated by religion, classconscious behavior on the part of Catholic miners grew from mid-century on.[24] In the late 1880s it was enhanced by the arrival of large numbers of men from the battles at Decazeville and the Alès basin, who brought union and strike experience with them.

The pinch of the new regime was first felt in Le Bousquet (a soft-coal mine supplying the glassworks) in late 1891, where a new manager put an end to gleaning coal on the premises, ordered foremen to speed up production, and sought thereafter to cut piece rates. Two strikes followed in rapid succession, the second joined by the glassworkers. Although the results were indecisive, a tremendous well of solidarity arose both there and over the mountain at Graissessac/Camplong. In both communes, politics followed suit, as socialist municipalities were elected for the first time. Graissessac, the heart of the company with 1,955 employees, now became the chief focus of cost-cutting policy. The goal was to reduce the work force by 300, while altering work schedules to streamline underground and surface activities. The latter provoked lesser job actions, but the union's key concern was to negotiate rotating work-week reductions and other measures of short-term relief for the beleaguered firm.

The company, however, sought permanent downsizing and proposed a plan that would "protect" locally born people, while shearing away what it perceived to be "outside troublemakers." It soon became clear that its goal was to fire union activists, whatever their origin, and take full control of the external labor market and internal personnel usage. After a series of "disciplinary" firings, the works superintendent at Graissessac, Robert Parisse, announced a plan, after the workers had taken an overwhelming strike vote, to fire 250 people immediately. It completely ignored union and local officials' proposals to reach some compromise. Indeed, it raised the number of dismissals to 287 on 1 June 1894. After some jockeying on both sides, the company magnanimously reduced the number to 226. Who were they? Sixty-six were locals, 35 more from Hérault and perhaps 20 from the nearby lower Aveyron. So much for the protection of community people. Over at Le Bousquet, 46 were fired, of which 27 were men in key union positions. Although a detailed analysis of this sort was not made for Graissessac, a significant number of those fired there were also union activists.

The workers thus had no choice—or so it seemed. The company, holding significant backlogs of unsold coal, clearly wanted a strike, and it got one.

The Graissessac strike became one of the great labor struggles of the era, although less marked by violence than many. The solidarity among the strikers and within their communities created an atmosphere of confidence and calm self-assurance that kept explosive tensions to a minimum. The company's "security" forces did what they could to foment physical conflict. Besides house to house "visits," they escorted scabs through populated areas to provoke reactions by taunting the surly strikers. Company staff also joined in the fun. Mme Castan, the wife of the production supervisor, took a turn operating the briquette machine and then "paraded" around Graissessac, accompanied by her husband, drawing out a "veritable hedge" of angry humanity. But the incident went no further. Overall, the unity and peaceful bearing of the strikers remained firm. Until the end (28 August), only 85 workers reentered the mines. Intimidation remained nonphysical. Although 133 strikers were arrested, the courts convicted only 9 people for anything more than "menaces." The women's auxiliary, formed on 17 May, utilized long-standing images of feminine instability combined with the clumsy chivalry of police and ably served as the chief enforcers of strike discipline.[25]

One could go on and on about the drama of the strike and the bravery and good sense of the strikers, but the simple point is that the company was perfectly happy to see it continue and remained determined to rid itself of troublemakers. As it said, rather amazingly, in an official report in late June: We have "turbulent people whom we have retained until this day out of charity or patience. Should we accept the rotation system they would retain their harmful influence on our personnel."[26] It succeeded entirely in its project. By late August, merchants no longer would extend credit, and resources from the outside were fast diminishing. The company had reduced its huge inventories substantially and was still not hurting in any significant way. The union ranks remained remarkably firm, rejecting a recommendation by the strike committee to return to work as late as 27 August. The next day, Socialist Deputy Eugène Baudin finally convinced the assembled strikers to end the stoppage.

The net results were clear: the company had saved Fr 752,000 in wages and had won total power over the labor market. It could hire and fire whom it wanted. To be sure, it lost clients in the short run. But even in the first six months of 1895, it made Fr 171,000 in profit, just 18,000 less than in all of 1892. In the years that followed, it restored its profits to the levels of the late 1880s.[27]

What happened to the workers and their union? In the end, 165 workers were actually not readmitted, but another 50 refused to return. The union was devastated. On December 15 1894, a knowledgeable official summed up the situation: "As a result of the ascendancy that the company has achieved over the workers, many of them have changed attitudes, lost interest, and attend meetings only rarely." The Municipal Council of Graissessac also collapsed, and the following year, Parisse was elected Mayor. Municipal socialism had lasted precisely two years in Graissessac. The same sad tale repeated itself in Camplong, followed, after a final stand by the glassworkers, by Le Bousquet. By 1901, in the entire basin, forty members of the miners' union continued to pay dues, and the glassworkers' union had evaporated.[28] Union-busting in Graissessac was now a matter of history.

What it meant for the company was several decades of a marginal, but stable existence. Its dividends went on at the 5 percent level, even though its share of French coal production had dropped from 5 percent in 1870 to less than 1 percent in 1914. But between 1900 and the war, it was famous for something—it had the highest mine accident and injury rate in the nation. And its wages were among the lowest. Such figures grew out of the triumph of 1894. The strike, in destroying the union, allowed the company to become the arbiter of its labor market. In time, the "free" market impelled more and more impoverished Spaniards to the wilds of Graissessac. In the commune of Graissessac, the Spanish population increased from 5 percent in 1911 to 18 percent in 1921 to 40 percent in 1931. In the census of 1926, Spanish-born miners outnumbered French by 198 to 147. The Spaniards lived in restricted neighborhoods, were slow to become citizens, and found little sympathy among the native born.[29] They worked hard, however, and, from the point of view of the company, possessed the ultimate virtue. As the Sub-Prefect of Lodève remarked to the Procureur General after the explosive strikes in 1919–20: "I noted a certain number of Spanish subjects in the tumultuous demonstrations and in teams impeding the freedom of work. Happily, with your powers, we can expel them from the country."[30]

The trend analyzed here was not unique to Graissessac. Décazeville, Carmaux, and especially Grand'Combe experienced the successive shockwaves of the southern French coal crisis: company reorganization, speedup, massive personnel cutbacks, militant strikes in response, and the internationalization of labor recruitment. But nowhere was this pattern so clear and nowhere, certainly, did a strike redound so perfectly to the advantage of the company, though the 1897 stoppage at Grand'Combe came close. Historically, Graissessac—despite its great promise as a coal basin—had suffered from one competitive disadvantage after another, a condition shared by the rest of Languedoc's piedmont industries. Among the major coal basins in France, its situation by the 1890s was the most precarious. Unfortunate as this may have been, for the historian, the troubled evolution of Graissessac allows one to put the larger problem into sharp focus. The clarity of its crisis provides an image, magnified by several powers and

The Padène mine at Graissessac, c. 1900

telescoped in time, of the fate that would befall industry across this entire region and, in the end, coal mining in all of France. It is also most useful in examining the limits of union militance.

Toward a Unidimensional Society

With the stagnation of the coal industry, nature's other bounty, the vine, came to lower Languedoc's rescue. Or so it appeared. The phylloxera, devastating as it seemed, most profoundly affected eastern Languedoc, the Gard, and the Montpelliérais in the Hérault. But by the time the parasite arrived in the Bittérois and the Aude, solutions had been found. Though largely inapplicable in the piedmont, as noted earlier, submersion, chemical treatment, but, above all, grafting to American phylloxera-resistant roots allowed for the rapid reconstitution of the vignoble of the west. Although suffering doubtless occurred, especially in the late 1870s, and early 1880s, the Hérault-Aude region had benefited from the earlier collapse in the east (the Gard never fully recovered) and then was able to meet the plague head-on when it arrived. It moved more slowly as well. Thus, a laborer whose own vines might be wiped out could find work in nearby communes not yet struck *and* get involved in the labor-intensive work of treatment or reconstitution in his own village or those already overrun. Harvey Smith has been able to demonstrate this phenomenon in detail for Cruzy, a village on the Hérault-Aude boundary, and Augé-Laribé made the point more generally long ago.[31] Careful studies have also shown that while the phylloxera may have given rise to some very large agribusinesses, there was not a dramatic expansion of great estates and a crushing of the micro-owner as a consequence of the phylloxera. Statistics, mainly compiled by Rémy Pech, demonstrate a significant decline in the number of *medium* holdings, that is, of the independent labor-hiring vintner, and an expansion of small and very small holdings. This meant that the middling sort, who often could not afford to hire labor needed for reconstitution, sold part of his land, sometimes to large holders who could, or more often to wage-earners/microholders who added on a few rows that they, like the hard-pressed seller, could pretty much care for with family labor. Thus, a degree of polarization occurred in the structure of ownership in this part of Languedoc. But vast masses of landless proletarians were not created.[32]

With the successful reconversion, western lower Languedoc entered a period of real prosperity during the 1890s. Then the problem of oversupply began to make itself felt. The reasons were simple enough: increasing yields coupled with ever-growing areas under cultivation; continuing influx of Algerian wine (originally promoted by the government because of the phylloxera); and market saturation. Languedoc wine, geared to volume, not quality, found little response in the export market and thus was inevitably limited by France's (admittedly large) drinking capacity. By 1900 working-class tables had fully assimilated vin ordinaire as a staple, but income and taste created limits. More important, French population growth was at a virtual standstill. Prices therefore plummeted and the *crise de mévente* more unfolded. The Révolte du Midi of 1905–1907 was the consequence. Although this upheaval would have an effect on government policy and the grand crisis of market glut would be alleviated, Languedoc entered into a permanent state of instability and dependency. The vine was the region's only significant resource and its product suffered from the "chronic maladaptation of supply and demand."[33] How these circumstances affected the political life of the region and the character of its labor movement underline deindustrialization's most ironic consequence: despite immiserization in the industrial areas and the insecurities of existence for those with jobs, the result was not a grand wave of labor militance, a "revolutionary situation." It was instead the growing tendency to cling to themes of regional solidarity, to bridge traditional class antagonisms, and to fall into a politics of seeking support from the existing state with little thought given to its transformation or overthrow.

One of the most troubling problems of regions experiencing significant industrial decline is the obvious weakening of the bargaining power of labor. The responses of working people, as individuals and through their organizations, depend on the seriousness of the crisis and on the options available. In areas where labor's economic and political organizations have created an independent, aggressive, even revolutionary force on behalf of the interests of the working class, the options are clearly more numerous, but the decisions often more excruciating.

One of the key issues to be faced is how to relate to voices or, indeed, entire movements espousing regional solidarity in face of what appears to be a hostile or uncaring national state. By their very nature, regionalist sentiments emphasize bonds that transcend class. On the simplest level, they can take form in a regional boosterism tapping rather shallow local roots, such as the contemporary "Say yes to Michigan" campaign. Even this, of course, creates real complications for a professedly class-conscious labor movement, for it implies a level of cooperation with the capitalist adversary (from support for import restrictions to wage concessions) that many militants abhor. But economic dislocation has often occurred in regions, like Languedoc, with deep histories of antagonism toward the national state, areas culturally and linguistically distinct and regarded by many of their inhabitants as their true, ancestral homeland. The experience of deindustrialization can, in part, be blamed on the dominant central state, thought to favor more powerful interests at the expense of the internal "nations" facing hardship. And this is not always a figment of the inhabitants' imagination, as we have seen in the case of Languedoc. Welsh, Scottish, and Quèbeçois nationalist movements have all blossomed under conditions of industrial decline in part attributable to central state economic policy. This is not to say that deindustrialization is a necessary precondition for modern regional nationalism. (Autonomy movements in Spain, for example, are the strongest in Catalonia or the Basque region, economically progressive areas.) The concern here is with the general problem of regionalism's historic impact on class-conscious labor movements. Obviously, the "regional defense" can be highly militant and trouble the powers that be, but the historical record strongly suggests that no matter how "popular," leftist, and pro-working class such sentiments might have been, they inevitably denatured the class consciousness of the mainstream labor movement, which found it necessary to abandon or at least play down its commitment to class-struggle politics.

Let us examine how this process sorted out in Languedoc. Experienced as a completed cycle, it has much to say to deindustrializing regions today.

The heart of the old industrial region of the Hérault, Lodève, as we have seen, "achieved" a kind of stasis at a lower level of output and existence. Politically, it passed through a period in the 1870s and 1880s of frightened conservatism, relying on the good offices of its most influential resident, Paul Leroy-Beaulieu, to try to extract new contracts (or at least maintain the old) from the government in his role as deputy from its arrondissement. Leroy-Beaulieu, also a famous political economist, had married Michel Chevalier's and Emma Fournier's daughter and became the new baron of Monplaisir after Chevalier's death in 1879. After the new, scaled-down social equilibrium had been reached by 1890, the exclusive concern for economic survival passed. Still, there were constant pressures, and Lodève's deputy had a critical role to play in fighting for contracts against other equally needy towns such as Châteauroux and Romorantin. Leroy-Beaulieu, now a member of the Collège de France, seemed increasingly unwilling to carry out the routine cajoling and arm-twisting involved. Moreover, political opponents documented his father-in-law's "betrayal" of Lodève back in 1865. Challenged first by Paul Vigné d'Octon, a prominent radical physician and novelist, in the cantonal election early in 1890, he was barely returned to his post in the departmental Council. Then in the national election later in the year, he was defeated by Ménard-Dorian, a member of Lodève's old elite in the Teisserenc circle whose nebulous politics made little difference to voters now well-versed in the sins of Michel Chevalier. After three tense years in which two more small companies fell by the wayside, Vigné d'Octon mounted a strong campaign for the seat Ménard abandoned, and defeated Leroy-Beaulieu and the Opportunist mayor of Lodève, Fulcran Hugo-unenq. Vigné billed himself alternatively as a Radical-socialist and independent socialist; he had the support of Jean Jaurès and ties to what was left of a labor movement in the arrondissement. But, through his wife, he was also friendly with the area's old elites, especially the long-time adversaries of Chevalier, the Teisserencs.[34]

To be sure, the election of Vigné d'Octon marked a new shift to the left in the old woolens district's politics, but it was a left that coupled nostalgia for the démoc-soc era of mid-century with a strong focus on defending the beleaguered region. Vigné d'Octon represented it perfectly. Vigné was only thirty-four years old when he entered the Chamber. Born in Lodève, his first political ideas were forged in his father's bakery on the rue Blaquerie, which catered to a worker and petty bourgeois clientele who lived along the Soulandres. The Epi d'Or was a "foyer of republicanism" in the late 1860s. The elder Vigné had been born in Octon and served as a journeyman baker during the 1848 era in several wool towns, including Clermont, where he encountered the artisan poet, Peyrottes, and his circle of humanist socialists. The woman he married, Appollonie Azaïs, hailed from Avène and was a deeply believing Catholic, a fact in this region that did not preclude a left political perspective. Paul's first teacher was a "former Christian brother who became a Republican" and his further education mixed classical, Revolutionary, and Christian themes. For a brief while, after the tragic death of his father in late 1871, he enrolled in a seminary, but soon gave up theology for medical studies. Vigné carried out his military service as a shipboard doctor and quickly became fascinated by the cultures of the colonial peoples he encountered in his travels. He developed expertise in tropical diseases and a passionate opposition to French imperial control, which he likened to the Bonapartist despotism that his father taught him to hate. Vigné also had a tragic love affair with a Guadaloupean woman; it ended with her accidental death and would be the subject of his first novel.

Upon his return to France in 1889, after a tour of duty in a Senegalese hospital, Vigné married a young widow whose parents had previously forbidden their relationship: she was the daughter of the Chatelain of Octon. But now, given his growing literary fame and professional standing, family opposition dissolved. By virtue of this marriage, he became Vigné d'Octon and immediately entered the high echelons of regional society. He thus found himself in a perfect position, financially and socially, to enter politics. Undoubtedly, his radical opinions on class and race raised the eyebrows of the elites, but his central message united support up and down the social ladder: to defend the economic interests of Lodève with every ounce of his energy. And this he did. Unlike Leroy-Beaulieu, Vigné had an intimate knowledge of the military and was not afraid to dirty his hands. As his biographer put it: "he threatened the Minister of War with an *interpellation à scandale* in which the intrigues of several well-known persons and the connivance of certain bureaux would be revealed. The newspapers, also alerted, began to gossip."[35] In an age when scandal had almost become the life-blood of the nation, it was not long before an internal inquiry was undertaken, and Lodève found itself much more secure in its contractual relations with the government.

Vigné went on to a long and stormy career, situating himself between the Radical-socialists and the SFIO. Besides a continuing ardent defense of his city's industry and consistent support for the vine, he championed reform in France's colonial regime. A believer in France's civilizing mission, however, he never preached decolonization per se, but sought humane policies of education and health and looked forward to the gradual achievement of autonomy for Francophone colonial peoples. His novels and stories reflected his fascination with the unique values and mores of his region, but also a vision of harmony within the broader human family that could be created through (essentially Christian) love. In many respects he provided a kind of left-wing complement to the paternalist management ideology that had conquered in deindustrialized Lodève. Desperation and departure had undermined any real possibility of a militant response by workers. Lodève, along with her ancient sister cities in the wool trade, has lurched on, under a survivalist mentality, in moribund mediocrity until this day.

But what about the new world of the vineyards of the coastal plains and of its key cities, places like Béziers and Narbonne? If the textile areas rapidly lost their militance, how would the class-struggle concepts of the workers' movement sit with its burgeoning proletariat? The answer depends on shifting historical circumstances and can be gauged, above all, by looking at the evolution of electoral politics and the content of socialist appeals in the vineyard area.[36]

The history of socialism in lower Languedoc is complex. During the 1870s and 1880s the left tradition of the 1848 era was largely transmuted into success for Radical Party politics of the Clemenceau stripe. Its most consistent line was lay education and anticlericalism. But dissatisfaction with the Radicals' tepid support for measures of social reform began to pave the way for a revived interest in socialism. Content of socialist ideology varied widely, ranging from the vague romantic humanism of a Vigné d'Octon to the orthodox Marxism of Ernest Ferroul of Narbonne. Also a physician, Ferroul, after trying a variety of alliances with left Radicals in the late 1880s, was converted to Marxism by Jules Guesde and just as explicitly affirmed the doctrine of the class struggle and working class revolution before and after his election to the Chamber in 1890. As he put it rather bluntly in 1894:

> No longer do we have royalists, bonapartists, opportunists, or radicals; there are only two parties: those who possess and those who do not possess. The first lives and grows rich at the expense of the other. The workers are the great majority and can be the masters. One calls us *les partageux* [the dividers of wealth]. This is not so; we want it all.

He went on to condemn faith in parliamentary reform and called for a "pitiless struggle" against the bourgeois government.[37]

Between these extremes, southern socialism exhibited a bewildering variety of tendencies, but passed through phases not atypical of France as a whole.[38] During the later 1890s when the Dreyfus affair put the very existence of the Republic in question, it coalesced around a reformist parliamentary socialism. In Languedoc, the prosperity of postphylloxera viticulture added to the moderation, although the militance of syndicalist port workers, building tradesmen, and miners kept the revolutionary perspective alive. But the great crisis of overproduction and low prices in wine that unfolded after 1900 fueled a revival of the socialist left, and the perspective of a Ferroul had renewed meaning. As usual, he cut to the heart of the matter. Speaking to microholders and agricultural proletarians, he underlined the contradictions of capitalism. For example, in 1906, he said: "The better the harvest, the fuller our caves, the more miserable is the worker. Nothing more clearly demonstrates the vices of our social organization. . . . Shall we wait for the collective appropriation [of the means of production] to fall from heaven?" He then called for a general strike "to bring the exploiters to their knees." In general, socialists supported agricultural worker unionism and their numerous strikes during 1903 and 1904. They called for the implementation of "socialist wine cooperatives," which would allow the small proprietors to compete, but also the inclusion of the landless in the management and the benefits of production.[39]

Thus, as the crisis in viticulture grew, socialist propaganda focused, rather stridently, on the class struggle. But already in 1906, contradictory tendencies were in evidence. For example, when Socialist Marcel Cachin ran against a key Radical, Louis Lafferre, for parliament, he certainly attacked the smoke screen of anticlericalism because it obscured "the fundamental realities of class relations" and stressed collectivism, but he also laid out a detailed immediate program for dealing with the wine crisis, which included controls over fraudulent production, the legalization of industrial alcohol distillation, the reduction of rail freight-rates, the control of Algerian and Tunisian production, and increased tariffs on certain foreign wines. All of this of course would benefit workers only if the owners passed on the savings. This campaign may be regarded as the first elaboration of the "*défense viticole*" theme that would soon swamp any reference to class-interest socialism.[40] That a Marxist of such impeccable credentials as Cachin lent his name to it underlines the pressures that were beginning to mount in a region so totally dependent on a single cash crop and one that had lost its industrial base.

Then came the massive explosion in 1907 in which hundreds of thousands of growers and workers took to the streets to protest the total collapse of wine prices. From their inception in April, meetings and confrontations with the forces of order had demonstrated a class harmony that many socialists found disturbing. For two years, however, owners had been promoting, with considerable success, "mixed unions" that in other circles would be called "yellow" or "company" unions. But here, because of the immense numbers of wage earners who also owned or rented some vines, because of the intimate and cooperative nature of the work that brought all but the largest owners into the fields with their workers, and because of the constant social intercourse of village life (again only the elite and absentees remained aloof from it), such efforts to focus on the crisis in general and overcome "passing" grievances between *patron* and *ouvrier* did not have quite the same odor. The socialist press warned the workers not to confuse their interests with those of the "possessing classes," but to no avail. As the demonstrations multiplied, corporatist themes were sounded by some leaders, royalist politicians jumped on the bandwagon, and a catharsis (the word had a literal meaning here!) of general southern resentment against the state exploded. It became the "revolt of the Midi," of the region against the nation.[41] Its armed suppression, in which Radical boss Clemenceau had demonstrators gunned down by occupying troops, only enhanced the power of the idea.

In a spectacular about-face, Ferroul emerged as the most ardent proponent of the regionalist focus and, in fact, became the key voice for the "claims of Oc." It was he who issued the call for a great organization that would bring together grower-dominated *Comités de défense viticole*, an appeal made in the socialist newspaper of the Aude and capped off with a free-form verse:

> Divided, we see what our lot has been. United, we can bring about our triumph. Sons of the soil of the Midi, none of you has the right to remain deaf to the call of our motherland.

On 22 September 1907, the Confédération Générale des Vignerons (CGV) was founded and Ferroul became its first president. On the podium with him were the major owners of lower Languedoc, although the statutes of the organization stressed its cross-class character. And indeed, thousands of microproprietors and workers did join it, no doubt encouraged by the socialist Ferroul's presence.[42]

On the other hand, it is clear that Ferroul himself was responding to a social and cultural reality. The defense of the vine was perceived by a majority of the common people of lower Languedoc as *the* critical need, and the concept of an Occitan "revendication" against France and the French struck chords deep in their collective memory. This became increasingly clear in the development of socialist electoral politics before the war. Most socialist leaders in lower Languedoc joined Jean Jaurès in condemning

Ferroulisme, as his collaborationist politics came to be called, but as one moved toward the elections of 1910, it became clear that the most fruitful appeal to the electorate, rooted in chauvinistic sentiments that vilified Paris and the north, was "the defense of the interests of the Midi." Although the wine crisis began to pass, the mévente had demonstrated the extreme fragility of the region's economy, and the repression of 1907 had shown how unfeeling and how powerful the central state could be.

Clemenceau and his Radical majority stood as the symbol of that state— of French power. The inheritors of centralizing democracy, of Jacobinism, they were the punishers of the south, and not only of its economy. Lay education, while welcomed by a majority who distrusted the Catholic church, was also a *French* education that mocked what the schoolmaster called the "pâtois" spoken daily by the mass of the people and taught that the Albigensian Crusade, which led to the thirteenth-century conquest of Languedoc by the Kings of France, was a glorious event and that the anti-Paris revolts thereafter, from the Protestant Croquants and Camisards to the popular royalism of the nineteenth century, were evil manifestations of *lèse-nation*. Many Languedocians viewed Radical deputies as lackeys of northern interests, living the high life in Paris, and only "parachuting" down to their home base around election time. Several, such as Louis Lafferre and Justin Augé in the Hérault, were fully compromised because of their support for Clemenceau in 1907. Others were condemned for their silence. It was, of course, a golden opportunity for socialism—at least for socialism as a parliamentary party.

Let us now explore how it drifted away from class-struggle politics toward electoral regionalism. *Le Devoir socialiste*, the official organ of the Socialist Federation of the Hérault founded early in 1909, allows one to follow the trend. The weekly newspaper devoted most of its copy to two subjects: the wine industry and parliamentary politics, particularly as it related to "the interests of the Midi." Increasingly, the latter phrase was simply used as if it were synonymous with *la défense viticole*. As Joseph Railhac, an Independent Socialist from Lodève, put it: "As for our meridional interests, the duty of your representative will be to assure the regularity of the wine market," as if there were no other meridional interest.[43]

Recognizing that the approaching national election of 1910 offered unprecedented possibilities, the socialist leadership in the Hérault published primers on campaign tactics. Particularly important was the approach made to peasants. Many militants, said a December 1909 editorial, "are frightened at the thought of propagandizing in rural areas" because their experience was largely with urban, propertyless proletarians. But it is not difficult if one understands the peasant's mentality: "limited to the horizons of his own area" and "highly individualistic," he does not often understand how capitalism affects him. But do not throw theory at him. Instead, show him concretely how the middlemen gobble up his profits and how the capitalist state supports them with laws harmful to his interests. Finally, avoid violent language. "What good does it do to frighten his peaceful and apprehensive character with brutal images?" What they were advising, of course, was to avoid the language of social conflict, and, indeed, they did not mention class in the entire article. The complexities of rural social structure, especially in the wine country, made such discussion difficult indeed.[44]

The socialist paper continued to stress the need for socialist cooperatives, the practical road to a "collectivist future." It also maintained that the SFIO was still the party of "social revolution." But it no longer called for a positive revolutionary movement, emphasizing instead "revolutionary" preparation to defend the republic if threatened. In short, it was reassuring its potential peasant clientele that no sudden upheaval was in the offing, at least, if not fomented by the reactionary right. Still, a quiet "economic revolution" was "underway," and the productive classes were beginning to understand the march of history: this was "what the privileged classes fear the most."[45]

The point was clear: electoral politics would light the way to a gradual "social revolution." The campaign of 1910, however, produced SFIO candidacies that were more moderate even than the pronouncements of the socialist press. Social revolution was hardly mentioned. Virtually the entire focus was on the sins of the Radicals occupying the current seats. (Two of them, Paul Pélisse of Lodève and Benjamin Razimbaud of St. Pons, both of whom had supported the revolt of 1907 in any case, declared themselves "Independent Radicals" and fast friends of the vignerons.) Three socialists in the Hérault won Clemencist Radical seats: Camille Reboul in working-class Montpellier and nearby wine and fishing villages; Céléstin Molle in the district including Sète and many wine villages stretching north from it; and Edouard Barthe in the poorer Béziers second district that encompassed major wine centers, such as the cantons of Pézenas, Montagnac, and Murveil, but also industrial Bédarieux and the mines of Graissessac. In every electoral district in the Hérault, the Clemencists were thrown out, with Bézier's Mayor Henri Pech, an Independent Radical, demolishing Lafferre in Béziers I, and Pierre Leroy-Beaulieu, a conservative, but an ardent defender of the vine despite the laissez-faire predilections bequeathed to him by his father, Paul, winning in Montpellier I. Elsewhere in lower Languedoc the old Radicals fared badly, hanging on to only one seat each in the Gard and Aude, while socialists gained two seats. Overall, the SFIO saw its total deputation to the Chamber jump twenty-three seats to seventy-seven lower Languedoc accounted for five of them.[46]

The candidacy, indeed the political personality, of Edouard Barthe exemplified perfectly the trend in southern socialism toward a species of regional boosterism. Barthe was only twenty-eight in 1910. Born in Montblanc, a village in his district, of conservative parents, he went to Montpellier to secondary school and the University at the turn of the century. He took an active interest in politics, was radicalized as a young Dreyfusard, and concerned himself with worker education projects, a subject to which we shall return. He ran in the cantonal elections in 1904 as an antirevolutionary "Independent" socialist and again for deputy in 1906, doing rather well in both. We cannot be certain, but it is likely that he was then a latter-day Proudhonian. He had unquestionably taken courses with Célestin Bouglé, until 1901 a professor at the University and later Proudhon's foremost historian.[47]

Barthe, who became a pharmacist in Sète, finally joined the SFIO in 1908, but retained his Independent connections. His choice as candidate was frankly based on this, and throughout his campaign he sought, and generally gained, the support of these more moderate socialists. He won a crushing victory, outdistancing Augé 9,550 to 8,150. The character of his campaign would set the tone for successful regional socialist politics in the future.

He focused heavily on Augé and his record, underlining his ties to Clemenceau and his votes on bills that compromised the "honest" wine growers. He also stressed Augé's membership in the "Camarilla" of Freemasons, who comprised the Radical party leadership in the south and throughout France. The "petite chapelle," as the Masonry with its secular but mystic rites of reason was called, supposedly ran French political life through its cliques of loyal members. The only thing unusual about the tactic was that it was traditionally the domain of the antirepublican right and implied a certain sympathy for the Catholic cause in France. The socialists had legitimately criticized the Radicals for their hyper-anticlericalism and the Charter of the SFIO did not endorse the radicals' goal of making church schools illegal in France. But in 1910, Barthe and other socialists made new political hay on the issue of the Freemasonry and unquestionably won Catholic, even royalist, votes as a result. The *Petit Méridional*, the region's Radical daily, accused him and others of making unabashed appeals to the right and blamed the socialist gains largely on conservative votes.[48]

Barthe campaigned in every nook and cranny of his district, always asking the same question: "When was the last time you saw M. Augé? At the last election, right?" And when Augé scheduled campaign stops, Barthe would scurry there to confront him. He had eyes and ears everywhere, keeping him abreast of his opponent's doings. Moreover, Barthe knew his district thoroughly, while Augé's long years in Paris left him ignorant of many nuances of local politics. A classic situation arose at Murveil, a large wine village that had given the Socialist candidate exactly fourteen votes in the last election and split the rest between Augé and a conservative. Barthe got wind of a campaign appearance by Augé at Murveil scheduled for 5 P.M. while on the way back from a noon-time stop at a mountain commune and arrived in Murveil at four. After an "apéritif d'honneur" with the local Independent Socialists, who agreed to fly the SFIO flag in front of their little office on the town square, Barthe headed for the hall where Augé was to speak. The latter's people reluctantly agreed to a "conférence contradictoire," wherein each would speak and then react to the audience.

The debates that followed were not uplifting. Augé called Barthe a "jackal" and alluded to his "purchase" of his candidacy with a generous contribution to SFIO coffers. He also claimed that he, Augé, had really opposed Clemenceau, calling his leader a "revolutionary of yesterday." After being stopped by the audience with laughs and hisses, Augé ceded the lecturn in the steamy room to Barthe, who showed what the new socialist politician of the Midi was all about.

First, brandishing a copy of the *Journal officiel*, he enumerated Augé's votes during the crisis in favor of Clemenceau: "Date by date, vote by vote, he demonstrated the acquiescence of the loyal ministerial deputy even while the murder of the Midi unfolded," wrote a sympathetic journalist covering the Murveil confrontation. Barthe proceeded to dredge up a minor scandal about Augé's alleged failure to pay full taxes on some nearby property and his closeness to the judge deciding the case. Radicals in the audience now hooted, but Barthe persisted and "revealed" Augé's part in the cover-up of the investigation concerning the distribution of property confiscated from the disbanded religious orders. He quickly followed with the accusation that his adversary illegally sold *piquette*, cheap, vinegary wine that could not even be marketed as vin ordinaire. So much for his respect for the laws protecting the wine industry!

This feast of vituperation moved into high gear when Barthe accused Augé and departmental Radical officials of forcing the removal of a loyal socialist deputy mayor in Murveil and replacing him with a turncoat. The latter, a dignitary on the platform named Hugounenc, screamed that this was not so and Barthe then turned on him: "You are nothing but a scab! Elected a councillor of the arrondissement on the socialist ticket, you betrayed your flag and your party. This," Barthe now fingered the deputy mayor's sash, "is the price of treason!" The meeting then exploded, and Barthe was carried into the night by his exultant fans singing the *Internationale*. After a quick *grenache* at the SFIO café, he headed for Causse-et-Véran for another meeting. Such political vaudeville performances became Barthe's stock-in-trade. Socialism, with its austere educational campaigns, would never be the same.[49] The final vote at Murveil was Barthe 328, Augé 257.

It should not come as a surprise that Barthe would be accused by the Radical press of avoiding the discussion of socialist doctrine because he was a *tête vide* "incapable of explaining his socialist ideas because he has none.[50] But he was certainly capable of trumpeting the cause of the wine growers. He chided Augé for avoiding connections with the Confédération Générale des Vignerons. The Radical deputy was afraid to do so because he did not want to seem too close to the large growers, but Barthe, the socialist, proudly displayed his allegiance at every opportunity. His victory speech summed up what would become his life's work and the essential orientation of southern socialism thereafter: "I shall struggle with all my power to make our bourgeois Republic into a democratic Republic that will be just and equitable, tolerant and good." The language was important: he did not speak of "revolution" at all. More crucially, he said, "I shall never forget that the lot of the humble folk of our area is intimately tied to the prosperity of viticulture: while I give my strongest support to socialist organization, everyone can be assured that I will put a large part of my activity into the economic revival of the Midi."[51]

Barthe thus developed a thesis that would remain central to the socialist message. There were certainly doubts raised by party members—even in the flush of victory, the *Devoir socialiste* quoted Marx and reminded its readers (and Barthe, Reboul, and Molle) "to beware of personalities and remember that Parliament is only a vehicle"—but the tide of expediency overwhelmed them. Compère-Morel, a socialist deputy from Nîmes and a party theoretician, even argued that in France the agrarian population, that is, "the workers of the land and the small holders above all: the small owners, lease holders, and sharecroppers," were "the most solid, strong, and faithful element in the socialist army."[52] Most important, Barthe was able to defend his relationship with the owner-dominated CGV with relative ease. He argued for conciliation between boss and worker wherever possible and found ready support from departmental socialist leadership. This story, headlined "Barthe and the Working Class," appeared in the Hérault socialist paper in September 1911: the agricultural workers' union of Florensac thought that they had won the employers' agreement to form a committee to establish a new wage schedule, but the proprietors, tipped off that the workers were unprepared to strike, backed away from the discussions. Local socialists contacted Deputy Barthe, who "did not hesitate to leave his young, pregnant wife to go where duty called." After talking with union leaders, he went to the mayor and got the principal proprietors to assemble. He discovered that many were still willing to negotiate. He then called a mass meeting of 2,000 Florensacois. Addressing the owners, he "sought to reawaken their humanitarian sentiments, which often sleep but nevertheless exist in the hearts of all men; to the workers he spoke as a friend, warning them that the strike is a two-edged blade that should be used only when all hope of reconciliation has disappeared. Wildly applauded by the entire crowd, Barthe concluded . . . with a final appeal to reason and to the unity of all the inhabitants of Florensac."[53]

Barthe and his allies in the Chamber did their work well. The years after their election saw notable gains for the wine industry in the south; Barthe himself emerged as the major "wine deputy" in France, becoming secretary of both the Customs Committee and the Alcoholic Beverages Committee in the Chamber and the Reporter for most of the key legislation affecting the Midi, including the creation of a bureau for the suppression of fraud with fifty regional inspectors, a law in 1912 controlling sugaring and artificial fermentation, and statutes giving greater legal protection to the agricultural workers' unions. Barthe delivered. He summed up his four years of work when he ran for reelection in 1914 as follows: "I have fought obstinately to defend viticulture because I know your needs; I am a son of the land who loves his native soil."[54]

This collaborative perspective did not sit well with all militants. The unions were divided, but they generally opposed Barthe's and Ferroul's embrace of the CGV. In February of 1913, Paul Ader, president of the regional agricultural workers' union, attacked them in *La Bataille syndi-caliste*. Reboul, who was not a member of the CGV, responded in *Le Devoir socialiste*. His feeling was that the Socialists made a mistake by their direct association with the CGV and hoped that workers would pull away from it. Nevertheless, it should not be thought of as an organization of the enemy. He had spoken before a meeting of the CGV, and Ader had chastised him for it. In one sentence he then summed up the dilemma of a region chained precariously to a single product for survival. "I went there, although a socialist and therefore a partisan of the class struggle, because I realized that above all else, there is the defense of the common nutrient [the vine] of both antagonistic classes." At the banquet that followed, Reboul claimed that he "returned to his proper character and situated himself on the terrain of the class struggle, making known to all these assembled proprietors the grievances and recriminations of all their workers." Reboul went on to say that the CGV should serve as a good example to workers in their own organization, somehow missing the point that if he were really serious about the class struggle, he would do whatever possible to undermine the power of the proprietors' association.[55]

But such an option no longer seemed possible. The powerful logic of economic reality was turning Languedoc socialism into the voice of the region's last, best hope, the vine. Its position was increasingly legitimated by the revival of an *Occitan* cultural militance that socialists only hesitatingly embraced, but nevertheless benefited from. In April 1913, the first poem in the language of Oc appeared in *Le Devoir socialiste*. Entitled "*A Padou*," it told of a poor farmer (whether a landowner or a leaseholder was not mentioned) who loved his land but faced losing it and was receiving no help from the government. It was not translated. The editors obviously assumed that most of their readers could understand it.[56] The impact of Occitan nationalism on Languedoc socialism is difficult to gauge. The problem is that in this era, *Occitanisme* was above all a doctrine of the right, although various countercurrents existed. Even so, in light of socialism's electoral emphasis and its desire to throttle Radicalism at any cost, even a nod toward reactionary Occitanisme might produce right-wing protest votes for socialism.

The history of the Occitan revival has been best told by Robert Lafont and his disciples in the Institute for Occitan Studies, although they have overlooked important links with the early twentieth-century socialist movement.[57] At the deepest level, its popular appeal is straightforward: Occitan, in its various dialects stretching from the Alps to the Pyrenees, was the language of the people. Elites, especially the eighteenth- and nineteenth-century bourgeoisie, disdained it as they sought to identify with the national culture, be it Jacobin, Bonapartist, or Orleanist. Legitimists, largely of aristocratic stock or with pretensions to such, took a paternalistic interest in the ancient culture. Occitan history was a living source of protest for anyone dissatisfied with the regime in power. Above all, the glory of the troubadours of the twelfth century and the brutal suppression of their culture under the excuse of extirpating the Cathar heresy in the thirteenth century provided grist for the mill of regional resistance. The issue was complicated for the Catholic right, however, because the Inquisition had been the instrument of anti-Cathar repression, and early modern secessionist movements had been animated by Protestants.[58]

The formal Occitan cultural revival led by Frédéric Mistral after 1854 first took a strong "albigist" and federalist-republican perspective, but turned to the right after the Commune. The revivers of Oc, called *félibres*, thus generally identified with aristocratic values and thought in terms of a feudal decentralization of France. There was, however, a "félibrige rouge" centered in Montpellier (Mistral lived in Avignon) that emphasized the individualism of the Cathar and Protestant tradition, but, above all, integrated the ideals of decentralization, communal autonomy, and reciprocal justice so dear to Pierre-Joseph Proudhon into their world view. Louis-Xavier de Ricard founded an Occitan-language almanach called *La Lauseto* (The Swallow) that fought both Mistral's politics and his Provençal grammar and lexicography. Although it is difficult to determine the impact of this school, it is clear that many leftist intellectuals of the 1890s and after drew sustenance from it.[59] But running beneath the conflicts of the félibrige were the day-to-day humiliations of "pâtois"-speaking children in schools where Parisian French was the only language spoken or the linguistic confrontations with northern-trained managers in many commercial and industrial enterprises.[60] A popular Occitanisme, largely without ideological content, certainly existed.

In the first decade of the twentieth century, as the economic difficulties of the region became more glaring and the impatience with Jacobin-Radicalism grew, institutions promoting regional culture and folklore also developed. Local historical societies flourished. At Béziers, Lodève, Pézenas, Sète, Lunel, and Montpellier, active attempts to educate the people in the ways of Oc were made. For the most part, these organizations were the work of conservatives and Catholics who represented the Mistral tradition. Charles Maurras, the founder of the *Action Française*, emerged from this movement and established a strong base in Languedoc for his protofascist organization. He actively sought working-class support on the basis of regional chauvinism arguing, for example, that "the Republic crushes all our organs of economic and social defense, delivers the region to the greed of the [wealthy] and the pillage of the Jews, Freemasons, and foreigners (*métèques*), crushes the rights of [regional] minorities under the force of the majority, and is the enemy of the true *Patrie* and destroys its prosperity. Long live the King, Protector of Languedoc."[61]

While such propaganda no doubt had some effect, a more important thread of Occitan nationalism can be seen in the workers' education movement that sprang up in the Hérault from the late 1890s, with its principal seats in Montpellier and Béziers. Each sent emissaries throughout their areas.

The municipal library in Montpellier has retained several printed documents pertaining to the *Société d'enseignement populaire* there, allowing us to glimpse the organization and ideology of such an association. It was founded in 1898 with the specific mission of fighting for the "social republic" in face of the reactionary mood created by the Dreyfus Affair. The key figures were all professors at the University of Montpellier or *lycées* in the city, led initially by the eminent Jewish physicist, Benjamin Milhaud, and a protegé of Durkheim, the socialist philosopher Céléstin Bouglé. Through an agreement with the Bourse de Travail of Montpellier, they would hold courses once or twice per week in the syndicalists' meeting hall, appropriately located on the boulevard Louis Blanc.[62]

Although neither Bouglé nor Milhaud were versed in Occitan ideology, both were admirers of Proudhon's views on political federalism and artisanal independence (though not his anti-Semitism). In his inaugural address to prospective sponsors, Bouglé delivered a respectful critique of Marxist "economic determinism," arguing instead for the importance of knowledge and will as forces of change for the working class.[63] Other leaders, however, espoused strong regionalist sentiments. Louis Planchon, who became the *de facto* president of the organization after Bouglé was called to the Sorbonne in 1901, was a biologist specializing in the flora of the region. He also took a loving interest in the "worker-poets" who published in Occitan during the mid-nineteenth century, symbols, as they were, of popular cultural resistance. In an article on one of them, Bigot of Nîmes (of whom a statue was erected in 1903), Planchon discussed the type of worker revealed in his poetry—the "Rachelan" of Nîmes or the "Travaydou" of Montpellier: "A courageous man in the full meaning of the term, honest, obliging, and good, sympathetic toward the unfortunate, gaining his livelihood but just barely, and, despite setbacks, full of dignity and simplicity; hardworking and sober, he nevertheless values good wine. One should not demand too much of him intellectually, however, for he prefers the gay and carefree life." While Planchon admired the warmth of this personality, he emphasized that like Bigot himself, workers can make something of themselves through intellectual development. This is the key to their betterment as a class, a sentiment that Proudhon would have endorsed.[64]

Another key figure in the Society was the geographer Ernest Roussel, son of a literary critic who had devoted his life to the study of Occitan literature.[65] Roussel studied Languedoc urban geography and economic life in ancient and medieval times, but also took as his special task the critique of Maurras and right-wing Occitanism, finally publishing a point-by-point refutation of Maurras's historical analysis in the 1930s. It was Roussel who brought the "people's félibre" of Montpellier, François Dezeuze, into the coursework of the society, devoting whole evenings to his yarn-spinning, but also capping off other classes with his poems and songs.[66]

Almost from the very beginning, the courses included lectures on regional subjects, but after Planchon and Roussel took over full direction of the society's affairs in 1907, they occupied a large place in the curriculum. We only have detailed listings for 1913–14 and 1920–21, but in both years, despite the press of world events, almost half of the classes dealt with an aspect of regional life, and half of those focused on Occitan history and culture. The latter, which invariably attracted "overflow crowds," included geographical lectures on the peopling of Languedoc, presentations on the Occitan language, performances by Dezeuze and others, and discussions of great Languedoc artists and of the old crafts of the rural south. The lecturers from Montpellier also gave courses in the towns and villages of the department.[67]

Overall, while it is impossible to analyze "influence," it is clear that a popular Occitanism with an enthusiastic working-class audience existed. It was consciously leftist, although explicitly antirevolutionary. Proudhon's federalism and his glorification of the independent and intelligent artisanal worker and peasant combined with the song and story of Occitan tradition to create a quite palatable ideological mix. Certainly it was compatible with the "new socialism" of an Edouard Barthe. Indeed, it is clear that Barthe had known these educators and was exposed to this ideology during his days in Montpellier.

The class struggle and the proletarian revolution had no place in such an outlook. The mentality of Occitanisme in its left-wing manifestation stressed moral uplift and social mobility. The highest goods were the spirit of Oc and oneness with the *pays natal*. The regionalist socialism of a Barthe fit perfectly with such views.

Socialism in Languedoc was not therefore totally devoid of class consciousness, and after the first World War, it shared in the radicalization of the French labor movement as a whole. But officials there were convinced that the militance was largely limited to trade-union goals and did not, like many of their colleagues elsewhere, fear political upheaval.[68] And they were right. In the end, a majority of Languedoc representatives voted against joining the Third International, thus running against the national trend. If they discussed the revolution, it was in these terms: "The Revolution," wrote Jean Félix, the head of the Federation of the Hérault, "is the substitution of economic harmony for disorder and waste and is not of necessity accompanied by violence." Barthe and other socialist "députés de vin" continued to get elected. And if they spoke for the workers, it was not to promote the class struggle, but to *protect* them. In 1919, sounding like a xenophobic voice from the 1840s, Barthe condemned the owners—yes, indeed—for hiring Spaniards while there was a "general malaise among native Frenchmen of our region." Because of this "lack of solidarity" on the owners' part, there are "many unemployed fathers of families in our villages." He proposed to restrict immigration.[69] This pathetic admission of defeat was not lost on some local socialists. In response to a Barthian "synthesis of the meridional defense" printed in the *Devoir socialiste* in May 1920, G. Bertrand wrote:

> And when our elected socialists offer reforms to the peasants without. . . avowing to them that they ought to count only upon the coming seizure of power by the proletariat, I protest that [these deputies] are nothing but ostriches blind to the meaning of socialism.[70]

In 1921, Bertand, himself an elected official as a member of the departmental General Council, reluctantly joined the group of socialists who organized the Communist Party of the Hérault.

Overall, the lesson of the Languedoc experience with deindustrialization and economic readjustment in a highly specialized and often precarious form of production is straightforward. Vigné d'Octon, Ferroul, and Barthe represented the dominant mode of thinking among a restructured working class, whose members made the perfectly rational choice of opting to defend what had been salvaged from the economic whirlwinds that overwhelmed their region. That generation saw silk and woolens disappear, the vine beset by the phylloxera, vineyards reconstituted at great cost, and, finally, overproduction (in addition to Algerian competition) drive prices hopelessly low. In the meantime, the coal industry, especially in the Gard and Hérault, went into a nosedive. Working out a common defense with the great and powerful and pressing the state to provide protection and guarantees made more sense—or so it seemed to a clear majority of them—than raising the banner of revolution. As a result, the Languedoc wine industry was saved. The great producers and especially the shippers benefited the most. But many villages formed cooperatives, which allowed for the profitable marketing of wine by many medium and small producers. Still, here too, the larger growers benefited disproportionately, and the landless and the semilandless were left out in the cold. "Socialist cooperatives" were forgotten about. The social structure, the distribution of wealth, social mobility, educational opportunity—all this changed remarkably little under the reign of the "wine deputies," whether they were radicals, socialists, or communists. Indeed, Languedoc slipped into a kind of comatose social state that only very recent developments have begun to alter. The society paid an enormous price, but the logic of the historical process of selective regional deindustrialization makes alternative scenarios seem utopian.

It would be absurd to argue that these Languedoc workers suffered from a case of "false consciousness." Indeed, the very character of the forces of production had produced the responses they made. Barthe and Ferroul were not pied-piper traitors to the revolution, but leaders responding to quite rational decisions being made by tens of thousands of workers who felt that they had no other choice than to defend their turf first, a defense helped along by long-standing cultural traditions of Oc, but by no means created by them. The economic realities of surviving in a region stricken by deindustrialization made a politics and labor relations of class collaboration seemingly inevitable.

It is important, finally, to underline the distinctiveness of Languedoc's socialist politics at the time. As Tony Judt has argued convincingly, the SFIO in the Var and in much of the rest of France remained largely true to its ideological mainstays of class struggle and revolution even when addressing the peasantry. His analysis provides a welcome alternative to the Claude Willard tradition and the general European explanation for the "failure of the revolution" after the first World War that simply lays the blame at the

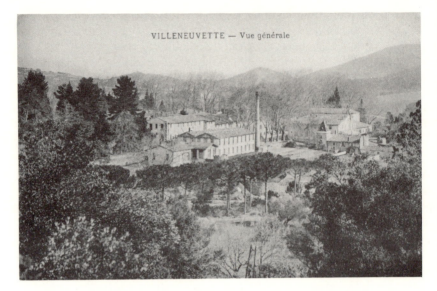

VILLENEUVETTE — Vue générale

Returning to nature: The last days of Villeneuvette

doorstep of socialist electoralism and bureaucracy. In the Var and other areas where socialism attracted a strong rural following, the ideology's condemnation of capitalism struck responsive chords among small holders coping with the vicissitudes of increasingly specialized production for volatile markets. Unlike Languedoc, however, their destiny was not necessarily tied to the fortunes of large growers, nor was the regional economy so excessively dependent on one crop. Thus, in 1920 Languedoc was almost unique in its experience of deindustrialization and subsequent agricultural over-specialization. But in time, area after area where socialism had sunk strong rural roots—Judt argues that peasant support was the secret to the SFIO's success—faced similar circumstances, pushing the farmers toward an increasing conservatism and with them, socialist politics. As Judt puts it, by the 1960s,

> [t]he French Socialists were thus the victims of their own origins. Committed to and dependent upon an electorate that was both shrinking and conservative, but which identified paradoxically with the very revolutionary character of socialism, in its negative incarnation, they came truly to follow a practice that had lost touch with its theoretical base. They could neither revise the first nor abandon the second; as a result the very features of French society which had ensured the rise of Marxist socialism in France also served to orchestrate its decline.[71]

The larger dynamic at work, however, is the unevenness of capitalist development and the ability of capital to play regional and sectoral hop-scotch with a mobility far exceeding labor's. For in whatever economic sector or geographical region one may identify, the long-term pattern has been progress followed by decline. The progressive phase is accompanied by rising labor militance and the establishment of some sort of class-conscious politics and/or trade unionism; the declining phase then sees that same movement pushed to a defensive, hat-in-hand conservatism, while the vital elements of capital migrate elsewhere. Joseph Schumpeter long ago labelled this overall capitalist dynamic "creative destruction." He was not (fundamentally) concerned about its impact on labor. This, of course, is what this book has been about.

Conclusion

This study has sought to capture the dynamics of economic growth and decline in what was arguably the first region to experience full-scale deindustrialization under modern capitalism. It suggests a number of hypotheses about the process generally, building blocks, perhaps, toward the construction of a theory of deindustrialization and its place in the general history of political economy.

One must begin with the concept of the region itself. Too often, the essential unit of macroeconomic analysis has been the "nation"-state. This was certainly understandable for much of the nineteenth and twentieth centuries, when it appeared as if historical understanding had, above all, to account for the "triumph" of "the" modern state, especially "the great powers." But recently, indeed in the twenty-year span of this book's gestation, this view of the state and of the locus of power has altered significantly. The international dimensions of economic relationships have become glaringly obvious, while accepted boundaries, units of sovereignty, are threatened with drastic alterations. What is at work in the latter arena is the fascinating combination of the growing power of supranational entities, such as the European Union, with the shrill claims of ethnic regions within existing multiethnic states for autonomy or independence. Although the outcome is in no way certain, traditional concepts of the Western state and of Western capitalism, are under challenge. In short, a multiplicity of pathways of state development, as well as a multiplicity of "alternative" forms of economic organization and change, now come more easily into the historian's view.[1] In this new environment, the region as both a cultural and an economic entity takes on a significance hitherto obscured.

There is little doubt that the focus on the economic performance of states has masked important phenomena observable only if one examines the interplay of regional economies. One must insist on the word "interplay," because it is also impossible to generalize about large-scale economic and social processes from the history of a single region, though regional study can obviously provide many insights into patterns of development and decline.[2] The central point is this: the dynamism of accumulation in capitalist economies (and hence the essence of the system) is rooted in a fact that regional analysis makes clear—capital mobility exceeds that of labor. The ability to relocate investment in new regions (and new sectors) within a nation or far beyond its borders has been the key to the remarkable resiliency of the capitalist system. Labor—or rather, the people who do the work—can obviously "vote with their feet," a phrase to which Ronald Reagan gave new meaning, but just as obviously cannot relocate as easily as capital. And those who do decide to make the move exert downward pressure on the already lower wages of the receiving area by their very numbers, and their attitudes and modes of behavior (including class consciousness) are often mistrusted by its inhabitants. The culture and institutions of the receiving region are just as crucial factors in the mind of the capitalist as lower wages, and regional authorities often provide as amenable a context as possible to attract capital. Today in the United States, this involves competition among states and cities (especially in the form of tax breaks),[3] but in the more fiscally centralized states of Europe in the nineteenth century, the principal activities were intensive propaganda campaigns and insider lobbying to woo capital and to create advantages that the central government could provide.

Conversely, regions that fall out of favor for ideological/political reasons or due to weakening economic clout (usually both) find their already dangerous position made more so. The first of the many tragedies associated with deindustrialization is that disadvantages due to market forces are usually accentuated by those at the helm of the state through whose intervention a reversal or forestalling of the downward slide might otherwise have been effectuated. The contemporary experience of the American Midwest, the Ruhr, Lancashire, and Lorraine (among others) confirms this point. It is clear that the state and its laws have played just as important a role in aiding the "natural" play of deindustrialization and regional hopscotch so critical to the ongoing viability of capitalism as it has in the generation of industrialization in the first place. Indeed, one region's deindustrialization, obviously, is another's industrialization—or reindustrialization. Odette Hardy-Hémery, who has done for France what Barry Bluestone and Bennett Harrison have for the United States, ironically laments the current industrial revitalization, due significantly to state *planification*, of the far south (including the Montpellier area) and its dolorous impact on her region of choice, the Nord/Pas-de-Calais.[4]

The survey of the life and death of industrial Languedoc allows us to give specificity to the place of one region in this evaluation of capitalism's trajectory. It is certainly a cautionary tale, one which, if taken as the inevitable way of the world, is disheartening for those on the left. But it also points up the extraordinary complexity of the interplay of politics and economic life and thus urges us to consider what that politics must become if the dominion of the grand systemic forces of our time, capitalism and the state, is to be challenged.

Languedoc's diverse economy and the entrepreneurial verve of its merchant capitalists, its strategic significance, and its uncertain loyalty to France made it the object of royal solicitude under Louis XIV. Nowhere was the Colbertian system more fully elaborated, and nowhere did mercantilism pay better dividends, as the draps de Levant trade became the jewel of France's foreign commerce. Simultaneously, the landed elites of Languedoc were placated with favors and power to generate a quite stable system of government under absolutism.[5] In the eighteenth century the Languedocian economy continued to flourish and a new dimension emerged—the military cloth business dominated by Lodève. It perfectly complemented the Levant trade because demand for its products fluctuated inversely with that of the latter, generally troubled by warfare. If in the later eighteenth century, the inspection system and other aspects of state control sapped entrepreneurship in the principal towns of the Levant trade, Bédarieux burst into this sector, guaranteeing quality, while the others wallowed in cost-cutting product degradation. Meanwhile, Lodève's capitalists used the corporative system and the unequal legal policies of state institutions to undermine the power of the producers guilds, but also found themselves pressed to innovate organizationally by a state bent on making them better capitalists. As a consequence, the army-cloth city became a model for industrial relations and capital deployment (though the machine age was still in the future) and, with its neighbor Bédarieux and more distant Mazamet, led Languedoc woolens into the industrial era. The woolens industry did not collapse and went on to honor and profit in the nineteenth century even though its overall market share slipped. Thus did the state and capital intertwine to expand and then save the woolens industry of the south.

These developments did not move forward without response from those who actually made woolen cloth. The urban weavers and finishers saw their privileges and power erode as their occupational, social, and geographical solidarity increased, but their immediate reaction was to hope that they might become capitalists under a regime that would end privilege altogether and create a level terrain of equality of opportunity. This is what the French Revolution meant to them economically—that capitalism would be fair. Some of their types indeed made their way, and their politics helped them do so in the brief Jacobin era. But soon another view of economic life prevailed, typified by the policies of Chaptal. Although not a revival of privilege per se, it privileged money—on the quite rational assumption that those who already had it would better know what to do with it. At the same time, Napoleonic policy encouraged technical progress and pressed southern manufacturers into the machine age. The would-be capitalists of the laboring classes faded, and their jobs—especially those of the finishers—were further degraded. State and capital again combined neatly and submerged the Jacobin version of a plebeian public sphere.

During the July Monarchy, class confrontation of the sort described in *The Communist Manifesto* unfolded, as a settled, mature, united, and sophisticated working class moved toward an era of militancy with few parallels in Europe. But the source of emotional and cultural solidarity was most un-Marxist (or so it would seem): a populist Christianity that distinguished clearly between a Christianity of domination and an egalitarian *vrai christianisme*, to use Etienne Cabet's words. Explosive and innovative strikes led finally to the tightening of employer solidarity and their will to unite behind a technological solution to the labor problem: mechanical looms would discipline these people once and for all. And the state, though at first ambivalent and indeed tending toward a thoughtful, Guizotian version of equitable policy, finally rendered the capitalists its support. The very essence of the bourgeois monarchy was revealed in the Prefect's simple realization that the regime needed these men's votes. And so the great strike of 1845 in Lodève was crushed, and workers were finally moved to violence—for the first time in this long history. But the coming of the Second Republic seemed again to promise that capitalism might again be made just, that Christian values and the market economy were compatible. When it turned out that they were not, workers veered rapidly toward democratic socialism. Meanwhile, the Republic turned bourgeois, heading down the path toward that deformed and manipulative version of the public sphere in which a plebiscitory state controlled the masses through violence and was met with violence. Nowhere was that violence as frightening as in industrial Languedoc. But it was thoroughly repressed with the Languedocian bourgeoisie cheering on the troops.

And so these industrial notables now expected their old relationship with the state to be reestablished. It was not. Why this was so boiled down to two basic factors. First, Languedoc workers (and many peasants) left an indelible impression on the nation and the Bonapartist political class: a murdered Procureur-general whose assassins were never prosecuted because the people of Lodève refused to testify, a gendarmerie demolished, after which the people of Bédarieux created their own social republic amid the ashes of authority. Here a plebeian public sphere had actually existed, and bourgeois France blanched. If the economy of the region suffered, well, perhaps they all—including the capitalists—deserved it. The parallel with America's United Auto Workers' constant challenge to Detroit's auto barons topped off by the great rebellion of black Detroit in 1967 cannot be ignored. "Reputation" does have an impact on consumer decisions—and government policy. Second, and more concretely, the national power structure, the arteries of influence, had changed with the Second Empire. We have seen in some detail how the state—not the abstract, reified structure often evoked by social theorists, Marxist or not, but real, flesh and blood officials pressured by clearly identifiable businessmen—failed industrial

Languedoc in the matter of rail connections, and how northern interests simultaneously undermined the financing of southern-led projects. The fate of an economically weakening and politically suspect region was sealed by the mid-1860s, when the first big firm, that of Lodève's most famous resident, Michel Chevalier, pulled out. Again one is reminded of the slashed federal programs, the attack on the unions, the encouragement of plant relocation in return for subsidies (Chrysler), the tragic efforts by municipalities to keep businesses from leaving (the General Motors Poletown project), the refusal to aid alternative reindustrialization programs (Youngstown), and all the rest that characterizes the recent history of the industrial heartland of the United States.

But, like many of the business and political leaders of this area, the regional bourgeois of Languedoc persevered. The rail battles prove it, but so do the efforts to adapt to other industrial processes and develop new projects. The vine was certainly available for investment and many of the wealthy in lower Languedoc did so, building economies in Montpellier, Béziers, and Narbonne around commerce in wine. But the Hérault's industrialists did not seem to do so. Their postmortem inventories do not show significant investment in vine land. Mazamet went on to an industrial future with an innovative new process, Lodève fabricants tried new lines, and Bédarieux and Montpellier businessmen invested in coal mining and glass blowing. The enterprising Leenhardt family, not popular perhaps with the Graissessac workers, nevertheless proceeded precisely like their rivals elsewhere to invest in new equipment, organizational reform, and new procedures. They were met with—and broke—a great strike in 1894. Raymond Dugrand, though clearly correct that the vine took over the economy of lower Languedoc, nevertheless underestimates the ongoing commitment to industry and economic diversity among the Hérault business community. In view of the historical depth of that community, this should hardly come as a surprise.

Finally, there is the end of the story—a deindustrialized Languedoc. The process was blessedly slower than it usually is today, and the vine, despite all the problems it encountered, *was* there. Still, the human impact parallels contemporary circumstances. The shift to a heavily female work force and to large contingents of foreign labor characterizes the ongoing efforts of Lodève and Graissessac to stay afloat. Family income becomes more important, and men take jobs outside the industry, only to become rivals to service artisans, driving their wages down. Many people leave, but they tend to be those on the margins of the main industry because the others are more rooted in the community, and experienced women can still find industrial work. The population ages. Fewer children are born, not only due to the out-migration of young adults but because of conscious restriction to adjust family size to the new circumstances.[6] Safety standards in industry deteriorate and unions, if they exist, fight almost exclusively for job maintenance.

Most obvious, however, is the enormous loss of basic self-esteem among working people that accompanies deindustrialization. Scrambling to hold their heads above water, men watch their traditional places as primary bread-winners erode. Young people hoping to leave are held by family obligation to contribute to the pool. Wives are overworked and frustrated on the job and off. Most residents resent foreigners who work for less and will not join the union. All find their former solidarity with friends in the service indus-tries disappearing. Languedoc industrial workers, like their counterparts in Flint, Oldham, Duisberg, and Joeuf today, just want to get through the day and make it to some kind of retirement. Labor militance is the furthest thing from their minds. One of the great ironies of differential regional deindustrialization, which is the standard form of capitalist "crisis," is that it hardly leads to revolution, but rather engenders quiescence, the internal-ization of despair.[7] Although the traditional Marxist might counter that this is not the "general crisis" that will stimulate the final conflict, most crises, in fact, are not general; in the one that perhaps most clearly was, that of the 1830s, the unemployed, to the disappointment of the militants, acted in much the same way.[8]

Now in Languedoc, of course, as indeed in virtually all other deindus-trialized areas, another form of economic activity came to the rescue. But what was lost was industry, and an ever-narrower dependency on a single and, for many, alien form of work in the vine fields developed. As we have seen, industrial workers rarely found employment in the vast vineyards of the plain, where hiring of more robust, and hopefully more docile, Aveyron-nais peasants with agricultural experience was more likely. But everyone knew that the vine was the future. A job on the railroad or in construction in Montpellier or on the docks in Sète was still dependent on the prosper-ity of the vine. And so, there unfolded the curious history of "le Midi rouge," where red had more to do with wine than politics. Socialism meant coop-eration with large growers to gain—what?—government action on behalf of the ubiquitous vine. The state intertwines with Languedoc's new capi-talist economy, and the great wine companies call the shots for "socialist" deputies.

Is this outcome, and the tamed working class that accompanies it, in-evitable? Do we revise our understanding of the way capitalism works and throw up our hands in despair? Some will say no and peer through long-term trends to visualize a generalized crisis of Western capitalism as deindus-trialization overwhelms entire states.[9] But perhaps efforts already made—though certainly not in the United States—in response to regional political movements that go well beyond the bogus regionalism of an Edouard Barthe, have rectified some past wrongs. In France, contemporary socialist leadership was significant in revitalizing the south, for example. But this still tends to occur at the expense of other regions—precisely why Hardy-Hémery writes.

What is required is a labor movement that understands the national and international dimensions of deindustrialization, that can turn the knowl-edge gained from the history of Languedoc and others like it into the will to confront the national state—and now, the European Union or the "free-trade"-zone politicians of North America—with a unified, interregional solidarity. But for what purpose? Action at the point of production? Perhaps. But, in fact, if this study has shown anything, it is the significance of *politics* in shaping and orienting the economy. And what might a counter-politics be? Let us recall the vision of those plebeians of 1848–1851, who understood that only the conquest of the state by the people would make capitalism fair—or alter it beyond recognition. But theirs was not just a "labor movement." Certainly not by 1851. Class-conscious workers and their organizations had originated the movement and continued to play a critical role, but they were joined by small peasants angry about mortgages, paltry credit facilities, taxes, and false promises from the state, by families despairing the loss of infants in unhealthy urban environments, by women who understood how they were being used at the workplace and in the society at large, by ordinary Occitans at once embarrassed by and resentful toward bilingual elites and French-speaking officials, by Christians whose religious values were offended by bourgeois versions of their religion and the ill-treatment of priests who practiced Christ's real message. In short, it was a vast presence of people seeking to decolonize and reclaim their life-worlds, people who subscribed to a politics of open democratic debate, a politics of demonstration as well as representation, a politics committed to harnessing economic and administrative systems to their needs and to their vision of the good life.

That we should return to the world of 1848 to conclude this book should not come as a surprise. It was the moment in modern Western history when the universal potential of the Enlightenment—of Jürgen Habermas's "path not taken," that of communicative, interactive rationality in the public sphere—was blocked by the triumph of a system of domination and control that fused capitalism and the bureaucratic state. It is important to stress that the movement struggling against it and struggling for the realization of that potential was not simply a labor movement, not simply a class struggle, though it was partially that to be sure, and certainly not simply the first effort to fulfill some preordained destiny of a collective subject, but a multipolar struggle of *le peuple*—one that remains a most illuminating model for movements of social transformation today.

Notes

Preface

1. See Christopher H. Johnson, "Patterns of Proletarianization: Parisian Tailors and Lodève Woolens Workers," in *Consciousness and Class Experience in Nineteenth-Century Europe*, ed. John M. Merriman (New York, 1979), 64–84.

2. Gérard Cholvy, "Histoire contemporaine en pays d'Oc," *Annales: Economies, Sociétés, Civilisations*, hereafter *Annales: ESC*, 33 (1978): 863–79.

3. Christopher H. Johnson, *Maurice Sugar: The Law, Labor and the Left in Detroit, 1912–1950* (Detroit, 1988).

4. See, especially, Saskia Sassen, *The Mobility of Capital and Labor* (Cambridge, 1988) and Patricia Fernandez Kelly and Saskia Sassen, *A Collaborative Study of Hispanic Women in Garment and Electronics Production* (New York, 1990).

5. Claude Fohlen, "En Languedoc: vigne contre draperie," *Annales: ESC*, 4 (1949): 290–97.

Prologue

1. This section of the book largely summarizes work that I have published previously. For details and extensive documentation, the reader is referred to the following studies: "Deindustrialization: The Case of the Languedoc Woolens Industry," *Rapports, Section A2: la protoindustrialisation; VIIIᵉ congres international d'histoire économique, Budapest, 1982*, ed. Pierre Deyon & Franklin Mendels (Lille, 1982), I, ch. 22; Italian translation in *Quaderni storici* 18: 52. (aprile 1983): 25–56; "Capitalism and the State: Capital Accumulation and Proletarianization in the Languedocian Woolens Industry, 1700–1789," in *The Workplace before the Factory: Proletarianization in the Age of Manufactures*, ed. Leonard Rosenband and Thomas Max Safley (Ithaca, N.Y., 1993), 37–62; and "Artisans vs. Fabricants:

Urban Protoindustrialization and the Evolution of Work Culture in Lodève and Bédarieux, 1740–1830," *Mélanges de l'école française de Rome* 99:2 (1987): 1047–1084.

2. Quoted in Pierre Boissonnade, "Colbert: son système et les entreprises industrielles d'état en Languedoc (1661–1683)," *Annales du Midi* 14 (1902): 6. See also Boissonnade, *Colbert: le triomphe de l'étatisme*, (Paris, 1932).

3. Henri Monin, *Essai sur l'histoire administrative du Languedoc pendant l'intendance de Basville (1685–1718)* (Paris, 1884), 285, 306. On the place of the landed elites in Languedoc's stagnant agrarian economy and in the political power structure of the system built by Louis XIV, see, respectively, Emmanuel Le Roy Ladurie, *Les paysans du Languedoc* (Paris, 1966) and William Beik, *Absolutism and Society in Seventeenth-Century France: State Power and Provincial Aristocracy in Languedoc* (Cambridge, 1985).

4. R. Ferras, H. Picheral, and B. Vielzeuf, *Atlas et geographie du Languedoc et du Roussillon* (Paris, 1979).

5. Archives Nationales (AN), F^{12} 1379.

6. See also Boissonnade, "La Production et la commerce des ceréales, des vins et des eaux-de-vie en Languedoc dans la seconde moitié du XVIIIe siècle," *Annales du Midi* 17 (1905): 329–60.

7. See, especially, Monin, *Essai*, 347–64; also, Le Roy Ladurie, *The Peasants of Languedoc*, trans. J. Day (Champaign, Ill., 1974), 265–86.

8. Leon Dutil, *L'Etat économique du Languedoc à la fin de l'Ancien Régime* (Paris, 1911), offers the most detail. J. Pégeire, *La Vie et l'oeuvre de Chaptal* (Paris, 1931).

9. Pierre Léon, "La Réponse de l'industrie," *Histoire économique et sociale de la France*, II (Paris, 1970), 224–25.

10. Le Roy Ladurie, *Paysans*; Louis Dermigny, *Sète de 1666 à 1880* (Sète, 1955) and "Le prix de vin en Languedoc au XVIIIe siècle," *Annales du Midi*, 76 (1964): 505–28; Georges Frèche, *Toulouse et la région Midi-Pyrénées au siècle des lumières (vers 1670–1789)* (Toulouse, 1974); Charles Carrière, "La Draperie languedocienne dans la seconde moitié du XVIIIe siècle: contribution à l'étude de la conjoncture levantine," in *Hommage à Ernest Labrousse* (Paris, 1974), 157–72; Carrière, *Les négociants marseillais au XVIIIe siècle*, 2 vols. (Aix-en-Provence, 1973); James Thomson, *Clermont-de-Lodève* (Cambridge, 1985); Dutil, l'Etat; Emile Appolis, *Le Diocèse civil de Lodève* (Albi, 1948); Paul Marres, *Les Grandes Causses*, 2 vols. (Tours, 1936).

11. François Crouzet, "Les Origines du sous-développement économique du Sud-Quest," *Annales du Midi* 71 (1959): 3–21; André Armengaud, "A propos des origines du sous-développement industriel dans le Sud-Quest," *Annales du Midi* 72 (1960): 75 ff. (He emphasizes the great difference between upper and lower Languedoc in this regard.)

12. Rolande Trempé, *Les Mineurs de Carmaux*, 2 vols. (Paris, 1978); Joan Wallach Scott, *The Glassworkers of Carmaux* (Cambridge, Mass., 1974); Rémy Cazals, *Les Révolutions industrielles à Mazamet, 1750–1900* (Paris, 1983); Donald Reid, *The Miners of Decazeville: a Genealogy of Deindustrialization* (Cambridge, Mass., 1985).

13. Claude Fohlen, "En Languedoc: vigne contre draperie" *Annales: ESC*, 4 (1949): 290–97; Raymond Dugrand, *Villes et campagnes en Bas-Languedoc* (Paris, 1963), especially his "Conclusion générale"; and Gerard Cholvy, "Histoires contemporaines en pays d'Oc," *Annales ESC*, 33 (1978): 863–79.

14. Dermigny, "Le prix de vin," 527.

15. It is especially instructive to read Dutil side by side with Ernest Labrousse et al., *Histoire économique et social*, II, (Paris, 1970) and Labrousse, *La Crise de l'économie française à la fin de l'ancien régime et au début de la Révolution* (Paris, 1944).

16. Guy Chaussinaud-Nogaret, *Les Financiers de Languedoc au XVIIIe siècle* (Paris, 1970) and L. Dermigny, "La Banque à Montpellier au XVIIIe siècle," *Annales du Midi* 93 (1981): 17ff.

17. Dutil, *L'Etat*, (398) presents the following graph of the total Levant trade controlled at Montpellier (this includes all the manufactories of the future departments of Aude, Tarn, and Gard, as well as the Hérault); army figures are drawn Archives Communales de Lodève (ACL), 2 F 6. A "ballot" is bail of 10 bolts.

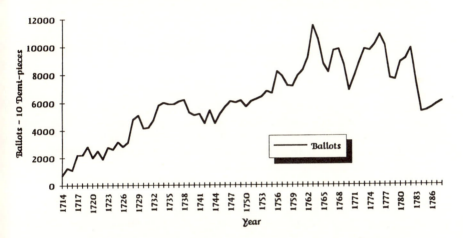

18. See recapitulation (1789–1822) in H. Creuzé de Lesser, *Statistique du département de l'Hérault* (Montpellier, 1824), 558–59.

19. See AN, F¹² 4487A and below, pp. 18, 47–49, 67–69.

20. See above, note 1.

21. Serge Chassagne, "L'Industrie lainière en France à l'époque révolutionnaire et imperiale (1790–1810)," in *Voies nouvelles pour l'histoire de la Révolution française* (Paris, 1978), ed., M. Vovelle, 163–64.

22. Mémoire contenant les éclarcimens résultans des opérations que Le Mazurier a eu ordre de faire, dans la fabrique de Lodève pour parvenir à y établir le bon ordre par un réglement," 7 November 1740. Archives départmentales de l'Hérault (ADH), C 2389.

23. Bossenga, "Protecting Merchants: Guilds and Commercial Captialism in Eighteenth-Century France," *French Historical Studies* 15 (Fall 1988): 693–703.

24. Pierre Lebrun, *L'Industrie de la laine à Verviers pendant le XVIIIe et le début du XIXe siècle* (Liège, 1948) and D. T. Jenkins, *The West Riding Wool Textile Industry, 1770–1835: A Study of Fixed Capital Formation* (Edington, Wilts., 1975).

25. Bernard Devic, *L'Industrie de la laine dans la vallée du Jaur, 1789–1851* (St. Pons, 1968) and AN, F¹² 2301.

26. The main source for what follows is the "Recensement de l'an VI," ACL, 1 F 2. Besides the normal census information, it provides commune of origin,

approximate date of migration to Lodève, and ownership information on the dwelling. For details, see Johnson, "Artisans vs. Fabricants," 1057–61.

27. By contrast, only 2 percent of wage earners of Daniel Roche's sample for Paris in the 1775–1790 period owned their flat. Roche, *Le Peuple de Paris* (Paris, 1981), 108.

28. ADH II E 39–40 (Etudes Géraud, Martin, Clainchard, samples, 1796–1835, Ventes).

29. Of 115 marriages of weavers (1796–1810) for which the father-in-law's occupation is listed, 28 wed service artisans' or tradesmen's daughters.

30. *Cartulaire de la Ville de Lodève*, ed. Ernest Martin (Montpellier, 1900), hereafter CVL, "Drappiers" of 1608, 310; "Relevé des fabricants en An III," AN, F^{12} 1389–90. Lists of merchant-manufacturers throughout the seventeenth and eighteenth centuries are numerous. Coupled with marriage records (1746–50, 1766–70, 1786–90) they reveal the turnover, or rather, the lack of it, in the patronat of Lodève.

31. See, for example, "Copie de la lettre de l'Administration du District de Lodève," 29 Prairial An II, AN F^{12} 1389–90.

32. Thomson, *Clermont-de Lodève*, Conclusion

33. This information is drawn from the census of An VI and from a sampling of notarial entries 1800–1830 (ADH, II E 40 [Etudes Gérard, Martin, Ecudéry, Clainchard]). Thanks are due to M. et Mme Boisse de Black of Pégairolles for the use of their genealogy charts of the Black and Teisserenc families.

34. Twenty-six single women over thirty years of age of fabricant families living alone with a servant were found in the census of An VI.

35. See Emile Appolis, *Le Jansenisme dans le diocèse de Lodève au XVIIIe siècle* (Albi, 1952).

36. Information compiled from the census of AN VI.

37. See Thomson, *Clermont-de-Lodève*, 355–430. On Bédarieux, the key materials are in AN, F^{12} 752, 754, and 1384.

38. Thomson, "Variations in Industrial Structure of Pre-Industrial Langue-doc," in *Manufacture in Town and Country before the Factory*, ed. Maxine Berg et al. (Cambridge, 1983), 61–91 and AN, F^{12} 754.

39. AN, F^{12} 754.

40. "Mémoire," 5 December 1789, AN F^{12} 652. "Mémoire sur le cotton," Intendant Balanvilliers to de Montaran (Conseil de Commerce), 3 January 1787. AN, F^{12} 557. "Wise regulation" was the theme of the major northern woolens towns, however. See F^{12} 652, 8 February 1790 (Elbeuf) and 16 March 1789 (Louviers); F^{12} 678, October 1789 (Sedan).

41. AN, F^{12} 652, petitions of 31 March and 15 April 1790.

42. *Adresse et pétition des habitants des lieux des Graissessac, Camplong, Boussagues, les Nyères, Lassalles et autres lieux de la baronnie de Boussagues contre l'exploitation exclusive de leurs mines de charbon. A l'Assemblée Nationale* (1790) in ADH, L 4533.

43. "Relevé des soumissionnaries de [l'an II] . . . ," AN, F^{12} 1389–90. On the social origins of these new men, see Michel Fabreguettes, "Mémoire" de 7 Thermidor An IX (25 July 1801). An, F^{12} 2301; on dyers become fabricants, Archives communales de Lodève and biographical information drawn from diverse notarial records, ADH, II E 29–40 and mutations par decès, 17 Q^3.

44. A mémoire of "Cincinnatus" (1795), AN F^{12} 3678 2, excoriated the Jacobin "butchers," but, in fact, seems to have had little effect.

45. On the politics of the Revolution and relations between Lodève and the state, see Georges Ferre, "La vie politique à Lodève de 1788 à 1793" (unpublished Diplôme d'études supérieure, [DES] Université de Montpellier, 1971) and Christopher H. Johnson, "Ordinary Revolutionaries: Business and Politics in Lodève, 1789–1795" (unpublished paper, Wayne State University), and a briefer account in Johnson, "Artisans vs. Fabricants," 1067–73. The essential documentation is found in AN, F^{19} 430–31; F^7 4561 and 3678 2; AF II 182; especially D III 104; "Relevé, AN, F^{12} 1389–90; F^{14} 828 (communications); F^{12} 2301 (Febreguettes' "Mémoire"); F^7 8849; and F^{14} 824.

46. This was the case throughout Languedoc and led to bloody conflicts. See Gwynne Lewis, *The Second Vendée, 1789–1815*, (Oxford, 1979).

47. AN, F^{12} 652.

48. "Mémoire" of Lodenait to Roland (Min. Int.) on roads, 29 December 1792, AN, F^{14} 828; État des Manufactures, Fabriques et Usines existants dans la Commune de Bédarieux, 4 Frimaire l'An 3, in ADH, L 4265.

49. ADH, L 916–18, 960, 5639; AN F^7 3678^1.

50. Gérard Cholvy, "Religion et politique en Languedoc méditerranéen," in *Droite et Gauche* (1975): 49–51.

51. For the details of this key struggle and the role of Chaptal, see Johnson, "Artisans vs. fabricants," 1071–77. The main documentation is a dossier of some 500 pages in AN, F^{12} 2301.

52. See Christopher H. Johnson, "The Protestant Nailmakers of Graissessac and the Revolutionary Struggle for Economic Liberty, 1789–1830" (unpublished paper) for details.

53. *Bulletin des lois* (1791). On the general problem of the struggle for control of mining rights, see Marcel Rouff, *Les Mines de Charbon en France au XVIIIe siècle* (Paris, 1922); Reid, *Miners of Decazeville*, 9–15; and René Garmy, *La "Mine aux mineurs" de Rancié*, 2nd ed. (Paris, 1970).

54. "Extrait du registre des procès verbaux de la Mairie de Camplong," 19 Nivôse An 10 (8 January 1802), AN, F^{14} 7694. This carton and the two preceding it in the Public Works series contains hundreds of documents relating to Graissessac.

55. *Aux Consuls de la République* (Béziers, 1802).

56. See below, pp. 154–56.

57. On the impact of the Concordat, see AN, F^{19} 5688; on popular Catholicism, X. Rame, *Essai historique et médical sur Lodève* (Lodève, 1841), 17ff, and Johnson, "Ordinary Revolutionaries," 25–27.

58. Chassagne, "L'Industrie lainière en France," 166.

59. Georges Clause, "L'Industries lainière rémoise a l'époque napoléonienne," *Revue d'histoire moderne et contemporaine* (1970) (special issue): 574–95.

60. Marres, *Les Grandes causses*, II, 69–80.

61. Thiomar J. Markovitch, *Les Industries lainières de Colbert à la Révolution* (Geneva, 1956), 310.

62. This figure is estimated from our precise knowledge of Lodève (30,000), Carcassonne (11,500), Clermont (10,000), Bédarieux (6,000), Mazamet (15,000?), St. Pons (4,000), Riols (2,500), and an extrapolation based on previous relationships for the rest; figures are drawn from Markovitch; ACL, 2 F 6; and Etienne Baux, "Les draperies audoises sous le premier Empire," *Revue d'histoire économique et social* (1960): 418–32.

63. Markovitch, *Les Industries lainières*, 227–30, 264–69.

64. Chassagne, "*L'Industrie lainière en France*," 163–64. Ternaux and Croutelle were famous entrepreneurs in the Rémois *nouveautés* trade.

65. AN F^{12} 4476 A. It should be noted that far less of the "Levant" production now went to the old Echelles; North Africa (particularly under the "favorable circumstances," as one official put it, that now existed in Algeria), Italy, and Greece were prominent markets.

66. Chassagne, "*L'Industrie lainière en France*," 155, n. 60.

67. Robert L. Heilbroner and Aaron Singer, *The Economic Transformation of America, 1600 to the Present*, 2nd edition (New York, 1984). The rapid revival of Germany after the Nazi takeover is one striking example, but the centrality of military production and government investment in technological development related to it in the boom years prior to the First World War is a more important one.

68. Estimates based on figures from diverse reports, AN, F^{12} 2301, 2302, AF IV 1177, ADH 132 M 2.

69. ACL, 2 F 6. Retrospective report of Mayor Belliot, January 1848.

70. Marres, "Le Lodévois," *Bulletin de la Société languedocienne de géographie*, 98 (1975): 297.

71. Eric N. Sigsworth, *Black Dyke Mills, A History* (Liverpool, 1958), 1–30.

72. Mémoire by Costaz, 1 Nivôse 12, AN, F^{12} 2301.

73. This tale is drawn from a dossier of correspondence, dated 18 April 1809 to 12 January 1812, in AN, F^{12} 2301 and Creuzé de Lesser, *Statistique*, 561–62. Causse retained an operation in Lodève, however.

74. Creuzé de Lesser, *Statistique*, 562.

75. Desgarets to Min. Int., 16 August 1814, AN, F^{12} 2301.

76. *Metiers à rouets* (fly-shuttle looms) are the norm in the listings for the detailed "Tableau statistique de la Ville de Lodève in 1838," ACL, 2 F 6.

77. See best summary of both the payment problem and the condition of the industry in 1814 is by Sous-préfet Desgarets, "Mémoire," June 1814, F^{12} 2301. It was estimated that the state owed Lodève manufacturers eight million francs. See also AN, AF IV 1177, 8, and 9; ADH, 132 M 2.

78. Délibérations du Conseil d'Arrondissement de Lodève, 28 juillet 1819, ADH (non-classé). Quoted (incorrectly) by Marres, "Le Lodévois," 298.

79. A sense of this can be gained by comparing occupations of immigrants from these outworking villages in the 1770s and 1780s and in the 1820s. Almost all the former were listed as *brassiers* if they were male. The women were domestic servants or married to brassiers or petty tradesmen. Marriage records for 1822–29, however, show twelve of twenty-five grooms from these villages alone listed as *fileurs*. Census of An VI and Mairie de Lodève, Etat civil de Lodève, Mariages.

80. See the five major statistical reports upon which this analysis is based— 1824, 1838, 1843 in ACL, 2 F 6; 1831 (ACL, 7 F 1); and 1848 (*Enquête*, A.N. C 954—Hérault, Lodève).

81. "Statistique" of 1838, ACL, 2 F 6 lists precise locations of mills and numbers of workers.

82. These comments are largely drawn from my analysis of petty crime in the Lodévois, 1830–1840, ADH, 2 U^{8b} 18, Tribunal de Lodève, Registres de jugements correctionnels. On wage differentials and currents of temporary migration, the *Enquête* of 1848 (A.N. C 954 [Hérault]) is invaluable.

83. See in particular AN, F^{12} 2303 (*Inventions divers*), but throughout the

official correspondence on draps de troupe and other matters as well are interspersed materials demonstrating the critical role of the state in subvening new technology.

84. See correspondence from Sedan and Louviers on cropping machinery conflict of 1 Brumaire, An 12, AN, F¹² 2301 and 31 August 1813, AN, F¹² 2302.

Part I

1. Creuzé de Lesser, *Statistique*, 472 ff and 560 (quotation).
2. AN, F⁷ 9786. The letter was dated 22 March 1822.

Chapter 1

1. The best account is Lewis, *The Second Vendée*, 153–218.
2. See above, pp. 15–18.
3. Report of 5 May 1815, AN, F⁷ 9663.
4. Prefect Aubernon to Min. Int., 19 November 1814, AN, F¹ᶜ III Hérault 14.
5. Chevalier de Brevannes to Min. Int. (Lainé), 6, 22, and 26 October 1815, AN, F⁷ 9663.
6. The political history of this period has been examined in detail, but space did not permit its inclusion. Primary documentation was found in the following sources: AN, F⁷ 9663 and 6687, F¹ᶜ III Hérault 14, and F¹² 2301; ADH, 5 U 248.
7. Drawn from quarterly reports in AN, F¹² 1577.
8. Reports of Creuzé de Lesser 25 November 1817 ff, F⁷ 9663.
9. This was the single most prevalent crime to come before the Lodève criminal court during the Restoration, ADH, 2 U⁸ᵇ 16–18.
10. AN, F⁷ 9663.
11. Fifteen came before the *tribunal correctionnel* of Lodève, ADH, 2 U⁸ᵇ 16, in 1830–32, a prosperous period, there was only one case. *Ibid.*, 18.
12. Etat civil, Lodève, Marriages, Naissances: summary figures for the relevant years.
13. R. Hortus, "Etude démographique de Lodève, 1800–1851" (DES), Montpellier, 1968. Táble, 206.
14. Oustry fails to provide numbers. I counted twenty-four grooms from Lodève, fourteen from Clermont and eight from St. Chinian in the period 1814–1830. Etat civil, Bédarieux. Jean-Marie Oustry, "Demographie et économie de Bédarieux, 1800–1831," DES, Montpellier, 1973, 20–23, 66ff. The quotation is from a gendarmerie report, ADH 39 M 93.
15. Hortus, "Etude démographique," 206.
16. AN, F¹² 1577; ADH, 132 M 8 (Draps).
17. On costs of hydraulic works, see deliberation of the Chambre consultative du commerce de la Ville de Lodève, December 1829, F¹² 2301.
18. ACL, 2 F 7.
19. See a report on weaving from 1830, ACL, 2 F 7.
20. Examples are drawn from the municipal registry of business agreements, ADH, 17 Q² 12, 1827–1830.
21. AN, F¹² 2414; petition dated August 1830. He had signed the agreement on 2 February 1830.

22. All these documents are gathered in a single carton of some 500 items, "draps de troupe," AN, F[12] 2301, which was much more useful than the highly technical materials housed at the Archives historiques de la Guerre.

23. ACL, 1 G 73.

24. His antecedents had been wool merchants and his father, a fabricant of modest proportions. The file relating to his bankruptcy included a day-to-day "journal" and all of his books dated back to 1818. ADH, 2 U 47 Tribunal de Commerce de Lodève (unclassified).

25. The basic structures are still there; general descriptions of the woolens merchants' houses can be found in notarial inventories.

26. See Gauffre's bankruptcy file in ADH 2 U 47 Tribunal de Commerce (unclassified).

27. Letters of 7 and 25 February 1828, An, F[12] 2301; and ADH, 17 Q[2] 12.

28. ADH, 17 Q[3] 20, déclaration du 22 Mai 1834 and II E 40/401, Inventaire après decès de Guillaume Rouaud.

29. Report of 2 January 1818, An F[7] 9663; on mineworkers, Creuzé de Lesser, *Statistique*, 521.

30. For parallels, see Rudolph Braun, *Industrialisierung und Volksleben* (Zurich, 1960), vol. II.

31. See below, pp. 214ff.

32. Robert Gély conveniently provides a table pulling together prefect reports on the industry during the period 1812–1844. "L'Industrie de laine Bédarieux de 1789 à 1851" (DES), Montpellier, 1969, 211–12.

33. Archives Communales de Bédarieux (non-classé).

34. Creuzé, 564 and mayor's report (April 1822) ADH, 132 M 8.

35. Gély, "L'Industrie," 133ff.

36. Guy Bechtel, *Un Village du Languedoc au XIXe siècle: Colombières sur l'Orb, 1803–1802* (Olargues, 1981), 142ff.; Bernard Devic, *L'Industrie de la laine dans la vallée du Jaur*, ch. 5.

37. ADH, 114 M Mons, 1836. I have made a detailed analysis of the demographic history of Mons that makes the last point clearly. Bechtel asserts the same for Colombières, *Un Village*, 43. C.H. Johnson, "Family Structures in a Changing Economy: Weavers and Vintners in a Nineteenth-Century Languedoc Commune" (paper in possession of the author).

38. On wages, see Creuzé, ADH 132 M 8.

39. ADH, 2 U 47 (Cauvy).

40. Renaud de Vilback, *Voyages dans les Départements formés de l'ancienne province du Languedoc* (Paris, 1825), 482.

41. Rivière to Min. For. Aff. 45, 10 May and 7 June 1817, AN, F[12] 2302.

42. Creuzé to Min. Int., 19 June 1819, AN, F[7] 9663; Creuzé, *Statistique*.

43. ADH, 162 M 8, "Fraudes sur l'aunage des draps," letter from Min. Int. Bequey to Creuzé of 30 November 1816, and responses of 18 February 1817ff.

44. Hortus and Dugrand both emphasize this. The extent to which it was true in general is a central issue in this book.

45. AN, F[12] 2301.

46. *Ibid.*

47. AN, F[12] 1577.

48. Gély "L'Industrie," 211–12; Hortus, "Etude démographique," gr. 21 and p. 206.

49. ADH, 132 M 8.

50. AN, F⁷ 9786.

51. Technically, the kind of machinery used for wool spinning amounted to a larger version of the simple jenny. The French "mule-jenny" was a misnomer. Harold Catling, *The Spinning Mule* (Newton Abbot, 1970), 142–43.

52. Tessie Liu, *The Weaver's Knot* (Ithaca, NY, 1994).

53. Paul Mantoux, *The Industrial Revolution of the Eighteenth Century*, revised ed. (New York, 1962), 264.

54. See E.P. Thompson, *The Making of the English Working Class* (London, 1963), 557ff.

55. See above (Mons analysis).

56. AN, F¹² 2302, letter of 31 August 1831.

57. ADH, 39 M 96.

58. For a brief period during the Empire, Captier jeune installed a longitudinal, which does not seem to have provoked any trouble. It was removed under circumstances that elude us. See Hortus, "Etude démographique," 126.

59. He was praised highly by Sub-Prefect Desgarets, who noted his award under the Empire in his 1814 report, AN, F¹² 2301.

60. Partnerships for army contracts were often temporary, and partners did not have control over what one did in his own factory.

61. AN, F⁷ 9786; F¹² 2301; ADH, 39 M 98.

62. He had this in mind from the beginning—the quote is from his first report of 6 May (F⁷ 9786).

63. A career bureaucrat, he served all régimes from 1800 to 1848. He was the architect of the restrictive press laws subsequent to the assassination of the Duc de Berri in 1820. Letter of June 1821 to the Prefect, AN, F¹² 2302.

64. ADH, 58 M 45.

65. An, F⁷ 9786 and ADH 39 M 98.

66. The number of "ouvriers divers," which includes tondeurs, laineurs, laveurs and presseurs, was 300 in 1821, 500 in 1828. In 1838, that same category had 1400 people in it for a total production of 40,000 bolts; see Hortus, "Etude démographique," gr. 21 and p. 206.

67. ADH, 2 U⁸ᵇ 18.

68. Fernand Rude, *Le Mouvement ouvrier à Lyon de 1827 à 1832* (Paris, 1944).

Chapter 2

1. Sources for Figure 2:1: Bédarieux, Gély, "L'Industrie," 211–212; Hortus, "*Etude démographique*," gr. 21; ACL, 2 F 6.

2. See below, ch. 3.

3. Bédarieux, too, had a social club gathering the notables of the town, but exclusion was more religious than genealogical. ADH, 58 M 29.

4. ADH, 39 M 125; see below, p. 56.

5. ADH, 132 M 15.

6. Mayor's report of 23 August 1830, AN, F¹² 2301.

7. *Echo de Lodève*, 7 September 1845.

8. ADH, 39 M 122 and 119; AN, F¹² 2301.

9. Gély, "L'Industrie," 178–84. AN, F⁷ 9663.

10. See John Merriman, "Introduction," *1830 in France* (New York, 1975) for the reasons why we really must think of the whole period 1830–35 as a revolutionary one.

11. AN, F14 7699; ADH, 39 M 107 and especially 2 U^{8b}18 (Tribunal du premier instance de Lodève).

12. ADH, 39 M 107 and 2 U^{8b} 18. Conflict also arose between the lay secondary school director and the Catholic elites, which ended in his dismissal. Moreover, primary education remained firmly in the hands of the Frères de l'Ecole chrétien. AN, F^{17} 3484.

13. ADH, 39 M 114.

14. Rouaud also willed Fr 1,000 to the poor of the parish of St. Pierre. Mutations, ADH, 17 Q^3 24. See T. Tackett, *Priest and Parish* (Princeton, 1979), 196–98, for an excellent discussion of confraternity rivalries in a rural setting during the eighteenth century.

15. Sous-préfet Brun reported in 1834 that "there exists no republican or legitimist association in Lodève." ADH 39 M 114.

16. ADH, 58 M 16 and 29. On Miquel, see A. Rivez, fils, *Notice sur M. Miquel, curé-doyen de l'église Saint-Alexandre de Bédarieux* (Montpellier, 1853).

17. See the proclamation of the new Préfet Fumeron d'Ardeuil promising help to distraught workers. F^{1c} III Hérault 14.

18. ADH, 39 M 107.

19. ADH, 39 M 109.

20. ACL, 2 F 7.

21. AN, F^7 4017.

22. This same ambivalence runs through much of the working-class press at precisely the same time in England. See G. Stedman Jones, "Rethinking Chartism," in his *Languages of Class* (Cambridge, 1983), 143ff. On Parisian workers' Saint-Simonism, see Jacques Rancière, *The Nights of Labor: The Worker's Dream in Nineteenth-century France*, J. Drury, trans. (Philadelphia, 1989), chs. 6, 7, and 8.

23. Etienne Cabios, et al., *Affaire des ouvriers de Bédarieux*, ADH, 39 M 108.

24. AN, BB^{18} 1221; ADH, 39 M 125. ACL, 1 F 7.

25. The literature is enormous; see Michael Sonenscher, *Work and Wages* (Cambridge, 1989), ch. 9, for the latest analysis.

26. E. Le Roy Ladurie, *Le Carnival de Romans* (Paris, 1976); Charles Tilly, "Charivaris, Repertoires, and Urban Politics," in *French Cities in the Nineteenth Century*, ed. John M. Merriman (London, 1982) and Tilly, *The Contentious French* (Harvard, 1986), 308–12.

27. These remarks were stimulated by William Reddy's contrary perspective, which questions whether such actions should be labelled "strikes" at all. See his *Rise of Market Culture* (Cambridge, 1984), especially 189–92, and my review in *Social History* (spring 1986): 259–63.

28. ADH, 39 M 125 and ACL, 1 F 7 (placard).

29. ADH, 39 M 125 and the retrospective report of 13 July 1858, ADH, 39 M 230.

30. ADH, 58 M 29 and 16.

31. ADH, 39 M 120.

32. AN BB^{18} 1376.

33. ADH, 17 Q^3 18.

34. For more detail, see below.

35. AN, BB^{18} 1376. Conseil des prud'hommes' deliberations for Lodève have not been preserved for 1815–48 period; in any case, materials from the late Empire indicate that few disputes went to judgement. ACL 7 F 2. On the importance

of the prud'homale courts' hearings, where preserved, see *Le Mouvement social*, no. 141 (spring 1987), especially Alain Cottereau's study, "Justice et injustice ordinaire sur les lieux de travail d'après les audiences prud'homales," 25–59.

36. AN, BB[18] 1386. On Paris, see Octave Festy, "Le Mouvement ouvrier à Paris en 1840," *Revue de l'école libre des sciences politiques* (1913): 266–97, and Christopher H. Johnson, *Utopian Communism in France* (Cornell, 1974), 66ff.

37. On Guizot's vision of governance, see Pierre Rosanvallon, *Le Moment Guizot* (Paris, 1985), passim.

38. ADH, 39 M 125.

39. Frank Manuel, "L'Introduction des machines en France et les ouvriers: la grève des tisserands de Lodève en 1845," *Revue d'histoire moderne*, 18 (1935): 209–225 and 353–72.

40. ADH, 39 M 125; *Echo* (not a complete run), Bibliothèque Nationale, annexe de Versailles; *L'Indépendant: Journal du Midi*, Bibliothèque Municipale de Montpellier; and AN, BB[18] 1429.

41. Sigoyer (S) to Prefect Roulleaux–Dugage (RD), 1 February 1845 (ADH, 39 M 125) and Sigoyer to Min. Int., 9 February 1845 (AN, 18 BB[18] 1429). All archival citations below, unless otherwise noted, are from these two cartons.

42. S to RD, *ibid.* (Clermont) and Barbot reported by S to RD, 7 February 1845, ADH (Lodève).

43. Commissaire de police de Clermont to S, 10 February 1845, ADH; *L'Indépendant*, 16 and 26 February 1845.

44. Confidential exchanges between Roulleau-Dugage and Sigoyer, 17 (RD), 19 (S), 23 (RD), 24 (Couzin, deputy mayor, to S), 26 (S), and 28 (Lieutenant Gendarme to S) February 1845, ADH.

45. S to RD, 26 February 1845, ADH.

46. S to RD, 4 March 1845 (ADH) and Passy to RD, 6 March 1845 (AN).

47. RD to Passy, 13 March 1845; Passy to RD ("très confidentielle"), 18 March 1845, ADH. Manuel "L'Introduction," 352–56; Justice had received the same message from Procureur général Massot (AN).

48. S to RD, 15 March 1845.

49. *L'Indépendant*, 27 March 1845.

50. S to RD, 24 March 1845 (ADH).

51. Quoted by Manuel, "L'Introduction," 358, probably drawing from an excerpt in *L'Atelier*. The original is missing from the BN Versailles run of the *Echo*.

52. S to RD, 24 March 1845 (ADH).

53. S to RD, 29 March; RD to Passy 1 April (on the mechanical loom association); S to RD, 7 April (on workers' economic situation; included the idea of sending unemployed to Algeria); RD to S, 9 April; S to RD 14 April; Couzin to RD 12 April (all concerning the petition); copy of *Mémoire* (23 April 1845), all ADH. Letters of Massot and Béard (Proc. du Roi at Lodève), 4–15 April 1845. AN. The fabricants' memoire was also sent to the Minister of War, whose interest in the end of the conflict was manifest (see copy in BB[18] 1429, AN). Also, Manuel, "L'Introduction," 364–66.

54. S to Rd, 19 and 21 April, 1845, ADH. The weavers were now "unapproachable," according to Sigoyer. Manuel did not have this crucial documention available to him.

55. S to RD, 3, 8, 10 May 1845, ADH.

56. Sent 11 May 1845, S to RD, ADH.

57. S to RD 15, 17 and 18 June 1845. 39 M 125, ADH.

58. ADH, 58 M 45 and ACL, letter of 4 January 1847, 2 D 82.
59. S to RD, 2 July 1845, ADH, 39 M 125.

Chapter 3

1. T.J. Markovitch, *L'Industrie française de 1789 à 1964*, III (Paris, 1966); Devic, *Vallée du Jaur* (1968); Claude Fohlen, "En Languedoc: vigne contre draperie," *Annales: ESC* 4 (1949); Cazals, *Les Révolutions.*
2. The results of this inquiry are found in AN, F^{20} 501.
3. Four towns simply provided numbers for their entire *fabrique*, not individual firms.
4. Most firms listed many more.
5. David Gordon, *Merchants and Capitalists: Industrialization and Provincial Politics in Nineteenth-Century France* (Alabama, 1935), 55ff; Reddy, *The Rise of Market Culture*, 89ff.
6. *Statistique gènèrale de la France: Industrie* (Paris, 1846) (Hérault, Ardennes) confirms the comparative significance of the Hérault industry.
7. Liste électorale censitaire: Département de l'Hérault (1846), ADH, 4 M. Occupations are listed as the elector wishes them to be.
8. ADH, 17 Q^3 25, Declaration, 19 May 1848.
9. See below, pp. 74–75.
10. 17 Q^3 39, Declaration of 22 October 1858.
11. Jean-André Tudesq, *Les Grands Notables en France (1840–1849)*, 2 vols. (Paris, 1964) and Adeline Daumard, *La Bourgeoisie parisienne de 1815 à 1848* (Paris, 1963); Alfred Cobban, *The Social Interpretation of the French Revolution* (Cambridge, 1964), 90 (citing Sherman Kent (1937)); Lenore O'Boyle, "The Middle Class in Western Europe, 1815–1848," *American Historical Review*, 71 (1966): 826–45.
12. Tudesq, *Les Grands Notables*, I, 88.
13. Ibid., 278–9.
14. For 1846, ACL, 1 G 84.
15. Tudesq, *Les Grands Notables*, I, 90.
16. *Industrie* (1846), Hérault.
17. It was common practice to give property to heirs before one's death.
18. ACL, 1 G 84.
19. See the arrangements completed by widow Valz for a steady income (Fr 2500 lease) for Prémelet, a small domain with vines and olives, orchards and meadows outside Lodève. ADH, II E 40/455 (Etude Maurel), 27 January 1847.
20. Probate declaration of René Fournier of 2 March 1858, ADH, 17 Q 24; Mayor's report of March 1862, "liste de fabricants," ACL, 2 F 6.
21. ADH, II E 40/435 (Etude Géraud), no. 258; Partage, succession de Jean-Fulcran Teisserenc-Dessalle, 8 September 1834; ACL, 1 G 84.
22. ADH, II E 40/424–439.
23. See Bonnie G. Smith, *Ladies of the Leisure Class* (Princeton, 1981), ch. 2, for a discussion of earlier nineteenth-century business involvement by women in Lille.
24. ADH, 115 M (Lodève, 1851).
25. See P. Roux and Henri Tannières, "Les licencements aux etablissements Teysserenc-Harlachol," *Revue de L'économie méridionale* (1956): 172–78.
26. Jules and Adolphe Teisserenc's leased their finishing in the midst of the

strike of 1834 to Adolphe's father-in-law, Jean-Pierre Fabreguettes, the beginning of their strategic withdrawal from direct participation in the industry.

27. ADH, II E 40/401, no. 267 (22 October 1833), /434, no. 364 (26 November 1834).

28. ADH, 2 U 47 Tribunal de Commerce de Lodève, Faillites (unclassified).

29. The Teisserenc-Calvet history has been reconstructed from the following documents (all ADH). 17 Q³ 15 (Jean-Fulcran Teisserenc, 12 January 1814); 20 (Jean Visseq, 3 May 1832); 21 (Jean-Pierre Fabreguettes, 5 April 1837): 23 (J.J. Teisserenc, 23 January 1841); 23 (Louis T.G. Calvet, 12 January 1841); 30 (Louis Calvet, 1 May 1860). II E 40/435 (Géraud), Partage, 6 September 1834 (Jean-Fulcran Teisserenc family), /332 (Géraud) Mariage, 6 Pluviose an 11 (JFT/Thérèse Faulquier); /415 (Géraud), Inventaire, 4 September 1813 (JFT); /429 (Géraud), Mariage, 18 June 1827 (Adrien Calvet/Zoé T.); /401 (Clainchard), Obligation 23 September 1833 (Hector T./J.F. Portier); /403 (Clainchard), Obligation 14 February 1835 (Hector T./Latreille); /401 Quittance, 24 April 1833 (J.T./Archimbaud); 402 (Clainchard), Quittance, 184 (1834) (Calvet/Lucas, house loan); 401, Vente, 22 October 1833 (Calvet/Cauvy vines); 434, Vente, 26 November 1834 (Calvet/Faulquier vines); Obligation, 17 June 1834 (Hector T./Causse); Bail à ferme, 10 February 1834 (A., J., P., E. Teisserenc/Fabreguettes).

30. Their interest in mechanization was clear. They possessed:

(1) A complete manufacturing establishment consisting of:

1 wool-washing and drying room
15 scrubbing or carding machines
7 slubbing billies
24 mule-jennies
24 weaving looms
1 fulling mill with 2 troughs (2 hammers each)
1 fulling mill with 4 troughs, Louviers style
1 power gig-mill
2 hand gig-mills
9 cropping tables with power-driven equipment
7 cropping tables with hand-shears
1 hydraulic press

(2) A dyeworks composed of:

4 vats
4 boilers

(3) A second pressing works containing:

1 hand gig-mill
7 cropping tables equipment not specified but probably hand-shears
3 presses again probably hand-operated

(ACL, 2 F 6).

31. Spinning mill: seventeen men, seven women, eighteen children. Weaving: eighteen men, forty-two women (ACL, 7 F 13).

32. Rather amazingly, Jean Walch presents none of the following information in his biography, *Michel Chevalier, économiste saint-simonien* (Paris, 1975).

33. Henri Leroy-Beaulieu, "Les propriétaires de Monplaisir, à la rencontre de la technique, de la politique et de l'économie," in *Hommage à Jacques Fabre de Morlhon*, ed. J.D. Bergasse, (Montpellier, 1978).

34. See Cameron, *France and the Economic Development of Europe*, 318–20.

35. Essential documentation for the Barbot and Fournier story: "Gaspard Barbot," *Echo de Lodève*, 7 September 1845; Etat civil de Lodève, mariages 1846; ADH, II E 40/452 Mariage Chevalier/Fournier; 17 Q3 24, Mutation Barbot, 25 February 1846; 25, Mutation Eugène Fournier (died 13 December 1846); 29, Benjamin Fournier (died 30 May 1855); 17 Q3 30, René Fournier, 27 August 1858. We shall return to Chevalier and Leroy-Beaulieu.

36. See Martin's fascinating introduction, in "Les faillites de Niort" (Thèse de troisième cycle, E. Le Roy Ladurie, director, Ecole des hautes études en sciences sociales, 1983.)

37. It is intriguing to consider that Rouaud's tenure as mayor, his respect in the community, the trust accorded him in affairs, and his place in the church were totally untroubled by all of this.

38. Even so, Joseph Rouaud was asked by Marie Christine Rouaud, widow Claparède, a G. Rouaud niece, to represent her interests in the estate.

39. René Nelli, *La Vie quotidienne des Cathares du Languedoc au XIIIe siècle* (Paris 1969); cf. Jack Goody, *The Development of Family and Marriage in Europe* (Cambridge, 1982), passim. On the desire to keep property together whatever the cost, recall Pierre Clergue's remarks about the *domus* of Montaillou: "if only one could marry his sister." (E. Le Roy Ladurie, *Montaillou* (New York, 1979), chs. 2–3.)

40. There were many instances of Lodève daughters—as with Melanie Teisserenc or Flor Ménard—who married men from elsewhere, particularly Montpellier, and they went to live with their husbands, creating useful external ties, but the in-migration of new manufacturers ceased.

41. AN, F⁷ 6696 ("Sociétés particulières formées à Lodève").

42. ADH, 17 Q³ 24, 7 August 1845; 25, 1 January 1847.

43. Etienne died in 1833 leaving a good deal of money to Joseph and his brother. 17 Q³ 20.

44. Letter of 21 February 1825 to Min. Int. AN, F⁷ 6696.

45. ADH, II E 40/400–402. They had twenty-one employees in 1834.

46. See above, p. 30.

47. 17 Q³ 19.

48. These remarks are largely generated from the census of the Year VI (above, p. 12).

49. ADH, II E 40/434 (10 February 1834); /401 (23 September 1833); /402 (16 October 1834) (9 January 1835); /426 (15 August 1825); 17 Q³ 20 (J.A.J. Visseq, 3 May 1832) for an idea of the continuing level of wealth of the Visseq family, however.

50. The history of Valz and Gauffre is to be found in the multiple transactions recorded by Lodève's notaires, ADH, II E 40/399–434.

51. ADH, II E 40/401 (4 December 1833); 17 Q³ 20 (22 May 1834); 2 U⁸ᵃ 34 (Jugements du Tribunal civil de Lodève, audiences of 9 June, 8, 9, 14 July, Jugement du 16 July 1834).

52. Jean Lambert-Dansette, *Quelques familles du patronat textile de Lille-Armentières, 1789–1914* (Lille, 1954), makes the point most forcefully. See also C. Fohlen, *Une affaire de famille au XIXe siecle: Méquillet-Noblet* (Paris, 1955) and more generally, Roger Priouet, *Origines du patronat français* (Paris, 1963). David Sabean stresses the role of widening kin connections for land-owning peasants in Württemberg scrambling to keep abreast of rapidly developing market

conditions in agriculture. *Property, Production, and Family in Neckarhausen, 1700–1870* (Cambridge, 1990), especially chs. 15–16.

53. ADH, 17 Q³ 22 (7 August 1838) and 24 (15 June 1844).

Chapter 4

1. L. René Villermé, *Tableau de l'état physique et morale des ouvriers employés dans les manufactures de coton, de laine et de soie*, 2 vols. (Paris, 1840); Ange Guépin, *Nantes aux dix-neuvième siècle* (Nantes 1832); William H. Sewell, Jr. *Work and Revolution in France* (Cambridge, 1980), 223–32 (critique of Villermé); *Echo de Lodève*, several issues, 1844.

2. ACL, 1 I 8 (Maisons de tolérance, vagabondage, mendicité); 7 (jeu de hazard); 9 (crimes et delits); Q 21 (enfants trouvés, filles mères); Q 2, 8 (assistance, ateliers de charité); ADH, 2 U⁴ᵇ 13–14 (crimes, including sexual). But illegitimacy in Lodève was consistently less than 5 percent, premarital conceptions rare, and rates of fathers confirming paternity nearly 100 percent.

3. Etat civil de Lodève, mariages and naissances, 1830–1847.

4. On this topic, the best work for France is on the second Empire; see Georges Duveau, *La Vie ourière sous le second Empire* (Paris, 1946), ch. 3 and Pierre Pierrard, *La Vie ouvrière à Lille sous le second Empire* (Paris, 1965), but little concrete work on the problem exists for the July Monarchy.

5. In Lodève, a "factory" weaver working the loom by himself, made as much as a Carcassonne family, while his wife and teenage daughter together made a minimum of 1.50. Figures from Villermé, *Tableau*, I, 326, 334, 338. Historical information on rates was gleaned from government reports on strikes, especially that of 1845, ADH, 39 M 125 and ACL 7 F 1.

6. *Statistique générale, Industrie* (Paris, 1846).

7. Some forty deaths of males fifteen years and over were not. ADH, 17 Q³ 22 and 23.

8. Adeline Daumard, *Les Bourgeois de Paris aux dix-neuvième siècle* (Paris, 1970), 17ff.

9. According to Villermé, this was the going rate.

10. Arbouy's and Fulcran's detailed declarations are in ADH, 17 Q³ 23, 7 January 1841 and 17 June 1842.

11. On butchers, see John Merriman, *The Red City* (New York, 1985), 12–18.

12. ACL, 1 F 6.

13. ACL, 1 G 84.

14. Villermé, *Tableau*, I, note 1, 328. ACL, Q 18. On worker attitudes toward savings banks, see Rancière, *The Nights of Labor*, ch. 2.

15. ADH 2 U⁴ᵇ 13–14.

16. An examination of succession evaluations and notarized sales records shows a range of twenty to thirty francs per *are*.

17. Villermé, *Tableau*, I, 331.

18. 320 is the total number of deaths declared in this period, while 279 appear in the succession registers.

19. Two at twenty, two at fifty, one at eighty.

20. AN, F¹² 4465ᴬ.

21. *Echo de Lodève*, 23 February 1844.

22. ADH, II E 40/418, Etude Clainchard (entry 104, March 1826) and 4/398 (entry 59, 4 February 1830).

23. *Ibid.*, 27 February and 9 March 1816.

24. X. Rame, *Essai historique et medical sur Lodève* (Lodève, 1841), 24–29 (B.N. Tc⁶ 22.).

25. Dugrand, *Villes et campagnes*, 439–41.

26. Compiled from ADH, 114 M 2 and Bureau de l'état civil (Lodève) 1823–1874, summary-copy in possession of author.

27. William Coleman, *Death is a Social Disease* (Madison, Wisconsin, 1982).

28. See the remarkably detailed summaries of death by age and by month (and causes after 1853) in ACL, 1 F 6. See also ADH, 113 M 64. Military recruitment statistics support this picture, with Lodève canton's rejection rates running 12 percent higher than the departmental average and 7 percent higher than the national. City figures alone would doubtless have been higher still. A.N., F⁹ 192.

29. Rame, *Essai historique*, 47–48; Villermé, *Tableau*, 326; for maps, blueprints, and so forth of factories and their location, see the detailed reports related to water-rights conflicts, see A.N., F¹⁴ 6134 (Cours d'eau Hérault—Lergue, Solandres).

30. Although differing from Tilly's perspective to an extent, this paragraph (and much more in this book!) owes a great deal to years of reading and discussing his work, summed up best in *The Contentious French*.

31. A.N., BB³⁰ 401 (Lodève).

32. Clothing workers generally were the most politically involved of all trades in the 1848 era. Lodève had ten tailor and thirty shoemaker shops in 1848 (A.C.L. 2 F 7) and 138 clothing workers altogether in 1851 (ADH 114 M 3—1851 census (summary)).

33. The arduous task of searching through état civil indexes and then *mutation* records for these individuals and members of their families, especially in a town where so many names are similar, was carried out with the full-time collaboration of Lois Johnson. The following section owes a great deal to her fine work.

34. Echo de *Lodève*, 11 November 1844.

35. 17 Q 39 and Etat civil Lodève, Mariages, 12 December 1838; contract, II E 40/452 (Clainchard).

36. "Noms de principaux chefs des ouvriers," 17 June 1845, ADH, 39 M 125. Noël Maizou was also on this list.

37. In an enormous literature, the reader should begin with *Interest and Emotion: Essays on Love and Power in the Peasant Family* ed. David Sabean and Hans Medick (Chicago, 1983); Colin Heywood, *Childhood in Nineteenth Century France* (Cambridge, 1989); Gaye Gullickson, *Spinners and Weavers of Auffay* (Cambridge 1987); and books and articles by those mentioned in the text and cited elsewhere in this book.

38. AN, F⁹ 192.

39. This is not to gainsay Rancière's important insight in *The Nights of Labor*, but "opportunism" of any sort seems remarkably low in Lodève. This city's character as a kind of Marxist caricature remains, and remains to be reckoned with.

Chapter 5

1. *Echo de Lodève*, 28 February 1847. "Soupes économiques" were established in Lodève (*ibid.*, 7 March). Tribunal de Lodève, ADH, 2 U⁸ᵇ 18 (1847). "Enquête sur le travail agricole et industriel de 1848," cantons of St. Gervais, Lunas, Le Caylar, Gignac, and Aniane, AN, C 954 (Hérault).

2. Roger Price, *The Modernization of Rural France: Communications Networks and Agricultural Market Structures in Nineteenth-Century France* (New York: 1983), 126–195 (see map of "subsistance disorders," 144).

3. Enquête, AN, C 954, cantons of Bédarieux and Lodève.

4. I first read Lodève's Enquête response in 1969. It was the document that piqued my interest in the city's social history.

5. *Ibid.*, questions 4, 5, 6, 13, 14, 15. ADH, 174 M 9.

6. See Joy Parr, *The Gender of Breadwinners* (Toronto, 1990).

7. ACL, 2 D 82. "Menuisiers de Lodève à M. le Maire, 13 mars 1848." A petition from twenty-eight unemployed locksmiths (*serruriers*) involved in construction metalworking voiced a parallel theme in criticizing the new city administration's contracting procedures by which they had been by-passed not only on repair jobs at the church and hospice, but, above all, in the construction of the slaughterhouse.

8. ADH, 39 M 134.

9. See above, ch. 2. See map of Lodève, p. 46.

10. My sample of the census of 1851 put the number of contre-maîtres at less than .5 percent of the woolens work force, and they were less overseers than technicians used to repair machinery.

11. *Commis* were limited to wool purchase, subcontracting operations, cloth sales, and payroll.

12. Prosecution for the occasional after closing-hour forays and "serenades" shows that the cafes had customers any evening.

13. Cadastral maps from the era (Mairie de Lodève) pinpoint the locations of *marchés*, *lavoirs*, and *fontaines* of the city.

14. The reader would be enthralled, as I was, by the exhibit at the Le Vigan Folklore Museum on the final victory over wolves in the Cevennes during the nineteenth century.

15. Enquête de 1848, AN, C 954, Lodève (Hérault), question 21.

16. *Echo de Lodève*, various issues, 1841–47. Edward Berenson, *Populist Religion and Left-Wing Politics in France, 1830–1852* (Princeton, 1984), 69–72.

17. On Brée, AN, BB[18] 1408 dos 5802 and 1434 dos 667. See also Katherine A. Lynch, *Family, Class, and Ideology in Early Industrial France* (Wisconsin, 1989), 44–48.

18. Ferdinand Fabre, *Ma Vocation* (Paris, 1989), 12ff.

19. On Thibault, see Cholvy, *Religion et Société au XIXᵉ siècle: la diocèse de Montpellier* (Lille, 1973). The only secondary study on Valibouze and other republican priests in the Hérault is Appolis, "Les Catholiques sociaux dans l'Hérault sous la Seconde République," *Actes du 85ᵉ Congrès nationale des sociétés savantes, Chambéry-Annecy, 1960* (Paris, 1961): 291–305. The essential contemporary source is Anon. [F. Gelly, editor of *L'Indépendant du Midi*], "Valibouze" in *Les Candidats à la députation nationale pour le département de l'Hérault* (Montpellier, 1848).

20. See above,

21. *L'Indépendant: Journal du Midi*, 11 and 20 February 1845.

22. On Roussac and his work, see Appolis, "Catholiques sociaux," 303.

23. *Echo de Lodève*, 20 April 1848.

24. Jürgen Habermas, *The Structural Transformation of the Public Sphere*, trans. by Thomas Burger (Cambridge, Mass., 1989), xviii and *passim*; *The Theory of Communicative Action* (Boston, 1989), II, trans, by Thomas McCarthy (Boston, 1989), 332ff.

25. Claude Delpla, in André Armengaud and Robert Lafont, *Histoire d'Occitanie* (Toulouse, 1983), 737.

26. AN, BB[18] series, especially 1389, reports from Aude, Gard, and Hérault, *passim*.

27. In part this is due to what seems to be inadequate documentation and poorly maintained newspaper collections. See Sylvie Vila, ("Les Milieux populaires et la République dans l'Hérault," Theses du 3e cycle, Paris I, 1976). One finds none of the depth in Vila's work achieved by Maurice Agulhon in *Une ville ouvrière au temps du socialisme utopique: Toulon de 1815 à 1851* (Paris, 1970) and *La Republique au village* (Paris, 1971).

28. Leo Loubère, *Radicalism in Mediterranean France: Its Rise and Decline* (Albany, N.Y., 1974), 29. On the history of Montpellier see, Gérard Cholvy (director), *Histoire de Montpellier* (Toulouse, 1984), 296–300 (section written by Roland Andréani).

29. *Echo de Lodève*, 27 February 1848.

30. P.G. Renard to G.S., 1 March 1848, AN, BB[30] 362.

31. Lunel, AN, C 954 (Hérault).

32. Renaud to G.S., 1 and 9 March 1848, AN BB[30] 362.

33. Nationwide, tax riots were far and away the most normal acts of protest in the wake of the revolution in Paris. See Albert Soboul, "Les troubles agraires de 1848," *1848*, 1 (1948): 181; Remi Gossez, "La résistance à l'impôt: les 45 centimes," *Société historique de la Revolution de 1848, Etudes*, 15 (1953): 89–132; Ted Margadant, *French Peasants in Revolt: The Insurrection of 1851* (Princeton, 1979), 42–48; P.G. to G.S., 9 March 1848.

34. Gelly, "Valibouze" (note 19 above).

35. *Echo du Midi* (the legitimist paper), quoted in *L'Indépendant*, 8 October 1848.

36. *Echo de Lodève*, 9 and 16 April 1848; Appolis, quoting the *Echo du Midi*, "Catholicisme sociaux," 301.

37. Letter of 2 June 1848, printed in *L'Indépendant*, June 1848.

38. "Les Ourdisseurs de Lodève à M. le maire," (protesting their exclusion) 8 March 1848, ACL, 2 D 82.

39. *Abattoir* shares are found in many death inventories of Lodève's economic elites.

40. ACL, 2 D 82. "Les habitants du Faubourg Montbrun à Monsieur André, Jules, Maire de Lodève" [March] 1848.

41. Habermas, *Communicative Action*, II, 355–73.

42. Renard, Procureur général de Montpellier to Min. Justice, 10 March 1848 and 9 March 1848 (on St. Guilhem), 6 April 1848 (Béziers), 26 July 1848 (Olargues), in A.N., BB[30] 362. See also the summary list of incidents ("Etat des émeutes, désordres graves, cris sédicieux, emblèmes sédicieux, menaces, sociétés secrètes, avril 1848-aout 1851, Département de l'Hérault") ADH, 39 M 132, and John Merriman, *The Margins of City Life: Explorations on the French Urban Frontier, 1815–1851* (Oxford, 1991), 113ff.

43. Martin, Proc. de la Rep. (St. Pons) to Proc. Gen. Roger, Reports of 2 and 3 May 1848, Montpellier, AN BB[30] 362.

44. The foregoing incidents were reported by the Procureur Général at Montpellier to Min. Justice on 16 May, 18 May, 31 May, and 25 June. AN, BB[30] 362.

45. Peter Amann, *Revolution and Mass Democracy: The Paris Club Movement in 1848* (Princeton, 1975), 326–27.

46. This was the conclusion of Atger's inaugural address of 17 March, quoted in Emile Appolis, "Un democrate social sous la Seconde République: Marcel Atger," *Actes du 87ᵉ Congrès nationale des sociétés savantes: Section d'histoire moderne et contemporaine* (Paris, 1963), 369–70. Emphasis added.

47. *Ibid,* 373.

48. *L'Indépendant* (8 June 1848).

49. Reports to Min. Guerre (extracts), 29 June 1848, AN, BB³⁰ 362.

50. *L'Indépendant,* 27 and 29 June, 4 and 7 July 1848.

51. Fabre, *Ma Vocation,* 6–7.

52. Proc. Gen. to Min. Justice, Letters of 20 and 29 July 1848, AN, BB³⁰ 362.

53. See above, p. 50.

54. Proc. Gen. to Min. Jus., 5 Aug. 1848, AN, BB³⁰ 362.

55. *Echo de Lodève,* 6 August 1848.

56. Election list in ACL, 2 D 82. In an 27 August letter from Paris, Jules André characterized the new group as "good and honorable citizens."

57. Hortala to the Prefect, 11 [July] 1848, ADH, 174 M 9.

58. See above, Ch. 1, n. 32 and Ch. 2, n. 1. See, on these elections, Robert Gély, "L'Industrie de laine à Bédarieux," 50–51.

59. *Ibid.,* 51; ADH, 16 M 5; *Echo de Lodève,* 10 September 1848. This kind of alliance was first used in the Second Republic and would be a socialist tactic during the Third. Royalism hardly gained by it.

60. ADH, 39 M 127, letter to Prefect, 29 July 1848.

61. *Ibid.,* Prefect to General of Line Division of Lnaguedoc, 30 September 1848.

62. *Ibid.,* Police commissar Nougaret to the Sous-Préfet, 20 October 1848. (Gély, in citing this, makes the date 20 September.)

63. ADH, 58 M 16 (Sociétés dissoutes), report of 14 February 1850, and 58 M 29 (Soc. demandées), letter from Belagou seeking authorization, 7 November 1848. Also, Gély, "L'Industrie," 53.

64. Margadant, *Peasants,* 142–46. Census of 1851, ADH, 115 M Bédarieux I, "Recapitulation générale" and nominative analysis.

65. ADH, 12 M 3 (Election results). Mayor Sicard to Sous-Préfet, 15 December 1848.

66. Jean-André Tudesq, "L'Election du Président de la République en 1848 dans l'Hérault," *Annales du Midi,* 67 (1955): 131–42.

67. Merriman, *The Agony of the Republic: The Repression of the Left in Revolutionary France 1848–1851* (New Haven, CT, 1978); Margadant, *Peasants* ch. 9; Loubère, *Radicalism,* ch. 3; Agulhon, *L'Apprentissage de la république* (Paris, 1973), ch. 4, and Roger Price, *The French Second Republic* (London, 1972), chs. 3–4.

68. Petition from "les honnêtes gens" of Limoux of 25 December 1848 and letter from Procureur de la République to Proc. Gen., 19 January 1849, AN, BB³⁰ 362.

69. *L'Indépendant* (October 1848), quoted in Appolis, "Catholiques sociaux," 302.

70. *Echo de Lodève,* 10 September 1848.

71. Judge de Paix to Prefect, 22 July 1848, ADH, 174 M 9.

72. ACL, 2 D 82.

73. Proc. Gen. to Min. Jus., 12 and 19 December 1848.

74. The entire speech was printed, with approval, by the *Echo de Lodève*, 10 December 1848.

75. Proc. Gen. (Gilardin) to Min. Jus. (Barrot), 22 May 1849, BB[30] 362.

76. Merriman, *Agony*, 130–34.

77. Adam to Proc. Gen., 19 May 1849 (AN, BB[30] 362) and election results, 13–14 May 1849, ADH, 15 M 9.

78. *Ibid.* and Listes nominative 1841 and 1851, ADH, 115 M Mons and Olargues.

79. Enclosure in report, Sous-Préfet (Béziers) to Prefect, 23 January 1849, ADH, 39 M 128; see Berenson, *Populist Religion*, 85–89, on the origins of la Solidarité républicaine.

80. Report of March 1849 (copy), AN, BB[30] 362.

81. Margadant, *Revolt*, chs. 6–8, provides the best overview of the mechanisms and processes of this phenomenon, first given its sharpest local analysis by Philippe Vigier in *La Seconde République dans la région alpine*, 2 vols. (Paris, 1963) and Agulhon in *La République au village* [Paris, 1970]).

82. ADH, 39 M 128. See also ACL, 2 D 82 (*Sociétés*).

83. Sous-préfet to Préfet, letters of 1, 2, 4 and 13 February 1849, ADH 39 M 129; 2 U[8b] 18, Procès de 13 Feb. 1849.

84. Adam to Gilardin, 27 February 1849 and Gilardin to Barrot, 23 March 1849, AN, BB[30] 362. Min. Int. Faucher to Gilardin, 14 March 1849, ADH, 39 M 129.

85. Adam to Gilardin, 27 February 1849, AN, BB[30] 362.

86. AN, BB[30] 362. Gilardin to Barrot, 23 April 1849. *Ibid.*

87. Adam to Gilardin, 20 March 1849 (a report separate from that on Paulhan, but the latter obviously was on his mind). *Ibid.*

88. Appolis, "Catholicisme sociaux," 303.

89. Commissaire Raynaud to Préfet, n.d., ADH, 15 M 9.

90. This is from the first detailed commissaire de police report of 22 May 1849. AN, BB[30] 362. Unless otherwise noted, all citations below are from the large dossier on the affair in this carton.

91. Gilardin to Barrot, 22 May 1849.

92. Gilardin to Barrot, 28 May 1849.

93. Reports of G. Pech, Juge d'Instruction (27 August 1849), and the Avocat General of Montpellier (4 September 1849).

94. Génie (A.G.) to Barrot, 22 Sept. and 4 Oct. 1849.

95. Dessauret to Rouher, 30 June 1850.

96. Even in death, Adam remained the enemy. A statue of him was planned for the city but never realized due to local opposition. ACL, 2 D 83: Rochet (sculptor) to Jourdan, 4 June 1849 and Martin (judge) to Jourdan, late June 1849.

97. For example: a major demonstration occurred in Montpellier on 19 May; the doors of the prefecture were broken down and calls for a new regime were lodged. Similar incidents occured in Bédarieux and Clermont. In the latter, a partial election for the municipal council in June produced six (out of six contested) new seats for "Socialists." Reports of 19 May (AN, BB[30] 362) and 26 June (ADH, 39 M 132), 1849.

98. "Emeutes, désordres graves, cris sédicieux, emblèmes sédicieux, menaces, violences, sociétés secrètes, avril 1848-aout 1851," provides a guide (ADH, 39 M 132). See also BB[30] 362: reports of 4, 15, 16 April 1850; BB[30] 380, Re-

ports of 31 January, 9 March, 11 April, 3 May, 14 October, 29 November, 30 December 1850; 9 April 1851. ADH, 39 M 128, report of 1 July 1850 (dog harassment); ACL, 2 D 84; 25 January 1850—troops of the line called out to control a charivari.

99. Etat des Emeutes, etc., nos. 82 (13 July 1850) and 113 (25 December 1850), ADH, 39 M 132.

100. ACL, 2 D 84.

101. Letter of 5 February 1850 from a Parisian manufacturer wishing to bid on its machinery. ACL, 2 F 6.

102. Margadant, *Peasants*, 252–54, 279–82.

103. AN BB[30] 362.

104. Sous-Préfet to Préfet, 14 February 1850, ADH, 58 M 16.

105. Reports of 20 September 1850, 15 March and 13 April 1851, ADH, 39 M 128; also 58 M 16.

106. Gély, "L'industrie de laine à Bédarieux," p. 70; ADH, 58 M 16 (on Miquel).

107. La Résistance au coup d'état du 2 décembre 1851 dans l'Hérault," *Actes du 77ᵉ Congrès des sociétés savantes, Grenoble, 1952* (Paris, 1952), 497–514, especially 504–13. This and Margadant have provided the main narrative of the events of 4 February.

108. Appolis, "La Résistance," 508.

109. *Echo de Lodève*, 11 Jan. 1852.

Part II

1. See especially correspondence relating to the appointment of local and departmental officials and to *notables* in general. ADH, 39 M 220 and 221.

2. For the Granier *faillite* see ADH, 2 U Faillites Lodève, non-classés; Jean Bouvier, *La Naissance d'une banque: le Crédit lyonnais* (Paris, 1986).

3. An, Fᶜ III Hérault 9.

4. Gramsci suggests this analysis in his prison notebooks but reserves any detail for the bourgeois regime in Russia in the age of the Dumas.

5. Gordon, *Merchants and Capitalists*, 118–59.

6. Space does not permit detailed examination of the political and economic twists and turns of the 1850s, summarized in the previous paragraph. Aspects of this history will be treated in the following chapters, of course. Documentation is quite voluminous. The key A.N. cartons are Fᶜ III Hérault 9 and 15, which contain both sub-prefect to prefect reports and reports from both to the Ministers of the Interior. The main documents are the following (A.N. carton number in parentheses): Prefect Durand St. Amand to Min. Int., 1 January 1853 (9); S.P. Alazard to Durand, 1 November 1852 (9); S.P. de Vésins to Prefects, 1 November and 29 December 1852, 1 January, 1 March, and 1 July 1853 (9), 30 June, 2 and 8 November 1854 (15), 1 July 1855 (15), April 1857 (15), 29 March and 8 July, 1858 (15); Prefect's reports of Oct. 10 and 31 October 1856 (9) and 2 December 1857 (15); January 1859 (9); S.P. of Béziers to Prefect, 27 April 1859 (9). See also AN, BB18 362; *Echo de Lodève*, 1 January 1853; and ACL, 7F1 (Dos. Prix de vente en detail).

7. Fᶜ III Hérault 15, sub-prefect reports, Lodève and Béziers, 29 March 1858.

Chapter 6

1. Robert Locke, *Les Fonderies et forges d'Alais* (Paris, 1978), 16ff. On the other areas see Pierre Guillaume, *La Compagnie des mines de la Loire, 1836–1854* (Paris 1965); Michael Hanagan, *The Logic of Solidarity* (Illinois, 1980); Reid, *The Miners of Decazeville*; Trempé, *Les Mineurs de Carmaux*; Joan Wallach Scott, *The Glassworkers of Carmaux* (Cambridge, Mass., 1974).

2. Locke, *Les Fonderies*, 33ff; Scott, *Glassworkers*, 73ff; Reid, *Miners*, 114ff; J.M. Gaillard, "La Compagnie des Mines de la Grande-Combe," in *Mines et Mineurs en Languedoc-Roussillon* (Montpellier, 1977), 191–93.

3. ADH, 39 M 107.

4. See Christopher H. Johnson, "The Revolution of 1830 in French Economic History," in John M. Merriman, *1830 in France* (New York, 1975), 171ff.

5. Thibaud/Bonnard, "Rapport," 24 April 1834 (103 pp.), A.N. F[14] 7692. See also Bayle, Fanjaud et Cie, *Demandeurs en Concession des Mines de Houille de St. Geniès de Varensal (Hérault)* (Paris, 1834), in F[14] 7699; also F[14] 7704 for Thibaud's further correspondence.

6. Lodève manufacturers did, too. In a failed bid for a concession in 1844, René Fournier joined two proprietors with former Lodève connections. AN, F[14] 7699.

7. Fabre, *Ma Vocation*, 8–9, 4–5.

8. Tableau des produits de exploitation des 4 Concessions de Houille depuis 1811 jusqu'en 1832," AN, F[14] 7699.

9. "Rapport." See also dossier St. Gervais, AN, F[14] 7699; Bernard, Avocat, *Résumé des mémoires et observations des héritiers Delzeuzes* (Montpellier, n.d.), 9, in F[14] 7699, and "Rapport de l'ingenieur ordinaire" (c. 1827) Castenet-le-Haut, F[14] 7698.

10. Papiers Simon, ADH, 6 J 12 (Mines de Fer de Maurian), 6 J 13 (Mines à cuivre) and 6 J 14 (zinc) and 6 J 15 (Verrerie, Le Bousquet).

11. Napoleon Garella summed them up in his report of 1843 (below, note 15); also, ADH, 2 S 1687.

12. Chef de la division chemin de fer au Ministre des Travaux publiques (Min. T.P.), n.d (1842), AN, F[14] 9268.

13. AN, F[14] 8230. Retrospective report by the Directeur du Bureau des Mines to Min. T.P., April 1863); and ADH, 8 S 98 (Usquin to Préfet de l'Hérault (PH), 21 April 1845, and following official correspondence).

14. Garella, *Etude du Bassin houiller de Graissessac (Hérault) jusqu'a en 1834* (Paris, 1843); 27–31, 62.

15. Garella, 87; "Rampe d'access à la route départementale pour l'exploitation de la mine no 5 situé au Bousquet," ADH, 2 S 1687.

16. Garella, 99.

17. Garella, 102–103; Report of 1852 (no exact date given) by Dupont, then mine engineer for Alais, ADH 2 S 98.

18. Simon to the Prefect of the Hérault, 2 July 1850, 22 and 31 May and 12 December 1851, ADH 2 S 98.

19. Report from the Maritime Prefect to the Min. T.P. included in a general report of 13 July 1852, AN, F[14] 9268.

20. Correspondence from Carteret and Graissessac company (Simon) to Min. T.P., 15 and 17 March, 24 April 1852.

21. *Compagnie des chemins de fer du Midi. Statuts* (Paris, 1852) in AN, 78 AQ 6. The Béziers-Graissessac *Statuts* were found in ADH, 5 S 36.

22. Acte de 26 fevrier 1853 Mᶜ Olangier, notaire, Paris, ADH 5 S 236.

23. Both (and much more) were revealed in later official correspondence as the company got into deeper and deeper trouble. See below, p. 165–66.

24. ADH, 6 J 6.

25. See David Cohen, *La Promotion des Juifs en France à l'époque du Second Empire*, 2 vols. (Aix-en Provence, 1980).

26. See Nancy Green, *The Pletzl of Paris* (New York, 1986), 68–78.

27. Carteret to Prefect to Min. T.P. (25 June 1853), AN, F¹⁴ 9268.

28. *Extraits de correspondance pour MM Moulinier et autres contre M. Boucaruc* (Montpellier, n.d.), in ADH, 2 S 98. *Echo de Lodève* (November 1853).

29. Things had been delayed also by the company's reluctance to pay the government engineers associated with the project, a normal—and often abused—condition. See correspondence between Boucaruc and the Prefect, 17 June 1853–18 January 1854 in ADH 5 S 236.

30. See François Caron, *Histoire de l'exploitation d'un grand reseau: La Compagnie du Chemin de fer du Nord (1846–1937)* (Paris, 1973).

31. Juge de paix (Béziers) to Sub-Prefect (Béziers), 11 November 1854; Sub-Prefect to Prefect, 24 November 1854; Report of P. Grillan, Com. de Police (Bédarieux) to Sub-Prefect, 25 November 1854; Léon, Report to Min. T.P. (on regulating pay procedures, or rather not doing so), 28 November 1854—copy to Prefect; de l'Espine (Board Chairman, Cⁱᵉ de Graissessac-Béziers), 1 December 1854; Report, Gendarmerie, Sub-Prefect to Prefect, 5 and 7 December 1854; Letters from Prefects of Nièvre, Puy de Dome and Allier to Prefect (Hérault), 12–14 December 1854; background to arreté de mise en demeure: Dubois (Rail Division Director, Public Works) to Prefect, 26 December 1854; Léon to Prefect, 16 February 1855; Arreté, 19 February 1855; Sub-Prefect to Prefect, 19 February 1855; André Gauze, foreman, to Prefect, 25 February 1855; François Combes to Prefect, n.d.; the Gandell bankruptcy: Sub-Prefect to Prefect, 30 June 1855; Gandell to Sub-Prefect, 29 June 1855; Gendarme report, 25 June 1855; Engineer Kauffmann to Sub-Prefect and return 4 July 1855; Franqueville (now Director of Railroads) to Prefect, advising the employés to go to court, 25 July 1855. All ADH, 5 S 236. Gandell finances detailed, Min. T.P. (Magne) to Joseph Orsi (six-page letter) 31 January 1855 sent first to Dubois (Note: "examine with care and return to me"); Prefect to Min. T.P., letter of June-July, 1855. Finally, we must record the words written on 9 July 1855, by Léon, the Chief Engineer in Public Works, on the subject of the Gandell *employés*: "L'Administration ne peut pas attacher la même importance au paiement exact des employés qu' à celui des ouvriers, car les retards de paiement n'offrent pas, dans les deux cas, les memes dangers pour la tranquilité publique." Ah, the plight of the petite bourgeoisie! All in AN F¹⁴ 9268.

32. AN, F¹⁴ 9268, especially *Première Assemblée générale des actionnaires de la Société anonyme du chemin de fer de Béziers à Graissessac: Rapport aux actionnaires* (Paris, 3 Février 1854); Dubois, Directeur général des Chemins de Fer to Min. T.P., 30 January 1855; Min. T.P. to Joseph Orsi, 31 January 1855 (and *pièces justificatrices*); and "Etat de la situation de MM Gandell Frères jusqu'au 31 October 1854.

33. See his report of 1851 on the Béziers-Graissessac via the Orb valley in ADH, 2 S 98.

34. A point made by Boucaruc in a letter to Min. T.P., 26 June 1855, AN, F[14] 9268.

35. F[14] 9268—copies of Kauffman and Magne letters to Boucaruc.

36. 10 March 1859, F[14] 9268.

37. Report of 12 January 1857, 5 S 236.

38. Sub-Prefect (Le Massy), Béziers to Prefect, letters of 9–11, 13, 15, 28 June, 7, 21, 27 July, 28, 31 October 1857. Giacoletti to Commissaire de Police (Special) 27 July 1857, all 5 S 236. On the image of the people of the upper Orb, Inspector Couret wrote (10 March 1859) to his Minister: "In this half-savage country, the agents show the passengers a kind and polite attention nearly unknown."

39. Cordoën's letter, Rouher's response (27 January 1858), complaints from shareholders, the first Boucaruc trial summary (18 May 1859), followed by a series of reports by Thouret, the Chief Financial Inspector for the Railroad Division of Public Works, 7 June–12 August 1859, all deal with the Boucaric affair, AN, F[14] 9268. 1867 trial record in ADH, 5 S 236.

40. The last is from the Annual Report to the stockholders of 26 March 1858, ADH, 5 S 236.

41. A leader of the shareholder's rebellion (copy) to Rouher "in November 1857." AN, F[14] 9268.

42. ADH, 5 S 236, letter dated 19 April 1858.

43. This meant that the sequester officer in Montpellier, Chaperon, would be all the harsher with small claims that did not go to court. See his treatment of the claim of Jacquinot, a worker, for Fr 150 (1 October 1858), ADH 5 S 236.

44. See below, pp. 186–193.

45. Report of 18 October 1861; the foregoing narrative is drawn from twenty-eight detailed reports by Thouret, 7 June 1859–28 May 1862; intermixed are other papers, especially petitions, sent to Rouher. AN, F[14] 6298.

46. The Director of Mines to Min. T.P., 12 April 1865, S.A. application, F[14] 8230.

47. La Tour Concession application, 1846, Moulinier Dossier, F[14] 7702.

48. ADH, 2 S 98.

49. Simon to Prefect, 12 December 1851, ADH, 2 S 98.

50. Simon to Prefect, 31 May 1851; Mayor of Camplong to Prefect, 14 March; Prefect to Sub-Prefect, Béziers, 24 March 1853; ADH 2 S 98.

51. Correspondence of 1858, 1869, and 1870 on these issues, *ibid.*

52. It was he who attempted to excuse early indiscriminate waste disposal by emphasizing "stronger and stronger competitors . . . from the mines of Alais, Bessèges, and Carmaux." (Simon to Prefect, 22 May 1851, ADH 2 S 98.)

53. Com. Pol. Béd. to Prefect, 14 June 1858, ADH, Subprefect (Béziers) to Prefect, 18 July 1855, ADH, 39 M 230; Thourel to Min. T.P., 23 June 1863, AN, F[14] 6298.

54. Report of F. Carrière 24 June 1858, ADH, 2 S 98.

55. F[14] 8234 (dos Hérault) March 1862.

56. On the first Assembly, ADH, 6 J 12; on improvements, 2 S 98.

57. Adapted from E. Gruner, *Atlas du Comité central des houillères de France* (Paris, 1893).

58. AN, 78 AQ 6 (Report, 1866). On the trials of the Pereires in this era, see Rondo Cameron, *France and the Economic Development of Europe* (Princeton, 1961), 192ff.

59. Jules Maîstre, Membre de la Chambre de Commerce de Montpellier, "Rapport," Euquête sur les houilles, AN, C 3100 (Hérault), 1874.

Chapter 7

1. See, above all, Cameron, *France*, 214ff.

2. Le Baron Ernouf, *Paulin Talabot, sa vie et son oeuvre* (Paris 1886).

3. Marcel Blanchard, "La politique montpelliéraine des chemins de fer," *Essais historiques sur les premiers chemins de fer du Midi languedocien et de la vallée du Rhône* (Montpellier, 1935), 215.

4. Louis Girard, "L'Affaire du chemin de fer Cette-Marseille (1861–63)" (unpublished these complémentaire du doctorat d'etat, 1949 Bibliothèque Nationale).

5. Emile Pereire, *Rapport du Conseil d'Administration a l'Assemblé générale des actionnaires* (Paris, 1862), 40–41; and *ibid.* (Paris, 1861), 44, AN, 78 AQ 6.

6. Girard, "L'Affaire," 42. And see below, p. 181 ff.

7. Girard, "L'Affaire," 26. On the general background of local developments, Prefect (Gard) to Min. T.P., 4 March 1859. AN, F^{14} 9054.

8. This became an issue in the Corps legislatif in July 1856. The Préfet de Police, Piétri, to Rouher, 10 July 1856 and Rouher to Napoleon III, 11 July 1856, AN, 45 AP (Papiers Rouher) 5. Also Emile Pereire to Napoleon III, 21 July 1856 complaining about Rothschild attacks on his company, 45 AP 3.

9. "Voeux du Conseil Municipal de 14 Mars 1857" (Lodève), AN F^{14} 9049. Most of the materials of the publicity mills of both sides are to be found in this fat carton, which, along with F^{14} 9050 through 9055, hold the bulk of the documentation collected by the government.

10. Although a road was finally built in the late nineteenth century along the "Pas de l'Escalette," only in the late 1970s, well after my research was underway, was it modernized, allowing rapid auto and truck travel up to the open land above.

11. Duviol, agent-voyer de l'Arrondissement, "Mémoire déscriptif à l'appui de l'avant-projet d'un chemin de fer de Montpellier à Rodez en passant par la ville de Lodève, 24 avril 1858" contains all the basic information. AN, F^{14} 9050. The Duponchel report is also included here.

12. F. Chalmeton, *Nôte sur les houillères du Gard* (Nîmes, 1866), 3–4.

13. H. Peut, *Des Chemins de fer et des tarifs differentiels* (Paris, 1858), 3–6.

14. M. Tardy, "Chemin de fer de Montpellier à Rodez: Rapport de l'Ingénieur en chef," Montpellier, 29 July 1858. AN, F^{14} 9050.

15. Undated letter with the mass of petitions and letters, 1857–58, from Lodève, AN, F^{14} 9049.

16. *Ibid.*

17. See the technical report on the "chemin de fer de Nîmes à Rodez" in F^{12} 9050.

18. Piétri was a confidante of the Emperor's and a key figure in Second Empire history. See *Le Dictionnaire de biographie nationale.*

19. "La géographie des chemins de fer en France," *La Pensée géographique* ed., M. Denis (Paris, 1966), 587–602.

20. *Voeu du conseil municipal de la ville de Cette en faveur du Chemin direct de Rodez à la Méditerranée* (Montpellier 1861) [meeting date: 23 September 1861], 30. See also on past antagonism, Dermigny, *Sète*, 111–13.

21. Both documents in AN, F^{14} 9049.

22. AN, F¹⁴ 9049. All the letters and petitions and clippings may be found there. For the later construction, see F¹⁴ 9052.

23. Prefect Piétri (Hérault), quoting the Hérault Committee, to Rouher, 12 April 1862; Emile Pereire to Rouher (undated, but later in 1862); Commission d'enquete de l'Aveyron, *Chemin de fer de Rodez à la Méditerranée, Procès verbal de la séance du 6 mars, 1862* (Rodez, 1862), 25, 27 [Peut's address to them is quoted extensively]. On the question of the PLM's actual disinterest in the Millau-Nîmes, an earlier brochure by Peut (27, January 1862, same carton) laid it out very clearly. AN, F¹⁴ 9049.

24. Talabot, *Rapport du Conseil d'Administration à l'Assemblé générale du 24 avril 1862* (Paris, 1864), 45ff. AN, 77 AQ [Compagnie du chemin de fer de PLM] 158. My emphasis.

25. Rouher's report was included (logically) in the papers of the PLM for this period and quoted joyously in Talabot's *Rapport* to the shareholders, 26 May 1863 (Paris, 1863). 77 AQ 158.

26. Lataud to Simon, July 1863, ADH, 6 J 12.

27. F¹⁴ 9255 and 78 AQ 14, *Rapport* (E. Pereire), 16 Mai 1862.

28. Talabot, *Rapport* (1863), 77 AQ 158.

29. See, for example, Phyllis Deane, "The Role of Government," in *The First Industrial Revolution* (Cambridge, 1965); Robert A. Lively, "The American System," *The Business History Review* (1955); and Carter Goodrich, *Government Promotion of American Canals and Railroads, 1800–1890* (New York, 1960). In France, there was considerable tension in the ministries between control for administrative purposes and promotion for economic growth, one that can also be seen under the Old Regime. But the impetus from progress conscious engineers, especially, often gave the nod to the latter. Unfortunately, state officials were not immune to pressure to support monopoly in the name of "bon ordre." See Yves Leclerc, *Le Reseau impossible, 1820–1852* (Geneva, 1987) and Christopher H. Johnson, "The Revolution of 1830 in French Economic History" in *1830 in France*, ed. J. Merriman; also see the interesting overview of Pierre Rosanvallon, *L'Etat en France de 1789 à nos jours* (Paris, 1990), 199–225.

30. David Pinckney, *Napoleon III and the Rebuilding of Paris* (Princeton, 1972), 197–205.

31. Arthur Louis Dunham, *The Anglo-French Treaty of Commerce of 1860* (Ann Arbor, Michigan, 1930), 57ff.

32. Chevalier to Rouher, 4 May 1862, AN, 45 AP 3.

33. Charles de Franqueville, *Souvenirs sur la vie de mon père* (Paris 1873), 252–54.

34. *Ibid.*, 251ff.; Gustave Noblemaire, "La vie et les travaux de M. Charles Didion (Mai 1883)," in *Hommes et choses de chemin de fer* (Paris 1905), especially 17ff.; Ernouf, *Talabot*, 30–35, 160ff.; AP, 45 AP 3, Bartholony to Rouher, letters of 1862 especially.

35. See above, p. 182.

36. Franqueville, *Souvenirs*, 256–7.

37. *Ibid.*, 255–60.

38. *Rapport sur les chemins de fer d'interêt local au Conseil général de l'Hérault* (Montpellier, 1873), 7.

39. See the *Journal de Montpellier* and the *Echo de Lodève*, May 1862–August 1863.

40. Various reports and correspondence 26 March 1862–30 April 1864 in AN, F¹⁴ 9255.

41. The petition and related materials (including copies of most of the reports relating to Lodève) are in ADH, 5 S 443. I was unable to ascertain what happened to the petition in Paris.

42. Reports from Rabieux (applying for a freight station) on the situation of the Agde-Lodève 1873–1874. In AN, F¹⁴ 9255.

Chapter 8

1. Jean Mercadier, socialist mayor of Lodève, wrote a glowing brochure, in which Chevalier's life and death at Montplaisir are viewed as a sort of Saint-Simonian fulfillment, *Michel Chevalier, 1806–1879: Promoteur du tunnel sous la Manche et du persement de l'Isthme de Panama* (n.d., n.p.). As noted, neither Walch nor Dunham seemed aware of these events. Paul Leroy-Beaulieu married Chevalier's daughter and their descendants still have an estate in the area. Leroy-Beaulieu himself, however, lived under the cloud of Chevalier's action. An attack on his father-in-law hurt his electoral chances in 1890. "Les ouvriers de Lodève et M. Leroy-Beaulieu," *L'Indépendant* (13 April 1890). Clipping and related materials, A.N. C 5507.

2. Min. Guerre to Prefect 30 April 1863, AN, Fˡᶜ III Hérault 15; Min. Guerre to Min. Int., 25 Aug. 1868, *ibid.*, Maine et Loire 12, presents the general policy promoting the "development of competition."

3. Letter, Subprefect to Mayor, 16 December 1861; Min. Int. to Prefect, 21 January 1862; Rouquet et al to Mayor of Lodève, 31 October 1863. ACL, 2 F 5.

4. Lodève's waters were subject to significant seasonal variations.

5. AN, F¹⁴ 6135 (Lergue, Lodève), Arrêté préfectoriale of 23 August 1855.

6. The transition to steam is a measure of industrial progress, but there were many places where steam engines were not needed for a long time because of the efficiency of water power. See, for example, Tamara Haraven and Randolph Langenbach, *Amoskeag: Life and Work in an American Factory City* (New York, 1978). More important, steam engines were used only as a partial motive force until they generated greater horsepower.

7. See petitions (AN, F¹⁴ 9049) and *Echo de Lodève*, 1857–1862 relating to the rail issue (above, p. 181 ff).

8. Copy (as an electoral flyer against Leroy-Beaulieu, 13 April 1890) in AN, C 5507. Also letters and telegrams, 5–26 May 1865, among the Prefect, Min. War, Min. Int., Sub-Prefect of Lodève, and Mayor Teisserenc provide the essential public information. Teisserenc only hints at Chevalier's chicanery in his official report of 26 May. All in ADH, 194 M 2.

9. A flurry of dispatches on 5–8 May 1865 show their concern, ADH, 194 M 2.

10. The story is from Teisserenc's mémoire, but official correspondence corroborated Teisserenc's visit and a dozen copies of the crucial telegram are in the archival dossier concerning the matter. ADH, 194 M 2.

11. Rapport de M. Hugounenc, Extrait des régistres des déliberations du Conseil municipal de Lodève, 19 juin 1868," ADH, 194 M 2.

12. Petition of Summer 1870 (undated) signed by sixteen owners of riverside businesses and land, ADH, 7 S 207, and the other related documents.

13. Dugrand, *Villes et campagnes*, 399, 400, 402ff. Fohlen "En Languedoc," 290–97.

14. For the ranking, see F. Morin, E. Wattez, E. Cohen, "Qui possède les 200 premières enterprises françaises?" *Science et Vie: Economie* (July–August 1987): 43–72 (52).

15. C. St. Pierre, *L'Industrie du département de l'Hérault: Etudes scientifiques, économiques et statistiques* (Montpellier, 1865), 184–87.

16. Gordon, *Merchants and Capitalists*, 62. Power looms were skyrocketing in numbers in the 1860s, going from 500 in 1861 to 4000 in 1870.

17. Dugrand, *Villes et campagnes*, 399; St. Pierre, *L'Industrie*, 8. As regards spinning, Dugrand gives the mysterious figure of forty spindles per machine, which could only be a figure derived by including all hand-jennies and spinning wheels, which were no longer employed at all in Lodève in production other than for thread purchased by hand-loom weavers attempting to survive in direct sales to consumers in the area. Dugrand does not cite a source.

18. ACL, 2 F 5—*enquête* of 1862. St. Pierre offers an excellent set of tables (214–15) that demonstrate the continuing power of the Hérault woolens industry, which has a total output in 1864 of Fr 18,042,000 (Lodève, 6,970,000).

19. Dugrand cites an apparent 1865 printing of Armand Audiganne's *Les Populations ouvrières et les industries de la France*. Audiganne's studies were in fact made in the early 1850s and largely published in the *Revue de deux mondes* and first printed in book form in 1854. A second edition (which I have used) appeared in 1860 (Volume II). Besides a wealth of information of workers' conditions of life and work, attitudes, and values, Audiganne also rendered judgments about the potential of the various regions and industries he studied. Much of it was rather impressionistic, but there was nothing disparaging about his remarks on Languedoc woolens (contrary to what Dugrand implies). Instead, he predicted (incorrectly for the most part as it turned out) that if woolens manufacturers continued to produce "*à bon marché*" but with "solidité" and employ labor-saving machinery where possible, "sur son terrain, avec la main d'oeuvre à bon prix, avec les forces hydroliques que lui offre liberalement la nature, la draperie du pays est à peu près invincible." Audiganne, *Les Populations*, 1860 ed., II, 230.

20. St. Pierre, *L'Industrie*, 28. Dugrand, *Villes et campagnes*, 399.

21. Hector Teisserenc, *L'Industrie lainière de Lodève* (Paris, 1908); Marres, "Le Lodévois" (part 2), *Bulletin de la Socété languedocienne de géographie* (1924), 166.

22. See note 18 above, table.

23. See Robert Mandel, "André Godin and the Familistère de Guise, 1817–1888" (unpublished Ph.D. diss. University of Toronto, 1978).

24. One may still examine the essential layout of the village. Plans of the nineteenth-century project are located in Papiers Maistre-Villeneuvette, ADH, Serie J.

25. St. Pierre, *L'Industrie*, 200–02.

26. See above all, Cazals, *Les Révolutions industrielles à Mazamet*, 165–74. Also Audiganne, *Les Populations*, II, 187–88; André David, *La Montagne noire: essai de monographie géographique* (Carcassonne, 1924), ch. 5; E. Cormouls-Houlès, *Mazamet en 1930: un centre d'activité économique du midi de la France* (Paris and Toulouse, 1931); Gaston Mercier, "Le Développement industriel et commercial de Mazamet," *Mémoires de la section des lettres, Académie des sciences et lettres de Montpellier*, 2ᵉ Series, V (Montpellier, 1912), 71–92.

27. Audiganne, *Les Populations*, II, 196–201; Cazals, *Les Revolutions*, 146–61; A.D. Tarn, IV M² 32, 44 and 46.

28. Cazals, *Avec les ouvriers de Mazamet dans la grève et l'action quotidienne, 1909–1914* (Paris, 1979).

29. The key families in Mazamet (Houlès, Olembel, Bénézech, Boudou, Gau, Puech, Rives, etc.) of the eighteenth century were those of the nineteenth. Also, see Devic, *Vallée du Jaur*.

30. The Clermont Chamber laments the passing of grain production and attributes the triumph of the vine partly to climatic changes.

31. Thomson, *Clermont*, 412–19 (Flottes); the following Lodève manufacturing families had known roots in Clermont: Ménard, Fraisse, Marréaud, Rouquet, Delpon, Palouzie, and Arribat. They were not the most important (with the exception of the Ménard), however.

32. Chambre de Commerce de Clermont l'Hérault, "Mémoire sur la décadence de l'industrie du Midi," 4 Mars 1871, AN, F¹² 4506.

33. C. H. Refrégier, "Démographie et économie à Bédarieux, 1831–72," Mémoire de maitrise (Gustav Laurent), Université de Montpellier, 1977.

34. Refrégier, Tables B-4 and B-9. Age pyramids, tables A-5, A-6.

35. See above, p. 48, for contacts between them and its significance in the boom years of the July Monarchy.

36. See, for example, the response to their petition of October 1862 in F¹ᶜ III Hérault 15.

37. Audiganne, *Populations ouvrières*; ADH 109 M 24.

38. Refrégier, Table 33.

39. Faillite de Gaston, Cadet, née Cavaillé, filateur, 1858–59 ADH 2 U⁴⁷ 148.

40. Mutations par decès—Bédarieux, ADH, 6 Q³ 18 (4 mars 1858–10 mai 1860).

41. ADH, 6 Q³ 13–23.

42. AN, F¹² 6804.

43. The essential sources: a fat dossier entitled "Situation de l'industrie drapière à Lodève à la suite de la suppression de l'epoutiage [sic] à la main" (August 1868–March 1869), ADH, 194 M 2, and ACL, 2 F 5 (diverse correspondence, 1866–70).

44. Various comments about éffilochage appear in both the collections cited in footnote 43 above. The sorting of scraps by quality and color required considerable labor and helped some in providing jobs for women. By 1873, 125 were at work in this industry, largely in two main firms (AN, F¹² 4506). See also Fulcran Teisserenc, *L'Industrie lainière dans l'Hérault* (Paris, 1908), B.N. 8⁰ F 20093), 123–24.

45. See 1875 correspondence from Puech, Fournier et Vallat—the company so badly burned in the Barbot-Fournier pullout—pleading with a contractor in Paris for more time on delivery owing to a flood of the Lergue, ACL, 2 F 5.

46. A separate analysis of age and causes of death reveals this ironic fact. Just when medical practice begins to have an impact on averting the tragedy of child death, the local economy fell apart. Annual statistics in ACL, 1 F 7.

47. ADH, 115 M. Lodève, 1851 and 1872; ACL, 1 F 2, recensement de l'An VI. Marriage records examined for the years 1866–72 show the collapse of migration to Lodève by woolens workers; 90 percent of all marriages were among natives of the city and nearby villages. See C. H. Johnson, "Marriage patterns and Industrial Decline, Lodève 1866–72" (unpublished paper available upon request).

48. In general, although infant and child death, and for males, the toll of the First World War, account for many of the missing (and foreign emigration for a handful), the failures to report and common-law marriages unquestionably take up a substantial number. Still, the large majority (70 percent) of women among the 155 post–1945 "death only" contingent underlines the magnitude of France's loss of men from this generation in the war.

49. Second marriages in Lodève were too few to be meaningful, five men and four women, one each of whom also figure in the death elsewhere total recorded here.

50. Marres, *Les Grandes causses*, vol. II.

51. See below, ch. 9, n. 31.

52. Mahfoud Bennoune, *The Making of Contemporary Algeria, 1830–1987* (Cambridge, 1988), 43ff.

53. Dugrand, *Villes et campagnes*, 9ff.

54. My thanks to the Boisse de Black family of Pégairolles for sharing their genealogical knowledge and sources with me—along with their wonderful hospitality.

55. This was not entirely the case, of course, since *other* woolens towns bought thread from Lodève and Lodève itself increasingly imported its soap and dyes, formerly produced locally and often within the woolens firms.

56. Alain Cottereau, "The Distinctiveness of Working-Class Cultures in France, 1848–1900," in *Working-Class Formation* ed. Ira Katznelson and Aristide Zolberg (Princeton, 1986), 111–154.

57. Liu, *The Weavers Knot*; Walton, "Working Women, Gender, and Industrialization in Nineteenth-Century France: The Case of Lorraine Embroidery Manufacturing," *Journal of Women's History*, 2:2(Fall 1990): 42–65; Gullickson, *Spinners and Weavers*.

58. Rapport de M. Hugounenq, 19 juin 1868, Conseil municipal de Lodève, ADH 194 M 2.

59. On the latter, see ACL, 2 F 7, petition dated 14 November 1871.

60. Letter of 8 February 1871, Guesde Collection, 14/2, Internationaal Instituut voor Sociale Geschiedenis. My thanks to Bernard Rulof for sending me this citation.

61. See below, pp. 237–239.

62. *Enquête sur l'état des industries textiles* (November 1903–December 1904), A.N. C 7318: "Rapport de M. Vincent Vitalis" (n.d.).

63. Paul Clavel, *Regions, nations, grands espaces: geographie générale des ensembles territoriaux* (Paris, 1968), 409.

Chapter 9

1. See Johnson, "Mons-la-Trivalle," Forthcoming.

2. Alain Berger and Frédéric Maurel, *La Viticulture et l'économie du Languedoc du XVIIIe siècle à nos jours* (Montpellier, 1980), 43–44.

3. Loubère, *Radicalism*, 96ff. Raymond Huard, *Le Mouvement républicain en Bas-Languedoc, 1848–1881* (Paris, 1982), *passim*.

4. Leslie Moch, *Paths to the City: Regional Migration in Nineteenth-Century France* (Beverly Hills, Cal., 1983).

5. Huard, *Le Mouvement*, 403–29.

6. This is not to say that cross-class "regionalism" could not be useful to workers in struggle. See Reid, *The Miners of Decazeville*, 205–6.

7. Economists Berger and Maurel, *La Viticulture*, (1980) provide an excellent picture of the process. The following figures are drawn from their compilations, 128–39, especially charts, 133–35. See also, Dugrand, *Villes et campagnes*.

8. Dermigny, *Sète*, 111–26.

9. A. Solier, "Contribution à l'analyse des disparités démographiques intra-régionales: l'arrière-pays languedocienne," *Economie méridional*, 92 (1975).

10. Berger and Maurel, *La Viticulture*, 54ff.; and, above all, Rémy Pech, *Entreprise viticole et captalisme en Languedoc-Roussillon du phyloxera aux crises de mévente* (Toulouse, 1975).

11. "[T]he old maxim 'iron ore moves to coal' was undoubtedly true for most of the nineteenth century because of the very large quantities of coal used in production." R.C. Estall and R.O. Buchanan, *Industrial Activity and Economic Geography* (London, 1980), 228.

12. Reid, *The Miners of Decazeville*; J.M. Gaillard, "Un example français de ville-usine: La Grand-Combe, 1836–1921" (Thèse, 3ᵉ cycle). For an excellent overview and critique of this regional concentration, see Ann Wendy Mill, "French steel and metal-working industries: a contribution to the debate on economic development in nineteenth-century France," *Social Science History*, 9, 3 (1985): 307–38.

13. Scott, *Glassworkers*, 81, notes the temporary impact, however.

14. ADH 6 J 6 (statutes) and 6 J 10 (Simon-Usquin correspondence).

15. Reid, *The Miners of Decazeville*, ch, 3; Gaillard, "La crise économique et sociale dans le bassin houiller d'Alès à la fin du XIXᵉ siecle," in *Mines et mineurs*, 211–21; Scott, *Glassworkers*, 72ff.; ADH 6 J 6, "Observations sur la marché de charbon," anon. (possibly Simon or his lawyer), 1895.

16. AN F¹² 6804, "Cⁱᵉ de Quatre mines réunies de Graissessac—transformation en Société libre par le décret du 25 septembre 1894." *Rapport de M. Kuhnholtz-Lordat du 15 janvier 1894 à l'Assemblée extraordinaire des actionnaries* (Montpellier). This document and supporting materials, along with the documents retained by Simon for his own protection (ADH, 6 J 6), provide most of the information on the perspective and goals of the company in the early 1890s. It was upon the close reading of these materials that I developed the general analysis offered in this section.

17. ADH, 194 M 7, "Table arrivée le 21 juin 1894." See also the "bilan de bénéfices" generated internally and not submitted in 1894, which was located in the dossier cited in note 16 (AN F¹² 6804).

18. See Christopher H. Johnson, "Union-Busting at Graissessac: De-industrialization, Employer Strategies, and the Strike of 1894 in the Hérault Coal Basin," *Journal of Social History*, 19 (Winter 1985): 241–260.

19. Graissessac experienced a number of isolated incidents and one great disaster during its period of greatest growth. On the fire-damp explosion that claimed forty-five lives in the Ste. Barbe pits (14 February 1877), see Jean Tuffou, *Vivre en pays minier de 1870 à 1940* (Bédarieux, 1988), a marvelous photographic essay on the basin, 65–66.

20. On the process, see particularly David Gordon, Richard Edwards, and Michael Reich, *Segmented Work, Divided Workers: the Historical Transformation of Labor in the United States* (New York 1979), especially chapters 3 and 4; Alfred

Chandler, *The Visible Hand* (Cambridge, Mass, 1977), 207–314; David Montgomery, *Workers Control in America* (New York, 1979); Harry Braverman, *Labor and Monopoly Capital* (New York, 1974), 85–152; and Michelle Perrot, "The Three Ages of Industrial Discipline in Nineteenth-Century France," in *Consciousness and Class Experience in Nineteenth-Century Europe* ed. J. Merriman (New York, 1979), 149–168.

21. These dates refer to the moments when the first significant moves toward organization began. Even in 1886 at Décazeville, for instance, only 175 miners were union members.

22. See Susanna Barrows, *Distorting Mirrors: Visions of the Crowd in Late Nineteenth-Century France* (New Haven, 1981), ch 1, for a brilliant overview of the specter of the mob in the mind of bourgeois France.

23. ADH, 115 M Graissessac, 1851.

24. For details, see Johnson, "Union-Busting," 247–48.

25. ADH 194 M 7, "Rapport Sommaire" and *Le Petit Méridionel*, 17 May 1894 for the formation of the women's auxilliary.

26. Rapport et table, 21 June 1894, Compagnie to Prefect, ADH 194 M 7.

27. AN, F^{12} 6804.

28. ADH, 194 M 10 (report) and Jean Sanges' excellent analysis, *Le Mouvement ouvrier en Languedoc* (Toulouse, 1980), 251–2.

29. ADH, 115 M Graissessac, 1926; ADH, 194 M 18, 25, AN F^{12} 6804.

30. ADH, 194 M 36, letter of 3 April 1920.

31. Harvey Smith, "Phylloxera and Household Economy: Wine Estates and Petty Producers in Bas-Languedoc, 1870–1900" (paper presented at the Social Science History Association meeting in New Orleans, La. October 1987 [full version 81 pp.]) M. Augé-Laribé, *La Révolution agricole* (Paris, 1950).

32. Pech, *Entreprise viticole, passim*; Laura Frader, *Peasants and Protest: Agricultural Workers, Politics, and Unions in the Aude, 1850–1914* (Berkeley, CA, 1991), chs. 1 and 2; Berger and Maurel, *La Viticulture*, 54–58.

33. This is the title of Berger and Maurel's third chapter in *La Viticulture*, 67–100.

34. ADH, 1 E (Papiers Paul Vigné d'Octon) 1180; Helia Vigné d'Octon, *La vie et l'oeuvre de Paul Vigné d'Octon* (Montpellier, n.d. [1930s]), 35–38 (located in the Vigné papers).

35. Helia Vigné d'Octon, *La Vie*, 43–44; ADH, 1 E 1198–99, 1182 ("draps de troupe").

36. Among the many studies of the wine industry, its workers, and their relation to the labor movement, see Pech, *Entreprise viticole*; M. Tudez, *Le Développement de la vigne dans la region de Montpellier du xviiie siècle à nos jours* (Montpellier, 1934); Gaston Galtier, *Le Vignoble en Bas-Languedoc et du Roussillon*, 3 vols. (Montpellier, 1961); J. Harvey Smith, "Work Routine and Social Structure in a French Village: Cruzy in the 19th Century," *Journal of Interdisplinary History* (1975); Robert Laurent, "La propriété foncière dans le Bittérois à la veille de la Première Guerre mondiale," *43e Congrès de la F.H.L.M.R. (Béziers, 1970)*, (Montpellier, 1971); and especially Frader, *Peasants and Protest*. Finally, the key study on the labor movement as a whole is Jean Sagnes, *Le Mouvement*. For an interesting sociological analysis of the relationship between agarian economies and regional politics, see William Brustein, *The Social Origins of Political Regionalism: France, 1849–1981* (Berkeley and Los Angeles, 1988).

37. Rémy Pech, "Les thèmes économiques et sociaux du socialisme ferrouliste

à Narbonne (1880–1914)," in *Gauche et droite en Languedoc-Roussillon de 1789 à nos jours: Colloque* (Montpellier, 1975), p. 263.

38. On the evolution of socialist perspectives, see Sagnes, *Le Mouvement*, 51–93, for the region and Claude Willard, *Le Mouvement socialiste en France (1893–1905): Les Guesdistes* (Paris 1965) and Robert Stuart, *Marxism at Work: Ideology, Class and French Socialism during the Third Republic* (Cambridge, 1992), for the nation as a whole. Tony Judt, *Socialism in Provence, 1871–1914* (Cambridge, 1978) deals with the different evolution in the Var.

39. The Ferroul speech is quoted in *La République sociale*, 19 March 1906. On cooperatives, see Sagnes, *Le Mouvement*, 146–169.

40. Sagnes, *Le Mouvement*, 126–29 and especially Sagnes, "Gauche marxiste et gauche jacobine en Bittérois à travers les campagnes de Louis Lafferre," *Gauche et Droite* (1975), 235–54.

41. See Sagnes, "Le mouvement de 1907 en Languedoc-Roussillon: De la révolte viticole à la révolte du Midi," *Le Mouvement social*, 104 (1978); popular overviews include Félix Napo, *La Révolte des vignerons* (Toulouse, 1971) and Guy Bechtel, *1907: La Grande révolte du Midi* (Paris, 1976).

42. Verse in *La République sociale*, 22 August 1907. See Pech, "Le socialisme ferrouliste," 267–69, for the transformation of Ferroul and Aude socialism.

43. ADH, 15 M 59, Professions de foi des candidates, 1909.

44. *Le Devoir socialiste*, 6 December 1909.

45. Article by Jean Levabre, a Béziers SFIO leader and recent candidate in the cantonal election, in *ibid.*, 19 January 1910.

46. ADH, 15 M 58–62 (cartons concerning the elections of 1910); Sagnes, *Le Mouvement*, 126–134. Michèle Montcouquiol, "Les Elections législatives de 1910 dans l'Hérault" (DES, Montpellier 1969).

47. Little work has been done on Barthe. See *Livre d'or: Les 25 années de Parlement d'Ed. Barthe* (Montpellier, 1937). Biographical information is drawn from nonsocialist newspaper profiles, especially in clippings on the elections of 1910 and 1914, ADH, 15 M 61, 62 and 66 (the prefecture in these years was dominated by the Radicals). See also *Devoir socialiste*, 27 March 1910 and Barthe's 1914 campaign propaganda in ADH, 15 M 65.

48. See *Le Petit Méridional*, 4 April 1910 and (post-election) 4 May 1910. See also *L'Eclair* (the royalist newspaper), 27 March 1910, which printed Barthe's declaration of candidacy. Overall, there is little question that the conservative vote helped Socialists and that the latter did not discourage it. On the whole issue of the decline of Radicalism in lower Languedoc, see Loubère, *Radicalism* 181–234.

49. This adventure was reported in a brochure published under the auspices of the Barthe campaign committee and is an expanded version of an article appearing in the Independent Radical newspaper, *La Depêche du Midi*, 13 April 1910.

50. *Le Petit Méridional*, 13 April 1910.

51. *Le Devoir socialiste*, 15 May 1910.

52. *Ibid.*, 6 June 1910.

53. *Ibid.*, 10 September 1911.

54. ADH, 15 M 65. Professions de foi des candidates, 1914.

55. *Le Devoir socialiste*, 16 February 1913. *La Bataille syndicaliste*, 28 January 1913. Also see Laura Frader's excellent analysis in *Peasants and Protest*.

56. *Le Devoir socialiste*, 20 April 1913.

57. See above all, Robert Lafont, *La Revendication Occitane* (Paris, 1974). Lafont is a brilliant literary critic and has emerged as the philosopher of left-wing

Occitanisme. The Institute has produced a raft of studies, capped off by *L'Histoire de l'Occitanie*, a huge collaborative effort published by Privat, the main southern publishing house (located in Toulouse) in 1978. The position taken by most contemporary Occitanists favors neither separation nor autonomy, but a system of local self-regulation not dissimilar to the ideals expressed in books like L.S. Stavrianos, *The Promise of the Coming Dark Age* (New York, 1978). See especially Lafont, *Autonomie de la région à l'autogestion* (Paris, 1967). On the recent history of the left and Occitan literary movements in the twentieth century, one should begin with Henri Lerner, "Etre gauche dans le Midi," (ch. 6) and Jean-Marie Petit, "Présence des lettres languedociens," (ch. 8) in *Histoires du Languedoc 1900 à nos jours*, ed. Gérard Cholvy (Toulouse 1980).

58. Lafont, *La Revendication*, 60–74.

59. Geneviève Colomer et Daniel Alibert, "Les Félibres rouges de *La Lauseto*," Mémoire de Maîtrise, Montpellier, 1975; Lafont, *Mistral, ou l'Illusion* (Paris, 1954).

60. Eugene Weber, *Peasants into Frenchmen* (Stanford, Ca., 1976), 67–94, 303–39.

61. Affiche, "Action Française aux Languedociens," ADH, 39 M 289 (1908). On right-wing Occitanisme, see Victor Nguyen, "Asperçus sur la conscience d'Oc autour des années 1900," 241–57 and G. Cholvy, "Régionalisme et clergé catholique au xixᵉ siècle," 187–201, in *Régions et régionalisme en France du xviiiᵉ siècle à nos jours*, ed. C. Gras and G. Livet (Paris, 1977). Cholvy points out that the church tried to take advantage of popular resentment against speaking French by training priests in Occitan. Catholic unions in the Hérault used reactionary *félibres*, such as A. Arnaveille, to urge their members to scab. See police reports of 12 and 14 November 1910 on such activity during the great rail strike of that year (ADH, 39 M 289).

62. Anon., *Cinquantenaire de la Société d'Enseignement populaire de l'Hérault, 1898–1948* (Montpellier, 1948), 5–14. B.M.M., 25,577 (20).

63. C. Bouglé, *Plaidoyer pour l'enseignement populaire* (Montpellier, 1900). B.M.M., 55,207.

64. Louis Planchon, "Le poète nîmois Bigot et ses poésies languedociennes," *Revue des langues romanes* (1904): 305–14.

65. Roussel, fils, was a *professeur au lycée*. His father, also Ernest, was best known for his work on Louis Roumieux, a popular poet who wrote in Provençal, published in 1870. His own thesis, published in 1900, was on *Orange, ancien capitale* (Montpellier).

66. Dezeuze's best-known work in French was *Savoirs et gaités du terroir montpelliérain* (Montpellier 1935), but he wrote dozens of plays, hundreds of songs and poems, and several folkloric collections in Occitan. He is a pivotal figure in the growth of a leftist, popular Occitanism and needs a great deal more study. The Musée Fabre of Montpellier put on an exhibition of his drawings and manuscripts in 1981 and published a brief catalogue.

67. Anon., *Enseignement populaire dans l'Hérault* (Montpellier, 1901); Ernest Roussel, *La Mission d'une Université populaire après la grande guerre* (Montpellier, 1920) (this includes a retrospective analysis of course content); *La vie de la Société de 1920 à 1923* (Montpellier, 1923); Odile Azéma, "Culture et société à Montpellier de 1910 à 1914" (Memoire de Maîtrise, Montpellier, 1977), 71ff.

68. See especially the Prefect's report of 4 April 1920, "Mouvement social

et état des esprits," in ADH, 194 M 32. This carton documents the dramatic surge of syndicalist action in 1919, but confirms the Prefect's opinion that "Syndicalist organization is strong and active, but remains at this time sincerely oriented toward job-related concerns [*des intérêts corporatifs*]. This defense does not assume the form of a class struggle, nor does it have the acuity of a desperate life and death struggle."

69. *Le Devoir socialiste*, Félix: 8 July 1919; Barthe: 7 September 1919.

70. *Ibid.*, 25 May and 6 June 1920.

71. Judt, *Socialism in Provence*, 302.

Conclusion

1. See Charles Tilly, *Coercion, Capital, and European States, AD 990–1990* (Cambridge, Mass. and Oxford, 1990); Charles Sabel and Michael Piore, *The Second Industrial Divide* (New York, 1984); Sabel and Jonathan Zeitlin, "Historical Alternatives to Mass Production," *Past and Present*, 108 (1985): 133–76; David Harvey, *The Condition of Postmodernity* (Oxford and Cambridge, Mass., 1989); Paul Kennedy, *The Rise and Fall of the Great Powers* (New York, 1987); *The Changing Boundaries of the Political* ed. Charles Maier (Cambridge, 1987), "Introduction."

2. See the wise discussion of this problem in Yves Lequin, *Les Ouvriers de la région lyonnaise (1848–1914)*, II (Lyon, 1977), 473–75.

3. Barry Bluestone and Bennett Harrison, *The Great U-Turn* (New York, 1988), 102–08; Richard B. McKenzie, *Fugitive Industry: The Economics and Politics of Deindustrialization* (San Francisco, 1984); on the issue in the United Kingdom, see *The Politics of Industrial Closure* ed. Tony Dickson and David Judge (London, 1987).

4. Hardy-Hémery, *De La Croissance à la désindustrialisation: un siècle dans le Valenciennois* (Paris, 1984); Bluestone and Harrison, *The Deindustrialization of America* (New York, 1982).

5. William Beik, *Absolutism and Society in Seventeenth-Century France* (Cambridge, 1985).

6. For a detailed study of this phenomenon, see Elinor Accampo, *Industrialization, Family Life, and Class Relations: Saint Chamond, 1815–1914* (Berkeley, 1989), ch. 4.

7. For the problem in the contemporary West, see Paul Schervisch, *The Structural Determinents of Unemployment: Vulnerability and Power in Market Relations* (New York, 1983); *Deindustrialization and Plant Closure* ed. Paul D. Staudohar and Holly Brown, (Lexington, Mass., 1987), especially parts II–IV; Leonard Fagin and Martin Little, *The Forsaken Families: a timely and disturbing report on the effects of unemployment on family life in Britain* (Harmondsworth, Mx, 1984); on the political economy of class conflict in the United States, see Mike Davis, *Prisoners of the American Dream: Politics and Economy in the History of the US Working Class* (London, 1986); for a happier (rose-colored?) picture, see Charles Sabel, *Work and Politics: The Division of Labor in Industry* (Cambridge, 1982); for a thousand reasons why workers should fight back despite the circumstances and the odds, see Alex Callinicos and Mike Simons, *The Great Strike: the Miners' Strike of 1984–85 and its Lessons* (London, 1985).

8. See Dick Geary, "Unemployment and Working-Class Solidarity: the German Experience of 1929–33," in *The German Unemployed: Experiences and Con-*

sequences of Mass Unemployment from the Weimar Republic to the Third Reich ed. Richard Evans and Geary (London, 1987); Eve Rosenhaft, *Beating the Fascists? The German Communists and Political Violence, 1929–1933* (Cambridge, 1983); John Garraty, "Unemployment during the Great Depression," *Labor History,* 7 (Spring, 1976).

9. David Harvey, *The Condition of Postmodernity,* especially ch. 11 ("Flexible Accumulation—solid transformation or temporary fix?").

Index